Elija A. Ferrie
Nov. 1931

ELLEN TERRY
AND
BERNARD SHAW

ELLEN TERRY

AND

BERNARD SHAW

A Correspondence

EDITED BY CHRISTOPHER ST. JOHN

NEW YORK

G. P. PUTNAM'S SONS

The Knickerbocker Press

1931

MADE IN THE UNITED STATES OF AMERICA

TYPOGRAPHY BY ROBERT S. JOSEPHY

Note

SHORTLY after the death of Ellen Terry, her executors contemplated the publication of a volume of her letters, and appealed to her numerous distinguished correspondents to supply copies of those they had preserved. Mr Bernard Shaw, who had a very large number, sent them for selection. They were found to throw much light on the inner history of the London stage at the end of the last century, and to possess such rare personal quality, that search was at once made for Mr Shaw's replies. Fortunately, many of them had been preserved. When fitted into their proper order the result was a correspondence unique in the annals of the theatre, and with very few parallels in the literature formed by the scant records we possess of the intimacies of well-known public characters. Unlike many such correspondences, the letters were evidently written without a thought of their possible publication; and their publication therefore becomes an act of that supreme justice to the memory of a great actress which consists in letting her be seen as she never dreamt of showing herself, and indeed could not without impertinence have shown herself, except to those friends from whom she had no secrets and with whom she could drop her public work of making the heroines of romance seem real and living. This consideration overcame all the difficulties in the way of publication; and Mr Shaw consented to contribute the preface with which this volume opens to clear up the situation in which the correspondence began.

The letters have been edited by Miss Christopher St. John.

v

Preface

I N ALLOWING everybody who cares about Ellen Terry to read this correspondence, I must warn them not to judge it according to the code of manners which regulate polite letter writing in cathedral country towns. As a correspondence between a churchwarden and a deaconess its implications would make its publication impossible. But the theatre, behind the scenes, has an emotional freemasonry of its own, certainly franker and arguably wholesomer than the stiffnesses of surburban society outside. The difference is less than it used to be; for actors, like the members of the other professions, have made their way into the general body of society and been accepted as ladies and gentlemen of the professional class rather than as players; and just as it was becoming difficult fifty years ago to imagine a medical baronet or a vicar or a prosperous solicitor or stockbroker accepting a position of social inferiority in a Bloomsbury mansion or a country house, which they had nevertheless had to do within living memory of that time, it is difficult now to imagine an actor being at any disadvantage in ordinary professional society in respect of his occupation, however he may happen to be disqualified in point of education and social habits. If there is nothing wrong with his table manners, his dress, and his accent, nobody will venture to snub or patronize an actor merely because he is an actor; and if he is not qualified in these respects he is at all events no worse off than any other professional man who has not taken the trouble to make himself presentable.

This social acceptance of the actor did not become quite unquestionable, until Henry Irving insisted on its official recognition, even at the cost to his singular eminence of a much disrelished knighthood for himself, in 1895. The theatre into which Ellen Terry was born in 1848 enjoyed no such general consideration. Actors, like Jews, were a race apart; and like all segregated races they preserved manners and customs peculiar to themselves. My first youthful contacts with the stage were in connection with certain amateur enterprises; and I well remember the puzzled mixture of amusement and indignation with which a company of ladies and gentlemen of considerable social position who had engaged a professional London stage manager (the modern Producer had not then been invented) to direct their operations, found themselves addressed by him, all the ladies as Darling and all the gentlemen as Old Boy. No modern Producer says Old Boy; and Darling survives only as an elderly joke to turn away the wrath of irritable stars at critical moments; but to the stage manager of that day they were as conventional as the Sir and Madam of a well trained shop assistant.

But though that stage manager's Darling did not mean what it would have meant if it had been addressed to the same ladies by a Dean, it is none the less significant that the convention of the stage should have been one of personal endearment whilst in other professions it was one of cold politeness. That difference still exists, and will exist as long as acting remains an art. When I was a boy, interested much more in music than in literature, I managed to get admitted to the stage once or twice during an opera performance, and learned thereby that this is quite the worst way to enjoy it, and that anyone behind the scenes who has no business there is as great a nuisance, and is as little considered by those who have some business there, as Mr Pickwick at the Chatham review. But what is more to the present purpose is that, the opera being Donizetti's Lucrezia Borgia, and Maffio Orsini and his comrades having overwhelmed Lucrezia with their exposure of her infamies in the exciting finale to the first act, the curtain had no sooner descended and Maffio ceased to be Maffio and become Trebelli, and Lucrezia ceased to be Lucrezia and become Tietjens, than the two hurled themselves frantically into one another's arms in a transport of some emotion that was certainly not any of the emotions of ordinary life outside the theatre, but something peculiar to their work that insisted on the most rapturous expression they could give it. It cannot be explained by what people called the Italian temperament: Trebelli was a Frenchwoman and Tietjens a German. It was something *sui generis* that nobody who has not experienced it can credit, and that soon becomes second nature in those who have experienced it. The Initiates never resent its expression. When they say "he (or she) is one of us," they mean that the happy person is privileged to express any extremity of affection for an artist who achieves a fine piece of acting, and any extremity of disgust at one who wilfully acts basely. The measured public judgments of the critics cannot express this impulse or satisfy this need. The stage is not one fairyland but two: one for the public when the curtain rises, and another, which the public never discovers, for the theatre folk when the curtain falls. In that secret paradise genius excites a flush of adoration in the properly tuned recipient and is satisfied with nothing less. I adored Ellen Terry accordingly, and did not tell her so by halves. And it never occurred to her to say "Sir: how dare you insult a respectable female by such expressions?" *Honi soit qui mal y pense.*

Genius, I may add, is not commoner on the stage than elsewhere; but there, as elsewhere, it produces extravagance of language. The epithet beautiful is used by surgeons to describe operations which their patients describe as ghastly, by physicists to describe methods of measurement which leave sentimentalists cold, by lawyers to describe cases which ruin all the parties to them, and by lovers to describe the objects of their infatuation, however unattractive they may appear to the unaffected spectators. Within the magnetic field of the theatrical profession such hyperbole became conventional, and was finally used by the rank and file who had never felt the emotion until at last every actress was every stage manager's darling and every actor his old boy.

There is another peculiarity of the stage to be borne in mind. An actress is not a lady: at least when she is she is not an actress. Let me explain. A lady is—or in Ellen Terry's generation was—a person trained to the utmost attainable degree in the art and habit of concealing her feelings and maintaining an imperturbable composure under the most trying circumstances. An actress is a person trained even more severely in the art and habit of displaying her feelings so demonstratively that every occupant of the back row in a remote gallery can read them in her face and see them in her gestures. What to the lady is an emergency in which dissimulation is her first duty, is to the actress an opportunity for explosive self-expression, however skilled her guidance of the explosion may be. Modern frankness has reduced this difference; but it remains, and is accentuated by the slovenliness of modern middle class speech, which contrasts strongly with the distinct articulation of the actress who knows her business. Ellen Terry escaped the trials of our young actresses, who find themselves between silly producers who tell them that they must not articulate because it is not natural and not ladylike, and despairing authors who warn them that nobody in the theatre will know what they are saying unless they articulate very distinctly. When the author is experienced and wily, the lesson takes the form of a conversational remark that slovenly speech is middle class, and that great ladies owe much of their distinction to their scrupulous articulation, of which Queen Victoria, one of the most perfect speakers of her day, was a conspicuous example. To tell a young woman that if she speaks well she will be mistaken for an actress may spoil her for the stage; but there is a ready antidote in telling her that she may also be mistaken for a member of the royal family. Ellen Terry's articulation was perfect. Her slightly veiled voice reached the remotest listener in the theatre without apparent effort, though the nervous athleticism behind it was of championship quality.

actors

Howbeit, the fact remains that an actress, having to exaggerate to get her effects on the stage (on the film, by the way, the contrary is the case: an unnatural quietude and delicacy is the trade mark of the Movie Star), finally from mere habit exaggerates to get her effects off it; and the greater the actress the greater is her power of seizing on every emotional impulse and not only amplifying it as a microphone or a thermionic valve amplifies a sound, but uttering it with a muscular articulation which gives it an impressive driving power. The story of Mrs Siddons terrifying the shop assistant by the intensity with which she asked "Will it wash?" is quite probable. And the playwright, supplying the verbal material for this skilled speech, develops the same quality in his writing. The reader of this budget of intimate letters must therefore not be surprised, and certainly not scandalized, by the reckless way in which the two correspondents express their delight in one another. I do not mean that they were insincere: all that the writers set down they felt at the moment. But their profession freed them from many of the inhibitions to which people outside that profession have to submit; and their language must be interpreted without the inferences which would be drawn from the same language on the part of a governess corresponding with a divinity student.

Possibly a little allowance should be made also for the very objectionable tradition of eighteenth century gallantry into which I, as an Irishman, was born. "Remember," said the most attractive of my aunts to me by way of improving my young mind, "that the least plain girl in a house is the family beauty." An English actress once expressed contemptuous impatience with women who want to be placed on a pedestal and worshipped. An Irish actress who was present exclaimed indignantly, "I would not *look* at a man who did not place me on a pedestal." It was her right, by Irish tradition. Now I claim that no male writer born in the nineteenth century outside Norway and Sweden did more to knock

Woman off her pedestal and plant her on the solid earth than I. But as, like all reactionaries, I was steeped in the tendency against which I was reacting, it was part of my conventional manners to concede a pedestal to every woman as such; and naturally in approaching a woman so goddesslike as Ellen Terry I did not pause to consider whether this attitude would have earned the approval of Ibsen or Strindberg. I do not justify it: it is really a relic of relations between men and women which are not only happily outmoded but insufferable. Still, there it was for what it was worth.

It must be borne in mind too, that we were both comedians, each acting as audience to the other, and each desiring to please and amuse the other without ulterior motives or what matchmaking mothers call intentions. A word, however, must be said about Ellen Terry's ethical position. She once said that what had supported her through all her trials was the consciousness that she had never done anything wrong; and this entirely sincere claim was quoted to me as an audacious hypocrisy. Ellen Terry was never called an advanced woman, the reason being that she was born, as Nietzsche put it, on the far side of good and evil as defined by the Victorian code. Such a play as Ibsen's Ghosts had no mission for her, because she had not had to break Mrs Alving's chains, never having worn them. She did not fight prejudices nor argue with them: like Mrs Stetson's heroine she walked through them as if they were not there, as indeed for her they were not. This was partly individual character; but it must be remembered that in the old segregated theatre, religion and morality were homemade: the actress did not live in ordinary society and go out to her work like a doctor or lawyer or clergyman or man of business: she belonged to a little world apart, with morals of its own; and though actors, being human beings, necessarily had the same morals as other people to the extent of, say, nine tenths, yet there was a difference in the other tenth. For instance, in the outside world ladies were not economically independent; and in the rare instances where a lady was paid for working she never dreamt of being paid as much as a gentleman, and felt herself heavily compromised socially by being paid at all. On the stage not only was the actress self-supporting, but if, as often happened, she attracted the public more than her male colleagues she was paid more. Consequently, the trade union view of marriage, from which the unmarried woman who is not a celibate must at all costs be boycotted as a blackleg, had no meaning in the theatre. Outside it women were held to a strict licitness in their sexual

xi

relations on penalty of ostracism, loss of employment, and every other injury that could express total reprobation by all decent people. In fact, a woman incurring this penalty used to be described as "ruined" until Ibsen set us laughing at the epithet by applying it to a man. In the theatre illicit relations *as such* involved no penalty whatever. But please remark the italicized limitation. The notion that actors can behave wickedly without incurring the reprobation of their colleagues and being passed over and replaced by better conducted substitutes when any are available is a vulgar error. But the wickedness must be real wickedness, not mere disregard of the law. The result is that the standard of morals on the stage is in some important aspects higher than it is outside the theatre, where married couples regard the legal tie between them as justifying them in treating each other much worse than they dare treat an independent stranger. In the very important matter of sexual temperance a marriage licence is held to dispense with it as completely as is humanly possible. But it is impossible to keep in training for stage work on such terms. Behind the scenes self-preservation unites with lay opinion to make the life of the theatrical performer in many respects a model which might be followed in the most straitlaced suburb with considerable advantage to its matrimonial morals.

When a late well-known Roman Catholic critic declared that no woman could be an actress and "a good woman," he was perhaps sufficiently answered by Robert Buchanan, who exclaimed "What! No good women on the stage! There are thousands of them—and only about six actresses." When Dumas *fils* publicly assured a young lady of good family who wanted to become an actress that it was quite out of the question for a person in her social position, and when Charles Dickens, himself an incorrigible actor, imposed the same prohibition on his daughter, they were expressing a class prejudice, not a moral one; for the stage is socially quite promiscuous. As no extra money is attracted to the payboxes by the social standing of the performers, talent is everything and pedigree nothing. You must rub shoulders there with persons of every degree, accepting an order of precedence in which a person born in a caravan may be paid and estimated more highly than one born in a palace. It takes a revolution to produce such a state of things outside the theatre: inside it is readymade and inevitable from the nature of the institution.

All this has to be grasped before the lay reader can understand how Ellen Terry could be a woman of very exceptional virtue without having the smallest respect for the law. She did not care enough about it to have even a prejudice against it. If the man of her choice was free, she married him. If the marriage was not a success she left him. She had many enduring friendships, some transient fancies, and five domestic partnerships of which two were not legalized, though they would have been if the English marriage law had been decently reasonable. She was not in the least what is called a *grande amoureuse*. In the ordering of her life there was nothing of the infatuations and extravagances, the reckless expenditure, the fantastic equipment, the debts, the jewels, the caprices, the menagerie of strange pet animals and reptiles, and all the other affectations and fictions by which actresses' press agents advertise their mostly sober, honest, industrious, economical and monogamous principals. Ellen Terry did not know what an actress's press agent was. And she was no fool: she lived and died within her means. She was certainly no skinflint: she would have run through her money too generously if she had not given it to businesslike friends to keep for her; but she died solvent, an honest woman with no vices.

Emotionally she was not quite so fortunate. She ran through her husbands, and ended as her own mistress and no man's housemate, though she retained the affection of her first husband, who was much older than herself, and of her last, who was much younger. One may say that her marriages were adventures and her friendships enduring. And all these friendships had the character of innocent love affairs: her friends were her lovers in every sense except the technical one; and she was incapable of returning their regard cooly; she felt either warmly or not at all. And yet she was critical, and never lost her head when it was necessary to keep it. Her soft side was her mothering side, her sensitive pity. She was drawn to men of brains because they interested her, and because she was very conscious of the holes left in her mind by the curious patchiness of theatrical culture and the ladylike ignorance of her day; yet she could not resist men who were so helplessly outside the world of intellect that their devotion to her was childlike and their distress at being repulsed by her more than she could bear unless they were personally repulsive to her. She seemed a mass of incalculable contradictions to people who had no analytic sense of character, and expected to find people either All Whites or All Blacks. But she was really as consistent off the stage as she was competent on it.

It must be noted also that she was not stagestruck. Her parents were actors. Like her famous contemporary Madge Robertson (Dame Madge

Kendal) she found it as impossible to keep off the stage as it is for many stagestruck outsiders to get on it. You cannot say that Ellen Terry, like Garrick or Irving, was a player by irresistible vocation. She was a player by force of circumstances. I am not sure that she would have become a professional actress if she had not been born with a property spoon in her mouth. Her natural taste was for pictorial art, not for histrionics. Her first husband was a great painter. She left the stage without hesitation for the best years of her youth to keep house on £3 a week with Edward William Godwin, a distinguished architect with a craze for stage pictures and pageantry, and was induced to return to it only by an offer of £40 when she had two children to provide for. Although she was soundly skilled in the technique of her profession she never needed to perform any remarkable feat of impersonation: the spectators would have resented it: they did not want Ellen Terry to be Olivia Primrose: they wanted Olivia Primrose to be Ellen Terry. Her combination of beauty with sensitive intelligence was unique: a disguise would have been intolerable. Her instinct was for beauty and for sincerity: she had only to play a part "straight," as actors say, to transfigure it into something much better than its raw self. But she could take this transfiguration home with her and fascinate her friends with it. She was not the sort of actress who is a genius on the stage and a nobody off it. She could do without the stage both as artist and woman. In her letters she often speaks of wanting work and having to earn some money; but there is no trace of the desperate need to be acting at any cost felt by those who are so completely specialized for the stage that they hardly exist except in fictitious characters.

This is almost a family characteristic. Her sister Kate, when she was in the first rank of London actresses, retired after marriage apparently without hesitation or regret. Miss Phyllis Neilson Terry, Ellen Terry's niece, does not follow up her successes, though she seems to have every qualification for a repetition of the career of her aunt. Ellen Terry's son, Edward Gordon Craig, who succeeded with the greatest ease as an actor, cared so little for acting or for the drama that he gave up acting whilst he was still a juvenile, and engaged in a lifelong struggle to use the stage as a frame for the pictorial architecture in which his father delighted.

I must now say a word about my own theatrical antecedents, as they explain the grudge against the old Lyceum Theatre, against Irving, and even against Ellen herself, which comes out so strongly in our correspondence, as it did publicly and in presentably measured terms through the series of my criticisms in *The Saturday Review* which ran alongside the correspondence during its main period.

From my birth in 1856 to my Hegira to London in 1876, I lived in Dublin, where the theatre had hardly altered, except for its illumination by coal gas, since the eighteenth century. There were two theatres: the Queen's, which was then not respectable (I visited it, at most, twice, perhaps only once), and the old Theatre Royal, since unhappily burnt down, which maintained a stock company to support the stars who came to Dublin on their touring circuits, and to perform the Christmas pantomime and keep the house open in the occasional weeks left unfilled by the stars. As nobody nowadays has the least notion of what the old stock companies were like, and as my own plays are written largely for the feats of acting they aimed at, and as moreover both Ellen Terry and Irving were rooted like myself in that phase of the evolution of the theatre, I may as well say a word or two about them.

To begin with, the playgoers of their towns grew so desperately tired of them, and so hopelessly unable to imagine them to be any but their too familiar selves, that they performed in an atmosphere of hatred and derision that very few of their members had talent or charm enough to conciliate. The modern practice of selecting for the performances actors and actresses suited to the parts they had to play was impossible: the stock company was a readymade cast that had to fit all plays, from Hamlet down to the latest burlesque; and as it never fitted any of them completely, and seldom fitted at all, the casts were more or less grotesque misfits. This system did not develop versatility: it destroyed it. Every member of the company except the utilities, as they called the worst actors who got parts that did not matter, had his or her specialty or "line." Thus there were leading juveniles with an age limit of fifty. There were walking gentlemen, first and second light comedians, first and second low comedians, first and second old men, heavies who played all the villains, and, as aforesaid, utilities. There were leading ladies and walking ladies, singing chambermaids (soubrettes), heavies to whom Lady Macbeth was all in the night's work, a pair of old women of whom one played the great ladies and the other the comic landladies, and, of course, female utilities. Each claimed as of right the part which came nearest to his or her specialty; and each played all his or her parts in exactly the same way. The low comedian was traditionally cast for Roderigo; and Roderigo consequently was presented, not as a foolish Venetian gentleman about town, but as a clown. The king in Hamlet and

Ham Peggotty might have been twins except for the costume, because the heavy man had to play Ham, the juveniles being used up for Copperfield and Steerforth. On no other terms could stock actors play all the parts that had to be, not studied, but "swallowed"; for the stars and other travelling attractions came and went week after week, and had not only to be "supported," but eked out by farces to fill up what the playgoers of that time demanded as a sufficient program. At my first visit to the theatre I saw on the same evening Tom Taylor's three-act drama Plot and Passion followed by a complete Christmas pantomime, with a couple of farces as *hors d'œuvre*. Tom Taylor's Joan of Arc had Massinger's New Way to Pay Old Debts as a curtain raiser. Under such circumstances serious character study was impossible; and the intensive elaboration of an impersonation which an actor can achieve when he can repeat his performance without having anything else to do in the theatre was out of the question. The actress learnt, not how to interpret plays, but how to appear sweet and gentle, or jealous and wicked, or funny, or matronly, or deaf and palsied, and how to make up her face and wear wigs. The actor learnt how to appear sprightly, or romantic, or murderous, or bucolic, or doddering, and to make funny faces. In addition he had one step dance, which he displayed annually in the pantomime, and one combat, which served for all stage duels.

These qualifications are not to be despised. In the modern cases in which they have been lost without being replaced by any discoverable technical qualifications at all they may well be sincerely regretted. The stock actor, with his conscientiously articulated elocution which reached the back row of the pit effectively (it is really more satisfactory to hear an actor say meechee-yah-eeld and know that he means my child than to hear him say msha and wonder what on earth the fellow thinks he is mumbling), his pompous entrance which invited and seized the attention of the audience, his momentous exit on the last word of his last speech (your modern novice as often as not finishes in the middle of the stage and stops the play until the audience has enjoyed the spectacle of his walking to the door), could plead that he knew the routine of his business and did not need a producer to teach him the A. B. C. of it. But only those who have seen him, as I have, in his native element, and lived to witness the effect of entrusting to his skilled hands a part in a play by Ibsen, can imagine how completely he could kill the dramatic illusion of a modern play.

The truth is, the style of work at which he aimed was wholly rhetorical and hyperbolical. Actors of gigantic or intense personalities could carry it off; but it made commonplace actors ridiculous, though commonplace actors could with ordinary diligence under good teachers acquire its technique only too easily. The teaching could give them style; but it could not give them taste or good sense or power, without which style is an affectation and an impertinence. The invariable effectiveness of the stock actor was a worse offence than the ineffectiveness of the generation which supplanted him, because it enabled and even obliged him to substitute himself for his part in and out of season. His blatant force, when he had any, was less impressive than the so-called "reserved force" of his comparatively impotent successor, who made a merit of either having no force to reserve or not knowing how to use it. When he was thrown on the world in the long interval between the break-up of the stock system in the latter half of the nineteenth century and the beginnings of the local repertory theatres in the twentieth, his plea that he knew his business, far from recommending him to the managers with whom he sought employment, only sealed his fate as a plague to be shunned at all hazards.

Conceive me then, a future playwright, with no conscious prevision of that destiny, gathering my practical knowledge of the stage from a company of such actors as I have just described playing round a star on tour. Of the English speaking stars incomparably the greatest was Barry Sullivan, who was in his prime when I was in my teens, the last of the race of heroic figures which had dominated the stage since the palmy Siddons-Kemble days. Ellen Terry shrank from his acting as from a display of pugilism in which his trembling supporters had no part except to give him his cues and be played off the stage by him. His stage fights in Richard III and Macbeth appealed irresistibly to a boy spectator like myself: I remember one delightful evening when two inches of Macbeth's sword, a special fighting sword carried in that scene only, broke off and whizzed over the heads of the cowering pit (there were no stalls then) to bury itself deep in the front of the dress circle after giving those who sat near its trajectory more of a thrill than they had bargained for. Barry Sullivan was a tall powerful man with a cultivated resonant voice: his stage walk was the perfection of grace and dignity; and his lightning swiftness of action, as when in the last scene of Hamlet he shot up the stage and stabbed the king four times before you could wink, all provided a physical exhibition which attracted audiences quite independently of the play. To John Coleman and T. C. King and other provincial stars with whom he has been sometimes ignorantly classed by

London stage historians he was as Hyperion to a very thirdrate satyr. He was as proud as Lucifer, and as imposing; but he was the only actor I ever heard come before the curtain at the end of a play to apologize for having acted badly. He had opened on Monday night in Hamlet (he was at his best in Hamlet and Richelieu) after a very rough passage from Holyhead. Certainly some of the usual charm was lacking; but only very sensitive Barry Sullivan connoisseurs could have noticed it. With an unanswerable dignity he informed the applauding Dublin playgoers that he had done justice neither to them nor to himself, and begged their indulgence. They were awestruck; and then their applause had a note of bewilderment; for most of them had thought it all very splendid.

Yet this great actor—for such of his kind and in his prime he was—had no notion of what we now require as artistic production. He went into a provincial theatre as into a rag and bottle shop; made them drag out the old scenes that the people of the town had seen hundreds of times in all sorts of plays; and, by summary methods that involved a good deal of swearing and bullying, drilled the stock company in a day's rehearsal into giving him his cues and playing up to his strokes of stage business that night. At first he brought with him nothing but his costumes and swords. Later on, he travelled with a fairly good looking young leading lady (possibly in consequence of an experience with a local Ophelia who reduced me to such paroxysms of laughter that I narrowly escaped ejection from the theatre) and an old actor, Cathcart, who had supported Charles Kean, and who, as Richmond or Macduff, got the worst of all the stage fights except the final fatal thrust under the arm, and who relieved the star of the worst drudgery of rehearsal when advancing age compelled him to husband his still mighty forces. In spite of this relief and of his haughty sobriety and irreproachable private life Barry Sullivan died paralysed, exhausted by the impossible task of being superhuman for six nights in every week; for, clever as he was technically, he revelled in his work too keenly to keep within the limits of that passionless science of acting which enabled Salvini to make his audiences imagine him a volcano in eruption when he was in sober fact hardly moving, and Coquelin, without turning a hair, to get through a night's work that would have worn most of our actors to rags or driven them to stimulants to pull them through.

Had I passed my boyhood in London I should have seen nothing of the very important side of stage art represented by Barry Sullivan's acting. He had appeared there with Helen Faucit as Hamlet at the Haymarket Theatre, and been hailed by *The Times* as the leading legitimate actor of the British stage. But when he found, as Irving found later, that this meant being skinned alive by the London landlords, he shook the dust of London off his feet, and, first in Australia and then in the English provinces and in Ireland and Scotland, set to work with a fixed determination that, however scanty the audience, whoever once saw him act would come again. He soon secured crowded houses every night, and died leaving £100,000 at about the age at which Irving had to abandon his London theatre penniless and fall back on America and the provinces. Had Barry Sullivan produced Shakespear's plays as handsomely as Irving did at the Lyceum they would not have drawn an extra farthing (for a theatre can be no more than full) and he would have had to spend much more money on them.

I certainly learnt nothing from Barry Sullivan's exploits of how far the grand style in acting can be carried by women. Most fortunately for me, however, a visit was paid to Dublin by Adelaide Ristori, who completed my education in this respect, besides convincing me that an Italian stock company, when the novelty of its foreign conventions wears off, can become even more unbearably stale than an English one. The nearest English approach to a tragic actress was Ada Cavendish, whose performance as Wilkie Collins's New Magdalen made an extraordinary impression; but she only flashed across the sky and vanished, leaving no successor until Janet Achurch arrived fifteen years later and inaugurated the Ibsen movement. Both of them, like Edmund Kean, Robson, and many others, called to their aid powers that destroyed them. Ellen Terry did not visit Dublin, and was only a name to me when I came to London in 1876; but everything that the perfection of technical accomplishment could do with youth, cleverness, wit, and irresistible charm in drawingroom drama was demonstrated by Madge Robertson, who came with Buckstone and the entire Haymarket company from London, and struck the first shattering blow at our poor old stock company.

The stock company was hard enough to bear when there was no alternative; but when the London successes began touring through the provinces and the Irish and Scottish capitals, and were performed there not as now by secondrate companies giving a mechanical imitation of the original London production, but by the London cast which had created the success, the stock companies fell dead at their impact. To say that they perished unwept, unhonored, and unsung would be to give only the faintest idea of their death and damnation. When we who had seen them scrambling anyhow through all sorts of plays, in the way I have tried to describe, first saw finished acting, careful production, thorough identification of the performers with parts for which they had been carefully selected as suitable, with new faces, new voices, new clothes, and new scenery, a return to the stock company was impossible.

And now I come to the link between all this theatrical history and the present volume. Among these London successes which brought London productions unchanged to Dublin was a play called The Two Roses, by Albery. One of the characters was a selfish old humbug named Digby Grant. It made the success of the piece by a certain egotistical intensity, sinister and yet dignified in its indignity, which was not in the play but in the actor: an actor with a tall thin figure, which, if it could not be convicted of grotesqueness was certainly indescribably peculiar, and a voice which was dependent so much on the resonance of a cavernous nose that it was, compared to the powerful and musical chest voice of Barry Sullivan, a highly cultivated neigh. His name was Henry Irving. I instinctively felt that a new drama inhered in this man, though I had then no conscious notion that I was destined to write it; and I perceive now that I never forgave him for baffling the plans I made for him (always, be it remembered, unconsciously). His stage disguise was so perfect that I did not even know that he was still a young man: indeed the one effect he never could produce on the stage was a youthful effect: his Romeo was no younger than his Digby Grant. He was utterly unlike anyone else: he could give importance and a noble melancholy to any sort of drivel that was put into his mouth; and it was this melancholy, bound up with an impish humour, which forced the spectator to single him out as a leading figure with an inevitability that I never saw again in any other actor until it rose from Irving's grave in the person of a nameless cinema actor who afterwards became famous as Charlie Chaplin. Here, I felt, is something that leaves the old stage and its superstitions and staleness completely behind, and inaugurates a new epoch in the theatre.

The theatrical system to which the stock company belonged decomposed and broke up; and when I came to London it seemed to recede into a remote provincial past. I hastened to the famous little theatre off Tottenham Court Road, where the Scala Theatre now stands, to see the Cup and Saucer drama of Robertson handled by the Bancrofts. The play I hit on was Ours; and in it I saw Ellen Terry for the first time. She left on me an impression of waywardness: of not quite fitting into her part and not wanting to; and she gave no indication of her full power, for which the part afforded no scope. As her portraits had prepared me to find her interesting and singular (I have never been susceptible to mere prettiness) I was less struck than I should have been if she had been quite new to me. It was not until I saw her in New Men and Old Acres, which was made a success by her performance as The Two Roses had been made a success by Irving's, that I was completely conquered and convinced that here was the woman for the new drama which was still in the womb of Time, waiting for Ibsen to impregnate it. If ever there were two artists apparently marked out by Nature to make a clean break with an outworn past and create a new stage world they were Ellen Terry and Henry Irving. Nobody can really understand my correspondence with Ellen Terry twenty years later without grasping this situation.

What actually happened was an anticlimax which in its public aspect was a glorious success for both of them. Irving fascinated London in a play called The Bells under an oldfashioned management. His success was so great and so entirely personal that he was able to lift the theatre out of the hands of his manager and take its professional destiny into his own hands with all shackles cast off from his art, in the position as head of the English stage which he held almost unchallenged for thirty years. The earliest notable use he made of his freedom was to engage Ellen Terry as his leading lady. It was his first and last enlightened stroke of policy. For he immediately turned back to the old Barry Sullivan repertory of mutilated Shakespear and Bulwer Lytton, to which he actually added The Iron Chest of the obsolete Colman. From the public point of view he never looked back: from my point of view he never looked forward. As far as the drama was concerned he was more old-fashioned than the oldest of his predecessors, and apparently more illiterate than the most ignorant of them. The taste and judgment which enabled him to achieve so much beauty and dignity in scenery and costume and to rid his theatre of all the old vulgarities when he had Ellen Terry to reveal such possibilities to him did not extend to literature. He seemed the most pedantic of elocutionists, because his peculiar nasal method of securing resonance obliged him to pronounce our English diphthongs as vowels; and though he delivered Shakespear's lines (what he left of them) like one who had a sense of their music, he would cut a purple passage even out of his own parts quite callously. If any doubts remain as to whether an actor who could look so profoundly and venerably scholarly did not know the difference between

Colman and Shakespear, much less between Shakespear's poetry and Shakespear's verbiage, a glance at his acting version of King Lear will dispel them. His henchmen Bram Stoker and L. F. Austin wrote his letters for him; for he did not know how much more creditable to him were his own simple and natural compositions than their displays of cleverness. He took no interest in the drama as such: a play was to him a length of stuff necessary to his appearance on the stage, but so entirely subordinate to that consummation that it could be cut to his measure like a roll of cloth. Of the theatre at large he knew almost nothing; for he never left his own stage. I am exaggerating when I say that he regarded an author as a person whose business it was to provide plays at five shillings an act, and, in emergencies, to write the fifth act whilst the fourth was being performed; and yet, in spite of his intercourse with Tennyson, Traill, Wills, and Comyns Carr, I believe that this caricature of his attitude gives a juster impression of it than any statement of the sober facts. He composed his acting with extraordinary industry and minuteness: his Matthias in The Bells and his Charles I were wonderful mosaics of bits of acting thought out touch by touch. His Macaire and Louis XI will hardly be surpassed: they were limit achievements in their *genre*. Even in his Shakespearean impostures (for such they were) there were unforgettable moments. But he composed his parts not only without the least consideration for the play as a whole, or even for the character as portrayed by the author (he always worked out some fancy of his own), but without any for the unfortunate actors whom he employed to support him. A great deal of that absence of vulgarity which I have noted as characteristic of his management was secured by the simple method of not allowing his company to act. He worked hard to make them do what he wanted for his own effects; but if they tried to make independent effects of their own, he did not hesitate to spoil them by tricks of stage management. In this way he threw on himself the enormous burden of attracting the public singlehanded. He achieved the celebrated feat of performing Hamlet with the part of Hamlet omitted and all the other parts as well, substituting for it and for them the fascinating figure of Henry Irving, which for many years did not pall on his audience, and never palled on himself. If those present could have remembered Barry Sullivan's Hamlet in the eighteen-sixties or foreseen Forbes-Robertson's Hamlet of the eighteen-nineties some of them might have said that Irving's Hamlet was neither skilled classic acting nor Shakespear's Hamlet, and that compared to Sullivan he was a limp duffer and compared to Robertson a freak; but most of them would have paid their money none the less to enjoy the performance as an avatar of Henry Irving.

When I use the word duffer I mean that when he began to play heroic parts he had neither the physique nor the technique needed for this sort of work, in which the actor must persuade the audience that he is sustaining bodily and vocal exertions which are, as a matter of fact, physically impossible. When Salvini electrified London with his Othello, Irving had a golden opportunity of finding out how this can be done by a study of the Italian actor's very scientific methods; but he flatly refused to avail himself of it, whereat Salvini was somewhat shocked. International courtesy apart, Irving was probably right in classing himself with the unteachables who have to find and go their own way rather than with the apprehensive geniuses who learn from everything and everybody.

I, being interested in the technique of acting, and having learned from Barry Sullivan, Ristori, and Salvini, what could be done in the grand school, was very conscious of Irving's technical shortcomings, and greatly relieved when, on his production of The Lady of Lyons, I found that he had at last learnt the limitations of the stage and of human faculty on it. Except for an occasional relapse into whinnying, he was maintaining his dignity and allowing the imagination of the audience to do its proper share of the work. Later on I saw him as Macbeth, his first assumption of which had provoked something like a storm of derision from the unconverted. I found it a performance of refined beauty. It was not any conceivable historical Macbeth; but then neither is Shakespear's. And I have not the faintest recollection of any other figure in the play, from which I infer that Ellen Terry cannot have played Lady Macbeth on that occasion, nor of any particular scene except the banquet scene, in which the violence of Macbeth's defiance of Banquo's ghost was rather ridiculously beyond the actor's resources; but still his performance was a fine piece of work within its limits. Mr. Gordon Craig's idolatrous memoir of Irving, though its judgments are invalidated by the misfortune that the author had no external standards except those set him by Irving himself, gives the most vivid extant pen-portrait of him both as actor and man.

To me, however, Irving's thirty years at the Lyceum, though a most imposing episode in the history of the English theatre, were an exasperating waste of the talent of the two artists who had seemed to me peculiarly fitted to lift the theatre out of its old ruts and head it towards unexplored regions of drama. With Lyceum Shakespear I had no patience. Shakespear, even in his integrity, could not satisfy the hungry minds whose spiritual and intellectual appetites had been whetted and even created by Ibsen; and Shakespear in his integrity was then unknown in the theatre, and remained so until William Poel and Harley Granville-Barker rediscovered and revived him. The shreds and patches which Irving and his predecessors tore out of his plays and tacked crudely together for performances which were interrupted four or five times by intolerable intervals, during which the women in the audience sat in silent boredom whilst the men wandered about the corridors and refreshment bars, were endurable only by people who, knowing no better, thought they were assisting at a very firstrate solemnization, and were helped by that illusion to persuade themselves that they were enjoying the best that a great institution and two great performers could do for them. I knew better. Irving, wasting his possibilities in costly Bardicide, was wasting Ellen Terry's as well. Her only rival as a Shakespearean actress was the great Ada Crehan (who by a printer's error became famous as Ada C. Rehan); and her genius too was being wasted by Augustin Daly, another master-mutilator of the unfortunate playwright whom he professed to adore. But as Daly did not himself act, his hackings and hewings were very largely addressed to the object of taking all the good lines out of the other parts and adding them to Ada Rehan's; and she spoke them so harmoniously that when listening to her it was impossible to care much about anything but the mere music of her voice and Shakespear's, whereas at the Lyceum Irving's peculiarities were the first consideration. To him, professionally, Ellen Terry was only the chief ornament of his theatre. Besides, his method was so slow that it was almost impossible to act with him. She had to stop too often and wait too long to sustain her part continuously when he was on the stage.

All this enraged me. I can keep my temper as well as most people; for my double training as a critic of highly sensitive living persons and a propagandist of seditious, not to say subversive, political views, kept me constantly on my guard against letting my temper get the better of me or my manners the worse of me: in short, against the least indulgence of personal malice. Besides, I am tolerant in matters of morals which provoke most people to censoriousness; for to me a great deal of current morality is unsound and mischievous. But when questions of art are concerned I am really malicious. Retrogressive art and wasted or unworthily used talent (the theatre is full of both) make me aware that I am capable of something as near to hatred as any emotion can be that has no taint of fear of it. This correspondence shews how, because Irving would not put his peculiar talent at the service of the new and intensely interesting development of the drama which had begun with Ibsen, and because he wasted not only his own talent but Ellen Terry's, I destroyed her belief in him and gave shape and consciousness to her sense of having her possibilities sterilized by him. Then her position became unbearable; and she broke loose from the Ogre's castle, as I called it, only to find that she had waited too long for his sake, and that her withdrawal was rather a last service to him than a first to herself.

The castle did not long survive her departure. Irving, himself poorer and the landlords of the Lyceum Theatre richer than when he entered it, went to the provinces to exploit his great reputation and retrieve his fortunes as Barry Sullivan had built his up. When he died, he was buried as a prince of the theatre, in Westminster Abbey, with only one dissenting voice, which I, by good luck, succeeded in silencing. His singleness of interest and purpose, his industry, his imagination, and his intensity had triumphed over his ignorance and self-sought isolation, and almost made qualities of them, forcing his audiences to attribute to him every talent, every dignity, and every accomplishment. Those who understood the art of the theatre and knew his limitations could challenge him on every point except one; and that one was his eminence. Even to call him eminent belittles his achievement: he was pre-eminent. He was not pre-eminent in or for this, that, or the other talent or faculty: his pre-eminence was abstract and positive: a quality in itself and in himself so powerful that it carried him to Westminster Abbey. Unlike Macready, Forbes-Robertson, and many of the best actors, he was stagestruck, and cared for nothing but acting: a craze and a limitation if you will, but one which saved him from being half ashamed of his profession, as Shakespear (the actor as distinct from the author) was, and thus enabled him finally to extort from the Government for his art the same official recognition which was accorded as a matter of course to painting and music.

Ellen Terry, not at all stagestruck, was extremely unlike Irving. She had had her professional technique hammered into her in her childhood by Mrs Charles Kean, who would sit in the gallery and see to it that every word of Ellen's reached her there. Thus she had skill at the back of her beauty and charm. Success came to her without the asking. She never had to struggle, like Irving, against derision and dislike. The few and insignificant attempts that were made to caricature her were hopeless misfires, whereas caricature alone could give a truthful impression of Irving. The posthumous statue of him outside the National Portrait Gallery in London, though possibly quite accurate in its measurements, gives no notion of what he was like; and even the portrait by Millais is only Irving carefully drest up to be as unlike himself as possible, the ghostly impression of his Philip II by Whistler being more suggestive of him than either. Artists were so eager to do Ellen Terry justice, and found it so difficult, that they had neither the time nor the desire to mock her. All this smoothing of her path had its disadvantages. She was not hardened and given the grim but invaluable quality of tenacity by having to struggle with an implacable resistance. Her value was so promptly and easily admitted that she did not realize it herself at all fully. I have already said that she trifled with her career by leaving the stage for years to devote herself to Godwin, an eminent architect in full practice outside the theatre. Irving would not have left the stage for a night to spend it with Helen of Troy. She squandered herself on all sorts of people and all sorts of interests until she lost the habit and power of mental concentration to such an extent that the slightest distraction made her forget her lines on the stage. She told me once that her memory was all right, but that if on the stage she saw the smallest thing (she instanced a matchbox) that had not been in exactly the same place the night before, it interested her so much that everything else at once went out of her head. Her sister Kate told me impatiently that Ellen could learn her parts well enough if she chose, but preferred to scatter her mind before the girls who crowded up to her to adore her. She was physically restless: when I reproached her for fidgetting she said "Do you know, I have no weight on the stage: unless I have heavy robes I cant keep on the ground." She literally did not think enough of herself: that was why her greatest self-squandering of all, her devotion of herself to the support of Irving at the Lyceum Theatre, did not until it was too late present itself to her otherwise than as a quite eligible professional opportunity.

And so, in the end, my early vision of the two as ideal instruments for a new drama did not come true.

When reading the letters which follow it must be borne in mind that long and intimate correspondence can occur only between people who never meet one another. Swift's journal to Stella would not have been written if they had met every day as Ellen Terry and Irving did, instead of living in separate islands. Ellen and I lived within twenty minutes of each other's doorstep, and yet lived in different worlds: she in a theatre that was a century behind the times, and I in a political society (the Fabian) a century ahead of them. We were both too busy to have any personal intercourse except with the people we were working with. Our correspondence began when I was a professional critic of music through a move she made to help a young musician in whom she was interested. Now critics, like dentists, are a good deal occupied in hurting sensitive people in sensitive places; and as they have to do it in an entertaining manner, which no doubt gives them an air of enjoying it, they produce an impression of Sadism. And so I, being a critic, and, I hope, an entertaining one, had been classed by Ellen Terry as an unamiable person. This was fortunate for me, because instead of having to live up to an exalted estimate of my merits I had only to be commonly civil and helpful to produce a surprised and pleased reaction in my favor. Finding her delightful as a correspondent, and having some gifts in that way myself, I improved the opportunity to such purpose that we presently became occupied with one another in a paper courtship, which is perhaps the pleasantest, as it is the most enduring, of all courtships. We both felt instinctively that a meeting might spoil it, and would certainly alter it and bring it into conflict with other personal relationships. And so I hardly ever saw her, except across the footlights, until the inevitable moment at last arrived when we had to meet daily at the rehearsals of the play I wrote for her: Captain Brassbound's Conversion. By that time Irving had passed out of her life, and indeed out of his own; and Ellen's heart was for the moment vacant. I could not help speculating as to the possibility of my filling the vacancy. But Providence had other views. At our first serious meeting in the rehearsal room at the Court Theatre, Ellen and I were talking together before business began when the door opened, and a young American actor, James Carew, who had been engaged to play the part of Captain Hamlin Kearney, came in. "Who is that?" said Ellen, looking at him with quick interest. "That's the American captain," I answered. Without an instant's hesitation she sailed across the room; put Mr Carew in her pocket (so to speak); and married him. The lucky captive naturally made no resistance; and some of the letters in this volume shew how far the marriage was successful, though I cannot believe that James had any choice of his own in the matter. I was awestruck; for I had not believed it possible for even the

xxvii

most wonderful of women to choose her man at a single glance and bear him off before he had time to realize who she was. Shooting a lion at sight is child's play in comparison, because it does not matter which lion it happens to be: if you do not kill it, it may kill you; so—bang! But it matters very much which man it is when marriage is in question; and so swift a decision by a huntress who, far from being promiscuous in her attachments, was highly fastidious, made me marvel and say to myself "There, but for the grace of God, goes Bernard Shaw."

After the play was disposed of our meetings were few, and all accidental. One of these chance meetings was on a summer day in the country near Elstree, where I came upon a crowd of people at work on a cinema film. Ellen Terry was there, acting the heroine. She was astonishingly beautiful. She had passed through that middle phase, so trying to handsome women, of matronly amplitude, and was again tall and slender, with a new delicacy and intensity in her saddened expression. She was always a little shy in speaking to me; for talking, hampered by material circumstances, is awkward and unsatisfactory after the perfect freedom of writing between people who *can* write. She asked me why I did not give her some work in the theatre. "I do not expect leading parts," she said: "I am too old. I am quite willing to play a charwoman. I should like to play a charwoman." "What would become of the play?" I said. "Imagine a scene in which the part of a canal barge was played by a battleship! What would happen to my play, or to anyone else's, if whenever the charwoman appeared the audience forgot the hero and heroine, and could think of nothing but the wonderful things the charwoman was going to say and do?" It was unanswerable; and we both, I think, felt rather inclined to cry.

She became a legend in her old age; but of that I have nothing to say; for we did not meet, and, except for a few broken letters, did not write; and she never was old to me.

Let those who may complain that it was all on paper remember that only on paper has humanity yet achieved glory, beauty, truth, knowledge, virtue, and abiding love.

G. B. S.

Ayot St Lawrence
26th June 1929

Introductory Note

BY THE EDITOR

I CANNOT pretend to first-hand knowledge of all the events I have had to narrate in the notes to these letters in order to keep the reader intelligently placed as to their historical context.

The personal acquaintance I can claim with both correspondents began some time after the majority of the letters were written. But, fortunately for me, my relations with the one who is dead allowed me to acquire a great deal of information about matters discussed in the earlier phases of the correspondence. I knew Ellen Terry well in many different aspects. As the closest friend of her daughter Edith Craig, I had a place in her family circle. I was a member of the company she engaged, when after her partnership with Irving came to an end, she went into management. I was associated with her in a small way as a dramatist. She played the leading part in my first original play and in my first adaptation of a foreign play. But it was when we worked together on her memoirs (published in 1908 under the title The Story of My Life) that I had my best opportunity for becoming well-informed about her career, and familiar with her views as a woman and an artist.

I have been able to supplement all I learned from Ellen Terry directly by references to the surviving correspondent Bernard Shaw, who has given me valuable assistance in preparing the connecting narratives. His more important contributions to them have been put in a form which makes their authorship perfectly clear.

Besides Bernard Shaw's assistance I have had assistance almost as valuable from Edith Craig, who knows more about the famous Lyceum partnership from the inside than any living person. As my most intimate friend and housemate she has been continually at hand to help me. Gordon Craig has helped me too, through the medium of his book on Henry Irving, which throws light on many of the events discussed in the correspondence.

Apart from the connective tissue, my editorial work has been largely a work of omission. The cuts have, however, not deprived the reader of anything except business proposals that came to nothing, uninteresting itineraries, and a few personalities of no importance which might conceivably affect living persons. There has been absolutely no bowdlerizing, nor whitewashing. The portraits of the principals have not been dehumanized by the removal of shadows, spots, and wrinkles. Nothing that any future editor may unearth from the letters can make the smallest difference to the reputations of the writers. This, which can be said confidently of them both, can be said finally and incontrovertibly about Ellen Terry, since nearly all her letters have been preserved and found. Several of Bernard Shaw's have been destroyed or lost; and it is possible that some of them may yet come to light. But it is very unlikely that they will add anything to the picture, or take anything away.

At all events I have kept back nothing, and if it seems improbable that a famous actress should come through such a revelation with a character that would do credit to many a saint, I can only say that she does so on her own account and not through any contrivance of mine.

C. ST. J.

ELLEN TERRY

AND

BERNARD SHAW

Ellen Terry and Bernard Shaw

A CORRESPONDENCE

I: G.B.S. *to* E.T.

[Ellen Terry writes in her autobiography The Story of My Life (pub-lished in 1908) that her correspondence with Bernard Shaw began with a letter from her asking him "what he thought of the chances of a composer-singer friend of mine." It is clear, however, from the letter numbered III in this collection that her first move was a letter, not to Shaw, but to Edmund Yates, editor of The World, at this date the most fashionable of the London weeklies. Its critical and social feuilletons were famous, William Archer writing every week on the drama, Theodore Childs on Parisian life, Lady Colin Campbell on pictures and London society, and Bernard Shaw on music. Yates evidently drew his critic's attention to Ellen Terry's letter, but he has no recol-lection of this. He answered the letter, and his reply, which is not among the letters from him preserved by Ellen Terry, no doubt provoked its prompt destruction by its stiffness. (See Letter II.) Nevertheless, he went to the after-noon concert at which she recited and her young friend sang; and the corre-spondence began in earnest with the letter (I) in which he sent her a consci-entiously careful opinion of the young friend's prospects.

At this time Ellen Terry was 44, and still acting with Henry Irving at the Lyceum Theatre, where she had first appeared as Ophelia in 1878. Bernard Shaw, eight years younger, had already made two of his many reputations in the curiously separate worlds of music (as a critic) and revolutionary politics (as a Socialist orator); but in the theatre he was practically unknown. Ellen Terry was not personally acquainted with him, and was not to become so until many years later. The majority of her letters are written from her London home in Barkston Gardens, Earls Court. Bernard Shaw, in the early phases of the correspondence, was unmarried and living with his mother in lodgings in Fitzroy Square.

Though Ellen Terry's 200 letters to Bernard Shaw outnumbered his to her, it must not be inferred that she wrote the more frequently of the two. There is evidence that she destroyed several of his letters, and that a few were lost.

From the year 1896 until the correspondence came to an end in 1922, Shaw seems to have kept nearly all Ellen Terry's letters. One reason given by him for the preservation even of some he was asked to destroy will be found in the note to Letter XXVIII.

The poem Ellen Terry recited at the Lyric Club was The Captive by Monk Lewis.

Elvira Gambogi, like many musicians who fail to attain eminence as executants or composers, subsequently devoted herself to teaching. She was only one of many young artists to whom Ellen Terry was a generous friend.—Trebelli: Zelia Trebelli, the famous operatic singer who took the public by storm in the sixties. She died in August 1892.

This is one of the few letters from Bernard Shaw to Ellen Terry not written with his own hand, but typed, like his regular professional World articles.]

24 June 1892.
29 Fitzroy Square, W.

DEAR MISS TERRY,

I WENT to the Lyric Club today, and listened to your friend Miss Gambogi. The only thing I can do is to give you my exact opinion, which you can take for what it is worth, and communicate to her or not, as you may think best. In every respect except the purely musical one, you will understand the position better than I do myself. To begin with, you know that you do not hold your present position because you possess this, that, and the other personal attraction, but because you have made yourself one of the six best actresses in the fourteen thousand millions of people (I think that is the figure) in the world. And you therefore know that nothing short of being one of the six best singers in the world would enable Miss Gambogi to get praised as you get praised. At the concert, for instance, although I was morbidly alive to every weakness in Lewis's poem, guessing all the bads and sads beforehand, and being tickled beyond measure by the line beginning "My language &c.," yet you brought tears to my eyes, not, you will understand, by the imaginary sorrows of the lunatic (sorrow does not make me cry, even when it is real) but by doing the thing beautifully. My whole claim to be a critic of art is that I can be touched in that way. Now Miss Gambogi did not touch me in the least. I liked her at once: she is very amiable, very clever, and very good-looking. But—and now the murder is coming out—she is not interesting as an artist. She sang the bolero from The Sicilian Vespers prettily and fluently, just as she would, I dare say, repeat one of Ophelia's speeches if you taught it to her. What is more, she sang it intelligently. You know, however, that this is not enough. The quality of execution that makes apparently trivial passages interesting, the intense grip of one's work that rouses all the attention of an audience: these she has not got to anything like a sufficient degree to make a career for her; and what is more, she will never acquire them in drawingrooms or in the Lyric Club. What she does is not convincing to me: it is only a development of that facility in music which clever children acquire when they are brought up in a musical atmosphere. You must know how children who grow up amid theatrical surroundings catch up a certain familiarity with stage ways which inexperienced people easily mistake for genuine artistic talent. Bedford Park is full of such imps, who will nevertheless be hopelessly beaten in the long run by comparatively unpromising competitors. Now singing is to Miss Gambogi partly what acting is to the imps: more a picked-up habit than an art. She has got to turn the habit into an art—to put purpose into it—to make it the means of realizing herself, concentrating herself, throwing herself completely and exhaustively into action—I cannot express it; but you will perhaps recognize what I mean. I therefore think she ought to work on the stage if she can obtain an opening. All her drawingroom beauty and charm will vanish at once behind the footlights; and she will have to remake herself, build herself up from the foundation, instead of taking herself down from a peg as she was hung up by Nature, and wearing herself at the Lyric Club before audiences more or less packed. She has a certain resemblance to Trebelli both in facial expression and musical style; and she might, if she worked hard enough, succeed her as Cherubino, Zerlina &c. Her voice is all stifled by singing into carpets and curtains: it wants large spaces to develop in; and what is true of her voice is true also of herself. She will never be a dazzling vocal executant any more than Trebelli was: her success, if it is to come at all, will be in sympathetic, intelligent dramatic singing. The most unpromising thing about her is her grace in her present uncultivated state. When Nature intends anyone to be a highly cultivated artist, she generally forces them on by condemning them to fiendishness or loutishness until they fulfill her intention. However, there must be exceptions to this, except perhaps as to the fiendishness.

I really must not make this letter any longer: you must be out of patience already. My verdict briefly is that as a drawing-room singer Miss Gambogi is no better than many others; and I would not walk a hundred yards to hear her sing again. But if she takes good care of herself and her voice, ten years work on the stage may make something of her. There is a certain humanity about her, to the development of which I should be sorry to prophesy any limit. At the same time, if she prefers to take things easy, and sing and compose in her present fashion, she may, with her social talent, get on very peacefully and comfortably, which you will perhaps tell her is better than being a great artist. If you do, you will be guilty of a most awful falsehood; but you must settle that with your own conscience.

My chief concern about this letter is the likelihood of its putting you to the trouble of acknowledging it. If writing is a trouble to you (my own correspondence drives me stark mad) pray do not mind me, or at least do not go beyond saying "Thank you for nothing" on a postcard.

Yours very truly,

G. BERNARD SHAW

II: E. T. *to* G. B. S.

[*In this letter, calligraphically beautiful like all letters written by Ellen Terry until the last years of her life when her eyesight, always a source of trouble to her, failed, many words and phrases, and a few whole sentences are underlined. It has been thought undesirable to let the usual method of representing a writer's underlinings in print be employed in this book. Italics, never a satisfactory equivalent for them, would give an entirely wrong impression of their significance in Ellen Terry's letters. Accustomed in speech to express her exact meaning by delicate nuances of tone and intonation, it is clear that when she wrote she felt the need of some sign for sound. She put a line, or two lines, on occasion three, under a word to convey the significance she could have given it with her voice. That was a far more subtle significance than a sign which stands merely for emphasis can convey. If all that Ellen Terry underlined were italicized, the reader might imagine that she had an epistolary vice, to which all Victorian writers were prone, and none more so than those of the female sex. To protect Ellen Terry from such misconstruction, her signs for sounds have not been reproduced, except when emphasis only is obviously intended.*]

29 June 1892

I AM exceedingly obliged to you for troubling yourself so much about my little friend. Your letter saddened me very much, for I do care for the girl, and long and long to help her. She's so alone, and so very, very little assertive. She *has* individuality; and I learn every day from her simplicity.

What fools we are in bringing up our children. This girl's father (who died a year ago) kept her all to himself in an old studio in Milan, and feared for her if she played with other children, or made acquaintance with man or woman! Her mother hated her from her birth, and has not set eyes on her now for the last 6 or 7 years. Consider her situation! But I see a peep-hole in your words for Blessed Hope. I will work to get her a few lines on the stage for a few shillings a week and at least then she will know the great happiness of occupation.

I didnt like you when you first wrote to me. I thought you unkind, and exceedingly stiff and prim. Now I beg your pardon most heartily. Although of course it matters no jot to you what I think, I must yet ask you to take my very bestest thanks for your long last splendid letter, and believe me most gratefully yours

ELLEN TERRY

III: G. B. S. *to* E. T.

[*Richard D'Oyly Carte, whose "provincial tours" of Gilbert and Sullivan Opera are referred to, was born in 1844 and died in 1901. In his earlier days he arranged concert and lecture tours. He left £240,000, more than double Gilbert's fortune, and more than four times Sullivan's.*]

1 July 1892

DEAR MISS TERRY,

JUST a hasty line—something sensible. Do you know D'Oyly Carte or Mrs D'Oyly Carte, who was Miss Lenoir? They always have several companies touring in a small way with their Savoy repertory; and they are the only people in the comic opera line in London, as far as I know, with whom Miss Gambogi's niceness would not be a disadvantage. Besides there are the possibilities of the New English Opera House, and of Carte's turn for operatic speculation. They might give her something to begin with. You ought to be able to make her speak English as well as the Dutch prima donna at the Savoy, Miss Snyders.

I am unfortunately quite unable to help her myself. As a musical critic I must not ask the most microscopic favor from any musical artist or entrepreneur.

I really did not mean to be stiff. Consider my awful situation. I had no right to go an inch beyond the business on which Yates wrote to me. I was presuming on the chance of your never having heard of me; but I was also running a considerable risk of your writing something of this kind to Yates:—"Sir: I wrote to you to ask you a trifling favor. In return, you have exposed me to a communication from the vilest of mankind, an enemy of religion and society, a shameless spouter of sedition in the streets, a wretch whose opinions about the womanliness which is the glory of my sex have made hardened profligates blush, a champion of the monster Ibsen, and one whom, to crown all, Mr Irving held up to public execration at a banquet in Liverpool for calling me an ignoramus. Henceforth, Mr Yates, we are strangers. I am, Sir, your obedient servant, Ellen Terry." Lots of people take that view of me, and go out of their way to print it. And from their point of view, it is perfectly true, all except the calling you an ignoramus, a calumny for which I will one day be even with Irving, who had better never have been born than quote my books without reading them.

I write in great haste, as I am up to my eyes in the election, my spouting propensities making me for the moment a much courted person. I am off to Bradford for a couple of days tomorrow; and I thought it better to suggest Carte in case you should take steps at once. I hope this letter is intelligible—I hardly know whether I am on my head or my heels. I am delighted beyond reason that my last letter was a good one. If the others were really stiff (which I am disposed to deny) your replies were angelic.

The stage is waiting for me at the corner of the square—open air meeting.

G. B. S.

IV: E. T. *to* G. B. S.

4 July 1892.
22 Barkston Gardens, S. W.

A ND TO think I thought you huffy! Coals of fire are burning my poor brains out! It's mostest kind to write to me so about my young friend, and I'll follow up the clue (Clew? my stylograph won't spell) about Mr D'Oyly Carte's provincial tours. In the midst of all your work to take so much trouble. Well, I can't begin to thank you, for thanks are not enough. *Did* you call me an "ignoramus?" Well, I forgive you for speaking the truth. But I must ask Mr Irving to tell me all about it. It delights me to be able to tell you that Miss Gambogi cleared £100 by that concert, the first money the poor girl has ever had. No more. You have no time, and I very little.

Thank you. Thank you. *Thank* you for all your beautifulness. If you

8

could ask me to do a little thing for you some day, I would do it, or I'd try to.

Yours sincerely,
ELLEN TERRY

V: G. B. S. *to* E. T.

[The book sent with this letter must have been The Quintessence of Ibsenism, first published in 1891, and reprinted, with a new preface and additional chapters, in 1913. The names of the Ibsen pioneers mentioned are not so well-known to-day as at the end of the 19th century, so some brief biographies are inserted for the benefit of 20th century readers. Florence Farr, who produced Rosmersholm at the Vaudeville Theatre in February 1891, was also a Shaw pioneer. She played Blanche in the first performance of his first play Widowers' Houses in 1892, and Louka in the first performance of Arms and the Man in 1894, which was given, I believe, under her management. She was concerned in the foundation of the Irish Literary Theatre in 1898. When Gilbert Murray's translation of The Hippolytus of Euripides was produced at the Court Theatre under the Vedrenne-Barker régime, she composed the music for it, and appeared as leader of the Chorus. Her recitals of verse to her own musical accompaniment on the psaltery pleased the poets, particularly W. B. Yeats.

Elizabeth Robins, who has had a distinguished career as a novelist, was at this time better known as an actress. Her chief successes were won in the Ibsen drama.

Janet Achurch (Mrs. Charles Charrington) a member of an old family of actors, had played a great variety of parts before she appeared as Nora in the first English production of A Doll's House in June 1889. Her association with Ibsen dates from this remarkable performance. She and her husband did valuable work in making his plays known in England. They were great friends of Shaw's. There are many references in this correspondence to Janet, who is ranked by Shaw in his notice of Little Eyolf in The Saturday Review as "one of the three best yet discovered actresses of their generation."]

5 July 1892

ONE LETTER more, positively the last, as writing to you is only a form of self-indulgence.

The word ignoramus occurs in the book which I send you herewith. I will not tell you the page; but I may say that it is so far from the beginning that I doubt if any human being has held out long enough to reach it, except a few who began at the end and read backward. When I wrote the book I had a terrible grudge against you, and I have it still. It arose in this way. I do not often find time to go to the theatre;

but I go when I can. One day I went into an afternoon performance, and found a poor ungifted, dowdy, charmless young woman struggling pathetically with Ibsen's Lady from the Sea. She was doing her best; and I thanked my stars that I was not a dramatic critic, and had not to go home and tell her that after all her study and toil she had done far more harm than good. That was the first act of my little experience. Act 2 was another visit to another theatre. There I found the woman who OUGHT to have played the Lady from the Sea—the woman with all the nameless charm, all the skill, all the force, in a word, all the genius—playing—guess what? Why, a charade the whole artistic weight of which would not have taxed the strength of the top joint of her little finger. And the silly public delightedly applauding. Worse than that, traitors calling themselves critics were encouraging her—allowing their brains and consciences to be cajoled away by her beauty—talking fatuously of her child's play as if it had been the best she was capable of. I was furious. If I had been a god, and had created her powers for her, I should have interrupted the performance with thunder, and asked in a fearful voice why she was wasting the sacred fire of which I had made her trustee. But I knew that she had made her powers for herself, and could be called to account by nobody for the use she had made of them. So I sat helpless, and went off in impotent rage. Since then I have never heard Nance Oldfield praised without vowing vengeance. And yet Charles Reade was better than Calmour. Oh, the Amber Heart, the Amber Heart, the Amber Heart! My wrath returns on me as I think of it all. Ask you a favor! Never by all that ought to be sacred to both of us as artists, not the smallest—not even the greatest.

I congratulate Miss Gambogi on the £100, but much more on having no father or mother, so that she can spend it all on making herself an artist, and be quite free into the bargain. To have friends, and to have no relations; do you call that a disadvantage? Happy girl! And I have helped her to clear a hundred pounds! Do you hear that, oh Rosmersholm Rebecca (Florence Farr), ruined by two enormously successful Ibsen matinées, and now honestly buckling-to at six lines in a *lever de rideau* to pay for your lodgings. Think of it, oh Hedda-Gabler-Karin (Elizabeth Robins), staring gloomily at the bank book that registers the cost of your courage and skill. What would you give for the half of it just now, oh cleaned-out and invalided, but still indomitable Nora (Janet Achurch)? And you, oh vanished and forgotten Ellida, I wonder have *you* a hundred pounds to bless yourself with?

And you, Nance Oldfield, what have you done to set against the records of these hardly used ones? Why (say you) created my incomparable self, sir. True, irresistible Ellen, quite true. That silences me. Farewell.

G. B. S.

[The gap in the correspondence between July 1892 and March 1895 has been bridged by Shaw with this interesting, but highly controversial piece of connective narrative.]

WITH this letter, in which G. B. S. unmasks the battery which he kept trained on Ellen Terry and the Irving management at the Lyceum Theatre until its end, the correspondence seems to have lapsed suddenly for three years.

When it was resumed Shaw's position was changed. He had abandoned musical criticism and broken into the theatrical profession —he can scarcely be described as pacifically joining it—by cobbling up an old and long discarded beginning of a play, and throwing it on the stage through Mr J. T. Grein's Independent Theatre (the first of the little pioneering societies which finally shook the regular theatres out of their worn-out grooves) and, as he himself put it, "at once becoming infamous as a playwright." It is impossible for the present generation of playgoers to imagine how this commonplace three-act comedy, of which the Independent Theatre could afford only one Sunday night performance and one matinée, could have kept the London press discussing it for a whole fortnight as it actually did. The explanation is that its commonplaces were at that time (1892) staggering and scandalous novelties. It presented, instead of the beautiful, amiable, gentle heroine who was then *de rigueur,* a husband hunting young virago who opened the conventional strong situation at the end of the second act by throttling her parlormaid in a transport of fury. And its theme was no love romance, but the then burning question of the Housing of the Working Classes. The effect of this at a time when the London theatre was occupied exclusively with theatricals, to the complete exclusion of politics, religion, speeches more than twenty words long, and anything nearer to human nature than Victorian shop window femininity, is now happily inconceivable. There was no question of Widowers' Houses being a good play or a bad one: it was vehemently denied that the thing was a play at all. It was dismissed by the critics as a revolting ineptitude by a pamphleteer without knowledge of the theatre, or naturally dramatic faculty.

The effect of the experiment on Shaw was to make him quite sure of himself as a writer for the stage. By 1895, when the correspondence with Ellen Terry was resumed, he had written four of the series of plays which he published three years later as Plays Pleasant & Unpleasant; and one of the pleasant ones, Arms & the Man, had been produced in the regular West End manner by Miss Horniman, the ostensible manageress being Florence Farr, and the leading actress Alma Murray, an ex-member of the Lyceum company. Another member of the Lyceum company, now Lady Martin Harvey, had played the throttled parlormaid in Widowers' Houses.

Another change had taken place in Shaw's situation. Edmund Yates died in 1894; and Shaw, severing his connection with The World and transferring himself to The Saturday Review (edited by Mr. Frank Harris), began the series of criticisms which first made the theatrical world acutely conscious of him. His attitude towards Shakespear soon made something of a scandal. Ellen Terry and Irving were the unquestioned heads of their profession in its admittedly highest department: that of Shakespearean art.

Applying to the British theatre the standards of philosophical seriousness and psychologic depth set upon by Goethe, Ibsen, and Wagner, and especially the new importance given to women in the dramas of the last two, Shaw dismissed the entire London drama, from Shakespear at its head to his own contemporaries, as too childish to claim any intellectual character whatsoever; and he seized every opportunity to revile Irving and Daly for wasting the talent of such greatly gifted actresses as Ellen Terry and Ada Rehan on pre-Ibsenite plays which were by his standards womanless.

This point became the central theme of the correspondence which follows. The G. B. S. of The Saturday Review (not yet, remember, the Bernard Shaw of Heartbreak House, Methuselah, and St Joan) did, as we shall see, gradually convince Ellen Terry that her Lyceum triumphs were, in the new searchlight thrown on the stage by Ibsen, a waste of her highest possibilities. Even Ada Rehan, who did not forgive Shaw his derision until she had lighted Daly's way to dusty death, succumbed finally to the iconoclast. Ellen alone took no offence. Laurence Irving, Henry's Irish-looking son, who made Shaw his friend, said to him, "All my people think you the most appalling Yahoo." That view was common enough among the actors then in fashion. It never misled Ellen Terry. Part of her remarkable mental endowment was a sure touch with men. It was easy to "get round her" by appealing to her pity, but impossible to deceive her. These letters shew that at a time when Shaw was posturing as a sort of half-saved Mephistopheles with a success that imposed on the whole theatrical West End, Ellen Terry, without hesitation or effort, went straight through the imposture to the real man and nursed him like a baby, though always taking his judgment seriously even when it did not jump with her own.

Her position had not changed since their first interchange of letters save as an actress's position must change as she approaches her fiftieth year, whilst the heroines whom she has to impersonate retain the gift of first youth and eternal beauty. Older and heavier parts, with the interest of which youth has very little if anything to do, become more and more necessary to her, whilst the conventional heroines, who are nothing if not young and beautiful, and are insipid and silly to an intelligent actress, make her feel more and more ridiculous. Even without a G. B. S. to prompt her Ellen Terry must have realized sooner or later that no new parts of the kind she needed were in the Lyceum repertory or in the least likely to be admitted to it, whilst actresses whose skill and charm she knew to be inferior to her own were receiving for their shabby little performances of Ibsen's plays in coterie theatres, eulogies that Mrs Siddons or Rachel could hardly have quite deserved. She could not condescend from the splendor and prestige of the Lyceum to the coterie theatres and their squalid bankrupt adventures; yet she was too wise, too experienced in the terrible evanescence of theatrical vogues, and too good a judge of men and women to be imposed on by the apparent permanence of the splendor and the prestige. Unlike the younger adorers of Irving, to whom he was immeasurably great because their standards of greatness were set by himself, Ellen Terry was pre-Irving and admired him rather as a wonderful innovator with an irresistible personality than as the genuine mother's milk professional that she was herself. She quite understood Shaw's pre-Irving views of acting.

The contrast between herself and Irving could hardly have been stronger. She, all brains and sympathy, scattering them everywhere and on everybody: he, all self, concentrating that self on his stage as on a pedestal. She, able to express herself effortlessly with her pen, raining letters all over the place on the just and the unjust: he, preferring to keep a staff of literary henchmen to write his letters and lectures, which sometimes did him only sorry justice. But the combination worked.

13

Everything went from her and everything came to him. They were extrovert and introvert, and thus to a sufficient extent complemented one another whilst the Lyceum sun was at its zenith.

Shaw was unlike Irving in all respects except that both of them were incorrigible actors, and unlike even there because Irving acted avowedly and in the theatre only, whereas Shaw made all the world his stage and was not supposed to be acting, in spite of his frequent clownings and the mask of mountebankery which Ellen Terry saw through so easily.

If we take it that a clever woman's most amusing toys are interesting men we must admit that Ellen Terry was fortunate in her two dolls. How far, and for what moments, they were anything more to her (and, after all, one can be very fond of dolls, as Ibsen had just pointed out) must be gathered from the correspondence.

VI: E. T. *to* G. B. S.

[*Apparently the recommencement of the correspondence was provoked by a newspaper paragraph. Ellen Terry always read her newspaper thoroughly, and made a habit of cutting out anything in it which interested her.*]

10 March 1895.
22 Barkston Gardens,
Earls Court, S. W.

DEAR MR BERNARD SHAW,

H ow SPLENDID! What fun. I wish I could be there. But for my wretched bit of work o' nights, I'm obliged to shut myself up. My Sundays are the only days in which I dare allow myself to be either interested or amused ('cos it delights and tires me so). And this note is to beg you to let me know if on any Sunday you discourse in public. Dont trouble to answer me now (woman's generosity!) but one line at the time, please, if you can remember it. I wrote you the other day and tore up the scribble. Woman's generosity again!

Yours sincerely and gratefully,

ELLEN TERRY

[*Newspaper cutting*]

Mr George Bernard Shaw is always one of the most vigorous and wittiest of speakers, but he should surely be more amusing even than usual next Sunday afternoon, when he is to address the Women's Progressive Society, who give an "At Home" at the rooms of the Ideal Club. For the subject of Mr

Shaw's lecture is to be "Feminine Meanness," and it is to be followed by an open discussion; and one cannot but think that even the courage of Mr Shaw will be pretty thoroughly tested during the course of the afternoon.

[*Postscript to letter*]

>There was a young man who said *Why*
> Cant I stick my chin into my eye?
>Perhaps I could do it
>If I put my mind to it,
>There's no knowing what you can do
>Till you try!

(I've got it wrong somehow, but it's *fine*, I think. E. T.)

VII: G. B. S. *to* E. T.

[*At the date of this letter, Ellen Terry was on tour in America with Henry Irving. It was their fourth visit; the first was in 1883. During their absence from London the Lyceum Theatre had been taken by Johnston Forbes-Robertson. In September 1895 he had put on Romeo and Juliet. "As to Juliet," wrote Shaw in The Saturday Review, "she danced like the daughter of Herodias."—The "beautiful little one-act play" referred to is The Man of Destiny (the sixth of Shaw's plays).—Ellen Terry's tomb is not in West-minster Abbey. The beautiful mural monument (the work of Paul Cooper) where her ashes lie, is in St Paul's Church, Covent Garden. Her epitaph is: "Ellen Terry. Actress. Born 1848. Died 1928."*]

1 November 1895

MY DEAR MISS TERRY,

THIS lonely critic's den, on which you have shed a ray from a news-paper wrapper, is wonderfully warmed up by it. It came just when it was wanted. I had just finished a magnificent article, not on the theatre, but on Church-going (of all subjects!), for a new quarterly; and the effort, complicated by the inexorable swing round of The Saturday Review weekly criticism, had left me *sore* with labor. At that exact moment your impulse to pet me for a moment came to hand, with heavenly effect.

I am interested in the bicycling, having lately tamed that steed my-self: but I utterly refuse to concern myself with your Beatrices and Portias and the like. *Anybody* can play Shakespear: you are wanted for other things. Mrs Pat Campbell entrances all London as Juliet, with a skirt dance. At the end, to shew that she is not going to give herself more trouble than she can help, she takes the dagger, and with a superb laziness, props it against the tomb and leans against the point, plainly conveying that if it will not go in on that provocation, it can let it alone. Then she lies down beside Romeo and revolves herself right over him like the roller of a mangle, leaving his sensitively chiselled profile perceptibly snubbed. Nothing will persuade me that Shakespear ever carries a modern woman with him right through: even Duse could do nothing with Cleopatra; and Mary Anderson, before whom the art of acting fled abashed (Lord have mercy on us, miserable sinners!) did as well as anybody else in Perdita. By the way, if you *will* let Shakespear steal you to decorate his plays with, why not play Hermione? Leontes is a magnificent part, worth fifty Othellos (Shakespear knew nothing about jealousy when he wrote Othello), as modern as Ibsen, and full of wonderful music—"I have tremor cordis on me" and so on.

To my great exasperation I hear that you are going to play Madame Sans Gêne. And I have just finished a beautiful little one act play for Napoleon and a strange lady—a strange lady who will be murdered by someone else whilst you are nonsensically pretending to play a washerwoman. Besides, your place is not *after* Réjane. I was asked to do an English Madame Sans Gêne as an opera, for Florence St John. That was suitable enough: I said I'd do it if I had time, which I never had (time meaning will). If they had asked me to do it for Ellen Terry, I would have obliterated them from the surface of the globe. Will your tomb in Westminster Abbey have nothing but reproaches for an epitaph?

G. B. S.

VIII: E. T. *to* G. B. S.

18 November 1895

I F YOU give Napoleon and that Strange Lady (Lord, how attractively tingling it sounds!) to anyone but me I'll—write to you every day! (I always feel inclined that way.) Ah, but be kind, and let me know that "lady."

Yours E. T.

Dont be ill. So many "good souls" can do that easily, but if you (and a very few) are ill, it's different.

IX: G. B. S. *to* E. T.

[After reading The Man of Destiny *Ellen Terry telegraphed: "Just read your play. Delicious." The stage directions include a personal description of the Strange Lady which is an obvious pen-portrait of Ellen Terry.— "That villain Mansfield": Richard Mansfield first produced* Arms and the Man *at the Herald Square Theatre, New York, on 17 September 1894. This was the first American production of a play by Shaw.]*

28 November 1895

MY DEAR MISS TERRY,

VERY well: here is the Strange Lady for you, by book post. It is of no use now that it is written, because nobody can act it. Mind you bring it safely back to me; for if you leave it behind you in the train or in your dressing room, somebody will give a surreptitious performance of it: and then bang goes my copyright. If the responsibility of protecting it is irksome, tear it up. I have a vague recollection of curl papers in Nance Oldfield for which it might be useful. I have other copies.

This is not one of my great plays, you must know: it is only a display of my knowledge of stage tricks—a commercial traveller's sample. You would like my Candida much better; but I never let people read that: I always read it to them. They can be heard sobbing three streets off.

By the way—I forget whether I asked you this before—if that villain Mansfield plays Arms and the Man anywhere within your reach, will you go and see it and tell me whether they murder it or not. And your petitioner will ever pray &c. &c.

G. BERNARD SHAW

X: G. B. S. *to* E. T.

[We gather from this letter that Ellen Terry had started on her Man of Destiny campaign. She writes in The Story of My Life: *"Henry at my request considered it, although it was always difficult to fit a one-act play into the Lyceum bill." The reference to the possibility of Irving's buying the play or offering advances on it is significant. Shaw tells me that Irving probably thought he was "bidding for a bribe." Shaw certainly suspected him of thinking so. "Irving's princely manner of buying literary courtiers," he writes, "was well known to me. The sequel proved that Irving, though contemptuously willing to pay me for control of the play, never had any serious intention of producing it." The first part of the letter refers to Laurence Irving's play* Godefroi and Yolande. *It was first produced at Chicago, and according to Ellen Terry in spite of its unpleasant theme (leprosy) "splendidly received."]*

17

ELLEN TERRY: what do you mean by this? Have you no respect for my years, my talent, my reputation, my feelings, that you play these games on me? Here is a newspaper—a miserable American newspaper—containing a monstrous statement that you insist on playing the part of a—a—no: I cannot write it, speak it, think it. Far be all such horrors from you for ever and ever and ever!

"And he went out from his presence—a leper white as snow."

How could you have the heart to threaten me with such a thing? Do you want me to go out from your presence also white as snow, blanched by a tormented, wounded heart? Wretch! perverse, *aluminium*-hearted wretch! I do not know any other way of expressing the lightness, the hardness, the radiance of that centre of your being.

Ugh! It is not an idea, but a pain too deep for surgery.

Let me shake it off. To business!

DEAR MADAM,

MY ATTENTION has been called to certain marginal notes made by you upon a copy of the Chicago Tribune dated the 25th ult. Among other flattering and irresistible expressions, whose probable insincerity I forgive in consideration of the exquisite pleasure they give me, I note a statement, apparently referring to my Napoleonic play, that "H. I. quite loves it, and will do it finely." Now I have to observe on this, first, that if the matter is one of love, the only initials I care for are not H. I., but E. T.; and second, that if H. I. has any serious intentions I should like to know whether they are honorable or not. For, having no idea that His Immensity had any sort of interest in the play—having sent it to you, I swear, out of pure vanity, to steal another priceless millionth of an inch of your regard by shewing you what a clever fellow I am—I might at any moment have parted with it to Mansfield or another, both for England and America. It has had one or two very narrow escapes, chiefly through my own laziness. Will you therefore befriend me to the extent of letting me know seriously whether H. I. wishes me to hold the play for him, as its production by him would of course be quite the best thing that could happen to it. If so, there is one thing that he ought to know, as he is commonly supposed to prefer to buy plays from the author. As long as I remain a dramatic critic I can neither sell plays nor take advances. I must depend altogether on royalties and percentages on actual performances. Otherwise, you see, I should simply be bribed right and left: already I could increase my income considerably by making "adaptions" for managerial shelves. It is bad enough to have my conscience telling me that with regard to you, towards whom it is my duty and my point of honor to be sternly impartial, I am hopelessly won over —won without a struggle—; but what would you think of me if I were accessible to money? At the same time, I am boundlessly accessible to the meanest commercial considerations when I can grab at them in an effective attitude of incorruptibility. You will detect at a glance the adroit mixture of flattery and business in this letter. I am eager for business—keen on it—because it will be an excuse for more flattery—because I can gratify my desire to talk nonsense to you under cover of filling my pockets. I *must* attach myself to you somehow: let me therefore do it as a matter of business. Gold, be thou my idol henceforth!

By far the best way to exploit my reputation (small, but intense) would be to produce the piece in New York. They think more of me in America than in England, thanks to Arms and the Man. But then I should not be able to rehearse it—to teach you and H. I. how to act —to see you every day for ever so long. Besides, if the play starts in America I shall have to get up a copyrighting performance here.

But it is all nonsense: you are only playing with me. I will go to that beautiful Mrs Patrick Campbell, who won my heart long ago by her pianoforte playing as Mrs Tanqueray, and make her head twirl like a chimney cowl with my blarney. *She* shall play the Strange Lady—she and the passion-worn Forbes. Yes, it shall be so. Farewell, faithless Ellen!

G. B. S.

XI: G. B. S. *to* E. T.

[*The play Bernard Shaw wrote for William Terriss was The Devil's Disciple. The effect made by Ellen Terry in the scene in Wills's Olivia where Olivia strikes Thornhill (played by Terriss) is shown not only in this letter, but in Shaw's You Never Can Tell, which contains a stage direction founded on Ellen Terry's "business" in that passage.—Penley: W. S. Penley, the comedian who succeeded Beerbohm Tree as Spalding in The Private Secretary. He built a theatre in Great Queen Street which was called after him. Its present name is The Kingsway.*]

26 March 1896

Do you see this?*
    Well, that is a Röntgen photograph of my heart, taken immediately after your telegram declaring that The Man of Destiny cannot

* There is a rough sketch of a badly broken heart in the manuscript of the letter.

possibly be performed until the 31st December 1897 (that is what next year means). What laziness! what procrastination! what indifference! Nothing to be done but put an advertisement in the paper, send around the corner for a stock scene and a few foreign looking uniforms, call a rehearsal or two, and engage an extra force of police to cope with the crowd at the doors. And yet you tell me it cannot be done for two years. Do you suppose that a trumpery toy of that sort can be put away in a drawer all that time, and then be taken out and enjoyed as if it were the brightest of novelties. Not a bit of it. Next year, when you look at my script, you will ask yourself with a sinking of the heart, whether that flimsy stuff is what you thought a part worth playing, and H. I. will ask you what you meant by committing him to such tomfoolery. I myself will writhe at the thought of an exposure of my folly on the stage as I writhe when I am asked to republish one of my novels (I once wrote novels). I hate the play already now that my Strange Lady has faded away into the unreal Future. There is no Future: there is only the Present. Do you suppose I will let you treat me as you treat Shakespear—play me centuries after I am dead? No: I will make no bonds and bargains for next year: by then my gold will have turned into withered leaves in your portmanteau. Let 1896 perform its own plays: If you do not want me until 1897 you had better have an 1897 play—I have an idea for a little play about King Pippin and his wife, with a lovely medieval French court for a stage setting—and let The Man of Destiny be done by Penley and Madame Anna Ruppert in London, and in America by Mansfield, who has had the audacity to ask me for another play, after heaping villainy on me over my Candida. I see that he was sagacious enough to pit Shaw against Shakespear by putting up Arms and the Man at Chicago against Macbeth, and that you did *not* give your understudy a chance by going to see my play. Alas! you do not really love me.

Terriss (this is a secret) wants me to collaborate with him in a play the scenario of which includes every situation in the Lyceum repertory or the Adelphi record. The best act is The Bells. He is arrested either for forgery or murder at every curtain, and goes on as fresh as paint and free as air when it goes up again. I talked it over with him whilst he was dressing for a matinée at the Adelphi. I noticed that his chest was black and blue. He caught the expression of pity and horror in my eyes as I caught sight of the bruise, and said, with a melancholy smile, "Ah yes, Ellen Terry! You remember the third act of Olivia at the old Court? I was Thornhill. The marks have never come off. I shall carry them to my grave." I did not tell him that I also had received heart wounds in those days which I shall carry to my grave. Neither, by the way, did I decide in favor of the collaboration. But I seriously think I shall write a play for him. A good melodrama is a more difficult thing to write than all this clever-clever comedy: one must go straight to the core of humanity to get it, and if it is only good enough, why, there you have Lear or Macbeth.

The most depressing rumors are about here as to the next Lyceum production—Julius Cæsar or some such obsolete rubbish, with Wilson Barrett as Pontius Pilate. Will nothing persuade H. I. that Queen Anne is dead? There is Peer Gynt ready to his hand. Can he read it without swearing to be the first man to drown that cook and peel that onion on the English stage? And how beautiful you would be as Solveig! Million millions! Is H. I. blind? is he deaf? or is he no actor at all, but only a Shakespear-struck antiquary that he passes by the great chances of his life as if they were pieces of orange peel laid in his path expressly to capsize him?

But what use is it to talk? We have no theatres, no drama, no actors, no nothing. And you will play nothing for me until next year, like the old tavern sign "Credit given To-morrow." Very well, then: but the delay raises my terms. This year, three pounds (as your telegram offers) of sterling gold. But next year the three pounds must be equal pounds of your fair flesh, to be by no means cut off and taken in what part of your body pleaseth me, but to accumulate to my credit until the forty-fifth performance or so, when I will take it all in a lump, if I may libel it by such a very undesciptive word. But even then I shall only have the shrine, useless unless the inner lamp shine on me. For one ray of that every year you shall have all the plays in the world and be a thousandfold underpaid.

Great Heavens, my work, my work, my work! How is that to get done if I turn from it every moment to write to you!

G. B. S.

XII: G. B. S. *to* E. T.

[The letters from Ellen Terry at this time are missing. There are none from her between November 1895 and May 1896.—Of Schubert's 603 songs, ten

are settings of words by Sir Walter Scott. The Ellen and the Huntsman songs are from The Lady of the Lake.]

6 April 1896,
Stocks Cottage, Aldbury, Tring.

THERE is a song of Schubert's in which the gentleman (who is, I think, Scott's Imprisoned Huntsman translated and retranslated and translated back again from English to German) wants "to sun himself in Ellen's eyes." That is what I am going to do for a while this evening in my Easter cottage. The weather has frowned; but Fortune has smiled. Ten splendid things have happened: to wit, 1, a letter from Ellen Terry; 2, a cheque for my Chicago royalties, swollen by the dollars of the thousands of people who were turned away from the doors where Ellen was acting and had to go to Arms and the Man *faute de mieux*; 3, a letter from Ellen Terry; 4, the rolling away of the clouds from the difficult second act of my new play, leaving the view clear and triumphant right on to the curtain; 5, a letter from Ellen Terry; 6, a beautiful sunset ride over the hills and far away, thinking of Ellen Terry; 7, a letter from Ellen Terry; 8, a letter from Ellen Terry; 9, a letter from Ellen Terry; 10, a letter from Ellen Ellen Ellen Ellen Ellen Ellen Ellen Ellen Ellen Eleanor Ellenest Terry.

Who has told you that Mrs Pat is to have my Strange Lady? He lies in his throat whoever he is. And yet I suspect Henry Irving—oh, I suspect him. Why, you ask, should everybody think everybody else corruptible? Because everybody *is* corruptible: is not that simple? He would buy me in the market like a rabbit, wrap me up in brown paper and put me by on his shelf if I offered myself for sale—and how else does a critic offer himself except by writing his little play, or his adaptation or what not? And it would be such a sly way to send it through you. Oh, twenty thousand million devils!—But, "it *is* not so, and it *was* not so, and indeed God forbid that it should be so." You see the devil can quote Shakespear for his own purpose. If he wants to do the play the least bit in the world, why, I know his value, and will reserve it for him though the next best man covered his offer ten times. But if not, do not let the rabbit be bought and wrapped up. He will not produce it for your sake: no man ever does anything for a woman's sake: from our birth to our death we are women's babies, always wanting something from them, never giving them anything except something to keep *for us*. After all, why

22

should he be fond of people? People are always talking of love and affection and the like—just as they talk of religion—as if they were the commonest things in the world; but the Frenchman was nearer the truth when he said that a great passion is as rare as a man of genius. Has he ever loved you for the millionth fraction of a moment? if so, for that be all his sins forgiven unto him. I do not know whether women ever love. I rather doubt it: they pity a man, *mother* him, delight in making him love them; but I always suspect that their tenderness is deepened by their remorse for being unable to love him. Man's one gift is that at his best he *can* love—not constantly, nor faithfully, nor often, nor for long,—but for a moment—a few minutes perhaps out of years. It is because I have had a glimpse or two that I am such a hopelessly impious person; for when God offers me heaven as the reward of piety, I simply reply, "I know. I've been there. You can do nothing further for me, thank you."

You boast that you are a fool (it is at bottom, oh, such a tremendous boast: do you know that in Wagner's last drama, Parsifal, the redeemer is "der reine Thor," "the pure fool"?) but you have the wisdom of the heart, which makes it possible to say deep things to you. You say I'd be sick of you in a week; but this is another boast: it implies that you could entertain me for a whole week. Good heavens! with what? With art? with politics? with philosophy? or with any other department of culture? I've written more about them all (for my living) than you ever thought about them. On that plane I would exhaust you before you began, and could bore you dead with my own views in two hours. But one does not get tired of adoring the Virgin Mother. Bless me! you will say, the man is a Roman Catholic. Not at all: the man is the author of Candida; and Candida, between you and me, is the Virgin Mother and nobody else. And my present difficulty is that I want to reincarnate her —to write another Candida play *for* you. Only, it wont come. Candida came easily enough; but after her came that atrocious Man of Destiny, a mere stage brutality, and my present play brings life and art together and strikes showers of sparks from them as if they were a knife and a grindstone. Heaven knows how many plays I shall have to write before I earn one that belongs of divine right to you. Some day, when you have two hours to spare, you must let me read Candida to you. You will find me a disagreeably cruel-looking, middle-aged Irishman with a red beard; but that cannot be helped. By the way, you once spoke to me, although, as you were evidently woolgathering at the time, you wont remember the circumstance. It was at one of the performances at the new opera house which is now the Palace Music Hall. You were in the stalls; so was I; and it happened that we were almost the last persons to leave and were kept standing together for a moment waiting for the doorway into the corridor to clear. I was highly conscious of your illustrious presence and identity, but of course took care not to appear conscious. You seemed very much in earnest and even affected about something; and my theory is that you were in imagination impersonating some unfortunate young village girl of lowly station—Hetty in Adam Bede perhaps—and that you suddenly took it into your head that I was the squire, or perhaps the parson. At all events you most unexpectedly raised your eyes to mine for a moment and said, with the deepest respect, "Good evening, sir." I nearly sat down on the floor in confusion; but by good luck I managed not to wake you out of your dream. What I did was to instinctively fall into your drama (whatever it was) by saying "Good evening" so exactly in the manner of the squire acknowledging a salutation from the game-keeper's daughter (a most respectable, promising, well conducted young woman) that you passed unsuspectingly on up the avenue, with the squirrels and rabbits scampering away as you approached; and I watched you until you turned into the path leading to the dairy and vanished. I suppose you dont happen to remember, in the course of your transmigrations, meeting a squire or a parson with a red beard and a nasty expression about the corners of his mouth?

But I must not ask you questions, as you have written me enough to live on until you come back; and your precious forces must not be wasted in writing letters to me. I wish this ink—a penny a bottle at the village shop—were blacker and my writing bolder. If you have a magnifying glass, it will all come out beautifully legible.

The Independent Theatre people, having had Little Eyolf snatched back from their grasp by Miss Elizabeth Robins (who will produce it next October, probably, in partnership with Waring), want to produce Candida. Janet wants me to consent. I must be cruel only to be kind; and I insist on their having £1000 to finance it with, even for eight matinées spread over a month. They have only £400; so I think I am safe for the present; but they may get the money. If so, Candida may be the first thing you are to see on your return to these shores. But then, alas! I shall have no excuse for reading it to you.

G. B. S.

24

XIII: E. T. *to* G. B. S.

15 May 1896
New York

Y OUR lovely letters!
    I am to blame. Forgive me. My star has stopped dancing, and for a
while I am down—down. Just when I was downest, your letter came and
comforted sore eyes and sore heart. We sail for home on the 20th. Thanks
and ever thanks.

E. T.

XIV: G. B. S. *to* E. T.

[*The "eminent London manager": George Alexander (knighted in 1911).
He first played Valentine in the Lyceum production of Faust, succeeding
H. B. Conway as Faust in January 1886. The new play of "such extraordinary cleverness" that it was beyond Alexander's comprehension must
have been You Never Can Tell.*]

5 July 1896

DEAR AND ESTEEMED LADY,

M AY I venture to call your attention now that your tour is over,
    and you have absolutely nothing to do but tremble at the prospect
of learning Imogen, to my unhappy case. Probably you have forgotten all
about me: but you used to write to me years ago, when you were in
America, playing a leper, or lepress, and otherwise wringing my very
heart.

    My condition is this. I have finished a new play, of such extraordinary
cleverness that an eminent London manager, who once played Faust to
the most beautiful of all Margarets, writes, after reading it, "When I got
to the end, I had no more idea what you meant by it than a tom cat."
Now if I have soared in my later works beyond human comprehension,
I can only fall back on my earlier ones. What I want to know is whether
there was really anything serious in your notion that my Napoleonad
would be added to the Lyceum Knight's Entertainments. Or are you only
a flattering story telling Scheherezade? I do hate people who cant make
up their minds: they remind me of myself.

    Not that I particularly want to know, after all: but I am about to cele-
brate my 40th birthday: and I *will* be grown up: I *will* be serious: I *will*
be businesslike. Good Heavens, do you realize that I may die in the
workhouse (I have often thought I should like to die there, by the way)

if I do not look after my affairs. I am going to Bayreuth for the first set of performances (19th, 20th, 21st and 22nd); I am rushing back to the International Socialist Congress here; then to Brittany on business and holiday; then to Italy on holiday and business; then back to chains and slavery. I must—I *shall* settle my business before I go. Where is that play? where is that agreement? Am I an insect, to be treated in this fashion? You said next year, I think—the 1st January—or was it the 31st December?

Come, I will teach you the part without your opening the book once. I will get a tandem bicycle; and we shall ride along over the celestial plains, I dinning the part into your head until you pick it up as one picks up a tune by ear. That is how all parts should be taught and learnt: in my ideal company there shall not be an actress who can read. I once learnt a part (and actually played it too)—learnt it from the book. What galley slavery it was! I had rather write ten articles, or a thousand plays. Imagine learning live emotion—live thought—from dead matter—linen rag and printer's ink!

Just Heaven, is this business? No. I repeat, then, I demand, I insist, I—I forget what I insist on: what I want is only to kiss your hands, which cannot be insisted on.

But I grow unbusinesslike: farewell!

G. BERNARD SHAW

XV: E. T. *to* G. B. S.

[*"No. 29 F.": the house in Fitzroy Square where Shaw lived.*]

7 July 1896

IT APPEARS to me, now I'm here in this hot London, that I've never before found *real* hard work to do! All the morning yesterday in the scene-painting room up-aloft at the Lyceum, or I should have been sitting on your doorstep at No. 29 F. It was my intention to try and find you in the cool of the evening.

(Added two days later)

They came to do my eyes and in a few days I'm to be blinded for a fortnight. Just as I want a holiday and to look at the grass, and the Sea! *And* to finish studying Imogen. I think your bicycle suggestion is the best plan.

26

Now, quickly (whilst there's an eye left!), to business. H. I. came here last night and he will agree to produce The Man of Destiny next year, or forfeit rights, if that must be an imperative condition. He cannot produce it for a run, only (perhaps) for a few nights. Later on in '98 it can have a run backed up by a longer play. Three one-act plays we know quite well by experience is of little good, no matter *how good,* but one 1 Act play sometimes splendid. We certainly could do it in '97, but it would be impossible to give it a run. The management or policy of theatres entirely depends on circumstances and freaks of the public, and H. I. is no fool, and he knows that to guarantee a run at a fixed time is impossible (for any *one*-act play). He wants the play very much (and so do I want him to have it), and he would like to buy it, or pay nightly fees. Oh dear, I cannot write about business at all properly. You are off to Bayreuth. How delightful! I'd like to go too, but I'm off to Winchelsea, I hope on Tuesday, and after a rest shall be a new—and much younger—woman. It would do you so much good to wheel down to Sevenoaks, sleep there and come on next day to Winchelsea before going to Bayreuth. The whole journey is only 60 miles. I *am* done up! My eyes wont see, and my pen wont spell, so farewell. I spare you further reading of my scribble.

Yours—yours

E. T.

You cant imagine how I'm looking forward with delight to being blind for a short while. Folk are so sympathetic to a blind woman, and I shall have to be taken care of instead of taking care of folk.

XVI: E. T. *to* G. B. S.

[*The "first night" refers to Cymbeline, produced at the Lyceum in September 1896.—Mrs. Sidney Webb, the well-known socialist and sociologist, is the Mrs. Webb mentioned. She and her husband (now Lord Passfield and Colonial Secretary in the Labour Government of 1930) were associated with Shaw in the Fabian Society and were his closest personal friends.— The "confounded duck of a play": The Man of Destiny.*]

10 July 1896

No. "SHE" doesn't "enjoy" the visit of the eyesmith, except for the lovely rest that must ensue. No-one "arranges" *my* holidays, I have to "arrange" the holidays of all belonging to me (and all belonging to *them!*). And now because of my plague-y eyes I cant get away until the end of next week. Well, I'll meet you in Brittany or Heaven yet. Meanwhile go to Henry about that confounded duck of a play, or write him a line please, for a line clinches matters between man and man. Some women are such fussers.

Shakspere. Ah you mad (angry) thing. With justice you might scream out against a woman of my age playing the parts I do. I only do it to please H. I. and because I "draw." Facts are stubborn. Why do you object to Shakespere drawing the people to us better than anything else? We have had a good long success in it, you know (Unberufen!) "Fashionable crazes" dont last for over 20 years, and London, America and the great English Provinces have responded to our call in greater numbers during the past 2 years than ever before, and the warmth of the people makes one glad to live! (That's much, it seems to me). Why even on the common necessary ground that it pays H. I. to pay so many people in his employment you should discontinue a "goin'" on so against Shakspere. *You'll* see whether "nobody wants Shakespere in September." I know that from the first night for 100 nights the theatre will be full up. Cease your funning then about S. (Altho' I must tell you I argue all the other way with H. for my own sake only. Just selfishness.) No. No "young patriots" for me. No daggers of Judith. Charlotte Corday does not attract me, and I fear only the character of *the Mother* becomes me. Only I sternly refuse to be the "anxious" Mother on or off the stage.

Now I'll let you off, poor man. No, "rich," with Mrs. Webbs to "arrange" you. Do you think she'd arrange *me* if I asked her? I'd like to see a third person read your letters to me! I enjoy 'em too much to share 'em. Be I ever so blind, my letters shall wait for me.

Dont shiver, kind gentleman. No knife will touch my eyes. They will be sent to sleep for awhile and awake some day to see you in your Jaeger clothing standing beside me. *Women* should wear just one garment (of course of Jaeger wool) and they'd be ever so much healthier. But there, men love unhealthy women. Goodbye. Farewell, and dont write to me again. (Yes, do, in September).   E. T.

XVII: G. B. S. *to* E. T.

[*Not dated. Assigned to end of August 1896. While Ellen Terry was holidaying at Winchelsea in Sussex Shaw was holidaying with a party of Fabian friends at Saxmundham in Suffolk.*]

THERE are no clocks and no calendars here but surely it must be September by this time. If not, keep this letter until it *is,* and then read it.

By the way, do you know what people do with their eyes in my family? I was taught solemnly when I was a child to dip my face into a basin of cold water every morning, and open my eyes under water. Do this twice a day, and you will be able to pick up pins from the carpet when you are ninety. It was a favorite performance of my grandmother's.

The negotiations concerning The Man of Destiny did not get very far. I proposed conditions to Sir H. I. Sir H. I. declined the mental effort of bothering about my conditions, and proposed exactly what I barred, namely to treat me handsomely by making me a present of a £50 note every Christmas on condition that nobody else got the play, with an understanding that it should be produced at some date unspecified, when the tyrannical public would graciously permit the poor manager to indulge in it. To this I replied by proposing three alternatives. 1. My original conditions (virtually). 2. That you should have the play to amuse yourself with until you were tired of it without any conditions at all. 3. That he should have a present of it on condition of his instantly producing works by Ibsen. The effect of this on his mind was such that I have not heard from him since. Only the other day there suddenly flashed on me something that we have been forgetting all along—Madame Sans Gêne. If you are really bent on playing that ridiculous washerwoman, there is an end of The Man of Destiny, since H. I. cannot play two Napoleons, mine and Sardou's, on top of one another. Why on earth did we not think of this before? I see the hopelessness of dissuading you from the washtub. You will certainly be the very worst laundress that ever burnt holes in the drama; but that is just what attracts you: you like to play at your profession on the stage, and to exercise your real powers in actual life.

It is all very well for you to say that you want a Mother Play; but why didnt you tell me that in time? I *have* written THE Mother Play—Candida—and I cannot repeat a masterpiece, nor can I take away Janet's one ewe lamb from her. She told me the other day that I had been consistently treacherous about it from the beginning, because I would not let the Independent Theatre produce it with a capital of £400! What would she say if I handed it over to the most enviable and successful of her competitors—the only one, as she well knows, who has the secret of it in her nature? Besides, you probably wouldnt play it even if I did: you would rather trifle with your washerwomen and Nance Oldfields and Imogens and nonsense of that kind. I have no patience with this perverse world.

Bother: they insist on my stopping writing and bicycling off to Ipswich with them. I dont want to go to Ipswich.

G. B. S.

XVIII: E. T. *to* G. B. S.

[*The two grandchildren who were spending this August at Winchelsea where Ellen Terry owned a cottage for many years are Rosemary and Robin, the eldest children of her son Edward Gordon Craig.—Janet: Janet Achurch (see note to Letter V).—There was a Spanish dancer called Candida who was appearing in London at this time.*]

Tower Cottage,
Winchelsea, Sussex

I wish I could write neatly, tidily like you. *Cant.* Dear Gentleman I was very glad to see a letter from you to me, and I "kept it" till the last! What a muddle about this little play. I wish you'd just *give* it to him to do what he likes with it. He'll play it quick enough, never fear, but I see what he is thinking, the silly old cautious thing. He is such a dear Donkey! Darling fellow. Stupid ass! I cant bother about him and the part I want him to play any more (As he *only* can play it). You ought to have come down here long ago and read Candida (Why, she's a dancer!) to me. Now my holiday is just over and I'm only a ha'porth the better for it, and I might have been well, all along o' you.

Oh, but I've had the happiest time. A few visitors, and my 2 grandchildren all the time with me. You see I love benefiting things, and I *can* benefit the babies. I'm as alert as a fox-terrier when children are on my hands. Oh, I'd love to have a baby every year. I return to town on Saturday, and must put aside all thought of babies and sich like trash, and stick at work, rehearsing every day and every evening for a whole cussed month. The part of Imogen is not yet well fixed in my memory, and it is so difficult to get the words. The words! Panic will possess me the first moment each morning until I know those words.

Did you sleep after Bayreuth? Last time you wrote, you were going to sleep, tired out. I wish I could sleep for a month. I'm generally worn out for want of the blessing, sleep. Why do you live in Fitzroy Square? Little Mrs Moscheles has been down here. You know her, dont you? I wish Cymbeline were "cut," and I could read Candida. Drive down to Hampton Court some Saturday or Sunday and read it to me. Of course you are busy, but never mind. Let things slide and come before the fine warm days are fled. You'll like reading me your own work and I shall like hearing it. At least I suppose I shall! Although I fear mine are very dull wits, and second times of reading are best.

A heavenly day here. I wish you were here, and every-one else I like. Lord! There'd be "a damned party in a parlour"!

Thank you for your letter. Dont think that I want to hurt Janet. I would help her (I have tried). But Candida, a Mother! Attractive to me, very. I'm good at Mothers, and Janet can do the Loveresses.

Am I successful? You say so. I heard the other day you hated success-ful folk. I said "Fudge"!

Oh—good-bye.

E. T.

XIX: G. B. S. *to* E. T.

[*The "Irish millionairess": Miss Charlotte Frances Payne-Townshend, who in 1898 married Bernard Shaw. Millionairess was a Shavian exaggeration; but the lady was in fact very comfortably circumstanced and helped materially to found the London School of Economics.*]

28 August 1896.
Stratford St Andrew Rectory,
Saxmundham

Do you know I should not mind giving him the play to do as he likes with if that were practically possible, but it isnt—at least, not on terms that I could propose and he accept. We may all admire one another, enjoy one another, love one another, enter into all sorts of charm-ing relations with one another; but all this is the mere luxury of human intercourse: behind it all, if it is to be really worth anything, there must be a certain deep and sacred respect for one another that we are free neither to give nor to withhold. It stands as an inexorable condition that we must not violate. It does not vary according to brains or beauty

31

or artistic talent or rank or age or education; and the difference between the wise of heart and the fool is nothing but the difference between the person who feels it and acknowledges it and the person who doesnt. It is the primal republican stuff out of which all true society is made. (The lecturer here took a glass of water and moistened his tonsils amid applause.) Now do you not see—you who are a wisehearted person, for which be all your sins forgiven unto you—that this respect prevents me from offering Irving a present of my rights just as effectually as it prevents me from violently robbing him of his? People who respect each other always make strict and fair agreements, reserving their rights each for the other's sake as well as for his own. What would you think of a man of property who took advantage of your daughter being in love with him to marry her without a settlement?

There is another way of looking at it. You say H. I. is cautious, as well he may be; but that is a reason for his making very careful agreements. Quite the most reckless thing he could do would be to accept an undertaking that he is to do as he likes with the play. For observe, ladies and gentlemen (here the speaker assumed a forensic attitude), the author cannot divest himself of his rights without formalities more guarded and elaborate than any customary agreement need entail. I might play false at any moment, I might die; and my heirs might instantly sell their inheritance to Wilson Barrett. Miss Ellen Terry might alter her present indulgent attitude towards me, and drive me to acts of jealousy, revenge and despair. *He* might die. If he made a will leaving me the play, his wife might die; he might marry again; and then the will would be invalidated. In fact all manner of the most nonsensical complications might arise from our being too lazy and petulant to make up our minds as to what we mean to do. As for me, I had rather die than make up my mind about anything for my own sake; but I am in the hands of Necessity, and so is he. It seems to me that the sensible thing to do is to stop worrying him about it. As long as the negotiations consist in writing letters to you and getting answers to them, I am quite willing to negotiate; but that is very poor fun for him. You will find that what will happen will be that he will play Napoleon in Madame Sans Gêne; and Mansfield, who burns to contest his supremacy will play my Napoleon against him. Mrs Mansfield has just been over here on the warpath; and I feel pretty sure that a second descent on London is in contemplation. I cannot very well refuse to let Mansfield play Arms and the Man here, though he has only the American rights, and the program

32

will be freshened considerably by a new play. That will be the end of all our dreams about the Strange Lady. Poor Strange Lady!

To tell you the truth I have had a shock down here. In the evenings they make me read plays to them; and the other night I had to fall back on my Opus 2, a comedy called The Philanderer, now some years old. It turned out to be a combination of mechanical farce with realistic filth which quite disgusted me; and I felt that if my plays get stale at that rate, I cannot afford to postpone their production longer than I can help.

It is downright maddening to think of your slaving over Imogen. Of course you cant remember it: who could? Unless you really want to say the things a character in a play says, your soul is not interested, and without that sort of interest memory is *impossible*. To learn Imogen requires a Bishop's wife, not *you*. Great heavens, doesnt it make you fear that your faculties are decaying and your memory failing when you find that the lines wont come to you *eagerly,* but must be fixed into your head with hairpins, without any security for their sticking? Well, that is because Shakespear is as dead *dramatically* as a doornail. Your only chance of learning him without intolerable effort is to learn him by ear; for his music is unfailing. Never read your part; get somebody to speak it to you over and over again—to urge it on you, hurl it at you, until your mere imitative echo faculty forces you to jabber it as a street piano forces you to hum a tune that you positively dislike. And when you have finished with Imogen, finish with Shakespear. As Carlyle said to the emigrant "Here and now, or nowhere and never, is thy America" so I say to you "Here (at Fitzroy Square) and now, is thy Shakespear." Time flies; and you must act *something* before you die.

Curiously—in view of Candida—you and Janet are the only women I ever met whose ideal of voluptuous delight was that life should be one long confinement from the cradle to the grave. If I make money out of my new play I will produce Candida at my own expense, and you and Janet shall play it on alternate nights. It must be a curious thing to be a mother. First the child is part of yourself; then it is *your* child; then it is its father's child; then it is the child of some remote ancestor; finally it is an independent human being whom you have been the mere instrument of bringing into the world, and whom perhaps you would never have thought of caring for if anyone else had performed that accidental service. It must be an odd sensation looking on at these young people and being out of it, staring at that amazing callousness, and being tolerated

33

and no doubt occasionally ridiculed by them before they have done anything whatsoever to justify them in presuming to the distinction of your friendship. Of the two lots, the woman's lot of perpetual motherhood, and the man's of perpetual babyhood, I prefer the man's I think. I dont hate successful people; just the contrary. But I dread success. To have succeeded is to have finished one's business on earth, like the male spider, who is killed by the female the moment he has succeeded in his courtship. I like a state of continual *becoming*, with a goal in front and not behind. Then too, I like fighting successful people; attacking them; rousing them; trying their mettle; kicking down their sand castles so as to make them build stone ones, and so on. It develops one's muscles. Besides, one learns from it: a man never tells you anything until you contradict him. I hate failure. Only, it must be real success: real skill, real ability, real power, not mere newspaper popularity and money, nor wicked frivolity, like Nance Oldfield. I am a magnificently successful man myself, and so are my knot of friends—the Fabian old gang—but nobody knows it except we ourselves, and even we havent time to attend to it. We have never stopped to pick up Atalanta's apples, and can only afford a country house for our holidays because one of us has a wife with a thousand a year. This time we have been joined by an Irish millionairess who has had cleverness and character enough to decline the station of life—"great catch for somebody"—to which it pleased God to call her, and whom we have incorporated into our Fabian family with great success. I am going to refresh my heart by falling in love with her. I love falling in love—but, mind, only with her, not with the million; so someone else must marry her if she can stand him after me.

What a holiday this has been! I never worked so hard before in my life. Four hours writing in the morning; four hours bicycling in the afternoon every day.

I live in Fitzroy Square, on the second floor in a most repulsive house, because I cant afford to live anywhere better within reach of my bread and butter.

What do you mean by Hampton Court? Have you a place down there? or do you only drive about with H. I.? I once or twice have met you on Richmond Terrace or thereabouts with him, like two children in a gigantic perambulator, and have longed to seize him, throw him out, get up, take his place, and calmly tell the coachman to proceed. I can get down to Hampton Court any fine Sunday on my bicycle and read you Candida (if you really care about it—Mrs Webb says that C. is simply a woman of bad character, neither more nor less) if you will say where.

And now these epistolary follies must be suspended until Imogen is off your mind. I suppose I shall have to come up to town to slate it.

Farewell, then, until after Cymbeline, oh divine quintessential Ellen of the wise heart: we shall meet at Philippi, or in the Elysian fields or where you will.

G. B. S.

XX: E. T. *to* G. B. S.

[*More about The Man of Destiny apropos of Shaw's statement that there was another Napoleon in the field in Richard Mansfield.*]

3 September 1896. Savoy Hotel,
Victoria Embankment, London

VERY well then I'll go on with my rehearsalling (it nearly kills me always) and you'll go on whilst holidaying with your "falling in love." (If you pretend only, some day it will never be able to be real!) And so you and I are at the 2 best occupations in this strange old world. Nothing else worth doing. Love and Work. Farewell. I'm on the rack about this part—this Imogen—yet frightfully interested all the while.

Yours rather much,

E. T.

One word about the little play (and breathe it to a living creature, and ugh! what is there I wont do to you?). If you let the little man [Mansfield] play it, it will be of little count, for he's rather clever, but not enough clever. In the first place he'd play it as it is, uncut, and Lord help you both then! For, although I love every word of it, it is too long in certain places to *play-act* as it now stands. All well, as it stands, to read, but not to play-act.

Farewell until after the 19th (or 22nd?) and dont you dare to be there! But later, please, about a week after. Oh I shall shake from fright about the thing.

I'm at this hotel, 'cos it's so near (and dear!) and there's scarce time to get to my nice home as we rehearse all day and most of the night. Goodbye dear George! Give my love to The Cat.

35

[The Intelligent Actress's Guide to Cymbeline.]

6 September 1896

I REALLY dont know what to say about this silly old Cymbeline, except that it can be done delightfully in a village schoolroom, and cant be done at the Lyceum at all, on any terms. I wish you would tell me something about Imogen for my own instruction. All I can extract from the artificialities of the play is a double image—a real woman *divined* by Shakespear without his knowing it clearly, a natural aristocrat, with a high temper and perfect courage, with two moods—a childlike affection and wounded rage; and an idiotic paragon of virtue produced by Shakespear's *views* of what a woman ought to be, a person who sews and cooks, and reads improving books until midnight, and "always reserves her holy duty," and is anxious to assure people that they may trust her implicitly with their spoons and forks, and is in a chronic state of suspicion of improper behavior on the part of other people (especially her husband) with abandoned females. If I were you I should cut the part so as to leave the paragon out and the woman in; and I should write to The Times explaining the lines of the operation. It would be a magnificent advertisement.

There are four good lines in the part. First

"—how far it is
To this same blessed Milford."

which, like that whole scene, you will do beautifully.

Second, the exit speech, with its touch of vernacular nature:—

"Such a foe! Good heavens!"

Third, to leave the comedy lines for the more painful ones:—

"I'll hide my master from the flies."

Fourth, the only good line of pure rhetoric in Mrs Siddon's style:—

"Fear not: I'm empty of all things but grief."

Only, Shakespear, like an ass, spoils that line by adding, in words, all that the delivery of the line itself ought to convey. The words "Thy master is not there, who was, indeed, the riches of it" should not be spoken. If anyone says you left them out you can retort "I did not speak them; but I did not leave them out."

If you utter all that rubbish about false Æneas and Dido's weeping, I will rise, snatch the nearest family Shakespear, solemnly throw it at your head, and leave the theatre. The moment Pisanio says "Good Madam, hear me," cut him short with "Come, fellow, be thou honest"; and say it with something of the deep admonition which makes me remember your "Shylock: there's thrice thy money offered thee" since years and years ago. And when you have fairly started cutting the miserable attorney's rhetoric out of the scene, do it with a bold hand. Dont trouble about the Paragonese "Some jay of Italy" stuff, or the wretched impossible logic chopping. And oh, my God, dont read the letter. You *cant* read it: no woman could read it out to a servant. (Oh what a DAMNED fool Shakespear was!) You must manage it in this way. In the second scene of the third act, let Pisanio begin by reading the letter, from "Thy mistress, Pisanio, hath played the strumpet, etc." down to "lie bleeding in me." Then let him break off and exclaim "How! of adultery!" etc. down to "O my master, thy mind to her is now as low as were thy fortunes!" Then let him resume the reading of the letter to the end, when he will find himself with just the right cue for "How! That I should murder her . . . *I! her!* . . ." and so on. The audience will not forget what is in the letter after that; and when Pisanio hands it to you in the fourth scene, you can *play* the reading of it with the certainty that the audience will have the clue in their imaginations burning hot. The pantomime will be easy for you—it goes this way—the horrible shock of the first sentence—"*I* false!"—then the slow, significant look at Pisanio, the man who is to kill you (it is the majesty of death that raises you for a moment from your horror)—then the return to the subject of the accusation and the slipping away of consciousness. Then cut all the rubbish out of the scene which follows, thus:—

P. What shall I need to draw my sword? The paper
   Hath cut her throat already. What cheer, madam?

I. False to his bed, etc. (the whole speech uncut)

P. Alas, good lady (Imogen has nothing to do with this speech and
   should go straight on without hearing it)

I. *I* false! Thy conscience witness, Iachimo. (Everything can be conveyed in these 4 words)

P. Good madam, hear me—

I. (Turning on him with solemn sternness)
   Come, fellow, be thou honest.
   Do thou thy master's bidding, etc. etc. (the whole speech uncut)
P.   Hence, vile instrument
   Thou shalt not damn my hand.
I.   (Sharply, not much impressed by his rhetoric at such a pass)
                                Why, I must die;
   And if I do not by thy hand, thou art
   No servant of thy master's. Prythee despatch.
   The lamb entreats the butcher: where's thy knife, etc. etc.

All this will mean an intolerable load off your memory and off the real side of Imogen. Archer will complain in The World of the violation of the Bard's integrity; and I will declare in The Saturday Review that your dramatic instinct and delicacy of feeling have never guided you more unerringly than in rescuing the live bits of Imogen from the bombazine trappings of the Bishop's wife.

There is another point which puzzles me—in that other big scene—that nice Elizabethan morsel of the woman waking up in the arms of a headless corpse. I cannot for the life of me follow the business of that long speech without getting the words "A headless man" in the wrong place. For instance, you wake up, you sit up, half awake, and think you are asking the way to Milford Haven—*the blessed Milford,* since for the moment you have forgotten your unhappines. You lie down to sleep again, and in doing so touch the body of Cloten, whose head (or no head) is presumably muffled in a cloak. In your dim, half asleep funny state of consciousness, you still have the idea that you mustnt go to bed with anybody else but Posthumus, and you say "But soft, no bedfellow." Then in rousing yourself sufficiently to get away from this vaguely apprehended person, you awaken a little more at this very odd, dreamlike thing, that the bedfellow is covered with flowers. You take up a flower, still puzzly-dreamy, and look curiously at it. It is *bloody,* and then in an instant you are broad awake— "Oh gods and goddesses!" etc. But it is quite clear that you must not know that "this bloody man" is headless, as that would utterly spoil the point later on. He looks simply as if he had swathed his head in his cloak to sleep in. It is the blood under the flowers that makes him so horrible to be alone with. When you utter the prayer "If there be yet left in heaven as small a drop of pity as a wren's eye, feared gods, give me a part of it," I suppose you kneel and cover your eyes with your hands in the hope that when you remove them your prayer will be answered and the nightmare gone. You take down your hands and dare to look again. "The dream's here still. Even when I wake it is without me and within me, not imagined—felt." Now in the text, what follows is "A headless man!" That is what I cannot understand; and I believe it is an overlooked relic of some earlier arrangement of the business. For see how it plays if you omit it. Your attention is caught by the garment of Posthumus; you go on with the recognition step by step (confound those classical allusions; but they cant be helped); at last you lift the cloak to see the face, and then—"Murder in Heaven!" you go tearing, screaming, raging mad and rave your way to the swoon as best you can (a nice thing to play every night for 100 nights). But if you leave in the words "A headless man" the sequel is spoiled, and you are represented as being surprised at finding no face on a man, who, as you have already observed, has lost his whole head. Therefore, I submit that the "headless man" sentence must be left out.

These, dear madam, are the only ideas I have on the subject of Imogen. I daresay you know your own business better than I do; but no matter; your consciousness of your own view will only become more definite and determined if it contradicts everybody else's.

So you see I have no objection whatever to an intelligent cutting out of the dead and false bits of Shakespear. But when you propose to cut me, I am paralyzed at your sacrilegious audacity. I always cut myself to the bone, reading the thing over and over until I have discovered the bits that cant be made to play-act anyhow. *All* of Napoleon can be done, if only the right touch is found. If a single comma is omitted, that will be because the actor has been beaten by the author. And I always like to beat the actor, and to beat the public, *a little:* it is the only way to keep screwing up the standard. I own I have certain misgivings about H. I. as Napoleon. Swift brute force, concentrated self-assertion, and the power of letting the electricity discharge itself in the meaning of the line, instead of in the look and tone of the stage figure, are all just what he has not got. His slowness, his growing habit of overdoing his part and slipping in an imaginative conception of his own *between* the lines (which made such a frightful wreck of Lear), all of which are part of his extraordinary insensibility to literature, are all reasons why he should avoid me, though his feeling for fine execution, and his dignity and depth of sentiment, are reasons why I should *not* avoid him. However, when Cymbeline is off his mind, I shall make

39

him say Yes or No about The Man of Destiny. Meanwhile, I shall begin another play—a melodrama. After that I will write a real comic opera, to revive *that* industry a bit; and then I shall do whatever may come next.

You will observe how strictly I confine this letter to business. After the 22nd I decline further responsibility for my actions.

G. B. S.

XXII: E. T. *to* G. B. S.

[Tyars: Frank Tyars, a member of Henry Irving's company for many years. He was a sound and reliable actor, indispensable to Irving as a sympathetic coadjutor in parts which had to be played to enhance the effect of Irving's own creation. Of his Pisanio in Cymbeline, Shaw wrote in The Saturday Review: "There is no reasonable fault to find."]

7 September 1896. Savoy Hotel,
Victoria Embankment, London

YOU DEAR fellow. Now this is a real help! (Oh I forgot! I was not agoin' to write).

I shall begin to think myself a proper clever person, for I had already cut out nearly everything you tell me in your letter of this morning to cut, just because when I got the words into my thick noodle and began to *act,* I found I could not speak them or act them. As to the letter (which is fine to act, by *not* acting it) that difficulty I got over rather well by appearing to read it to myself. *Of course* she could not "read it to a servant." This is better than your way, suggesting that Pisanio should read it (pardon me, blessed man) because I can act better than Tyars (You know I can). If H. I. played Pisanio I'd suggest it at once, for he'd do it better than E. T.

I didnt think about the flower with the blood upon it (the "head-less man" scene). It's lovely, and I'll try to do it—*have* tried this minute (not successful, but it will come, for practice makes perfect, and how I will practise). I've cut that speech a great deal. Very many beautiful lines are gone, but oh dear friend I had to, for these emotional parts just kill me, and a sustained effort at that moment would probably make me mad. I should laugh—or die.

Gods! How you seem to feel with one! Because of the "screwing up the standard" I find heart to go on and on, and feel intense interest all the while. "Security is mortal's chiefest enemy." The sickening flattery one gets! If it made one smug, how unhappy! how wretched! And I see around me such great people sapped by it.

40

Now dont write to me (but thank you for writing) for I cant help writing then. You are very kind to me. I'm getting very well, know every word of my part! In tremors about that boy's dress (being fat and nearly fifty). Oh pray for me! Wish for me!

NELLEN TERRY

XXIII: G. B. S. *to* E. T.

[*Henry Irving's acting version of* Cymbeline, *which Ellen Terry had sent with her last letter, provoked this second penetrating essay on the play and more suggestions about the interpretation of Imogen for the actress to ponder. One surmises that Shaw had been surprised to find from Ellen Terry's annotations of the text of the acting version how profoundly she studied her parts.*]

8 September 1896

I HAVE read carefully through that copy, but, worse luck, I must either write hurriedly or miss the post, as some people have arrived here and I have had to spend a lot of time mending punctures in female bicycle tyres. Therefore brief and blunt must I be, O Ellen. Fortunately there is not much to say. Our brains evidently work in the same way. At the same time I begin to doubt whether you can really be an actress. Most of 'em have no brains at all.

You have only once slipped out of the character in your plan, and that is in the scene between Imogen and Iachimo in the 2nd Act. Imogen is an impulsive person, with quick transitions, absolutely frank self-expression, and no half affections or half forgivenesses. The moment you abuse anyone she loves, she is in a rage: the moment you praise them she is delighted. It is quite easy for Iachimo to put her out of countenance by telling her that Posthumus has forgotten her; but the instant he makes the mistake of trying to gratify her by abusing him—"that runa-gate"—he brings down the avalanche. It is just the same with Cloten: she is forbearing with him until he makes the same mistake. And Iachimo has nothing to do but praise Posthumus, and lay the butter on thick, and she is instantly as pleased as Punch, and void of all resentment. It is this that makes her pay him the extra special compliment of offering to take the chest into her own bedroom, *a thing she would never have done if she had not forgiven him* quite thoroughly—honest Injun. Therefore there is no subsiding storm, no "wary of him," no "polite—words, words, words." The words:—

41

> "—such a holy witch
> That he enchants societies to him:
> Half all men's hearts are his."

humbug her completely. The sun should come right out through the clouds when she says "You make amends."

You are unerring everywhere else.

On p. 4 the speech "O the gods! When shall we see again?" is really two separate speeches. When Posthumus puts the bracelet on your arm, look for a moment with delight at the present if you like, but that doesnt matter: the great thing is that you shiver with love at his touch on your arm, and say "O the gods!" as a sigh of rapture. It is when that subsides that you ask the question a woman always does ask—it being the nature of her sex never to be satisfied—"When will you come again?"

On the same page (4) comes the first quick transition. "I beseech you, sir, harm not yourself with your vexation" is thoroughly petulant and full of temper, Cymbeline having not only sent Posthumus away, but called him "thou basest thing." What she really means is "You may save your breath to cool your porridge, you old wretch."

On page 33—the last line—throw up your engagment and bid H. I. farewell for ever sooner than allow Pisanio to make "and too much too" a comic aside. It is a perfectly serious, tender, *nurselike* thing to say. Any Irish peasant would say "and too much too, darlint," quite naturally. I hasten on, lest I should use bad language.

I still think you should let Tyars read the letter. My reasons are that if you read it so as to convey your own feelings on seeing it you cannot also read it with the decision and point needed to enable the audience to take in the force of Posthumus's instructions to Pisanio. Further, I have a particular liking for the absolute truth of effect produced by the *acting* of the reading only, without the clumsiness of an aside, not to mention the force of effect derived from the audience's foreknowledge of what is happening to you; so that they can watch you without listening to the verbal instructions. However, I dont press that. Shakespear preferred to convey the foreknowledge by Pisanio's speech in the former scene, and the fact that his knowledge of his business was always a clever half-knowledge (the result of a hurry to get things done anyhow) is known to me only. So read the letter by all means; but just take another look at my way of cutting the following scene. At all events you must cut out "to pieces with me!" (p. 38) as it is not only unintelligible as it stands, but actually suggests a quite wrong idea. In the original it means "Now that there is another woman, to pieces with poor me!" As you have it, it represents Imogen as inviting Pisanio to carve her up like a chicken, which is ridiculous and spitefully out of character. And "Come: be honest—look" is nothing like so beautiful or expressive as "Come, fellow, be thou honest: do thou thy master's bidding etc." To cut out such fine bits and leave in such tawdry trash as "slander whose tongue outvenoms all the worms of Nile" is idiotic. The tearing of Posthumus's letters from her bosom seems to me very poor business—at least for you. Cut out the Roman courtesan on page 39: she belongs to the Bishopess side of the part, as you have noted.

But do *not* cut out the "clouted brogues" on p. 52; but rather "put thy shoes from off thy feet, for the place on which thou standest is holy ground." And I adjure you, do not cut out the prayer to heaven for "as small a drop of pity as a wren's eye" (54). You will find it a blessed relief (prayer is better than crying for that purpose) and to kneel and pray with your eyes covered will be beautiful. On p. 63 do not let them cut the speech of Lucius, "I do not bid thee beg my life, good lad, and yet I know thou wilt." It belongs to *your* part, your reply being important as a bit of play.

Generally speaking, the cutting of the play is stupid to the last extremity. Even from the broadest popular point of view, the omission of the grandiose scene about England and Cæsar for the queen, Cloten and the Roman, is a mistake. Cloten's part is spoiled. Every part is spoiled except "the governor's"; and he has actually damaged his own by wantonly cutting off your white and azure eyelids laced with blue of heaven's own tinct. Posthumus's exit on p. 32 is utterly spoiled by a fragment of another scene stuck in in the wrong place, lest Posthumus should complain that Iachimo was jealous of him and would not let him have that scene. The prudery of the cutting is silly: Pisanio says "disloyal" instead of adultery; Iachimo discreetly omits the lines "where, I profess, I slept not etc.," and Cloten's irresistibly turned remark that if Imogen doesnt like his serenade "it is a vice in her ears which horsehairs and calves' guts, nor the voice of unpaved eunuch to boot [a quite delightful bit of writing] can never amend"—is sacrificed to please the curates for whom the Lyceum seems chiefly to exist.

Forgive these splenetic remarks; but really H. I.'s acting versions of Shakespear are past all bearing. The man has no artistic sense outside

43

his own person: he is an ogre who has carried you off to his cave; and now Childe Roland is coming to the dark tower to rescue you.

This letter I positively forbid you to answer: I should not have written it if it did not bear on your present business.

Did I tell you the name of my new play: You Never Can Tell. The Haymarket people—Harrison, Cyril Maude & Co.—appear to be making up their minds to ruin themselves with it.

Hark, hark, the lark—no, the post. This hurried kiss—adieu.

G. B. S.

XXIV: E. T. *to* G. B. S.

[The implication of the quotation "her lord hath interest in them" is that Henry Irving will have a word to say about the playing of the "chest of jewels" scene. We see Ellen Terry in this letter pondering Shaw's suggestions with the intelligence which surprised him in an actress. Her attempt to persuade him to substitute "Nell" or "Nellen" for "Ellen" failed. He calls her "Ellen" throughout the correspondence.]

9 September 1896. Savoy Hotel
Victoria Embankment London.

How splendidly kind you are to me! (This is not a letter. Only *how* can I keep from saying thank you? I should burst.) I've read the scene with Iachimo (1) over again, just now, read it through your eyes, and I feel you are right. But it is a quick business to do! Much easier in (2) the Cloten scene. As to the chest of jewels (3) "her Lord hath interest in them"!

(4) Pretty business, the bracelet. I see it!

(5) No. Pisanio *means* to be serious enough.

(6) The Letter is the Awful Thing to do. I see the shoals, but praise be, blessed *you* see them as well.

(7) I'll alter "to pieces with me" in a way that's good to act. But I'm ashamed, for it is nonsense, as we have it, and *I* did it, not H. I.

(8) I had put back "the wren's eye." Could not spare it. It was too-oo-oo lovely. (And your "business" is exactly right. Bless you! If I were dark, and 30, I'd send you a kiss for it.)

(9) I'll suggest the "blue of heaven's own" etc. I'd not dare tell it was you, not yet at least.

Good-bye.
NELL (or NELLEN)
not *Ellen!*

Ellen! Ugh! It suggests a tartan and sword. How I entreat you not to write, for I'm weak-minded and cant do what I mean to do. Thank you for all.

XXV: E. T. *to* G. B. S.

[*Obviously written after a long and tiring rehearsal of Cymbeline during which Ellen Terry had been trying to get some of Shaw's suggestions carried out.*]

11 September 1896. Savoy Hotel,
Victoria Embankment, London

"'T̶IS now the witching hour of night." Churchyards yawn—and so do I. Oh the long speeches! Impossible to act except as soliloquy. (That cant be the way to spell it! *Why* wasnt I sent to school?)
Oh but I'm weary.

E. T.

I've got back "How of Adultery," "The Wren's Eye" and a few other things. Bless you, and good-night.

XXVI: E. T. *to* G. B. S.

[*This letter shows the interest every new production at the Lyceum excited in the nineties, and the "competition" Ellen Terry had to face in the tradition or memory of what some famous predecessor had done in a Shakespearean rôle. "Ted" is her son, Edward Gordon Craig, at this period a member of the Lyceum Company. He played Arviragus in Cymbeline.— The play by Bernard Shaw referred to is You Never Can Tell, which Frederick Harrison and Cyril Maude at this time thought of producing at the Haymarket Theatre.*]

15 September 1896

OH MY dear friends, the letters I get now each day! They come in swarms. Strange—to me—folk. *One* remembers (?) Mrs. Siddons's "Yes." Another Mrs Jones's Nose! I believe competition excites some actors. It crushes me. To try to do something as well as somebody else makes me so frightfully uncertain of touch, and I end by doing nothing. I fear it will be like that this time. The first few nights I shall make a sorry mess of it. Then people write to Henry too about what the "Imogens" have done. And he, like a dear old silly, gives me the letters, and I get frightened. *He* is frightened for everyone but himself, for he has not the ghost of an idea of how anyone acts in his theatre, unless

45

he's not in the play. I tell Ted to grossly flatter me all the while to keep my heart up, or I shall run away Tuesday morning. Shall I call a cab and go to America? Why all this to you the Lord knows!

Forgive, and may the weather be fine for your by-me-envied bicycle trip.

Dont think of your play just yet, or you'll forget to look at the grass as you ride by it. Oh, but I forget! You are only just now at the end of your holiday. I forget mine. It's so long ago. (What a lot of "Forgets"!)

Forget me not.

E. T.

XXVII: G. B. S. *to* E. T.

16 September 1896.

Stratford St. Andrew.

(last day—leave tomorrow)

THIS will never do. Read *no* letters (except mine) until after the 22nd. The one thing that is quite certain about Mrs Siddons's "Yes" is that she did not get it out of the letter of an amateur, or even a professional eighty years out of date. What is more, if you did it exactly like Mrs Siddons, you would do it wrong, because you are not Mrs. Siddons; and even if you are a worse actress—which cannot be proved—there is all the more reason why you should put her completely out of your head. Of course, if any trustworthy person remembers that Mrs Siddons made a great effect in such and such a line, it is quite worth considering where the tender spot she found in it lies, and then touching it in your own way; but very likely you would find that spot—if you detected it at all—one that has lost its tenderness with the wear and tear of the imagination and the growth and change of the human spirit since her time. Just imagine Duse (now *that's* acting if you like) playing Magda at Drury Lane in 1815. The thing is not more impossibly preposterous than Mrs Siddons playing Imogen at the Lyceum in 1896; and it is this absurd and monstrous effect that your good old people want you to produce. Did you ever see Cathcart playing Iago exactly as he used to rehearse it for Charles Kean? Nay, more horrible still, did you ever see Henry Irving, 20 years ago, trying to get Macready-Barry Sullivan effects in Richelieu? Or would you like me to rewrite The Man of Destiny in blank verse? Clear all superstitions out of your mind: there is nothing before you but Ellen Terry and Imogen; and the only letters that concern you are those which I shall write when I am 99 or so begging the newest leading lady of that time to do the wren's eye exactly as

Ellen Terry did it (for you must die before me and get my rooms ready for me in heaven and tell the cook about my vegetarianism)—or, better still, the letters of the old men who are now boys, and whose first Imogen you will be. If you have the heart to fob them off with anything out of Wardour Street—anything that is not the very ownest own of your sacredest self—you are a wretch.

After all, how easy it all is! You will have a huge house, all convinced beforehand that whatever you do will be the right thing, all idiotically loyal and enthusiastic and devoted, except a few with a deeper and not idiotic feeling, and yet none of them expecting more than you can give them by merely existing as you are. There will be no traditions, no comparisons, no compulsion to retain a scrap of the dead, stupid, rhetorical, stagey past. As for me, I shall be there on the first night (for The Saturday Review must have its article on Cymbeline all in type on Thursday) with my nostrils writhing in scornful derision of the whole wretched show. *I* shant expect anything from you; my expectations, on my honor, will be so cynically tiny that you cannot help surpassing them—surprising, delighting me. All the other nasty critics will be like that too; and it will be easier for your pride to annihilate us than for your soft side to face the nice ones, who will believe anything you do beautiful, even if you introduce a skirt-dance out of jealousy of Mrs Pat's Juliet. Of course competition paralyses you; but what great artist *competes?* As the Boyg says to Peer Gynt, "the great Boyg does not fight: he conquers." After all, the real thing that you fear is your own criticism; but dont waste fear on it. Cæsar, Napoleon, all the big achievers have said the same thing; guard against everything you can forsee; and then—take your chance. Take your own Imogen as if it were *the* Imogen and play it for all you are worth; and dont relax your determination or look back disconcertedly on a missfire in this or that line until the last word is out of your mouth and the curtain down. Then go home to bed, and sleep comfortably with *your* part of the work done. However, you know all about this as well as I do; only it is aggravating to have you talking about so small a business as Imogen (however large it may loom in the amateur imagination) as if you could possibly be unequal to it. Dont you see that the real difficulty is that *there is not enough in it* —not enough to absorb your whole power of work and fill your embrace and occupy every corner of your energy and affection—that Imogen, an old mechanical thing with a few touches of simple nature, is too cheap for you instead of too big? Good Lord! did you ever see Duse play

47

Shakespear? I did—Cleopatra! It was like seeing her scrubbing a scullery. Dont deceive yourself: what you have to do on Tuesday is to be a mother to Shakespear—to cover his foolishness and barrennesses, and to make the most of his little scattered glimpses of divinity. If you cannot believe in the greatness of your own age and time and inheritance, you will fall into the most horrible confusion of mind and contrariety of spirit, like a noble little child looking up to foolish, mean, selfish parents.

Oh, if people only would be modest enough to believe in themselves!

Ha! there they rang the bell for grub. I am hungry. I leave this place tomorrow (Thursday) and shall spend Thursday night at the Bath Hotel, Felixstowe. Thereafter as God pleases until Monday (or perhaps Tuesday) and then Fitzroy Square.

Must I really give up calling you Ellen after twenty years? Impossible: Ellen Terry is the most beautiful name in the world: it rings like a chime through the last quarter of the 19th century. It has a lovely rhythm in it. Not like "Jorj," which is so horribly ugly and difficult that all attempts to call me by it are foredoomed to failure. I am, and always have been, and ever shall be, by pre-eminent brevity and common-sense, simply

SHAW

XXVIII: E. T. *to* G. B. S.

[*Forbes: Norman Forbes-Robertson, younger brother of Sir Johnston Forbes-Robertson. He studied for the stage under Samuel Phelps. His association with Ellen Terry began when he played Moses in the first production of Olivia at the old Court Theatre in 1878. From 1879 until 1898 he played many parts in Irving's productions at the Lyceum. His Cloten is described by Shaw in his notice of Cymbeline in The Saturday Review as "a fatuous idiot rather than the brawny beefwitted fool Shakespear took from his own Ajax in Troilus and Cressida, but effective and amusing."— Cooper: Frank Cooper, a descendant of the Kembles. It was he who, as Laertes, first led Ellen Terry as Ophelia on to the stage of the Lyceum.—Lacy: the son of that Walter Lacy who was in Charles Kean's company at the time of Ellen Terry's first appearance, at the age of eight, in A Winter's Tale.—Webster: Ben Webster, a grandson of the famous actor Benjamin Webster. In 1895 he succeeded Johnston Forbes-Robertson as Sir Lancelot in King Arthur at the Lyceum. He remained with Irving until 1898. A list of the parts he played from his debut in 1887 at the St James's until 1930 (he is still on the stage) fills three columns of Who's Who in the Theatre.—Gene. Ward: Geneviève Ward. Born in New York in 1838, she began her stage career*

*as an opera singer. Shaw tells me she was accepted as a tragic actress on
the strength of the association with Ristori alluded to in this letter. He says
that her greatest achievement ("of which she was rather ashamed") was her
creation of Lona Hessel in the first London performance of Ibsen's Pillars
of Society. Shortly before her death in 1922 she was made a D. B. E.
(Dame of the Most Excellent Order of the British Empire) which called
public attention to the surprising fact that Ellen Terry's services to the stage
had never been officially recognized. It was not until 1925 that she was
made a G. B. E. (Dame Grand Cross of the Most Excellent Order of the
British Empire).—F. Robinson: Frederic Robinson, an actor whose chief
successes were gained in Australia. Ellen Terry's mischievous reference to
his stoutness is characteristic of her. She abhorred avoirdupois in man or
woman, and was genuinely distressed when in middle age her slender
figure became more ample. (It still remained youthfully lithe.) Her instruction to tear this letter up was, we see, disregarded. Shaw has attributed
his reluctance to destroy her letters to their pictorial character. It would, he
declares, "have been like tearing up the Luttrell Psalter."]*

16 September 1896

(Tear this up, quick, quick!)

I NOTICE you fall foul of the cast, but there's something good in
each one.
Now.

Cymbeline	(Macklin) Will look superb.
Cloten	(Forbes) Has brains.
Posthumus	(Cooper) A lovely voice, and never shouts.
Guiderius	(Webster) Shouts, but has a sweet face.
Arviragus	(Teddy) Has "some of the charm which for centuries be-longed" to his ma-ma.
Belarius	(F. Robinson) "What a proud stomach!" And one critic I know will discover that *at last* an actor has arrived in our midst who can deliver Blank Verse. Looks as if he were going to deliver something else. Oh! and as H. I. says: "You can *hear* him" (I wish I couldnt.)
Pisanio	(Tyars) Well, he always looks well.
Cornelius	(Lacy) Was a parson! So he must be "good."
Iachimo	(H. I.) Well, do you know I think we agree, you and I, that he's quite a decent actor.

49

Queen	(Gene. Ward) She was the pupil of Ristori. Hang it!
Imogen	A painstaking person, but I fear will look a sight.

Then *All* work with earnestness, are "sober, clean" and perfect (in their words). Except E. T. who will never know those Confounded Words.

Good morning! Isnt it a heavenly day, but *not* to "keep house." My vocal cords are all queer, and I cant speak to a soul. Hence this scribble to you, for I *must* cackle.

I've had a lovely tricycle given me, and havent time yet to *think* of it.

Dont write plays to be acted in a scene of 4 walls. Oh, the Open, the Open! Let *mine* (!) be in the open. Good-bye.

Yours ever gratefully,

NELLEN T.

XXIX: E. T. *to* G. B. S.

[*Ellen Terry had seen Arms and the Man at the Avenue Theatre (now the Playhouse) where it was first produced in 1894, the year it was written. —The question-mark after "met" should be noticed. The correspondents "met" only metaphysically until 1900, except for one odd little encounter mentioned by Shaw in Letter XII, and, of course, the vivid personal knowledge on his side gained as a member of her audience.—Ellen Terry's statement that she "understands nothing" of music should not be taken literally. She knew enough of it to read it easily and to be a fairly proficient pianist. Her musical ear was acute, and her musical taste discriminating. Her favourite composer was Bach. I remember that her aversion to the gramophone was finally overcome by a record made by Kreisler and Zimbalist of the Concerto for Two Violins in D minor.—The letter from G. B. S. referred to is Number XXVII.*]

18 September 1896.

Savoy Hotel

THE timeing plays (or rather the *not* timeing them!) is where one goes on the rocks for the first few nights, and it comes of not rehearsing, *for at least a week,* each act without a stop. One does that for the first time on the first night, and of course it's *wrong* at first.

I'm not good at knives and curses, but better at flying to lovers and enduring a good deal in the way of rocks and shocks.

What are *you* best at?

You seem to do everything.

50

But I remember you made me laugh, and amused me more than I was ever amused, when I saw Arms and the Man. But then Music (the which I fear I understand nothing of, but love the best of all). Are you best at that? Oh how frightful it must be to know a lot! No possible companionship, for most people know nothing at all! I'm nearly dead. Pray for me, "wish" for me. My head, and heart, and body all ache. I think I'm just *frightened*.

And, after all, as if anything mattered!

Why here's a letter from G. B. S. And he is a vegetarian, is he? I knew of his Jaegerish woolerish ways, but not of the carrots and beans.

Missfire! That's the word. That's what I am doing as I get older. And I shall have to give it up. *You* must advise me to, in public or private, I care not a ha'penny which, and strengthen me in my own opinion. You honour me by anything you say to me. I should like one thing, that you never mentioned me in print. It's different, it seems to me, now that we have met(?) But again, what does it matter? *How small*. Only it would be fun to me if you found all fault with me in the eyes of other people, and really, all the time, *liked* me, although with but as small a drop of liking as a wren's eye!

Ellen is a very small person even to consider for a moment such matters.

You have become a habit with me, Sir, and each morning before breakfast *I take you,* like a dear pill!

The only thing that distresses me (though it joys me too) is that you write back again quick—like thought—you kind Dear, when you ought not to waste yourself upon unconsidered trifles. Well, somehow you will be rewarded, I doubt not, and when Tuesday is past and gone, I'll only trouble you once in a long while, for my grandchildren shall have my time, and I'll take my comfort from them. (Selfish!) At present need, they are too much in the milky way for their drooping grandmother, and your desperately tired and grateful

ELLEN TERRY

P.S. I wont send this off until to-morrow, and so let you escape for a day.

XXX: G. B. S. *to* E. T.

[*The analysis of Duse's art referred to was made in an article in* The Saturday Review *in June 1895. One passage bears a very close resemblance to a passage in this letter. "... With the greatest artists there soon com-*

mences an integrating of the points into a continuous whole, at which stage
the actress appears to make no points at all, and to proceed in the most
unstudied and 'natural' way. This rare consummation Duse has reached."]

21 September 1896.
Underground—smoke, fog,
filth, and joggle-joggle.

I HAVE been bicycling about since Thursday—got your last letter but one at Felixstowe—did not get your very last until I reached Fitzroy Square, an hour or so ago, sopping like the policeman's helmet in The Area Belle when it is fished out of the copper. What with changing and bathing and getting the mud off the bicycle and unpacking and hastily opening my accumulated letters I have had no time to sit down to yours, but must perforce eat it standing up, like refreshments at Swindon. As to answering it, all I can do is to scrawl this in the hideous Underground train on my way to the theatre at Camberwell, where they have a real first night, if you please, "new and original" and all the rest of it.

Now I shall have to change at Aldersgate, and this will get all crumpled and blotted.

Ha! safe in the other train at last. And now, unfortunately, I have nothing to say.

Oh, quite as much as a wren's eye, I assure you. I always have, ever since I first saw you. But that's nothing; for there have been ever so many others from that point of view, whereas there has been only one Ellen Terry.

As to missing fire, why of course. Dont you understand the development of your own art yet? Why dont you read The Saturday Review? You would learn all about it. Damn this train! I cant write with its bumping and banging about, and here we are at the Elephant already. By the way, I write most of my plays this way.

However, as I was saying about missfires, missfires belong to the elementary stage of "making points." When you were a small baby, a very small baby, long before you could be trusted by yourself and were born, you had no bones. Then little stars and points of love began to appear in you like the specks of butter in churned milk. These points multiplied and grew until they all intergrated into a complete little skeleton, upon which Ellen Terry was built. Now that is how you become an actress. At first you try to make a few points and dont know how to make them. Then you *do* know how to make them and you think of a few more. When they miss fire, you are greatly put out. But finally the points all integrate into one continuous point, which is the whole part itself. I have sat watching Duse in Camille, analysing all her play into the million or so of points of which it originally consisted, and admiring beyond expression the prodigious power of work that built it all up. And now, said I to myself, I will shew what criticism is; and I gave my analysis duly in The Saturday—and sure enough there presently comes a majestic letter from a Secretary of State. The Signora Duse, it declared, was unaccustomed to be even conscious of the unspeakable littlenesses which her work called forth, whether in praise or blame, from the insects of the Press. But the S. D. could appreciate merit even in abject occupations; and as I had shewn some power of at least understanding the very hard work which the S. D. had devoted to her art, she permitted herself for a moment to betray a consciousness of the Press, and even to thank me. I was prodigiously pleased; but what I want to know is, does she corrupt every critic in the same way, just like you in *your* way!

Now Duse sometimes misses fire. I saw her great opening performance of Magda at Drury Lane. Everything came off like mad. I couldnt help going in to see it again when I accidentally found myself near the Savoy at a matinée of it. I positively and actually paid for my stall, a stupendous phenomenon. But observe, this time . . . all the great passages escaped her, slipped through her wretched fingers; and yet it was a great performance. She played for all she was worth at that moment; and it was more than enough for anyone who had not seen the other performance. Well, as I said before (you will have noticed that I am always saying the same thing over and over again—I have no doubt I have told you the Duse story at least 30 times) if you play Imogen to-morrow for all *you* are worth, under the circumstances, you cant fall below a good weekday performance, even if you are not in the vein for a regular Sunday one. Why be greedy? What would the golden moments be worth if they came always? There is always a great charm nowadays in you. I remember once feeling inclined to throw things at your head. It was during the revival of Olivia at the Lyceum. As it happened, you did not play well the night I saw it: compared with the old Court Olivia it was stale and spoiled. You no longer walked in the fear of the Lord, which is the beginning of wisdom. But all that seems gone now: you suffer and conquer in your work again.

The agony, the dread, is the price of the success. Would you cheapen it if you could?

As to not mentioning you in public, I understand the feeling: but I am not convinced. Before the world I must deal sincerely with you, however light a turn I may give my sincerity. I owe that to your dignity as an artist and to my profession. But in private I only want to please you, which makes me a liar and an actor. But you understand all this; only you are not quite as proud as you should be of the fact that you are a fully self-possessed woman and therefore not really the slave of love. You would not delight in it so if it were not entirely subject to your will, if the abandonment were real abandonment, instead of voluntary, artistic, *willed* (and therefore revocable) rapture.

But I am drivelling. All this is scrawled in trains, between acts, in fragments, to amuse you at breakfast. You will find that the grandchildren, like all children, have the qualities conventionally ascribed to old age. The ideal old person is a child, the ideal child is forty, the ideal woman is a man, though women lie low and let that secret keep itself.

Now I have got home; but it is midnight; and I must go to bed betimes to be prepared for the slaughter of Cymbeline. Your account of the cast is appalling. Can *none* of them act? Oh, your apologies for them! Your apologies for their existence! Do you realize what an incompetent profession it is?

I am surprised to hear that you saw Arms and the Man. They told me that your infants all came to see it, and vainly endeavoured to persuade you to venture. So I concluded that you had not ventured. By the way, when I used to read the play before it was produced, people used not to laugh at it as they laughed in the theatre. On my honor it was a serious play—a play to cry over if you could only have helped laughing.

Of course I am a vegetarian. Did you suppose I was in the habit of chewing the dead bodies of animals? Ugh! And yet I confess I once did it habitually, as recently as fifteen years ago; but not since then. I cannot tell you what I am best at; for best is a rank that I have not yet attained. I will send you an account of myself presently: there is one coming out in an American magazine; and next Sunday the best amateur photographer in London is going to try to make a pretty portrait of me. If the interviewer, who is a very clever fellow, hits me off at all, you shall have the magazine and a copy of the photograph together. The interview will let your imagination down astonishingly; but the effect of the portrait will depend on the expectations you have formed.

I am apprehensive about the effect of that nasty expression about the corners of the mouth. You will catch that expression vividly in the Saturday at the end of the week. For I shall corruptly praise you no matter what you do; but oh, wont I take it out of the rest!

It's past one: I am almost asleep.

A thousand successes! You will break my heart if you are anything less than PERFECT.

G. B. S.

XXXI: E. T. *to* G. B. S.

[*A vivid glimpse of Ellen Terry during the anxious hours before the first performance of Cymbeline. Seldom has anyone who has had the experience of being "inspired" come nearer an exact description of it. The words "I'm all earth instantly I get on the stage for this part" can be appreciated in the light of her description of herself in Letter XXXVI as "always in-the-air, light, and bodyless" when on the stage.*]

22 September 1896

A
H, BUT you are kind! But spite of all your goodness to me I shall do nothing to-night. It's not because I've left my effects to chance. I've settled what I want to try for but I'm *all earth* instantly I get on the stage for this part. No inspiration, no softness, no sadness even. Tight, mechanical, *hide-bound*. I feel nothing. I know some of myself. In a few days it will all be different. I think it is the result of physical weariness. My head is tired. I cant care, cant think, cant feel. *Can Not.* After the carefullest thinking and practising every detail of my blessed work, something comes upon me. (This is when things go well and right. It has nothing to do with my will.) I feel exquisitely, and then, then, I realize the situation (in the play) and all is golden.

But no "gold" to-night. Only dull mud. I cant help it, dear fellow. You see it has nothing to do with me. If I ever act well, it's accident. It's *divine,* isn't it? There's a double movement somewhere, for all the while one is receiving this gracious dew from heaven, this fire and warmth, one is turning oneself, as it were, to be basted properly.

Ah, cracked and stupid fool to take up this man's time because he's good to you.

H. I. will be wonderful and will look his best. He comes out of that box well, I tell you! I want to act a modern part. Oh, I am so ill, and stiff, and dull.

E. T.

XXXII: G. B. S. *to* E. T.

[The reader should bear in mind, apropos of the allusion to what Irving "did for Lear," that this thing he did seemed to some good judges magnificent. But the play had been terribly mangled in the cutting, and Shaw, whom we have just seen pressing the most unscrupulous cutting of Cymbeline on Ellen Terry, was implacable in his denunciations of Irving's blue pencil, and would not admit that the extraordinary figure invented by Irving had any relevance to Shakespear's creation. Shaw's estimate in these letters of Irving, as a man and as an artist, is frankly biassed, and should be compared with Gordon Craig's Henry Irving (Dent, 1930). The eternal strife of author and actor as to which shall be the instrument of the other probably had its part in this matter.]

22 September 1896.
29 Fitzroy Square, W.

Now LORD bless the woman, this is too much. Pray how long, oh stupidest, do your inspirations last? From nine in the morning until 12 at night perhaps! And do they ever come twice a day? Of course not. Then, if you felt ready for Imogen at breakfast, pray what chance would you have of feeling ready for her after dinner? Rather pray that your happiness does not come one second before the call boy. Pray for it as you would pray for a bad last rehearsal, since misfortunes do not come twice running.

But mind, inspiration or no inspiration, to-night or never Imogen must be created. Next week is nothing to me or to anyone else: Napoleon might have won the battle of Waterloo a week later. It is not your business to be happy to-night, but to carry the flag to victory. It doesnt matter whether you are tired, frightened, hurt, miserable: it wouldnt matter if you hadnt slept for a week and were heartbroken and desperate. Tonight will never come again: your enemy, *his* enemy, will be there in the stalls; and woe betide the Lyceum and its traditions and reputation if you do for Cymbeline what he did for Lear! If you come on with seventy-seven sharp swords sticking in your heart, I should still say you must play as if you were never to play again even if every word drove one of the swords an inch deeper. Therefore set your heart like iron, Ellen, and fight for your side tenderly—that is, strongly. Tomorrow never comes. "Cannot—tomorrow" is no answer to "Must—today."

After all, do you suppose you play the worse when you are not enjoying yourself? Ask the audience, and they will tell you that you play better. Ask *me,* and I will tell you that every mood has its value; and that the failure of inspiration, though it may take the happiness out of a few passages that are little secrets between some half dozen of us, gives force to other and perhaps harder passages. But whether or no, you are in for it now; and if anyone dares encourage you, WITHER him. A newspaper correspondent telling Nelson on the morning of the Nile to keep up his spirits would not be more monstrous than anyone encouraging you now. I am going to do my small duty; and you are going to do your greater one. Who talks of happiness until the day is over? And so—*avanti!*

Hitherto, you have only *coaxed* me. Tonight you must CONQUER me. I shall fight to the last, as if you were my mortal foe, but oh, with such a longing to be conquered.

And now I think I shall go out and get some lunch.

G. B. S.

XXXIII: E. T. *to* G. B. S.

[*Written after the second performance of Cymbeline. Although Ellen Terry had had a marvellous triumph as Imogen with the public and with the critics, she did not yet feel the breath of life in her creation. Shaw writes in his criticism of the production that Imogen's repulse of Iachimo brought down the house on the first night "though I am convinced that the older Shakespeareans present had a vague impression that it could not be done properly except by a stout turnip-headed matron, with her black hair folded smoothly over her ears and secured in a classic bun." He tells me that this description was inspired by his meeting with Miss Glynn (not the novelist, but the actress) at Lady Wilde's in the seventies. The concealment of her ears, and her Siddonian deportment, made an indelible impression on him.*]

23 September 1896. Savoy Hotel.
(Last night here. Barkston Gardens to-morrow.)

WELL, it was pretty bad again to-night. Only one scene better. I went to meet my love at Milford Haven really, instead of pretending. That was good. The rest pretty awful. Well, now an end of me, sweet sir, and thank you for your forbearance.

Am I to hear or read Candida? I think I'd rather never meet you— in the flesh. You are such a Great Dear as you are! And you are such a worker, and I work too for other people. My kids, and Henry, and my friends. And we both are always busy, and of use!

Next Sunday I go with Henry's cousin and perhaps H. to Richmond or Hampton Court (3 is a crowd!). I must get air, or I'll die. I'm thinking how *kind* you've been to me, and now I'll to bed, for I'm beat.

Yours, yours,

E. T.

XXXIV: E. T. *to* G. B. S.

[This letter, undated by Ellen Terry, bears the date below in Shaw's writing. It would seem, however, to have been written before the preceding one, and to refer to the first night of Cymbeline. A few rose-petals were enclosed, probably from a first-night bouquet.]

23 September 1896

WELL, they let me down very kindly, but—you and I know it was all rubbish, and as I only care for what "you and I" think, why—! You were a great dear to send me that last letter. Oh I'm asleep. Good-night, good-night. I'm glad they were kind. They love me, you know! Not for what I am, but for what they imagine I am. Oh you kind one, good-night.

E. T.

XXXV: G. B. S. *to* E. T.

[The article on Cymbeline was entitled Blaming the Bard. It remained "not half nasty enough." The writer paid a handsome tribute to Irving. "This Iachimo was quite fresh and novel to me. I witnessed it with unqualified delight. It was no vulgar bagful of 'points,' but a true impersonation, unbroken in its life-current from end to end, varied on the surface with the finest comedy, and without a single lapse in the sustained beauty of its execution."—The "Hurst" referred to was Irving's box-office man.]

23 September 1896
29 Fitzroy Square, W.

YES, that is all very well, but the real event is yet to come—the event that London is waiting for, to which the Lyceum business is the merest insignificant preliminary—that is G. B. S.'s article in the Saturday. I have to do that unaided and alone: nobody writes *me* sixteen or seventeen nice letters a day to encourage me, but no matter. If there is a thing I hate, it is ingratitude. Some people think of nobody but themselves. But I say no more.

My article is half written, and oh! isnt it nasty! All the natural malignity which I have been suppressing for weeks on your account is now simply boiling over. So it is to be "Madame Sans Gêne" after all. Oh VERY well, Sir Henry Irving. A homemade Napoleon isnt good enough for you, isnt it? Very good: we shall see. And you are going to play Richard III, are you? Then I think I know who is going to play Richmond: that's all.

I shall begin that article over again to-morrow: it's not half nasty enough.

I was greatly shocked by your entrance last night. You must have spent hours before the glass, getting up that success of personal beauty, merely to écraser Mrs Pat. Do you think, at your age, it is right?

I consider the way you went on with Posthumus postively indecent. Who is he, pray, that he should be made love to in that fashion? I consider myself to the full as good-looking a man.

Look here: I shall go again in a week or two. I am not satisfied: there is a crumple in the roseleaf here and there. You made one AWFUL mistake. You actually bawled out the words "a headless man!" before you had half seen him. Good heavens! you mustnt do that: it's ridiculous. You must simply start in horror, give the audience time to see in your face what is the matter, and then say "a headless man" in a frozen whisper. If you must make a noise, screech like mad when you start. Then it will be all right.

In playing Shakespear, play *to* the lines, *through* the lines, *on* the lines, but never between the lines. There simply isnt time for it. You would not stick five bars rest into a Beethoven symphony to pick up your drumsticks; and similarly you must not stop the Shakespear orchestra for business. Nothing short of a procession or a fight should make anything so extraordinary as a silence during a Shakespearean performance. All that cave business wants pulling together: from the line about "'tis some savage hold" to "Such a foe! Good heavens!" you ought to get all the business of peeping and hesitating and so on packed into the duration of the speech, spoken without a single interval except a pause after the call. Otherwise it drags. Mind, I dont propose that you should omit or slur anything, but only that you should do it with the utmost economy of time.

The scene of the waking up should be moonlit: full bank holiday sunlight is too prosaic to make Imogen's dreamy condition and the uncanny effect of the mysterious body covered with flowers credible. On

59

the other hand the low light in the scene where you read the fatal letter is not good. Somehow, at the Lyceum, the scenery is always imagined pictorially instead of dramatically.

How extra-OR-dinarily young and charming you have made yourself by that American trip! Or is it all tricks? Hurst put me five rows further back than usual. Heavens! am I the victim of a conspiracy!

Oh my article, my article, how am I to keep my style fresh if I sit up all night writing to you now that it is all over and I can be of no further use.

Can you recommend some horribly ugly person for the Strange Lady, now that Iachimo has deceived me? The villain! he has locked my play up for exactly a year. All your fault, yours, yours, yours, yours, and nobody else's. Ought to be ashamed of yourself.

G. B. S.

XXXVI: E. T. *to* G. B. S.

[*"The modesty of a soul confessing its defects" which St Augustine praises can be recognized in Ellen Terry's reply to Shaw's criticism of her Imogen. She was indeed entirely free from that human frailty which makes artists who criticize their own work resent their criticism being endorsed and amplified by others.*]

24 September 1896.
Savoy Hotel

YES, yes, yes, I see what you mean about the "headless man" bit; and the "5 bars' rest" in the Cave Scene is of course all wrong. I see it now, and will try and try at it. Delightful. Difficult to undo the wrong things which have been practised quite carefully, but I shall delight to try at it. You must understand I am the one person at the Lyceum who is never advised, found fault with, or "blackguarded" before the production of our plays! Henry finds fault with everyone, and rehearses and rehearses and rehearses and (da capo) them over and over and over again. Then our scenes (his and mine) come on, and he generally says "Oh we'll skip these scenes," and I am to be found up in the scene-dock doing it all by myself to myself, or being heard in the words by some girl or boy. Then Henry's scenes come on, and I watch those, and find fault with them (!), and this great advantage is lost *only* to me! Now if you had seen me rehearse, you could have stopped my stupidities. It is *frightful* not to be found fault with. Henry wont, cant find time, and the rest are silly and think me a very grand person indeed, and would

60

not dare (Fancy! not "dare" to *me,* and I never put on a ha'porth of dignity!)

I'm glad you think I looked well. I suppose I *must* look well on the stage, for they all say so. I'm glad. I think it is because though I may *seem* like myself to others, I never *feel* like myself when I am acting, but some one else, so nice, and so young and so happy, and always in-the-air, light, and bodyless.

You have "no one to help you" write that article? Poor dear man! Good-bye, dear Mr Fox! Oh! do send me something to read. No, I'm not to read for a few weeks. If you "cut up" my companions I'll kill you dead with my sword!

I'll shut my eyes and try at the Cave Scene all over again. How *stupid* I am. Thank you, and thank you, and no "five bars' rest" in thank you.

E. T.

XXXVII: G. B. S. *to* E. T.

[*Hawes Craven: chief scene-painter at the Lyceum. He was there when Bateman produced The Bells in 1871. It is not clear which play Shaw had "just begun." You Never Can Tell is dated 1895-97 and The Devil's Disciple 1896-97. Candida can hardly have seemed to Shaw "an overrated play" in comparison with either of them.—The "amiable woman, with semicircular eyebrows" is Florence Farr, who was an intimate friend of Shaw's (see note to Letter V).*]

25 September 1896.
29 Fitzroy Square, W.

Now this is positively my last letter. The thing is getting ridiculous. The article is finished and gone irrevocably to press. A mass of pounded, smashed, lacerated fragments, with here and there a button or a splinter of bone, is all that is left of your unhappy son, of H. I., of Shakespear, of Webster, and of the Lyceum stage management. On the latter point I want you to consider the article carefully with reference to that headless business. I am furious with myself for having omitted to urge upon you the importance of the scenic setting—I ought to have known that without a vigorous protest you would be put off with something between Bellinzona and Tintern, and two nice young men out of a studio, instead of a land of lions murderers and hobgoblins, with dreadful lonely distances and threatening darknesses. Why should you ask for a drop of pity on a nice pretty warm comfortable reassuring lovely day in the country, with "tea for tourists" obviously just round the corner? Great Lord, if I were a scene painter I'd have painted such an endless valley of desolation for you that at your appearance in its awful solitudes, lost and encompassed by terrors, everybody would have caught their breath with a sob before you opened your mouth. I should like to see Hawes Craven offering that cosy little hill and millstream to Mrs Siddons. The idiot! You would rank as the greatest actress in the world if only you were not surrounded by fools, duffers, blockheads, people with heads like croquet balls, solid all through. How would Iachimo like to play his scene in one of the bedrooms in Maple's shop window, with a nice new portmanteau to hide in?

Ellen: art is one and indivisible. If ever you play Shakespear again, dictate the scene plot before you think of anything else—even of your dresses.

Sir H. I. does not see why Sardou's Napoleon should exclude mine. He summons me to conference tomorrow (Saturday) at midday. I shall see him with the Saturday article (which he will get up at five in the morning to read) up to the hilt in his heart. Unfortunately, he will have the satisfaction of getting the better of me in personal intercourse. In correspondence I can always maintain an iron consistency. In conversation I shall get interested in *him,* and forget all about the importance of my rubbishy little play. What with the article and the interview combined, it is I, and not he, who will need to be taken to Richmond and petted. But women have no sense of justice in these matters. I hope his cousin will bore him to distraction.

Very well, you shant meet me in the flesh if you'd rather not. There is something deeply touching in that. Did you *never* meet a man who could bear meeting and knowing? Perhaps you're right: Oscar Wilde said of me: "An excellent man: he has no enemies; and none of his friends like him." And that's quite true: they dont like me; but they are my friends, and some of them love me. If you value a man's regard, *strive* with him. As to *liking,* you like your newspaper, and despise it. I had rather you remembered one thing I said for three days than *liked* me (only) for 300,000,000,000,000,000 years. How would you like to be an *amiable* woman, with semicircular eyebrows?

Candida doesnt matter. I begin to think it an overrated play, especially in comparison to the one I have just begun. You simply *couldnt* read it: the first scene would bore you to death and you would never

62

:ake it up again. Unless I read it to you, you must wait until it is pro-
luced, if it ever is. However, that can be managed without utter dis-
llusion. You can be blindfolded, and then I can enter the room and get
ɔehind a screen and read away. This plan will have the enormous advantage that if you dont like the play you can slip out after the first
speech or two, and slip back again and cough (to prove your presence)
ust before the end. I will promise not to utter a single word outside
he play, and not to peep round the screen.

G. B. S.

XXXVIII: E. T. *to* G. B. S.

*The interview with Henry Irving took place and is referred to again in
Ellen Terry's letter of October 2 (Number XXXIX).—"The Review": The
Saturday Review, containing the notice of Cymbeline.*]

26 September 1896

OH YOU perfectly charming being. You are just a Duck! Your letter
here for supper with my cold chicken pie, and I have not left
ɔff laughing all the while. I had been amused before I left the "work-
ɪouse" by hearing from H. I. that you were to meet to-morrow at 12:30.
Then he brought me home here, but didnt come in, and then your
ɘtter, and "the Review" to-morrow! !

Dont misunderstand my words, and call me up in your mind's eye
ₐs a sweetly pathetic picture who "Never met a man worth meeting
nd knowing"! That's not so. I've only ever met fine fellows and found
hey were *all* worth knowing, and have loved them all (dont misunder-
tand me) and I'm all tired out with caring and caring, and I never
ɘave off (which is so absurd). But I must hear your plays. Maynt I
ɪave Candida? Do you think I'll run away with her?

Well—it's just what I *am*. "An amiable woman." I have been told
ɔ of many. Ugh! Good-night, you poor old dear. You're splendid! Oh
ɔ be there to-morrow morning at 12:30, and I cant be. But I know H.
vill drive up here directly afterwards and tell me all about you, from
·is point of view! But he is such a clever old silly, and when we know
·eople *together,* he sees 'em through my eyes. Except critics!

Just read you again, and am bubbling with laughter. Thank God
'm alone here. The clock strikes one. Good-night—and good-morning.
  You Pet!

63

XXXIX: E. T. *to* G. B. S.

[Gordon Craig's actual age at this date was 24. "That other acty boy" was H. V. Esmond. He achieved fame as a dramatist as well as an actor. He died at a comparatively early age.—The Strange Lady is of course the heroine of The Man of Destiny.]

2 October 1896

OH DEAR G. B. S. how do you do? I've had a hell of a time since I was last with you, and I'm *so* glad to get back to you. Entertain me (I cant entertain you) for I have *not* come to stay. I'm not buried but I'm quite dead. My voice "went" the first night of C. and I've had to talk ever since. Oh "the Conference"! I could add a wee chapter to it. No, you could, if I tell you I was also there that morning! Intended coming straight into the office, but got no further than the doormat. Heard your voice and then skedaddled home again full tilt, and, oh I was laughing.

I *couldnt* come in. All of a sudden it came to me that under the funny circumstances I should not be responsible for my impulses. When I saw you, I *might* have thrown my arms round your neck and hugged you! I *might* have been struck shy. The Lord knows what I might or might not have done, and I think H. I. might not have seen the joke! (He thinks me crazy, but "good." It's t'other way on!)

Would not you like to be somebody's (anybody's perhaps!) pleasure for a few moments? Well, you have been my sole delight for the last six weeks, and I'm ever gratefully yours. By the way though, you dont play fair. Your "Saturday" was perfect, all but about E. T. You scolded her in private beautifully, but you should first have printed your letter to her. You know perfectly well that in the acting of this "Womanly woman" I'm prettty bad, and you might have said so in The Saturday plain and straight.

Yes. Ed'ard Gordon Craig *can* act, or *will* act. He had best be quick for he is a big boy for 7 and that's his age.

Ah, let him act in something of yours. Heavens! he's better than that other acty boy. Now when I'm clear of "velvet" friends who are flocking around me, I'm going to get to know the Strange Lady and to make acquaintance with a beautiful new tricycle I have, and to—oh do ever so many nice things, when I'm less exhausted.

Arent you going to send me Candida? Only to read. I wont steal it

64

but I want to know her. Now there's no *need* for you to write to me any more.

Oh aint it a dark day.

.

Good-bye.

XL: G. B. S. *to* E. T.

[*Winifred Emery: an actress who held a distinguished place in the English theatre in the nineties. Her father, grandfather, and great-grandfather (Samuel, John, and Mackie Emery) were all famous actors in their day. She married Cyril Maude, and in 1896 was appearing with him in productions at the Haymarket Theatre. It was there she created one of her most famous parts, Babbie in Barrie's The Little Minister. Harrison was the manager of the Haymarket.*]

2 October 1896

THIS is a nice way to behave. You coax everything you want out of me—my notions about Imogen, my play, and a beautiful notice in the Saturday, and then instantly turn on your heel and leave me there cursing the perfidy of your sex. However, it opened my eyes to the abject condition I was drifting into. I positively missed your letters. *I, I,* Bernard Shaw, MISSED the letters of a mere mortal woman. But I pulled myself together. I will not be the slave of a designing female. Henceforth I shall regard my morning's mail with the most profound indifference, the coldest calm. Let me tell you, Ellen Terry, that you make a great mistake in supposing that I am that sort of man. I am not: why should I be? What difference does it make to me whether you write to me or not? You should curb this propensity to personal vanity. My well ordered bosom is insensible to your flatteries.

Oh my dear blessed Ellen, let me stop talking nonsense for a moment. This play of mine which the Haymarket people want to do—You Never Can Tell (what do you think of the name, you who are so clever?)—contains parts for two twins, a boy and girl of seventeen or eighteen. The boy must be attractive, with a smart diction, an inimitable self possession, a refined gravity when mocking his elders, and an exquisite impudence. The other twin is Winifred Emery, who is youth personified (having no soul) and will hit off the callous prettiness of the sister to perfection. She does not want to play the heroine, her public reason being magnanimity, her private one that she doesnt understand the part and doesnt want to. Suggests Mrs Pat for it, to the horror and anguish of poor Harrison, whom I cruelly tell that I must have either

65

Mrs Pat or Elizabeth Robins. However, the boy is the difficulty. I suggested Esmond; but I suspect they have got to cross purposes with him by postponing his play to mine after announcing that they would open with it. I asked them whether E. G. C. would do. They said disconsolately that they believed he went about the country playing Hamlet. I suggested that he might be capable of acting in spite of that; but as none of us had seen him do anything like what we wanted, and Winifred does not want too young a boy (being a mature girl) nothing came of it. I do not know whether you are one of the mothers who believe that their sons can do everything, or one of those who believe their sons can do nothing; but saving your maternity, do you think he would do credit in a piece of smart comedy work? If the Esmond proposition falls through, and you will guarantee him up to the mark and capable of impersonating an extremely airy young modern gentleman of eighteen (at most) I am quite prepared to press him unless somebody likely to be the millionth of an inch better comes along, in which case your tears, your entreaties, your prayers will be in vain. There's a mother's part too—not a bad one—but if *you* will throw up Imogen and come to the Haymarket, you must play Gloria, the heroine. I anticipate an exceptionally brilliant failure this time.

You cannot read Candida: you know very well that you have been strictly ordered not to read until your eyes are better. Wild horses shall not tear that script from me, especially after your atrocious conduct in being at the Lyceum that Saturday and not coming in. There was no danger of your kissing me: no woman, however audacious and abandoned, would *dare* take such a liberty with a man of my majestic presence. I liked Henry, though he is without exception absolutely the stupidest man I ever met. Simply no brains—nothing but character and temperament. Curious, how little use mere brains are! I have a very fine set; and yet I learnt more from the first stupid woman who fell in love with me than ever they taught me.

I *wont*, WONT, WONT, WONT, WONT, WONT WONT let you read Candida. I *must* read it to you, if I have to do it through the keyhole. But I, too, fear to break the spell: remorses, presentiments, all sorts of tendernesses wring my heart at the thought of materialising this beautiful friendship of ours by a meeting. You were quite right not to come in on Saturday: all would have been lost. In some lonely place, by starlight—stop: I am getting idiotic. Miss Terry: your servant!

G. B. S.

XLI: E. T. *to* G. B. S.

3 October 1896

I SHOULD think you *did* miss my letters. I know it! but—I wish I could pick out the sting—you missed them in another way than you infer, you little minx! No more of that, my love, no more o' that. Wait until the 25th and tell that to the Marines when we all meet at Radlett! I'm at St Albans that Saturday to Monday, and will drive over (shall I?) by starlight! Meet me by moonlight—*"alone,"* for pity's sake. But this is foolery, and really I'm not going to write any more 'cept on business.

Ed'ard is engaged by Henry for the "run of the play," Cymbeline. (I give it 70 nights. H. says over a hundred, for the booking is fine for the next eight weeks.) I *should* like the boy to act in your play. *I* think he's going to do everything, but so many mothers are silly about their children, and *I* may be. Why not? I think Miss Emery hates everything Terry-ish . . . perhaps she would not have the boy.

Oh I dont like damp weather. I'm ill. Disgusting to have a body at all. No, I dont think I mean that. I love my body, but why does it ache most times. There's a conundrum! Where I may ever be now, I set folk talking of you. Then artfully hold my tongue, and *listen,* and am amused, and sceptical!

Dear fellow, Good-bye. On each of your fingers, good-bye, and on the end of your little nose, good-bye.

NELLEN

You have hit it! (Of course, you always do) in regard to H. "Character and temperament." He has so much *character*. You'd like him. That's it. *Character*. Here. Here comes my Sat. Review!

[*The enclosure in this letter, a newspaper cutting, shows that Ellen Terry had her spiteful gutter critics in the press.*]

Poor Ellen Terry! I saw her at Charing Cross Station last Saturday afternoon shortly before she got into the train, and she occupied the few moments before her departure by inspecting the papers and books on Smith and Son's bookstall. She appeared to me to be suffering from a certain nervous tick, which caused her head to be continually bobbing from right to left, and her eyes seemed to wish to evade the light. I wonder whether she is really ill?

This much however I did notice, that she is just as artificial off the stage as on, for not a movement of the hand or foot, nor a single expression in her face

m the mechanical obtrusive staginess that clings to many
they are away from the playhouse. She looked wonderfully
wish I had seen her on the boards only. I should then have kept
s. Whereas now!

s the comment written on the cutting.]

ou must keep yours! Now I never have illusions! From a pretty
tle paper called The Sphinx. Sent me by a friend.

E. T.

XLII: E. T. *to* G. B. S.

*[Shaw's estimate of his fellow critic Clement Scott appeared in the Saturday
Review in May 1896.]*

5 October 1896

BERNARD SHAW, what did you write in the S. R. a few weeks ago
about Clementina?

Although I always thirst for the sight of your pretty handwriting,
I know I'm greedy, and so, dont stop and write, but do send me your
"summing up" of the temperament, work, character, and style of Clement, who was so very vulgar in the "Era" of October 3rd.

I think I told you in my last screed that I believed "my son could
do everything." I got that all wrong somehow. I *know* he can do a good
deal, and hope and believe he will do much more, but—*You Never Can
Tell!*

(I'd written something else, but no: I've a Will, unless I give it to
somebody else, and wont speak of anything but "business") I was going to say that if E. G. C. were given a free hand with Peer Gynt everyone
else would believe in him, as well as his mother.

Blessings on your dear head.

NELLEN T.

XLIII: G. B. S. *to* E. T.

[William Morris died in October 1896.]

5 October 1896

I AM at my wits' end—telegrams every five minutes asking for articles
about Morris, and a million other worries. Last night I had to orate
at Hornsey; and a young lady got up afterwards and said, "I dont think
what I have to ask belongs to the subject of the lecture; but will **Mr**
Shaw tell us when his play will be produced at the Lyceum?"

Happy Morris! he is *resting*.

You remember the publication of Scott's criticisms of the Lyceum the other day. Well, I reviewed it: that was all. Not worth reading. Dead and gone journalism.

When I read your remark about Peer Gynt, I fainted away stone dead. In Heaven's name, how old is E. G. C.? What puts such audacious ideas into his infant head? If you're serious, he must be either much too good or much too bad for me. I expect it will end in my having to teach him his alphabet.

I have just been asked to stay at Radlett from Saturday to Monday —for the 25th. What am I to do—read you Candida? Did you say Radlett, or am I dreaming?

Oh, I cant write, I cant think, I am beaten, tired, wrecked. I should like to get away from this wretched place to some corner of heaven, and be rocked to sleep by you.

What did you say about Morris? Do you want an article about him? Look in the Chronicle to-morrow, and ask me no more questions: my brain wont work. I havent energy even to tear this letter up.

G. B. S.

XLIV: E. T. *to* G. B. S.

6 October 1896

I FEEL how tired you are feeling. Dont be vexed with me for writing yesterday. I wont tomorrow.

What a return I make you for all your goodness to me—to tire you, as the rest do. Forgive.   E. T.

You *must* work too hard I suppose? Wrong, wrong! Even on blessed Sundays? No more questions.

XLV: E. T. *to* G. B. S.

[*In an article on Morris in The Saturday Review Shaw writes that he never could induce him "to take the smallest interest in the theatrical routine of the Strand." Also that "nobody goes to the theatre except the people who also go to Madame Tussaud's." The other reference to the article in Ellen Terry's letter is elucidated by this sentence in it: "If you had told Morris what a pretty 15th century picture Miss Ellen Terry makes in her flower-wreath in Cymbeline's garden, you might have induced him to peep for a moment at that, but the first blast of the queen's rhetoric would have sent him flying into the fresh air again."—This letter contains the first*

69

reference in the correspondence to Ellen Terry's daughter "Edy" (Edith Ailsa Geraldine Craig), who after she left school became a music-student in Berlin, and was developing proficiency as a pianist under her master Alexis Holländer when rheumatism settled the doubtful question of her vocation. She returned to England and the stage on which she had appeared as a child. She played various minor parts at the Lyceum, and gained valuable experience there in every branch of theatre work. Subsequently she devoted herself to designing stage costumes and was hardly seen on the stage again except when Shaw, who had a high opinion of her capacity and deplored the fact that she was "too clever for her profession," insisted on her playing for him. When her mother's long artistic partnership with Irving came to an end, Edy became her stage director, and in that capacity accompanied her to America in 1907. She used this experience and training to found The Pioneers, under which name she produced play after play of the kind that the commercial theatre could not afford to touch (including, by the way, a war play of Shaw's), and, says Shaw, "by singleness of artistic direction and unflagging activity did more for the theatrical vanguard than any of the other coterie theatres." The only department in which she failed was the publicity department. This she neglected with the odd result that, as Shaw put it in a characteristic jibe, "Gordon Craig has made himself the most famous producer in Europe by dint of never producing anything while Edith Craig remains the most obscure by dint of producing everything." Inexact as the sally was, it is worth quoting as a richly deserved tribute to Ellen Terry's daughter even though it be at the expense of her more famous son.—Brandon Thomas: a popular actor, and author of the classic farce Charley's Aunt.]

10 October 1896

Now I see the use of there being so many people in the world, "mostly fools." To go to the theatre; (*and* Madame Tussaud's—a nasty one that!) I didnt ask you "why Morris didnt go to the theatre?" Poor creature, when he did go—Brandon Thomas, Henry Arthur Jones, *and* Shaw! But I must explain why I write to you this morning. It is to tell you that although I am dull as a great thaw, I perceive between the lines of your article this morning that *that* is to be the "weekly letter" until Christmas you promise me, and I wont look for any other, for you really must not waste your time on me. You bring my name into that article, force it in, and now I understand why it is a message to me to tell me I'm in your head and your heart, and that you cant get me out of them, and that all your work is for me (!) and that *that* is your weekly letter. *I mean this.*

I wont have you waste yourself on me. Even if I write, you need never read. The list of your attractions lengthens, when I note in your letter-card this, "I will write once a quarter until Christmas '98, and then once a year until the 20th century by which time I shall be faithless." Such constancy I never knew, and such an example I could never hope to copy. But, *Darling,* you are too cocksure of yourself. Ah, this foolery.

If you had written nothing about dear Morris but "You can lose a man like that by your own death, but not by his," we should all have been touched profoundly. The words made my tears pour out, and my heart smile, all at the same time.

When Rossetti died, it seemed as if all my family were dead. I was young then, and generally very sad. Now I'm old and much happier, and your words teach me the why and wherefore. We "cant lose" the few we love.

The Earthly Paradise was coming out at the time my children were born. I lived in the sweet country—in the middle of a common—and I forgot my pangs whilst reading The Watching of the Falcon on a certain bitter-sweet night in December when Edy, my first child, was born. They were playing in the church "O Rest In The Lord." I heard them as I passed through the village—alone,—feeling frightfully ill and afraid. I could never forget that music and that poem. It was all lovely—and awful. I am growing quite George Moore-ish.

So goodbye, you precious creature. Keep well.

Your lover, ELLEN

I think Arthur Symons might have left it unsaid that Morris's "art of verse was as the art of tapestry." One felt that all the time it was decorative, I know, but naughty to say it.

XLVI: G. B. S. *to* E. T.

[The comments on the photographs of Ellen Terry's son and daughter towards the end of the letter are interesting. "He will make a good actor or a good anything else" was only half prophetic, although Gordon Craig had all the family graces and talents for that art. He broke loose from the Lyceum Theatre when he was twenty-four, and rarely acted again. Happily he had other strings to his bow. He inherited his father's love of the stage as a frame-work for a pictorial art which could be made to respond with the most fascinating delicacy to the imagination of the artist in colour, in design, and above all, in lighting. According to Chambers' Encyclopedia, "he maintains that the art of the theatre has been enslaved by acting, music,

literature, painting and costume designing, whereas the stage director should work not for statement but suggestion, and should appeal primarily to the eye by colour and mass and movement, the words and other things being allowed to help out the meaning." Shaw has made an addition to this note, on the ground that it is "an inadequate tribute":

"Naturally the authors and actors who were mainly interested in 'the other things' could by no means be persuaded to accept this order of precedence. They sometimes bought his designs, sometimes stole them, and always admired them, but would never concede to his art the supremacy which he demanded for it. However, he had yet other resources. He could write as vividly, gracefully, and directly as his mother, with a fanaticism quite foreign to her; and his polemics have influenced stage directors wherever there is an artistic theatre in the world. Also he learnt enough of wood engraving to decorate the Cranach Press Hamlet, the finest printed book produced in English since the death of William Morris, with the silhouettes which were indispensable to its perfection. And so, though the dramatists of his day, with whom he had no sympathy, had other fish to fry, and he altogether refused to fry them, he abundantly justified my estimate of him as not only a good actor but a good anything else."

[When Edith Craig first appeared on the stage she was known as Ailsa Craig.—The play of Pinero's referred to is Bygones, produced at the Lyceum in 1895.]

12 October 1896

O H, DEAR! You've given me an attack of sentiment. "And he shall give thee thy heart's desire"—that has been singing through my head until I have had at last to betake myself to the piano and let it out, with a good deal more to the same effect.

Well, now it's over let me be sensible. Let me correct, coldly and accurately, the statements in your letter. It is quite impossible that my Saturday articles—about Arthur Roberts, for instance—should take the place of my letters to you. But you are right: I shall not write every week—not even every day, because good letters are rare and cannot come as regularly as the laundress. Besides, one must not weary you. Mind, I am not to be your lover, nor your friend; for a day of reckoning comes for both love and friendship. You would soon feel like the Wandering Jew: you would know that you *must* get up and move on.

You must enter into an inexorable interested relation with me. My love, my friendship, are worth nothing. Nothing for nothing. I must be *used,* built into the solid fabric of your life as far as there is any usable brick in me, and thrown aside when I am used up. It is only when I am being used that I can feel my own existence, enjoy my own life. All my love affairs end tragically because the women *cant* use me. They lie low and let me imagine things about them; but in the end a frightful unhappiness, an unspeakable weariness comes; and the Wandering Jew must go on in search of someone who can use him to the utmost of his capacity. Everything real in life is based on *need;* just so far as you need me I have you tightly in my arms; beyond that I am only a luxury, and, for luxuries, love and hate are the same passion.

I have wandered into describing myself as a luxury. This means that I am talking nonsense. What news have I for you?

Oh, I forgot. At the Fabian Society I have had a heroic victory. I rashly boasted beforehand that my side would be victorious—that the enemy would be smashed, annihilated, routed, scattered. And it all came off: *they were.* I made a tearing speech, and was insufferably pleased with myself. You are not interested in the Fabian, I know; but I mention this just to give you a glimpse of the street corner Socialist of whom you may have heard. If Teddy (that's what you call E. G. C. if I recollect aright) ever catches Socialism, and announces his intention of spending his Sunday morning at the Triangle, Limehouse, calling on the passers by to overthrow society, encourage him. A year at the street corner is an invaluable training to a young man, especially if he wants to play Richard III.

And now as to all my love affairs. One is just perishing under a bad attack of the Wandering Jew. Then there is my Irish lady with the light green eyes and the million of money, whom I have got to like so much that it would be superfluous to fall in love with her. Then there is Janet, who, on hearing of the Irish rival, first demanded, with her husband to witness my testimony, whether I still loved her, and then, on receiving the necessary assurance, relented and informed me that she had been faithless to me (with the said husband) to the extent of making Candida impossible until after next February, when she expects to become once more a mother. And then there are others whom I cannot recollect just at present, or whom you dont know anything about. And finally there is Ellen, to whom I vow that I will try hard not to spoil my high regard, my worthy respect, my deep tenderness, by any of those philandering follies which make me so ridiculous, so troublesome, so vulgar with women. I swear it. Only, do as you have hitherto done with so wise an instinct: keep out of my reach. You see, nobody can write exactly as I write: my letters will always be a little bit original; but personally I shouldnt be a bit original. All men are alike with a woman whom they admire. You must have been admired so much and so often—must know the symptoms so frightfully well. But now that I come to think of it, so have I. Up to the time I was 29, actually twenty-nine, I was too shabby for any woman to tolerate me. I stalked about in a decaying green coat, cuffs trimmed with the scissors, terrible boots, and so on. Then I got a job to do and bought a suit of clothes with the proceeds. A lady immediately invited me to tea, threw her arms round me, and said she adored me. I permitted her to adore, being intensely curious on the subject. Never having regarded myself as an attractive man, I was surprised; but I kept up appearances successfully. Since that time, whenever I have been left alone in a room with a female, she has invariably thrown her arms round me and declared she adored me. It is fate. Therefore beware. If you allow yourself to be left alone with me for a single moment, you will certainly throw your arms round me and declare you adore me; and I am not prepared to guarantee that my usual melancholy forbearance will be available in your case.

But I am really getting idiotic. All this time I have been trying to recollect something. Oh, to be sure: the photographs! I return them with many thanks. The young man is excellent: good chin, good mouth, not too long upper lip, good brow, and plenty of head above his ears. (A donkey has all his head below his ears, thus——*; whilst Ferdinand Lassalle, the cleverest man of the 19th century was like this——.* His ears were where his collar should have been.)

If Edward has a nimble tongue, he will make a good actor or a good anything else; perhaps he ought to be something else. There is not suffering enough in his face for the hero of Candida; but he might *act* that. Is the young lady Ailsa Craig? I dont recognize her, though I saw Ailsa in Pinero's play and remember her very well. I shall finish this letter by instalments in the course of the week. By the way, what place did you say? Was it Radlett?

G. B. S.

*Two rough pencil sketches.

XLVII: E. T. *to* G. B. S.

13 October 1896

O H, MAYNT I throw my arms round you *when* (!) we meet? Then
I shant play. And I cant "use" you any more, so there's an end.
And you are the only man I have ever used (and I havent used you
much).

Ted caught socialism long ago. He is susceptible and catches most
things, against the advice of my friends. I allow him £500 each year
so that he may be laid hold on by his whims and fancies whilst he is
very young (he's a baby) and get it all over very soon. He is a donkey,
but he's a *white* one. Edy is the clever party, but the most simple, single
person I ever met.

No more of these domestic details. With your 3 (or 30?) love affairs
on, and the Fabian, and the *Saturday* and the etc. etc. etcs., you must be
full up and it's not my moment. I'll wait until you "need" me, and then
I'll mother you. That's the only unselfish love. I've never been admired
or loved (properly) but one-and-a-half times in my life, and I am perfectly sick of loving. All on one side isnt fair.

Goodbye child.

Do you take snuff? I've a circular box with Napoleon on the outside,
and a strange lady inside, but the puzzle is to "find the strange lady"!

XLVIII: E. T. *to* G. B. S.

[*Ellen Terry finds a resemblance in a photograph of Bernard Shaw to a
Dublin jarvey. It was taken by the amateur photographer who Shaw says in
Letter XXX is "the best in London." He was Frederick J. Evans, a well-
known bookseller of Queen Street, Cheapside. His studies, architectural and
human, were highly prized in the nineties. He was a master of the subtleties
of platinotype.*]

16 October 1896

W HY, I knew you in a second! And you used to drive me wild
with delight in Dublin by exciting your horse to run away. Yes,
the "car man" took me out in all weathers. No fits of the "blues" when
you drove me out to Howth, and to that quiet, wonderful spot where
there was the monastery. Do you remember how the mare shied across
the road, and I fell out into the mud? And you washed my face for
me quite gravely and concernedly because I was all scratched.

So this is you, is it, G. B. S.? Well, turn your eyes round to me, and dont hide your mouth (for *that* tells all about one!). I dont believe this is like you! I'd like to ask Edy, but I darent! Is that your ear? I dont like it. It's rather like mine, but so much the worse for both of us. A lovely forehead, and top altogether. Two lines between your eyes. And your eyes? *Look at me!* Nicely cut nose. (This photograph must be defective. No "cutting" in the rest of the face, yet the nose so finely cut. Something wrong in the photograph, somewhere.) A jolly chin. A head shaped at the back like my Edy's. Turn round: I cant see. What is the nostril like? I can see it's not dull. (How I do hate a dull nostril.) Dont let the barbers shave you round the cheek and ear like this. And you are red! So am I, *now.* I was grey a little while ago, all on one side though. Looked like a half "restored" picture.

[In the original there is a rough (very rough) sketch with "Guess who this is! Yes of course!" written underneath.]

XLIX: G. B. S. *to* E. T.

[Hollyer: Frank Hollyer, one of the pioneers of "natural" camera portraits. —The play which "progresses" is The Devil's Disciple. It was finished in 1897, first acted in the same year, and published in 1901.—The artist to whom Shaw was sitting was Miss Nellie Heath. She studied first under Fred Brown (for many years Professor at the Slade) and later under Walter Sickert. She recalls that during one of the sittings Sickert called on her and that there was a lively argument between him and Shaw about the portrait in particular and art in general of which Sickert got the better. "I was tremendously attracted," says Miss Heath, "by Shaw's red ears, and red hair which grew on his forehead in two Satanic whirls." The portrait did not make her fortune. She sent it to the Royal Society of Portrait Painters' exhibition, but it was rejected; although another canvas of hers, which she considered far less interesting, was accepted. This Heath portrait is still in Shaw's possession.]

15 October 1896

JUST after my last letter was posted, when I was on the point of falling asleep, I suddenly recollected that your eyes were not strong, and that I had been inflicting a ream of tiny crabbed writing on you. Forgive me: man is by nature inconsiderate.

Here am I after spending the last hour—how, do you think? Why in remonstrating with William Archer. First, he complains of your not making Imogen a vindictive Scotchwoman—a point on which I turned you right into his line of fire. I wrote him an abusive letter about it; and now he sends me the MS. of his next week's World article, all in refutation of my letter, and in disparagement of your reading of the scene with Iachimo. He says he will destroy it if I object "personally." I have objected in the most personal terms I can command. Would you ever suppose that man to be a walking mass of shy sentiment, striving to express himself and only succeeding in cavilling over trifles?

The eyes of the portrait are averted purposely. The consequences of their looking at the spectator might be fearful. Suppose Edy picked it up by chance! The fatal spell would operate at once: I should have her here by the next underground train, insisting on my flying with her to the ends of the earth, and utterly disregarding my feeble protests that I adore her mother. I'll send you some other views as soon as I get proofs from Evans. What I want you to admire is the skill with which he has lighted the head so as to get rid of the usual photograffy look about the background. His interiors of churches are particularly fine; but he is now trying his hand at portraits. He is an odd little man, a wild enthusiast about music and acting. He adores Duse and worships you. I asked him had he ever taken you: he gasped at the notion of such bliss, but added misgivingly that Hollyer told him you were an unmanageable genius, and wouldnt keep quiet. If ever you want an unprofessional portrait, you may count on him, if he does not die of nervous anticipation immediately after arranging a sitting.

The play progresses—the new one—the melodrama—such a melodrama! I sit in a little hole of a room off Euston Road on the corner of a table with an easel propped before me so that I can write and be painted at the same time. This keeps me at work; and the portrait, for which I have to pay the artist's top price for millionaires ($£5$) is to make her fortune when exhibited. I do not usually allow myself to be got round in this fashion; but this girl did it without an effort. I suppose I am a great fool; but I shall turn the sittings to account in getting on with the play. As for her, she is delighted, and thinks me a most interesting and celebrated old man to have for a sitter.

So you see everybody sees me; but I never see you. I shall go to Cymbeline again, I think; but then you will be busy, and that will make me busy too—string me like a bow into the keenest observation, whereas I want— but no: I dont want anything. How could I look Edy in the face?

I am really sorry about the ears. They are a Shaw specialty. They stick straight out like the doors of a triptych; and I was born with them full size, so that on windy days my nurse had to hold me by my waistband to prevent my being blown away when the wind caught them.

Ah well, farewell—at least good night. I am glad I still have that deep shivering sigh left, ridiculous as it is. (I really am an A S S)

G. B. S.

L: E. T. *to* G. B. S.

[*Nan Finch-Hatton (afterwards Countess of Winchilsea): a close friend of Ellen Terry's. She was an excellent amateur pianist, and composed songs.*]

[Some time in October 1896]

WELL I wont write to-day, but shall take it out in thinking and I shall talk to you to-night when I come home from the theatre and have a quiet time with you. It's quite pathetic, your last card, saying you want to finish your work, and not write "nonsensical letters," and I suppose as long as I go on writing them, you'll reply so as not to make me feel "left." Well I wont post this until the end of the week so you will get some rest. You are very gentle and sweet to me. Sorry, though, you wont have the snuff-box with my picture in it.

But I've nothing you could ever "want and could get from no-one else," and I want nothing from you, dear fellow—nothing *more* I mean. I'm in your debt and dont mind that in the least since I love you. I want to tell you that I very nearly trotted round to you after the play the other night (the first night) but I stuck to my post like a heroine and I helped Henry with all the people, and oh, all the time I was just dying to go away to some quiet place—to you, or to hear some music from Nan Finch-Hatton, but you most of all, or something really nice. Glad I didnt now because of something you said in one of your blessed letters.

Wont you send me Candida one day next week? I'm dull and sick, very, and want an entertainment. Send it to me, like a good boy, as a reward for not letting you hear from me until the end of a week, and for not coming to Fitzroy Square, and—well just because I want it. There! I *am* wanting something "only you can give me"! For just entertainment, no other purpose. Not for Teddy, sir! *I* want to read you.

My curses of children have discovered your handwriting now, and Mistress Edy is exceedingly pert to her aged mother. She has drawn your picture which she says is a speaking likeness, and requests me to wear it inside my bodice. I send it to you.

78

A splendid idea! I wish you'd marry her! Nobody else will. (The ninnies are frightened at her!) Then you'd belong to me, and I'd have her back if you didnt like her! (No answer needed)

Later

Good morning. I must not send to you until Saturday. Here's a stamp-case for its little waistcoat pocket I want to send to you, but wont. Am learning RESERVE, and knitting against blindness in my old age.

Later

Your Ellen is very ill, and perhaps may not be fit to act to-night. She probably will though, for she often acts when she is unfit to stir from her bed.
Here's a picture from you! You darling! You knew I would be ill and just want that picture. Oh, the pangs and pains, but—your picture!

Later

Havent I been good to keep from posting my rubbish to you all these days. Peel off those covers (envelopes) one at a time, and go backwards to Monday. I loved you then. I love you now (on paper it hurts no-one). But I am learning RESERVE. I forgot.

Bad fellow! Hog-dog! to stay Archer on his wild and whirling way! I like the world to abuse me and flout me and scout me, and you *not*. Give my love to every bit of you. Especially the dear old ears. I love them best now, because you made fun of them. What do you think of Edy's picture of you? I *must* show her the one you sent. Edy knows you well! She has met those orbs and still lives! She was next you in the pit one night at Duse's Doll's House. I love Edy even better than you. I think I love her better than me.

Never alter your writing for my eyes. I'd crack them to read *you*.

LI: E. T. *to* G. B. S.

["Them all": the photographs of Shaw by Evans]

18 October 1896

I LIKE them all, the old ones too. I keep the grave one, please. I like that and the sparky one you sent me best. These two are from you. Now I'll get all the rest from Mr Evans.

I wonder will the Euston Road picture be good? I guess you are sitting just to help that girl. Oh I think I know your bad heart, Mr Shaw! I'll go and give her my profound opinion on the work of art some day when you're not there. Will she show it me I wonder?

I'm just going to read your Candida. I knew you'd send it me if I were ill. Women get everything if they're sick enough! I cannot *pretend* to be ill (except just say it on paper) and so I never get anything. Truly at present I'm not fit to be out of bed (where I've been for the last 3 days) and here am I going to a big stupid dinner to-night. What a fool I am! By the way why do you keep on calling yourself an "ass" to me? That's different.

Now for your play.

Yours—yours.

LII: E. T. *to* G. B. S.

19 October 1896

I'VE CRIED my poor eyes out over your horrid play, your *heavenly* play. My dear, and now! How can I go out to dinner to-night? I must keep my blue glasses on all the while for my eyes are puffed up and burning. But I can scarce keep from reading it all over again. Henry would not care for that play, I think. I know he would laugh. And that sort of thing makes me hate him sometimes. He would not understand it, the dear, clever silly. *I* cant understand what *he* understands.

Janet would look, and be, that Candida beautifully, but I could help her I know, to a lot of bottom in it. I could do some of it much better than she. She could do most of it better than I. Oh dear me, I love you more every minute. I cant help it, and I guessed it would be like that! And so we wont meet. But write more plays, my *Dear,* and let me read them. It has touched me more than I could tell of.

Yours E. T.

LIII: E. T. *to* G. B. S.

[*Satty: Miss Sarah Fairchild, a member of a well-known Boston family, united in the closest ties of friendship with Ellen Terry from the time she first visited America. The occasion when Shaw came to Barkston Gardens to read a play to "Satty" is described in Ellen Terry's reminiscences, but it is clear from a letter of Shaw's to her in November that the play was not* Arms and the Man *as Ellen Terry thought in after years, but* You Never Can Tell.—*The "new play":* The Devil's Disciple.]

Y OUR Mrs Webb is a dear (as well as all the other good things) I
should say, but Candida "a sentimental prostitute"! *Well!* "Some
said it thundered. Others that an Angel spake." You may wear your rue
with a difference! So your new play is "grim, gloomy, horrible, sordid"
etc. etc. You have to do that I know. Yes you have to do everything you
will, if you dont waste yourself on trifles like me (All trifles are not as
kind as I am). Anyway you are all dear, all very precious. You say
"your tiredness and illness are my opportunity." I do not quite understand that.

Now I'm going to read Candida once more, and again Mrs Webb's
explosion of opinion sets me a'thinking, and wondering whether—but
there, you certainly will not benefit by knowing what I think. How much
I do wish I could be invisible and see you at work.

Farewell E. T.

I passed your house yesterday on my way to see a poor little servant of
mine of years ago. She's dying. She liked to see me. I'll never forget
her look.

LIV: E. T. *to* G. B. S.

[Later in October]

M R STANLEY WEYMAN. Yes, I think crowds of novelists now-a-days
fancy they are the dear Musketeers all over again! I've just com-
menced reading The Seats of The Mighty and feel certain it will be
the same song over again.

My dear Sally Fairchild will meet you—this evening I imagine. A
very sweet girl is Sally (Satty we call her in America) but it is *detestable*
that she should be at Radlett on Sunday with you, and then come on
Monday (and all the other days), from you to me. I told her I had a
wilful hopeless passion for you, and had tendered you as a remembrance
a snuff-box which you scorned and refused. Now I have given it to *her*.
She'll show it to you.

I am dying to read Candida to Teddy, to Satty Fairchild and Edy,
and promise you I wont until you tell me I may. I will send you back
the 3 precious acts by next Saturday, if I may keep them until then.

Esmond could *look* Marjoribanks to perfection, and act it well, but
Teddy would appear to *be* Marjoribanks.

Do send me more to read. E. T.

LV: E. T. *to* G. B. S.

26 October 1896

D ARLING, I've not read your letter, but I must tell you I dislike folk who are not reserved, and will tell me of your *Janets* and things and make me mad, when I *only* want to know whether they think you would, if we met, have a horrible dislike of me when you found me such an old thing, and so different to the Ellen you've seen on the stage. I'm so pale when I'm off the stage, and rouge becomes me, and I know I shall have to take to it if I consent to let you see me. And it would be so pathetic, for not even the rouge would make you admire me away from the stage. Oh what a curse it is to be an actress!

Couldnt wait, and I'm half-way through your (horrid type-written) letter. Idiot, do you suppose that Janet is the only "she" who'd love to get your play bit by bit? Why that is *the* charmingest of all ways to know a play.

Isnt Satty a sweet? If you read to Satty and Edy on Saturday evening I shall be thinking of it all the while I'm acting, I know.

I passed your house again to-day (on purpose, I confess it). I was going from St Pancras to Kensington and took a turn round your Square. I'd like to go when you are there! But no, all's of no use. I cant compete 'cos I'm not pretty. Edy, I do assure you, is nicest, cleverest, best of all. *She* never tried to compete for anyone, and so probably she'll go to the wall unappreciated. She'd be a handful, but oh wouldnt I just be glad to get her back again if a man she chose wanted to get rid of her. I'd adore her to the scaffold.

Yours, you blessed thing,

ELLEN

LVI: E. T. *to* G. B. S.

became the darling of the gods in melodrama at the Adelphi. It was at the stage-door of this theatre that he was murdered by Prince, who was found insane at his trial and sent to Broadmoor. Ellen Terry writes of "Lord Terriss": "Sometimes he reminded me of a butcher-boy flashing past, whistling on the high seat of his cart, or of Phæthon driving the chariot of the sun—pretty much the same thing I imagine!"—Bram: Bram Stoker, Henry Irving's business-manager at the Lyceum. Author of the well-known "thriller" Dracula.—"The shay": Ellen Terry is referring to the carriage, drawn by a black horse called "Nigger," which she hired from a mews in Earls Court for many years.]

28 October 1896

O FF to Paris? Oh! With Janet? Or no incommoding females? Why dont you give yourself over to a play where there's no smile round the corner, nor a teeny-weeny smile at all, at all. With heat, and with pain and with tears unable to come out, and the pen tearing along at a grand pace. I wonder what you would write then? You are as cold as ice and quizical (cant spell it) when you make girls invite boys to sit on hearth-rugs and "amuse" them. Of course I like that play, too, but—

You say you are tired. I am sorry. I think I gather you are writing 2 plays at the same time. One for the Haymarket, and one for Lord Terriss. Why dont you help "the cause" by writing some scrap for me? The whole of Bernard Shaw thrown undiluted into 25 or 30 minutes. I act for so many "charities" and anything taking longer than 20 minutes kills me when I have to work at night as well. A bit of fun (or a bit of misery) strong colours to "take" the people would come in so "handy-like," as they say in the classics.

Oh G. B. S. you fine dear, be quick and get that picture out of hand. As I passed through Euston Road on a fine smiling day I wondered whereabouts you were. Quite close I felt certain sure. Now when you have some spare time, write *for* me, not *to* me. We need not waste time with solicitors and deeds and things as you and Henry and Bram did. Quick! I want a bit of you, of your brain—only you can give me that— and you must come and read it me in off minutes, going to your office, or to my office, in the shay. A real good idea that! It would not waste our time. If you leave Fitzroy Square, come and live in Kensington.

So Janet *really* "loves" you! What do *I* do? Goodbye. Dont get a cold crossing the silly bit of water. I wish I were coming.

Yours very truly, sweet sir, E.

LVII: E. T. *to* G. B. S.

29 October 1896

JUST back home from your doorstep (from the young painter's—Nellie Heath's—doorstep). I couldnt help going there, and when I got there I could not go in. Felt such a fool, and felt so very ill. Went up the third flight of steps, got shy, and ran back to my shay. I had Candida with me, so sent up one act of her by a rum little boy who stood staring at me and longing to earn pennies.

Oh I'm ill. I'll just go back to bed, and if you ever dare write me another unkind letter I promise you it shall not draw me out again into the cold and the hateful fog. I generally go and see Burne-Jones when there's a fog. He looks so angelic, painting away there by candlelight. I'm studying Richard III. Whilst they are slaving at the Lyceum at that, I'm going to (will you come too?) to, to—of all places in the world, Monte Carlo! I never was there. Edy would like the fun, and I may chance to, or loathe it.

I've ghastly aches all over me, a cold in every inch of my body, and oh, I'm acting so badly. The Americans call you Mr *Shore*. Goodbye.

LVIII: E. T. *to* G. B. S.

[*On the 29th Shaw had telegraphed that he was "horribly disappointed" to find in an envelope addressed to him a letter to someone else.*]

30 October 1896

I AM BETTER. Thank you for sending the letter back. *Yours* is still abroad. It went to a busy man at Brighton, and I dont think he would read it. I forget what I said in it.

I was going out of the fog in this Old Smokey to Brighton on Saturday night, to see an old lady, and think of you. But I'm torn to bits, for here's a girl whose sister is going to be operated on for Cancer, and she wants to come and stay the night with me "for comfort." Think of it! To be able to give "comfort" to *anyone* at the moment of their intense trouble. It flutters me (flatters me I suppose) and I guess I shall stay in town and have the girl with me. (She has no mother and I cant help feeling motherly to her.) If she comes, I want you to stay away. It's *your* night, and I could not come down to you, and I'm at heart so real wicked and selfish that though I'd be upstairs with her, I'd be all the while longing to run down to you, and she would be in too much sorrow to wrestle with the trouble.

Perhaps she'll come with me to Brighton. In which case you'll come here and read to those two lucky girls, Satty and Edy. "Pearls before Swine" I gently murmured when they told me. Farewell, sweet fellow. I'll telegraph you.

LIX: E. T. *to* G. B. S.

4 November 1896

E DY. I think you think she takes care of me! Of course she does in a way, because I care what she thinks and I love her best, but I'm not her child. Lord no! They are not *my* dolls, but the dolls of all the babies who come to see me and stay with me, and they particularly belong to Miss Rosemary Nell Craig, the daughter (2½ years) of my baby Teddy.

Edy *looks* a tragedy, and is about the most amusing, funniest creature living, a casual wretch. Oh she is odd. Envy was not in the mixture that made her up, nor me. (It's quite odd, and we cant help knowing it.) She says she could not live with any set of people in the world, that no one would put up with her but me ("Put up" with her!) She'll try and go away for a whole month sometimes, and hates it, and always gets into a difficult corner. . . . She's high, she's low. She's a perfect Dear. She loathes emotional people, yet adores me. I scarcely ever dare kiss her, and I'm always dying to, but she hates it from anyone. It "cuts both ways" I assure you, the having an impersonal person for a daughter.

When she was 3 years old (speaking of dolls) I saw her engaged in banging to pulp a brand new fine wax doll which was smiling at her. She says she remembers quite well its pink cheeks, horrid smile and blue ear-rings. Madame Tussaud's Exhibition filled her with disgust and contempt. She turned up the clothes of the waxen Princess of Wales. "Only a disgusting doll!" She would look like a murderess, the servants told me, if ever she was left alone in the room with a doll, and most people I'm certain used to think: "That child will come to a bad end." Until she was about 12 she lacked sweetness and softness. But oh she's really sweetness and softness indeed. Only she's odd. She doesnt spoil me, I tell you, but let anyone try to hurt me! Murder then, if it would save me.

I've prayed she might love, but I dont pray for that now. I'll tell you some day when we've time to meet.

How are you? I've been acting Imogen beautifully the last 3 or 4 nights now for a change, or it would kill me.

I cant gather anything about your visit here. I'm just told where you

85

sat, and that's all. To let the fire out! Three donkeys. Had you a stiff neck next day? I'm going to read Arms and the Man.

Your ELLEN

P.S. Edy says she'd never marry because she would not stay anywhere where she was not entirely happy. I heard she said once: "Not one minute would I stop with Mother, but that I do just as I like." (She thinks she does, but really she does as I like.) To my mind she never wants to be naughty in any way. One thing I desire. That she shall never be frightened at me. She's such a baby—and yet so clever.

LX: G. B. S. *to* E. T.

[*Peer Gynt was produced in Paris by Lugné-Poé of the Théâtre de l'Œuvre on 12 November 1896. Shaw, writing about the production in The Saturday Review, says: "The humiliation of the English stage is now complete. Paris, that belated capital, which makes the intelligent Englishman imagine himself back in the Dublin and Edinburgh of the 18th Century, has been beforehand with us in producing Peer Gynt."*]

4 November 1896

I MUST write three words in reply; but I am getting uneasy about your eyes: it cant be good for you to write so much. I believe I ought to break off the correspondence. I would, too, if I were sure you wouldnt at once find out how easy it would be to forget me.

I see that I saw Edy's future rather than her present. Somehow I expect you have spoiled them a bit—probably succeeding handsomely with the man, and overshooting the mark a little with the woman and making her cynical. I have a morbid horror of any ill treatment of children; but I believe that love and the more touching sorts of happiness are wasted on them: they are really not capable of them. Nobody is until they've earned them. In my own case I am afraid that though I was not ill treated—my parents being quite incapable of any sort of inhumanity—the fact that nobody cared for me particularly gave me a frightful self-sufficiency, or rather a power of starving on imaginary feasts, that may have delayed my development a good deal, and leaves me to this hour a treacherous brute in matters of pure affection. But I am quite sure that people with happy childhoods usually say—what is incomprehensible to me—that their childhood was the happiest part of their lives. Tell Edy that the two things that worthless people sacrifice everything for are happiness and freedom, and that their punishment is that they get both, only to find that they have no capacity for the happiness and no use for the freedom. You have a ready example to point this piece of maternal wisdom. You are not in the least free: you are tied neck, wrists and ankles to your profession and your domestic arrangements, and your happiness has been picked up in casual scraps on your way to your work. Edy on the contrary is quite free and has nothing to do but be happy. Yet who would choose her life instead of yours? Tell her to go and seek activity, struggle, bonds, responsibilities, terrors—in a word, life; but dont mention me as the prompter of this highly edifying lecture.

Teddy with two children—at his age! I give him up. You've ruined him. What use can the children be to him? How can he feel their weight on his arm if you support them? You dont agree with me? You know all that, and know that there's another side to it? Well, shall I marry my Irish millionairess? She, like Edy, believes in freedom, and not in marriage; but I think I could prevail on her; and then I should have ever so many hundreds a month for nothing. Would you ever in your secret soul forgive me, even though I am really fond of her and she of me? No you wouldnt. Good: then you love me better than you love Ted. Let me add, though, that I shared (and deepened) *my* mother's poverty—that is, lived virtually at her expense—for long enough. I began my literary career by writing five big novels and a host of articles which nobody would publish. My earnings for nine years were exactly fifteen shillings. So perhaps Ted is a genius like me. But has he produced the five books, or only the two babies?

After all, this worldly wisdom is great nonsense.

Since Imogen is in such good condition, and my millionairess returns from Ireland on Sunday, I think I'll treat her to a stall (cant very well take a millionairess to the pit) when I come back from the Parisian Peer Gynt, now fixed for Monday next.

By the way, make H. I. go carefully over Richard III and recut it.

[*Part of this letter is missing*]

LXI: G. B. S. *to* E. T.

[*The allusion in the first sentence of the letter is to some new photographs of herself Ellen Terry had sent Shaw.*]

5 November 1896

Yes: I'll give them away—if I want to.

Oh why, *why*, WHY did you send me that one with your back turned. Are you not satisfied to be my good angel? Must you be my everyday angel (cant write bad angel, dont believe it) as well? Those with your eyes in them are divine: it's like looking at the stars. But to turn your soul and your intelligence away from me and shew me nothing but how beautiful the outline of your cheek is, and the base of your neck, just to give me that lost feeling of unfulfillment—oh, wretch, you will provoke heaven too far some day, and then—stop: these things become detestable unless they are said plainly and bluntly.

I hereby testify that I, G. B. S., having this day inspected a photograph of Miss E. T., have felt all my nerves spring and my heart glow with the strongest impulse to have that lady in my arms, proving that my regard for her is a complete one, spiritual, intellectual and physical, on all planes, at all times, under all circumstances, and for ever.

The reading to-night was an appalling failure. The play's no use: I looked for my gold and found withered leaves. I must try again and again and again. I always said I should have to write twenty bad plays before I could write one good one; and yet I am taken aback to find that number seven is a phantom. I've been happy all the evening, but dead. I couldn't read; and there was nothing to read anyhow. Sattie saw that I was a mere rag: when Edy was gone she spread me out on the hearthrug on my back and relaxed me. You know the Annie Payson Call system: it means simply petting a tired man. There was what you call the warmth and peace of home, *your* home. If only you had taken off my burden I should have slept like a child. No: *I* shall never have a home. But do not be alarmed: Beethoven never had one either.

No: I've no courage: I am, and always have been, as timid as a mouse. Really and truly.

She doesnt come back until Tuesday. And she doesnt really *love* me. The truth is, she is a clever woman. She knows the value of her unencumbered independence, having suffered a good deal from family bonds and conventionality before the death of her mother and the marriage of her sister left her free. The idea of tying herself up again by a marriage before she knows anything—before she has exploited her freedom and money power to the utmost—seems to her intellect to be unbearably foolish. Her theory is that she wont do it. She picked up a broken heart somewhere a few years ago, and made the most of it (she is very sentimental) until she happened to read The Quintessence of Ibsenism in which she found, as she thought, gospel, salvation, freedom, emancipation, self-respect and so on. Later on she met the author, who is, as you know, able to make himself tolerable as a correspondent. He is also a bearable companion on bicycle rides, especially in a country house where there is nobody else to pair with. She got fond of me and did not coquet or pretend that she wasnt. I got fond of her, because she was a comfort to me down there. You kept my heart so warm that I got fond of everybody; and she was nearest and best. That's the situation. What does your loving wisdom say to it?

G. B. S.

LXII: E. T. *to* G. B. S.

[This is what her "loving wisdom" said to it]

6 November 1896

"PLAINLY and bluntly" you are a great silly Dear in the *me* part of your letter (but that part doesnt count).

If *she* does not dote upon the quintessence of *you,* she'd better marry your book! I wouldnt marry a book. I know it, because I told a man so once, and he went away, and very soon married another (another "book") and lived "happy ever afterwards"—until he died and she married again. And so it goes on and on, and that's all quite right and proper.

But somehow I think she'll love you quick enough. I *think* so, but it's what's in herself I can tell her, not what is in you. How very silly you clever people are. Fancy not knowing! Fancy not being sure! Do *you* know you love her? 'Cos if so, that would be safe enough to marry on. For if it came to the last second and she didnt love *you,* she couldnt kiss you, and then you'd know quick enough! I'm supposing she's a woman, not a—a—(I dont know what to call the thing I mean)—a "female that never knows"! Those are often married things, and they have children, and there are many such, but I pity their husbands.

It is borne in upon me that if she is your lover and you hers, I ought not to write to you quite as I do. She might not understand. I should understand it if I were the SHE, but it's because I'm not clever. I never was, and sometimes, looking at you all, I hope I never shall be!

One thing I am clever enough to know (TO KNOW, mind. I know few things, but I know what I know). It is this. You'd be all bad, and no good in you, if you marry anyone unless you know you love her. A woman may *not* love before marriage and really love afterwards (if she has never loved before). We all love more after union (women I mean, and surely, oh surely men too). *But a man should know.* (Get

89

off, scrawly letter, to him quick, for I believe if I read what I've said I'll put you in the fire. And that would be ridiculous, for I've thought it anyhow, ever so bad as it may seem (I'm not bad) so it may stand as it's written.)

I wonder I havent doubted you were earnest in asking me about this at all! Mind I believe you are speaking "sad brow and true man." Too sad. It makes me unhappy for you, and so I write. But now I think I wont be with you quite so much. Do tell me, have you asked her to be your wife? (Does she know that has a lovely sound?) If you have—! If not, why dont you—"use Sunlight soap and dont worry." (See advertisement.)

Patience is rich. "How poor is he who has not patience!" (Misquoted from the Shakespere you love.)

ELLEN

P.S. Dont trouble about your Haymarket play. You werent well perhaps when you read it.

LXIII: E. T. *to* G. B. S.

[*Only extracts from this letter and from the two following ones dated the 10th are given here, as some passages without Shaw's replies, which it would seem that Ellen Terry destroyed, are not clear.*]

7 November 1896

. . . OF COURSE though there's kissing and kissing. I'm a very "kissing" person, but some girls kiss "in conservatories." (Oh dont you know what I mean—the dancer they have met an hour ago, and the next one, probably, and the next *ad lib.!*) I never could have done that. Very many women kiss 2 men at the same time. Pigs! I'll never forget my first kiss. I made myself such a donkey over it, and always laugh now when I remember. Mr Watts kissed me in the studio one day, but sweetly and gently, all tenderness and kindness, and then I was what they call "engaged" to him and all the rest of it, and my people hated it, and I was in Heaven, for I knew I was to live with those pictures. "Always," I thought, and to sit to that gentle Mr W. and clean his brushes, and play my idiotic piano to him, and sit with him there in wonderland (the Studio).

LXIV: E. T. *to* G. B. S.

[Ellen Terry saw the visible world with the trained eye of the painter as many painters who knew her can testify. Her "chair" in this letter will recall Van Gogh's picture of just such a chair to many readers.]

10 November 1896

I FEEL so sorry for you sometimes. Perhaps it's "sorry" thrown away. Now nobody need ever be sorry for *me*. I'm so shallow, that although at this moment half of me is in true sadness about you, yet with my eyes I see a most lovely sight. The sun comes through the half-opened door of my bedroom and shines on a chair—slanting the shadows, *and* the feast to the eye! Certainly the chair is very beautiful, an old "kitchen chair," rush-bottomed, sturdy-legged, and wavy-backed. You know them. Thank the Lord for my eyes! I think they have got ill from over-enjoying themselves. It is happy *not to be clever*. E.

P. S. "He is just the vainest flirt." That is what they agreed about you yesterday. I wonder whether I know you in the least? Oh yes, I'm "faithful" enough to you.

ELLEN

LXV: E. T. *to* G. B. S.

10 November 1896

. . . YOU *are* in the blues! You are only a boy. 40 is *nothing* when it's Irish.

Blow Webb! Be strong. Dont waste your time on any women. Work. Shake the world, you stupid (darling). Give up picture-sitting, writing to elderly actresses (selfish beasts). Give up fooling. It's only because you are a boy, but it's not fair. It's horrid, and like a flirting girl who is more thoughtless, maybe, than wicked. But at 40 you ought to have felt the ache of dead-at-the-heart, the ache of it. I guess you have given it to this poor lady, and you couldnt do that if you knew the pain. But you're only a boy.

Dont be a fool (sweet) . . . Henry married her he knew he didnt love, thought he ought to, and he had better have killed her straight off. For a while at least think only of your dear work. I can scarce bear the reproach in your words: "I've not missed answering a single letter of yours." I take your most precious time, although I dont claim your love. . . .

91

LXVI: G. B. S. *to* E. T.

[The reproach to which Ellen Terry refers in the preceding letter had evidently made her refrain from writing for nearly a week. The "line" she sent at last is missing.—Madame Sans-Gêne was produced at the Lyceum Theatre in April 1897. Shaw wrote in The Saturday Review that "the part does not take Miss Terry anywhere near the limit of her powers."—Mrs Patrick Campbell played The Ratwife in the first production of Ibsen's Little Eyolf at the Avenue Theatre on 23 November 1896. In December, when the play was put on for a run, she succeeded Janet Achurch in the part of Rita.]

16 November 1896.
29 Fitzroy Square, W.

A h, a t last a line, oh faithless, jealous, exacting, jilting Ellen. You push me into the abyss and then desert me for falling in.

Well, I have been to Paris, and seen Peer Gynt done in the sentimentallist French style with tenpenceworth of scenery, and the actormanager in two nameless minor parts. And how did it go? Not, like Cymbeline and Co., by dint of everybody in the theatre making believe with all their might that they were witnessing a great work, but *really*. The scene where Solveig joins Peer in the mountains touched everybody to the marrow. The scene of the mother's death (with the lights going wrong, and everything as ridiculous as possible) was so enormously effective that if H. I. had been there, he'd have abandoned Richard III and substituted P. G. on the spot. Any of your Tuesday morning novices would have passed for a great actress in Solveig, the part is so interesting. The Strange Passenger got a round of applause; the Button Moulder was immensely appreciated; the house caught its breath and then came down with a gush when poor old played-out Peer said he would bury himself under the inscription "Çi git personne." What *is* Henry Irving thinking of, and what are you thinking of, that you are going to waste the precious remaining years of your careers on Madame Sans Gêne and baby comediettas like The Man of Destiny? However, if you wont do it, you wont. Only, *it will be done,* if I have to play it myself. Considering that *anybody* can get a reputation by playing Ibsen nowadays, whereas Duse herself cannot make Shakespear interest anybody above the level of a curate—but what is the use of saying all this to the one person who doesnt believe it. And by believing it, I dont mean merely holding up your hand and saying "Credo" (always an interesting attitude): I mean acting on the assumption that it is true.

92

Excuse me, Miss Terry, I grow tedious. Proceed with Madame Sans Gêne, by all means. I look forward to it with infinite interest.

Réjane's cast off clothes on my Ellen! That will be charming—charming.

"Never has Miss Terry been so winsome as in this, her latest, assumption of the rôle of the merry laundress etc. etc. etc. The production was characterised by all that gorgeousness which we are accustomed to associate with the Lyceum etc. etc. etc."

Quite so.

Can you hear my teeth grinding, miserable woman?

Even Mrs Pat plays the Ratwife sooner than not play at all.

Let us change the subject.

Your advice went straight to the mark. The moment I read that exhortation in your beautiful large print to sit in devout silence and feel beautiful and *do nothing,* I was up like a lion. Aha! were you made what you are, oh heartwise Ellen, with unshrivelled arms and fulfilled experience, by men who *spared* you, and sat in corners seraphically renunciating? . . .

I swooped on Paris, and swooped back like a whirlwind; and now, dear Ellen, she is a free woman, and it has not cost her half a farthing, and she has fancied herself in love, and known secretly that she was only taking a prescription, and been relieved to find the lover at last laughing at her and reading her thoughts and confessing himself a mere bottle of nerve medicine, and riding gaily off.

What else can I be to any woman except to a wise Ellen, who can cope with me in insight, and who knows how to clothe herself in that most blessed of all things—unsatisfied desire.

Farewell—the post is at hand; and this must away to-night.

Oh, I am all alive—possessed with a legion of spirits—alive, awake, all at your inspiration.

What do you say now?

Ha! ha! ha! ha! ! ! In mockery for all illusions—in tenderness for my dear Ellen.

G. B. S.

LXVII: E. T. *to* G. B. S.

[*Ellen Terry always rose to the happiness or success of her friends as she could not rise to her own. Envy, as she has said in an earlier letter, she "cant help knowing" was not in the mixture that made her up.*]

O H I see you, you two, walking in the damp and lovely mist, a trail of light from your footsteps, and—I dont think it's envy, but I know my eyes are quite wet, and I long to be one of you, and I dont care which.

The common usual things appearing so beautiful as you tell me. Yes, I know. It's a long time ago, but, praise be blessed, I'll never forget! Why you dear precious thing, if you are not as happy as she, you *are* wasting precious time. But you are happy, arent you? Tell me.

Your E.

LXVIII: E. T. *to* G. B. S.

[*The "little play"*: Journey's End in Lovers' Meeting *written by John Oliver Hobbes (Mrs Craigie) in collaboration with George Moore. It was first produced at a charity matinée, in 1894, when Sir Johnston Forbes-Robertson and William Terriss played the men's parts. Mrs Craigie watched this performance from a box with the Princess of Wales (Alexandra) and Henry Irving. Later on the play was put into the bill at the Lyceum. The story that Ellen Terry never saw Shaw in the flesh until he took his call after the first production of Captain Brassbound's Conversion by the Stage Society (1900) is contradicted by this letter. Apparently she had looked through the peep-hole of the Lyceum curtain and spotted the dramatic critic of The Saturday Review in the stalls. His letter criticizing the "little play" and Ellen Terry's performance is missing. "I shall always bless that play" she writes in her autobiography, "because it brought me near so fine a creature. I rather think I have never met anyone who gave out so much as Pearl Craigie."*]

26 November 1896

I KNEW you'd hate it. (Your ticket was to see The Bells.) I cant play a modern woman "in society." I dont like them, but I *had* a model. Men flirt with *her*. *She* flirts with her husband. Adores him, but he doesnt even look at her. He cant think of anybody but himself. What *do* you mean by "tricks"? But never mind. You should not have seen the little play. You will have to teach me your "strange lady," for fear I go wrong with her. No one has ever helped me in my acting (since Mrs Charles Kean in '58) except the public, and *you* with Imogen.

I've seen you at last! You *are* a boy! And a Duck! (I must not call you names now.) Edy told me last night your play (You Never Can Tell) was here, in this house! I'll read it to-night (busy this morning) if

94

I can hold my head up. The excitement last night about Henry made my heart beat, and then my head bursts.

And so that was you! How deadly delicate you look.

Sir, if ever I win money (I've only tried at silly babyish raffles and such like) I always send it to somebody or something. Many little sums have been left me in wills, and I always give it away. *Of course, you stupid!* A very poor woman got £70 from—someone (she didnt know who it was) and, my stars! it killed her! That's the way everything I do turns out wrong! Now I'm going to drive to Hampstead.

Farewell my dear E.

LXIX: E. T. *to* G. B. S.

[First impressions after reading You Never Can Tell.—"B. P.": The British Public. This abbreviation is not so often used now as in the nineties, and American readers at least may not find this note superfluous.]

26 November 1896

W HY my dear friend, it is tremendous. Frightfully funny. Interesting, Interesting,

INTERESTING.

Too much, just a *wee* bit too much of Dolly. I say this as a wary woman, and as if I had to play the part (supposing I was young again). Too much of a good thing bores folk, especially a funny thing.

Gloria is delightful. They are all immense. You never can tell, but I should say it would be a tremendous go with the B. P.

Yours E.

There are *bits* they must not play too fast to an English audience.

LXX: G. B. S. *to* E. T.

[The play Shaw had just finished was The Devil's Disciple. It was first performed in England at the Princess of Wales's Theatre, Kennington, on 26 September 1897, Murray Carson playing Dick Dudgeon; and in America at Albany on 1 October, with Richard Mansfield as Dudgeon. This American production was Shaw's first great box-office success. It fixes the date at which he was able to retire from regular breadwinning journalism as a well-to-do capitalist and an established playwright. The play was revived in London in 1907 during the Granville-Barker repertory season at the

30 November 1896.

I MUST write at least three lines to you. Do not be afraid of wasting my time: you are, on the contrary, saving my life. Here is the proof.

1st. I finished my play to-day. What do you think of that? Does that look like wasting my time? Three acts, six scenes, a masterpiece, all completed in a few weeks, with a trip to Paris and those Ibsen articles thrown in—articles which were so over-written that I cut out and threw away columns. Not to mention the Bradford election.

2nd. I am the centre of a boiling whirlpool of furious enquiries from insulted editors, indignant secretaries of public bodies (wanting orations) all over the country, the management of the Haymarket, and innumerable private persons, who have written me letters upon letters, enclosing stamped envelopes, reply paid telegram forms, and every other engine for extracting instant replies in desperate emergencies. For months I havent answered one of them. Why? Because I could write to no one but Ellen, Ellen, Ellen: all other correspondence was intolerable when I could write to her instead. And what is the result? Why, that I am not killed with lecturing and with the writing of magazine articles. (What the pecuniary result will be presently I decline to think; but now that the play is finished (in the rough) I shall try to earn a little supplemental money—not that I really want it; but I have always been so poor as to coin that nothing can persuade me now that I am not on the verge of bankruptcy.) I am saved these last inches of fatigue which kept me chronically overworked for ten years. The Socialist papers denounce me bitterly—my very devotees call me aristocrat, Tory, capitalist scribe and so on; but it is really all Ellen, Ellen, Ellen, Ellen, Ellen, the happiness, the rest, the peace, the refuge, the consolation of loving (oh, dearest Ellen, add "and being loved by." A lie costs so little) my great treasure Ellen.

What did I want so particularly to say? Oh yes, it was this. I have written to Terriss to tell him that I have kept my promise to him and have "a strong drama" with a part for him; but I want your opinion; for I have never tried melodrama before; and this thing, with its heroic sacrifice, its impossible court martial, its execution (imagine W. T. *hanged* before the eyes of the Adelphi!), its sobbings and speeches and declamations, may possibly be the most monstrous piece of farcical absurdity that ever made an audience shriek with laughter. And yet I have honestly tried for dramatic effect. I think you could give me a really *dry* opinion on it; for it will not tickle you, like Arms and the Man and You Never Can Tell, nor get at your sympathetic side like Candida (the heroine is not the hero of the piece this time); and you will have to drudge conscientiously through it like a stage carpenter and tell me whether it is a burlesque or not.

But now that I think of it, all this is premature. The play only exists as a tiny scrawl in my note books—things I carry about in my pockets. I shall have to revise it and work out all the stage business, besides reading up the history of the American War of Independence before I can send it to the typist to be readably copied. Meanwhile I can read it to Terriss, and to other people, but not to—well, no matter: I dont ask that the veil of the temple shall be rent; on the contrary, I am afraid, in my very soul, to come stumping in my thickbooted, coarse, discordant reality, into that realm where a magic Shaw, a phantasm, a thing who looks delicate and a boy (twelve stalls and a bittock off) poses fantastically before a really lovely Ellen. (Remember, I have stood where I could have stolen your hairpins without unbending my elbow, and you were talking like mad all the time.) But when the thing *is* typed, then you will read it for me, wont you? Perhaps before then I shall have been forced to break the spell by teaching you the words of The Strange Lady.

What shall I write next? A comic opera?

I have sat up again to write to you. Now the fire begins to burn low; and Iachimo in his trunk gets intolerable pins and needles. This grim cold is good for me, I suppose, since I am by complexion and constitution a Northman; but you I hope are warm as a summer island lying fast asleep in the Mediterranean. This sounds like a flower of literature; but I have bathed in the Mediterranean; and it was 80 degrees Fahrenheit.

Now I have finished my play, nothing remains but to kiss me Ellen once and die.

G. B. S.

97

LXXI: E.T. *to* G.B.S.

A H NOW you've got it into your head that I like *that* sort of letter best. Well I like your EVERY letter best. Some of the terms in your letters make me fly out laughing all suddenly, and they do me good. Why you *have* been good and busy! And this is the weather for working, isnt it? I am not a bit of the South. Not a bit. Northy, Northy-Polish. (That's where the true fire burns, in the North, I'm sure.)

"Fare thee well my Dove."

Yours truly,

ELLEN TERRY

LXXII: E.T. *to* G.B.S.

[Shaw had evidently asked Ellen Terry's advice in one of the missing letters about some alterations proposed (perhaps by the Haymarket management) in the first act of You Never Can Tell.—Miss Audrey Campbell: an enthusiastic amateur actress, and a plant of "vigorous habit" in Ellen Terry's herbaceous border of friends. After Ellen Terry left the Lyceum and formed a company of her own to tour the provinces Miss Campbell joined it. She made no other professional appearances on the stage, married in 1912, and died tragically (drowned in a pond near her Surrey home) in 1926, two years before the death of Ellen Terry.]

4 December 1896

I DARESAY there are folk who would think the old gentleman's teeth business was unpleasant. When I read it, I myself thought it was— unpretty, and I dont like ugly things. I remember you stay so long, so many pages, on the subject. "A Dentist's Operating Room." That gave me a turn at the beginning, but you didnt dwell upon it and were funny at once. Then too, a pretty young lady like Miss Emery is one thing, but an old grumpy man—well, I think I *would* alter it if I were you.

I'm better to-day thank you, and played quite well last night to my amazement. Oh I hope Miss T. will come. I should like to see her, but I promise not to look at her, if she doesnt like it, only at you! Why dont you both come round after the play up to my room? Mayhap she doesnt like playacting folk? I dont like some of 'em myself, but most of 'em I love. I wonder do you know Audrey Campbell? Or rather know of her? (She is my Beatrice model.) We have adored each other for the last 14 years. She is a sweet, and is, I think, a relative of Miss T.

She is not an actress. It's odd, but so many what are called "Society people" are very fond of me. I dont particularly hanker after them, but I dont know them well, perhaps that's the reason why.

I'm very sorry you get headaches. It frustrates one's work terribly if they get a hold on one. Dont write to me at night. All good be with you. E.

LXXIII: E. T. *to* G. B. S.

[*"Sixth-rate Kingsley": the reference is to a "Saturday" article by Shaw on a production of As You Like It at the St James's. His remark that on to magically fine speeches Shakespear "tacks lines which would have revolted Mr Pecksniff" elucidates another sentence in the letter. This is the first time Ellen Terry calls Shaw "Bernie," the name she always used when speaking of him to her friends.*]

5 December 1896

SHAKESPEARE "a sixth-rate Kingsley" is frightfully funny. Oh my dear Bernie, as if Shakespeare ever did write those lines: "If ever you have looked on better days" etc. *You know* he never wrote 'em. Why even I know that, or rather I hear the actor who played the part making up those lines to play off his pretty voice upon (Oh I hear, I hear him) and falling in love with himself as most actors do.

When I'm changing my frock at the side wing every night and getting into the boy's clothes I hear—"Oh, Imogen, Safe mayest thou wander, safe return again." Anybody, anybody, might have written that, but I could swear an actor who played Pisanio *did* write and put the lines in. One sees why the clever fellow did it. The donkey.

LXXIV: G. B. S. *to* E. T.

5 December 1896

WRETCH: you thought that play might be battered, and you did not say so. You thought two pennorth of flattery all that the occasion demanded. And you pretend to be my friend!

Very well: I'll come on Thursday to see Imogen. The difficulty is that you wont see Miss T. unless she shews herself to you. She is, normally, a ladylike person at whom nobody would ever look twice, so perfectly does she fit into her place. . . . Perfectly placid and proper and pleasant. Does not condescend to be anything more. And takes it all off like a mask when she selects you for intimacy. She is not cheap enough to be brought round to your room and *shewn* to you. She isnt an appendage, this green-eyed one, but an individual. No prejudices—has too much respect *for* you to put up with anything less *from* you. In a dressing room interview you can do nothing effective except by playing the charming woman of experience and talent receiving with affectionate interest, condescension, and a lovely artless childishness of delight, a young creature just venturing into the life you are queen of. You'd feel instantly with her that such a line would be actressy and that the dressing-room was the wrong *scene* for the right *line*. No: I wont go round to your room; and you know that perfectly well, you tantalising fiend, or else you wouldnt have suggested it.

Mind you tell me something serious about The Philanderer. How would you like to play Julia?   G. B. S.

LXXV: E. T. *to* G. B. S.

[*The fourth paragraph refers to the change in the cast of Ibsen's Little Eyolf. Miss Achurch who had played Rita in the first London production had been replaced in the part by Mrs Patrick Campbell.—Charles Kelly, (Charles Wardell) was Ellen Terry's second husband. Her first was G. F. Watts, the celebrated painter. Charles Wardell was a soldier before he went on the stage, and had fought (in the 66th Regiment) in the Crimean War. Ellen Terry first met him when both were acting in Charles Reade's play Rachel the Reaper. Their marriage took place in 1876. They continued to tour together, after Henry Irving engaged Ellen Terry as his "leading lady," when the Lyceum was closed.*]

7 December 1896

WHEN I wrote "Perhaps you and Miss T. will come round to my room after the Play," I said it in a kind of take-it-or-leave-it fashion, "pretending" a little. My real feeling was a somewhat earnest desire to hear the voice of the lady beloved of my friend. The attitude of my heart towards her, perhaps you do not understand, dear clever one. My heart is on its knees to her (my children's friends come in for that sort of thing, the lucky creatures!). And I suppose I am vain, for I fear I am so accustomed to folk wanting to know me, and not daring to ask to come (All manner of folk, not only "young creatures just venturing into the life you are queen of"—*those* I always receive). I am so accustomed I say to this that I—Well, I shall not go on Sir, for two reasons (1) I cant explain what I feel! And (2) you are laughing at me! And you may.

Of course I thought that play might be bettered, that you might better it. But as my eyes are very bad and I cant read for myself, my poor little reader, who will insist upon being a worm, got tired of repeating the passages over and over and over again, and since I suppose you have deeply considered every line, I concluded I was wrong (but thought I was right). The whole play was just splendid, but there were several little things in it wrong for stage production. At least I thought so. I will tell you of them if you like (without marking the MS.). Shall I?

What do you mean by saying (in re The Philanderer) it is dull and bestial? It's perfectly wonderful, with a swing in it from beginning to end. (No! Since I must be particular, I think there is a halt in the beginning of one of the acts, the 2nd or 3rd, which might be improved away!) "Would I like to play Julia" you ask. Heavens no! I couldnt. Comedy is my "line," and Julia is a very tragedy. I'm lazy, and couldnt tackle her now. A fine part. I could play it from the life, if I played it. For three years I lived with a *male* Julia. He was my husband, Mr. Wardell ("Charles Kelly") and I'm alive! But I should have died had I lived one more month with him. I gave him three-quarters of all the money I made weekly, and prayed him to go. Tut, tut!

Janet. Well, Edy says she was the only one of the three women who could act. But beg her to smile, and retire with great grace, as if she loved to leave—yet not to *overdo* it, as she does in her acting on the stage. Poor Janet! But tell her to wait. One gets everything if one will only wait, and she can. She is young and clever. There will be no money from that Eyolf for *anybody*. I hope I'll forget you and yours on Thursday or I'll not be able to act a bit.   NELLEN

The extra Sundayishness of this is because I have a baby and a kitten in my arms, and Rosy (Ted's other baby) is pulling my arm. I'm having a real good time.

LXXVI: G. B. S. *to* E. T.

[*W. B.: Wilson Barrett. Shaw writes in his notice of The Daughters of Babylon in February 1897 that "like all plays under Mr Barrett's management it is excellently produced."—"That Manxman affair": The Manxman by Hall Caine, one of Wilson Barrett's greatest successes.—Sam Johnson: a member of the Lyceum Company who had played with Irving in 1856 when he first went on the stage. He was highly popular as first low comedian in the stock company of the old Theatre Royal in Dublin during*

Shaw's boyhood. "An able actor," Gordon Craig says in his Henry Irving, "trusty and trusted."—De Lange: Herman de Lange, a Dutchman, and a clever actor of foreign character parts, who appeared in many of Charles Wyndham's productions at the Criterion. He played Giuseppe in The Man of Destiny at the Court Theatre in 1907.]

7 December 1896

OH, BOTHER the MSS., mark them as much as you like: what else are they for? Mark everything that strikes you. I may consider a thing fortynine times; but if you consider it, it will be considered 50 times; and a line 50 times considered is 2 per cent better than a line 49 times considered. And it is the final 2 per cent that makes the difference between excellence and mediocrity.

Do you know, that Manxman affair is really a good bit of work of its kind. If you were a critic you would know how one jumps at an opportunity of praising a man who will probably be wasting his ability in making a donkey of himself next time. And I wish you would send for W. B. to rehearse Journeys End. I dont say he could make Cooper act— no man can accomplish impossibilities—but he might at least devise some means of making those two look as if they had a fourteenth cousin's aunt's grandmother's housemaid twice removed who had once walked out with a callboy. Mind: I am not going to have Cooper for the lieutenant and Sam Johnson for the innkeeper in The Man of Destiny —dont think it.

The right men, by the way, would be Little and De Lange.

I cannot make up my mind about The Philanderer. Sometimes I loathe it, and let all my friends persuade me—Janet and Archer being the most vehement—that it is vulgar, dull, and worthless. Sometimes I think that it is worth playing. Now I say that if it is good enough for you it is good enough for the rest of the world.

She shant be brought round to your dressing room as an appendage of mine, to be exhibited as my latest fancy. Will you never understand what I mean when I say that I can respect people's humanity as well as love their individuality. I should feel nice standing there between you. Of course she is greatly interested in you, as everybody else is; and she is quite capable of understanding your feeling. But you must manage it for yourself if you want to see her. Her address is Miss Payne Townshend, 10 Adelphi Terrace, W. C. She has delightful rooms overlooking the river, over the London School of Economics (door round the corner, opposite the Caledonian Hotel). On Saturday, hearing that Janet, between the matinée and the evening performance, had no refuge but the Solferino, she promptly went to that haunt, yanked Janet (who was half dead) out of it, took her to Adelphi Terrace, put her to bed, and delivered her punctually in magnificent condition for the performance.

I shall miss the post if I add another word.

G. B. S.

LXXVII: E. T. *to* G. B. S.

8 December 1896

I'M AFRAID you took my last words to you as a further urging to bring Miss T. within my close range. You mistake. But that is done with, and you (and she) may rest quietly in the certain knowledge that I shall not even look through the curtain at you (or her). In fact I've only 2 minutes' pause in the play in which I've time to have a peep— just before the last act—and then most like I'll be occupied looking after the dresses of the young Princes in Richard III. By the way they will be little pictures (Miss Lena Ashwell and Miss Norman) and they will act very well. Lena *was* undisciplined, but she gains knowledge daily, can command herself a little, and I'm sure will do a deal—in time. The little Norman girl will do well too I think in the future, and she has more *style* than Lena.

I said I would not send to you for a week, but after to-day I may not use my eyes for a *longer* time than a week, and so—You say "I should feel nice standing there between you." You mean that "sort o' ironical," but why should *not* you feel nice? You need not answer, but that line of yours puzzles me. *I* should feel very nice, standing between two nice people.

I wonder if I'm going to be blind. (Hush, or it would make quite a pretty paragraph for an idle moment.) You would come and see me then, my dear, wouldnt you? I would ask you to come and lie to me then and tell me that you love me. You have an ear for music and could make your voice sound sincere.

LXXVIII: G. B. S. *to* E. T.

8 December 1896

JUST three lines. When you say those things about your being blind, I feel a deadly twitch that drags me all down into a writhing shuddering heap. Never write to me again; never speak to me ever at all; but keep your prosaic blessed eyes and dont torment me with the frightful beauty and mystery of a lovely blind woman.

If you dont look at her I will never forgive you. Oh, I cant explain; and you understand perfectly well. I want you to meet one another without any reference to me: I hate these contrived occasions. Well, never mind; wait until you can do something for her, or she for you: I can always wait: that's my secret—even wait for Thursday night. Only, *do* look at her; and yet how can you? E18 & 19 is six rows off.

Yes, Lena is a fascinating squawker. If only you can convince her that it is not possible to stand on her heels and point up to the flies with both big toes simultaneously!

I must stop: I have nothing to say, or rather no time to say it in. I love you. You are at liberty to make what use you please of this communication. Of course I will love you after Thursday; but the point is that I love you *now*.

G. B. S.

LXXIX: E. T. *to* G. B. S.

21 December 1896

You looked worried last night, like the photograph I have of you (which I know now is not much like you as you usually are).

I was worried, sick from excitement and the pain in my eyes. Now I'm starting. I wish you would not write about Richard III until you have seen it again! I'll be back in a fortnight perhaps. Be a good boy and dont forget your E. I wish you a careless New Year.

LXXX: E. T. *to* G. B. S.

[*After the first night of the production of Richard III which followed Cymbeline at the Lyceum, Ellen Terry went abroad for a short holiday. At the beginning of the letter she is referring to Shaw's notice of Richard III in The Saturday Review. Irving did not use Cibber's version of the play, so the lines quoted were omitted.*]

26 December 1896.
Prince of Wales' Hotel,
Monte Carlo

Yes "Hark the shrill trumpet
My soul's in arms and eager for the fray."
The lines always excited me, and I missed 'em the other night.

Oh Sir, you are a very devil. "A line or two at the right moment" is perfect Shaw. H. I. is always "out of temper" when I dont act with him, because I save him trouble, knowing exactly what he wants me to do to help him, and doing it, generally.

Darling (conventional merely), how are you? Oh, the sunshine here and the trees! I never met anything which seemed really to enjoy itself as much as I can do until I came here and met these trees. Good God, they are delicious. I want to kiss them. I *did* when the moon shone on them and Miss Lowe turned another way for a moment. I had to kiss *something* for I felt so extraordinary, and I hate to kiss women. I was never here before, but I pray I may come again. Oh, the sun and the light air! I'll bring you a little in a box if I can secure it.

You must be well to write like that about last Saturday. I was ghastly ill all the evening in the box. See how silly H. I. is directly I turn my back. To get ill! I'll be back the first week in the New Year. I wish you a graceful year and your heart's desire.

The Tables here don't amuse me. I play 2 or 3 francs each eve—win 2 or 3—lose 2 or 3, and then come out on the Terrace!

Your ELLEN

LXXXI: E. T. *to* G. B. S.

[*The "Good old W." mentioned is the late A. B. Walkley, at this time dramatic critic of The Speaker, and later of The Times. Partly owing to an accident to Irving which had kept him out of the cast Richard III had not done well at the Lyceum, and Olivia was now in rehearsal.—Kate Vaughan's dancing was the rage in the London of the nineties. Until her day, dancers in burlesques and popular musical shows had always appeared in tights. or short ballet-skirts. She made the innovation of dancing in a long skirt, and may claim to have been the pioneer in England of "skirt-dancing." Her graceful and original style was also a complete novelty.*]

1 January 1897

OH YOU dear little Darling to send off to me the same time as I was posting to you! (Dont write to me now whilst you are so busy. Take the time to breathe, and breathe meward. That's enough.)

Monte Carlo has "cured my troubles," yes, but not cured me of you. Dont want to be cured.

Yes, I saw The Speaker. Good old W.!

John Gabriel Borkman. I read 2 Acts to Henry last night, and he

105

read me the rest. "What a play!" You said so, and Henry too, but differently. Yes, a part for me.

Manchester! Oh! my dear Bernard, "how happy you make *those*." But poor Bernie, that hideous journey.

Dont be worn out my precious lamb. Do anything that will do you good. You're so clever. Think, and then do it.

Fancy, I've no time to sit down for 5 minutes and go over my dream of the South! I drove with my poor old dear down 26 miles into the country yesterday, left him for air, and have this moment come back by rail, 'cos I've two long rehearsals to-morrow.

Kate Vaughan's "Andante" movement in dancing. Yes, that's just it. I like her dancing best.

I'm aching to do a hundred pleasant things whilst I feel well enough to take pleasure in living, and these cussed rehearsals stop all my plans. I never felt tired once during my fortnight's holiday. What *donkeys* we all are to have all work and no play.

Bless you, dear Brightness,

I am

Your ELLEN

LXXXII: E. T. *to* G. B. S.

[Shaw had contributed a letter signed "Architect" to The Saturday Review on the subject of the restoration of cathedrals, the authorship of which Ellen Terry had guessed. Farrar was Dean of Canterbury at the time.]

9 January 1897

HELLS! what a day, and are you very well? And are you submissive? (The latest thing borne in on me is how strangely unsubmissive women can be about the what must be.) My copy of last Saturday's Review went to Paris for a little airing to find me, and missed me, so it happens I have only just read it.

"Architect"! If you didnt write that, you stood at "Architect's" elbow. Anyhow his are my sentiments, but how comes it it's all put in a Shawesque manner?

I fell upon poor Henry yesterday because while I was away my eyes got quite well and they lighted on a paragraph telling me how he would give a reading to help the Defamation of Canterbury Cathedral! And I knew he meant it quite nicely, for he's a very proper man. He has "promised Farrar" he says. Now if he'd help to restore *Farrar* I'd say nothing! But if he dares to give that reading, I'll go back to Monte

Carlo. I call that place "Little heaven—little hell," but it's heavenlier than heller.

This scrap is only to tell you my eyes are much better and look well. I know you'll like to hear that. And to say I hope you are well, and to send you some love. Now for a galley-slave's labour for a month or so, with thoughts of the sunshine of the South, and Shaw, and other nice things and people, to bear one up and make one "Submissive."

Thank you for your letter. Until I got it I never knew what had really happened to Henry. (At the present time by the way he is resting on the sofa and looking the living image of the younger Napoleon—your Napoleon.) You should come in and see him some day. He looks just lovely. To-day I'm going to take him down to Sevenoaks for some fresh air, leave him there, and come back Monday to rehearse day and night, for he's losing over £1000 a week and *that* must not go on. I shall not have time to write, so thank God for that.

Your ELLEN

I *like* that architect.

Out with the damned spots Pearson and Blomfield and all Deans and Chapters, but I hope the Review wont get into a law tangle for libelling the perfect gentlemen!

LXXXIII: G. B. S. *to* E. T.

[*Philip Webb: the architect of William Morris's famous Red House, and of many similar houses. He showed how old churches threatened with "restoration" could be preserved by grouting, a system just applied (1930) on a huge scale to save St Paul's. He was very highly esteemed in the Morris circle. He died in 1915.*]

11 January 1897

I FORGOT to say that I was not at "Architect's" elbow: he was at mine. Of course I wrote it (coached by Philip Webb), and you are the only person in London who has had the brains to find it out.

You are the only person in England, in the world, in the universe.

Oh, such piles of work—getting finally rid of that infernal article for the political book (undertaken for money, before Mansfield rescued me from indigence), writing a review of Borkman (H. I. is irreclaimable) for The Academy, and the inevitable Saturday. A nice week. Promise to let me kiss just the tip of your little finger before Easter next year and I will get through ten such weeks without a groan.

G. B. S.

LXXXIV: E. T. *to* G. B. S.

Now I really do wish you would tell me what you mean by the *success* of Little Eyolf. Dont answer now, whilst you are busy, but later on. The production caused pretty low behaviour among the— "artists," and calling in at the theatre one morning and observing the audience, I noted most of the folk there were in convulsions of laughter (the which they were politely trying to suppress).

From a monetary point of view was it a success?

I'm seeking information, wanting facts.

E. T.

LXXXV: E. T. *to* G. B. S.

27 January 1897.
Savoy Hotel

Oh I wish I had a Mammy. I'm so dreadfully comfortless. Expensive, dreary hotel, too tired out to sleep, and Ted's baby dreadfully ill leagues off at Bedford Park. The luxury of seeing it only for me on Sundays. The Cymbeline cheers me up always. It's fine to be somebody else for a few hours, and this writing paper is nice and sunny isnt it. Such little things cheer me. Send me a few lines, and tell me you are sweet and merry still. Last time you wrote, you were up, up, up!

The Haymarket play is finished right off, I know. Then what else? Terriss's? I've not enough time acting one play and rehearsing two others all day long to move far away home, or to read any paper or even to read my letters. I can think a little of "my Bernie," and I do, and wonder about 2 or 3 things. But send me a line or two for comfort, and tell me you are sorry with me a little.

I'm ill and worried and much overworked. But this yellow paper is *something* anyhow. Tell me of yourself. Dont talk of me. I hope I'll get some time soon to read something of yours. Much better fun than Doctors. Farewell, you sweet friend.

E. T.

LXXXVI: E. T. *to* G. B. S.

28 January 1897

Love you? Dont be silly. Of course I do and "twenty such" if there *were* twenty such. If only one year back—but I never compete. Is your knee really bad? I find when I am half way through your letter that I am puckering up my face and pitying you so. But then I remember, and laugh, for I cant believe a word you say. It's very kind to say you'll write me a line each day for a week, but dont, because I only care to hear from you when you want to send to me (that would be perhaps once in a year), or when I want a question answered.

Janet. Yes. Imitate me? I always think that a clever thing to be able to do, to imitate. Clever, and unfair (unfair to each). I never could imitate. I wonder whether I should've, if I could've!

Are you "up above the world so high" still? I'm rather grovelling just at the moment, being so tired that I'm unable to care for anything much, even *you,* my Bernie, writing so kindly to me.   E. T.

I've lately met with the most extraordinary cases showing the effects of the word according to Ibsen upon a young family and their friends, and I hold converse now and again with you, but cant answer myself for you. I wish you would take more points of view.

LXXXVII: E. T. *to* G. B. S.

[*Olivia was revived at the Lyceum on 30 January 1897.*]

29 January 1897.
Savoy Hotel

No, she cannot come? So.
     But keep this ticket, and either take someone with you or keep a breathing space by you, and put your dear little hat and coat on it.

I'm nervous with all these new people in the old play (and I so old!) I shant shape into it I fear until about Thursday or Friday. Go for bicycle rides, my heart, instead of writing to me, but call it my time no matter who is with you. (E. T.'s time, and enjoy it.)

E. T.

LXXXVIII: G. B. S. *to* E. T.

27 January 1897

No, I really cant write to you whenever I want to—how should I earn my living?

My nice flimsy bluish book that I got to write to you in is mislaid, so I have to use this vile thing. It's impossible to write in easy chairs and corners except in a book.

No, my knee isnt really bad: only it wont work properly. The bit of cartilage will presently get absorbed, or tumble out of the way, and then I shall be all right.

In this world you must know *all* the points of view, and take One, and stick to it. In taking your side, dont trouble about its being the right side—north is no righter or wronger than South—but be sure that it is really yours, and then back it for all you are worth. And never stagnate. Life is a constant becoming: all stages lead to the beginning of others. The Lyceum business, on its present plane, cannot be carried any further than it has been carried, consequently we have now reached a beginning. H. I. may think that he is free to abandon the drama to Wilson Barrett or Marie Corelli; but he isnt. The theatre is my battering ram as much as the platform or the press: that is why I want to drag it to the front. My capers are part of a bigger design than you think: Shakespear, for instance, is to me one of the towers of the Bastille, and down he must come. Never mind your young families: omelettes are not made without breaking eggs; and I *hate* families.

Did you ever read Morris's Sigurd the Volsung? If so, do you remember Regan the dwarf, who taught the people all the arts and lived on and on, the new generations not knowing that he had taught anything and ascribing all his work to Bragi and the rest of the gods. Well, what I say to-day, everybody will say to-morrow, though they will not remember who put it into their heads. Indeed, they will be right; for I never remember who puts the things into my head—it is the Zeitgeist. So I will give H. I. a bronze bracelet with this inscription:

"It is not for your silver bright
But for your leading lady."

Your reproaches are undeserved. I have not been unfaithful to you. But I am like the madman in Peer Gynt who thought himself a pen and wanted someone to write with him. That was wise of you. But the green-eyed one was also wise in her way—the way that was your way when you were at her stage of the journey. She used me too, and so far widened my life. I am not for all hands to wield; so I do not throw away my chances. You say you do not compete: well, you need not. *I* do not compete with all the men you love (more or less—I am convinced that with you a human relation is love or nothing); there I am, not possibly to be confused with any of them, and ten times better realised because of the knowledge you have gained from them than if you knew nobody but me. Just so you are not injured by the filling-up with Emeralds (schöne grune Augen) of that castle of my life which you left unfilled.

It is hard upon six, and I must fly to the post.
For to-day, adieu.

G. B. S.

LXXXIX: E. T. *to* G. B. S.

[*The 30th was a Saturday, and as in all Ellen Terry's Saturday letters,
there is a reference to Shaw's Saturday Review article. She questions the
validity of the reasons he gives in it for Ibsen's being kept off the stage, especially off the Lyceum stage. "First," wrote Shaw, "there is the inevitable snobbery of the fashionable actor-manager's position which makes him
ashamed to produce a play without spending more on the stage mounting
alone than an Ibsen play will bring in." Ellen Terry encloses this extract
in her letter with the comment: "Now this is very silly." In Shaw's opinion it seemed silly to her because she was so extraordinarily free from snobbery herself that she never realized how important a part it played in the
West-end theatre in her time. "It is a significant fact," he adds, "that in the
many volumes of Reminiscences published by the fashionable actors of that
day, their occasional appearances (under pecuniary stress) in the coterie
theatres, and in the plays of Ibsen, Shaw, and the young post-Ibsen authors
are hardly mentioned, and often entirely suppressed, even when they have
enabled the writers to do their best work. Such engagements seemed to them
a form of outdoor relief of which they were genuinely ashamed."*]

30 January 1897

I'M DEAD ill to-day, tired out and with a blinding cold.
You cant talk of Ibsen and Wagner in a breath. When jaded ill-
treated, *cheap*-treated Italian opera was at its lowest and dullest, Wagner
(raising hundreds of fiddles and everything else to do it) made the air
simmer with ravishing, expensive exhilaration. Now all the colour and
warmth we get into the Shakespeare plays would never, never (at this
particular time) be (oh, I cant express what I mean) never be *made up
for* to our audiences by substituting the tremendously powerful *bare*
hardness of Ibsen's Borkman. As far as the Lyceum goes, it's much too
big a theatre to play delicately any of Ibsen's modern plays.

I've not time to think thoughts about it, not brains to tell you the
little thoughts I have, but I sometimes long to tell you how impossible
it all is. A few weeks ago you talked of Ibsen and Wagner, but it's all
different. The matinée as you point out would be good, but (for myself) I find one part a day nearly kills me, and I want to live! *Practically*
the things you want wont work. A theatre supported by the State. Yes.
Then it could be done, but in these dull, dull times in England to show

grey instead of gold would not bring folk from their firesides. They would not come.

From your frightfully ill E. T.

I've no right to act to-night because I'm so ill. Ibsen would say I owe it to *myself* not to show my red nose and pouring eyes. But that theatre must be kept open.

XC: E. T. *to* G. B. S.

[*Frank Cooper played Squire Thornhill in the revival of Olivia in February 1897.—Sardou's Madame Sans-Gêne was not produced at the Lyceum until April, but we see from this letter that it was already in rehearsal.— Mr Mackintosh: William Mackintosh, who, after playing with Mrs John Wood and the Kendals (1875–88), joined the Lyceum Company in 1891, playing Caleb Balderstone in Ravenswood and Dogberry in Much Ado About Nothing. He then left, but returned this year to play Fouché in Sans-Gêne.*]

5 February 1897.
Savoy Hotel.

ACHING, every inch of me! I've had the 'flu, sir. I am acting all through with it. Isn't it dreadful? But I strike at rehearsals as well, and am not going to-day. So I can send a few lines to my neglected Bernie. I'm still stuck in this detestable hotel so as to be near my work.

I never said Borkman was a "poor" play. What do you mean? I say the effect on an audience would be to depress, to make unhappy, to make less hopeful some of us who long to dream a little. I think the theatre should gladden tired working people. I cannot imagine a greater happiness coming to me than to be well enough and free enough to just act "for nothing" all round England in little dull narrow-minded poky places—the people to come in for nothing (not to pay money I mean) and for me just to try to make them bright and happy for a few hours. But do you think I'd give them Borkman? (Understand, I love it for myself. That's different.) Poor dear people. No. They should have The Tempest with such lovely enchanting fairies, such graceful young things, such a lot of warm yellow limelight sunshine. They should have Much Ado, Merchant of Venice, Merry Wives, As You Like It, Olivia, Nance Oldfield, She Stoops to Conquer, Belle's Stratagem, one of the Ford tragedies, The Lady from the Sea, Pillars of Society (properly done) oh, and heaps and crowds of nice things. But mostly I'd choose out-of-door scenes, and warm, happy simple-worded and simple-thoughted plays, ending always happily, if possible!! It's very shocking all this, I believe you'll tell me, but for why, I cant think. And I would have mime, and lots of dancing. Dancing with meaning, with joy, with ecstasy in it. How I wish I had been a Dancer. I'd have danced myself and every-one I met with to bliss, to heaven!

Well I'm tired. Temperature right up (extraordinary for me) and stuck in this bed like a helpless idiot, and so much to be done. Oh one's disgusting body!

Sir, critic-man, brute, darling! I played *very* well last Monday, but axing your pardon, my acting on Saturday when you saw me was as dull as the weather. Visitors arrived, Henry, Mr Cooper (who plays much better the last few nights), and Mr Mackintosh. I'm going over the Sans-Gêne scenes with them. Not a single speech do I know yet, and my head is thumping and wumping. How *can* I learn the horrid words?

Thank you, kindest, for your letter, and you are such a Duck! I *see* you at that dinner-party. Now like enough I'll not write to you until Sans-Gêne is out, but don't feel *too* safe! For sometimes, such odd times too, I must send to you. Isnt it a shame that a woman should be com-pelled to overwork as I do? When will come some comfort, some little heaven? I suppose I've *had* it! Oh Lord, and then there's Edy, and the babies, and your letters. Well, well.

Kiss me quick and go my honey. Did you know I waited for you 4¾ hours after Olivia on Saturday? Did Miss Farr like the play I won-der? I feel certain I should like her after what you told me of her being "no trouble" to one. It means unselfish I think. Women as a rule think a mighty deal too much of themselves. I'm always trying not to be a nuisance to Henry in the theatre. Every little Miss there gives him more trouble than I do. And then I shake them, and he detests them, but endures.

Oh, sweetheart, good-bye.

E. T.

XCI: E. T. *to* G. B. S.

[*Johnston F.R.: Sir Johnston Forbes-Robertson. The play he had got was The Devil's Disciple. He produced it at the Coronet Theatre in December 1900 and subsequently presented it in the provinces.*]

Dear mr. conscience,

Well, I thought you were dead or very unkind, so concluded in charity you were dead. One thing I was certain of: that you knew I was very ill and that you did not write to me—Well, well, you have your hands very full at present so farewell for the present.

I often smile when I come across little things in the Saturday Review: The modern lady who dismissed Olivia with entire conviction as "beneath contempt"—*Who?* Why of course I know! Which play is it Johnston F. R. has got? Just tell me that. Dont write much just because you know I love to hear (you kind old conscience creature that's just why you did write to me). I'll get someone else just whilst you're so busy, but I hope he wont be nicer than you, because it would be so delightful to want to go back to you. The idea of Margate smiles upon me, and I will hie me thither next week for a week with my Tricycle and my Maid and the endless words of Sans-Gêne.

Good-bye, Sweetheart.

Your ellen

XCII: E. T. *to* G. B. S.

[*Mrs P. C.: Mrs Patrick Campbell. Miss P. T.: Miss Payne-Townshend.*]

Oh yes, I'm quite sure that I *am* "lonely," but another state may be worse, and I'm not intrepid now. And after all I have grandchildren and they want much, and I can give and give and that's what we women I think want most to do.

Dont talk to me of Leighton. (Poor man he's gone to glory, so a nice waxen Leighton, with peace be his.) I refused even Mr Watts's request to sit to him, I so detested his work. As for dear old Madox Brown he was the father of all the good late work. I loved him, and he loved me. Do you know the great hall in the Manchester Town Hall? Isnt it *FINE*? The last three panels I *could* not like so much as the rest. He told me I ought to like those the best, and I tried to, but couldnt.

You seem to mean Terriss's Play! Is it so good? But of course it is. I suppose you havent a copy for this ill old wretch to read down here, have you? And so now you love Mrs P. C.? Well she's a very lovely lady, and clever and amusing. I've always liked her, tho' I scarcely know her.

Where is Miss P. T.? Was it not she who could find nothing but contempt for Olivia? The rush of letters I got again, all fresh (as it was 19 years ago) about that play. They'd amuse you some of 'em.

I'm so ill my sweet. You neednt be sorry enough to write, but be a little sorry, for I've just overworked myself and could not have gone on one night more. Think of that! Here I am in a very homely lodging, with just my maid by me to read to me. The last 3 days in bed. Cheerful, isnt it? But here's a jolly fire and I make my tea myself and I have letters from *only* the best people and I ought not to feel lonely. In 2 weeks' time I hope to come for a little theatre going. Be happy and love me a little.   E. T.

XCIII: E. T. *to* G. B. S.

[*Lady Colin C.: Lady Colin Campbell. The Colin Campbell case was one of the most famous divorce cases of the last years of the 19th century. Lady Colin, the respondent, won it, mainly because Dr Furnival, the Shakespearean scholar, accidently saw a report of some of the evidence, and was able to upset it by establishing an alibi. She had been G.B.S.'s colleague on The World, and had a quaint habit of making him draft important letters for her on the ground that he could supply the "feminine touch" which she hated, but occasionally found useful.*]

26 February 1897.
1 Paragon, Margate.
Friday

WELL, well. Perhaps it's best to have a *very full* address for such a treasure as one of your old plays, so do add 1, Paragon, by all means, when you send me The Devil's Disciple (like a pet, as you are, all times).

Lady Colin C.—a mystery to me, but immensely handsome, and she's interesting. I wrote to her (what an Ass I am!) during the big trial. I felt so acutely sorry for her and for her mother. I'd never seen either of them. It was outrageous I should write. But I did! Isnt it centuries ago? Or was I old enough to have known better? I'm afraid you are really ill! Dont try your best to get a chill, sitting in Parks and things. I'm quite, quite ill now, unable to leave my room all this while, and all because like a fool I fought the Influenza, just for Henry's silly sake, and to keep the idiotic theatre open.

Now give up, like a good Dear, and nurse yourself awhile, and so avoid a long depressing illness. Even *I* am a *little* depressed, at last! Oh the Play! Send it me like a sweet boy and quickerley!

Your E.

Woking? Winchelsea is better. Take my cottage and invite the others there. *You* should have Edy's room, and she (Miss T.) mine, and the Webbs could have the big sunny one.

XCIV: E. T. *to* G. B. S.

[*Ellen Terry always gave begging letters sympathetic consideration. "I daresay it is a pack of lies," she would say, "but that doesnt prove there isnt a pack of trouble."*]

28 February 1897.
Margate

FORGIVE my enclosing this queer letter and oblige me by reading it. I have not so many £10's flying about unappropriated as some folk think, so I'm obliged to tear up most of the hundreds of letters of the kind which I receive. But I could not tear this up somehow.

I'm sure you wont mind troubling to read it for me. Dont bother yourself to give me any reason but just say Yes or No to me. Would you or would you not (if you were me) send him the money? I think the poor fellow is "off it," but I feel so ill myself, and if he is mad just from ill-health, why, how terrible. But I'm so laughed at for being constantly deceived, "taken in" as they say, that I'm sure I must be the uncleverest person in the world. I had such a beautiful birthday yesterday. Fly away time! Some rest I hope at last!

Yours, my Bernie,

E. T.

XCV: G. B. S. *to* E. T.

[*This letter, which is incomplete, begins with a reference to the cast of* You Never Can Tell.]

[Not dated. Assigned to 1 March 1897.]

MACKINDER for Phil, with, of course, Maude for the waiter and Winifred Emery for Dolly. I daresay it will be all "werry capital"; but though I shall do all I can at the rehearsals, I feel at present as if nothing could induce me to witness the performance.

Your letter has just come. Of course you know my advice before-hand—DONT. The gentleman is not slimy like the usual begging letter waiter: his frank opening "I wish you would lend (*"lend"* mark you!) me £10" is so good that I am half disposed to advise you to send him five shillings as a tribute to his cheek, and tell him why. But he betrays himself later on. There is no mistaking the approach of death and the longing for it, followed by "I Trust God I shall yet live to etc. etc." And the clergyman's letter, and the want of food and so on! No, dear Ellen: if you want to spend £10, get ten sovereigns and skid them out from the beach into the sea: they will do no harm then, and they will twinkle prettily in the sun if you make them ricochet successfully. Or if you want to "do good" with them, send them to one of the heaps of people who are disinterestedly in that business, and know how to do it. But *never* give it to a beggar, especially a beggar who begs well (practice being the secret of excellence in that as in other departments of acting). You need have no remorse in this instance: the gentleman's cant is unmistakable: he wont starve and he wont die; and I dont mind wagering that he wont work either. As to his sanity, I guarantee it. You cant even answer him, because if you lecture him, you must send him the money to shew that you are not taking a moral attitude to save your own pocket; if you write kindly, your sympathy is mere hypocrisy without the money; if you write "Dear Sir—No—yours truly, Ellen Terry," which would be quite proper, you will hardly feel that to be an improvement on silence. The waste paper basket is the proper place for all such appeals.

Winchelsea is too far off; and I swear I will never go there as I have gone to Barkston Gardens, only when you are away. You are the most utterly heartless wretch I have ever met.

What birthday did you say? 59th was it?

G. B. S.

XCVI: G. B. S. *to* E. T.

3 March 1897

Ellen: are you quite sure that you're not very ill? You should have got that play a couple of days ago: is it possible that you have been unable to—ah! I have it! There's no such address as 1, Paragon, and you trusted to the Post Office finding you out eventually, whilst you remained secure from my—but suppose you should really be ill. Why should I get suddenly anxious? A thousand things come into my head: your handwriting has not been steady: the wind has gone to the north and is now a dreadful March wind: you are alone in that bleak corner of the coast without anybody to smother you in sympathetic nursing.

I cant write. I am full of vague apprehensions—at least I should be if I ate meat or drank tea or did any of the usual foolish things (except loving you). The odd thing about being a vegetarian is, not that the things that happen to other people dont happen to me—they all do— but that they happen differently: pain is different, pleasure different, fever different, cold different, even love different.

Dont worry about Sans Gêne: let it be put off: Richard III will draw enough to pay forfeits until you are well.

I cannot think that March is quite the best—but I am talking like an old woman. Of course the sea air is good for *you,* always. O Miss P. T. has secured the house at Woking: that would be the place for you, I feel sure.

Stupid and impatient that I am, why was I in such a hurry to know you? If only I had waited I should have been a fresh interest for you now. Whereas by this you are quite tired of my letters. The only possibility of novelty in me now is to talk to me. Is there really and truly such a place as 1 Paragon in Margate?

Dearest and beautifullest: do write and pretend that you're quite well.

G. B. S.

XCVII: E. T. *to* G. B. S.

4 March 1897

VERY well then darling I am "quite well." Who could be ill after reading your lovely babbling nonsense? (Of which *of course,* I am "tired," oh, yes!) However I will confess I'm not *quite* well enough to read the Play, for I have a Nurse who is a tyrant and says I'm very unfit to do one little thing. She's pretty and clever but I get some letters worth all her nursing. They mend me more. Must not write. Am only half alive. But I love you with it, and Henry is coming down on Sunday.

Your ELLEN

I did telegraph that your play was safe, didnt I? Surely, surely. Nurse doesnt know I'm writing. Aint I *lawless!*

5 March 1897

OH INDEED! He's going down on Sunday, is he? Well, of course there's no reason why he shouldnt if you are well enough to receive him, even though you are not well enough to read my play. Why should I object? It's nothing to me, is it? Oh dear me, no: I assure you you are quite mistaken if you think *I* care. I am not that sort of person—quite the opposite, as you would know if you understood my real nature. I trust he will enjoy himself. Poor fellow, he looks as if some sea air would do him good: it's only to be expected at his age.

Of course that nurse tries to prevent you from writing to me. All these nurses have begun by being advanced young women and going to hear me lecture. Jealousy—simple jealousy and nothing else. She will burn that play if you are not careful, and perhaps intercept my letters as soon as she finds out which is my handwriting. Do you think I would send you the play if it would not do you good? Read it at once: it has a nice happy ending, and a breath of my heart's affection for you is imprisoned between every pair of leaves. Or stay—no—keep it until Sunday: and get Henry to read it to you; and then you can tell me which part suits him best.

I have simply stopped working, except for the inevitable Saturday article. I have been clearing up my table—*such* a job—two long days' work; but the green cloth has been reached at last. Even my bedroom table is clear. Whilst I am dressing and undressing I do all my reading. The book lies open on the table. I never shut it, but put the next book on top of it long before it's finished. After some months there is a mountain of buried books, all wide open, so that all my library is distinguished by a page with the stain of a quarter's dust or soot on it. The blacks are dreadful; for my window is always wide open, winter and summer. This work of cleaning up rests my mind, tires my back, and begrimes my face and hands. And now I begin to recuperate like mad. A few days ago I met Florence Farr. She was horrified; said I looked my age; pointed out that my moustache and two great tufts of my beard were grey. To-day they are bright scarlet; a keen sap of mischievous energy rises through all my capillaries; in a day or two more I shall be 29 again. This must be also coming to you: the air from which I can extract middle-aged vigor must be full of flowering youth for you. I no longer believe that you are ill: I can hear a distant noise like wind in the ferns, which must be stirring up your pores as they open and straighten to take in the first delicate draught of spring. Oh, if I were in Margate, I would squeeze them all shut again with one mighty embrace.

My mother calls to remind me that I have promised to post her letters in time. Yours too must go, with a radiating aurora of love for my Ellenest Ellen.

G. B. S.

XCIX: E. T. *to* G. B. S.

[The play referred to is The Devil's Disciple. William Terriss, with whom Ellen Terry thought no one could compete as Dick Dudgeon, was never to play the part. Richard Mansfield first played it in America, and Murray Carson in England (see note to Letter LXX).]

7 March 1897

YES, the 2nd Act was so tremendous, it "took it out of me" as they say. So I tried to *wait* for Act III and lay flat on the dining-room table for a while! Fidgeted, then got up and went at it again. "You'll re-write it"? Oh now *do* like a pet. No softening. No, no. Nothing of that kind. "Tell you how"?!! Why you have been working on it for months! How could I tell you "how" all in a minute, and with Sans-Gêne, and headaches and things. I'll get someone to read it to me over and over again, and then I'll tell you what I think. And if a lot of my "thinks" could be of a wee bit of use to you should not I be a proud lady! It struck me at once that those scenes between Burgoyne and Swindon (although they are excellent scenes *as scenes* and *for acting*) are irritating as interruptions, like Lovers talking of Ships or Icebergs that pass in the night when they dont feel quite like that. Then too 3 scenes in one act (and that the *last* act) is clumsy (Oh, excuse me! Ignorant and rude!), unfortunace. I think I've turned the corner and am getting better. But this ghastly weather is frustrating. Cant write. Oh, that 2nd Act! There has never been anything in the least like it. You *are* a Dear.

Edy could not do Essie. Essie does just *one* thing, three or four times over. It's not easy. I'm not easy. Good-bye my beautiful.

Your E.

Oh, for dear old Smokey! I want to go to the New Gallery and to Tissot's pictures. Do you know his studio in Paris? Do you know him?

People are so odd that I'm certain *no one* could compete with T. as Dick. The neat head and figure, and the charm, the arrogant manner. "Taking." Act II will find out the *woman*.

120

C: G. B. S. *to* E. T.

[The reference is to some photographs of Rosemary, Ellen Terry's eldest grandchild.]

7 March 1897

Bless me! that's a very remarkable infant. Just look at the energetic expression of her feet in the reading one and the "Kill Claudio" one. The reading one is very good: it shews the character in its initiative, aggressive, wilful aspect; but the one with the cap on, dressed for walking, is equally interesting, as it shews the *social* side of her—the receptive, sensitive, enduring side. Only, they oughtnt to smother her up like that in a stiff, thick, extinguisher of stuff an inch thick, with fur round her throat. They will make her "a delicate child" in no time at that rate. Let her neck alone and give her lissome clothes (all wool) so that she can use her spine and not go propping that extinguisher on her ankles with her spine and ribs held like an open umbrella. And teach her to hate and forswear fur for the nasty smelling, savage, cruel, thoughtless, bestial thing it is.

I observe that she has plenty of room between her eyes (shewing amiability and brains and character), that she is very unmistakably her grandmother's granddaughter (would you really say granddaughter on the stage?—Henry would, most conscientiously—or gran'daughter?); that she has great nervous energy and sensibility; that she has splendid *working, living* hands and feet, and not silly little ornaments; that she is much older and wiser than her father, and will probably spoil you as you spoiled him; and that she will be strong enough to make it impossible for anybody to hang her keys on her nose, in spite of a certain Terry tendency in this direction which has very nearly got the better of her gran'aunt Marion. And to think that this fellow-infant of mine will never know me except as "an old gentleman" named *Mister* Shaw! And will speak of you as Granny to future generations! What tragic lines that pet impostor of yours, William Shakespear, could have written on this profoundly foolish theme!

Does H. I. really say that you are in love with me? For that be all his sins forgiven him! I will go to the Lyceum again and write an article proving him to be the greatest Richard ever dreamed of. I am also touched by his refusing to believe that we have never met. No man of feeling *could* believe such heartlessness.

I did not see the paragraph you mention; but I saw another describ-

121

ing how you rushed on the stage after seeing Duse act Camille, and fell weeping into her arms. And yet you read my plays—much greater achievements than Duse's—and you do not rush to me and fall weeping into *my* arms. Well, no matter, since you are well again. Sleep soundly, since when you lay awake you thought of everything and everybody before me—oh, I have noted the order very feelingly. No room for more.

G. B. S.

CI: G. B. S. *to* E. T.

8 March 1897

JUST time for three lines. Get anyone but me to read that play to you *if you dare*. What do they know about it? I dont believe all the brutal environment of that little story is real to you; but it is to me. Ted isnt brutal enough for Richard's outbursts of savagery. Candida—a play which you've forgotten, but which you once read—has the part for him. The woman's part is not so difficult where she has anything to say; but the listening to the court martial—the holding on to the horror through all the laughing—that will be the difficulty. No: I wont rewrite that last act unless you tell me exactly how: I'd rather write you another play.

Mrs Webb and Miss P. T. want to know whether you would really come to Woking and, if so, whom you'd like to have meet you—a bishop or a politician or a philosopher. I can be sent up to town if necessary (I fancy I see myself going—*just*). They want to watch our embarrassment when we meet.

What ought I to do with that play? That is, if Forbes wont have it?

Take care of your reviving strength. I presumed on mine the other evening to ride eight or nine miles at wild speed on the bike; and next morning I was again a wreck.

Post hour—ever dearest—

G. B. S.

CII: E. T. *to* G. B. S.

[Ellen Terry is referring to an article by Shaw in The Saturday Review, entitled Madox Brown, Watts, and Ibsen. "W" in the letter is Watts, and "L" Leighton. Shaw likens the younger actor-managers, the "expectant Knights," to Leighton, and Irving to Watts. "Sir Henry Irving stands on the Watts plane as an artist and idealist, cut off from Ibsen by the deplorable limitations of that state, but at least not a snob, and only a Knight on public grounds, and by his own peremptory demand which no mere gentle-

*man would have dared to make lest he should have offended the court and
made himself ridiculous."—The actresses alluded to are Maria Saker,
Marianne Caldwell, and Mrs Charles Calvert. Mrs Calvert, who like
Ellen Terry began her career with Charles Kean, and in her prime played
many important Shakespearean rôles at the Princes Theatre, Manchester,
of which her husband was manager, returned to the London stage as a quite
forgotten and somewhat infirm old woman to play Catherine Petkoff in
Arms and the Man at the Avenue Theatre in 1894. Shaw was horrified at
her apparent unsuitability to the part of a dashing and overdressed matron; but she made good to such purpose that she remained until her death
the most efficient and irresistible impersonator of comic old ladies on the London stage. One of Shaw's verdicts on a comedy in which she appeared was:
Mrs Calvert first: Charles Hawtrey a good sixteenth: the rest nowhere.—
Louis Calvert, the most distinguished of Mrs Calvert's four sons, was well
known in London, in the English provinces, and in America as both actor
and producer when he was selected by Shaw to create the part of Broadbent in John Bull's Other Island (Court Theatre, 1905). Shaw says he at
first refused the part on the ground that he had "never appeared on the stage
in modern dress." It is difficult to reconcile this with Calvert's appearances in Ibsen's Rosmersholm and The Enemy of The People in the provinces (1890–94). However, his chief lines were Shakespear and costume
melodrama before he made one of the greatest successes of his career as
Broadbent.]*

13 March 1897

"**M**adox Brown—*A man.*
W.—Artist and Poet.
L.—Only a Gentleman."

"Gentleman!" Oh that word! Some day define the term, not for me
privately, but for your general readers.

To *me* "Gentleman" has always meant the highest and best. I think
it must mean differently to different people.

H. I. did not "demand" the knighting for *himself*. But he resented
the followers of his calling being left out in the cold. The authorities
could not be so absurd as to make, say Blank or Dash, Sir! (Altho'
I think it would have been good fun if the "honouring" (!) had been
amongst *women,* to have had a "Lady Saker," or a "Lady Caldwell.")

I'm so glad you hoist Mrs Calvert. I think she is immensely clever.

I'm back from Margate. Still not well. Isnt it maddening? And I'm
longing to get my work by the throat. When do you go to Woking?
Soft Woking, so sweetly smelling. I very nearly wrote and thanked

123

those ladies for their kindness in wishing me to share the rest and quiet of the place. Then I remembered how once before I was idiot enough to simply believe you serious when you put your sad and distracted condition before me and how I so nearly ran round to Fitzroy Square, and actually *did* get so far as writing you a most heartshaken blithering idiot's letter. Oh, I'll never forgive myself nor will you ever forgive me for being so dull.

Only, only I dont in the least mind being laughed at *by you!* Oh, did you think I meant Ted when I said I thought T. would make a great effect in Richard? I meant *Terriss!* He would not understand all the things he had to say (!) but (with the last act disciplined into shape) the Play and he together would be a frantic success. No, Master Bernie, I have *not* forgotten Candida, and you know it!

It appears to me your Haymarket Play is splendidly cast. (You told me if you remember.) That will be a great success. It *must* be.

Darling! I havent said that yet! And now I'll say it again. Good-bye,

Darling!

CIII: G. B. S. *to* E. T.

13 March 1897

S HE explains to me about the knighthood—to ME! Do you know, oh woman of little faith, that when H. I. formulated his demand at the Royal Institution, it was I, and nobody else, who understood and appreciated his position, and explained it to London when everyone else was either toadying or sneering.

And so you dont know what a gentleman is. Oh my third act, my third act! Ellen: Burgoyne is a gentleman; and that is the whole meaning of that part of the play. It is not enough, for the instruction of this generation, that Richard should be superior to religion and morality as typified by his mother and his home, or to love as typified by Judith. He must also be superior to gentility: that is, to the whole ideal of modern society. Leighton's plan was to give an elegant air to life, to soften and beautify what could be softened and beautified by fine art and fine manners, to help the deserving but not quite successful subjects by a little pretence, and to ignore all the horrors. Burgoyne pleads all through for softening and easing the trial by reciprocal politeness and consideration between all the parties, and for ignoring the villainy of his gallows, the unworthiness of his cause, and the murderousness of his profession. The

124

picture is completed by the band playing Handel's music, and the Christian clergyman reading the Bible to give the strangling an air of being an impressive ceremony. Oh, *cant* I make you understand, you who are a woman *in excelsis,* and—here! listen to this.

My dear Miss Terry, to me "LADY" has always meant the highest and best. As the most perfect lady in England you must ever command my respect and devotion.

That sounds nice and cordial, doesn't it? How am I to make you fully conscious of yourself? You wouldn't let Leighton paint your portrait. Why not, if a gentleman is the highest and the best? Surely Leighton would have made a perfectly gentlemanly picture of you. Watts was —*is*—an idealist of the finest as well as a gentleman and artist. Well, why did he not hold you? Bless your dearest eyes, my secret is that I learn from what you *do,* knowing that that is the reality of you. The dear silly old-fashioned things that *you think you think:* at these I laugh, though never at you.

Why do I worry you about these things? Well, what else can I do for you? Others have wakened your love: *that* wouldnt interest you. Beauty, success, lovely ways that enable you to play with men and women as Sarasate plays with a violin: all that you have gone through. My only chance is to awaken your wisdom, which is still asleep, and so stops at the end of my second act. But indeed I think I shall die lonely, as far as my third acts are concerned.

I was perfectly serious about Woking. They—Mrs Webb and Miss P. T.—discussed the idea a whole Sunday afternoon. I never deceived you about that or anything else; and I never laughed at anybody. (This is the holy serious truth.) But Mrs Webb has insisted on the lady at Woking leaving out 12 teacups instead of 6; and she, terrified at the notion of much company, is trying to back out of her bargain. I think, however, she has gone too far for that. If you come, bring 4 copies of Sans Gêne besides your own, and we'll get up rehearsals for you. We can all act better than the Lyceum company.

I see that my watch has stopped, and that I have lost the post. If it does not rain I will bike to Barkston Gardens and drop this into the letter box; and to-morrow you will see on your door-step a red stain wrung from my heart by the longing to go in—like Peer Gynt at the end.

I have also to go to the Haymarket to see the scene models for that wretched comedy.

125

In the morning to the Dock Gates, to harangue the *flaneurs* of that region until the public houses open.

On Monday to Manchester to see Janet's Cleopatra. *She* will let me see her off the stage.

I am being pressed to publish my plays. I think I will, and give up troubling the theatre. I only took to it to get closer to somebody; and she is the one person who will not endure my presence. Serve me right?

G. B. S.

CIV: G. B. S. *to* E. T.

[*Written after the first night of Henry Arthur Jones's play The Physician, produced at the Criterion Theatre.*]

25 March 1897

DEAREST AND EVEREST,

I COULD not go any nearer to you tonight (even if you had wanted me to—say that you did—oh say, say, say, say that you did) because I could not have looked at you or spoken to you otherwise than as I felt; and you would not have liked that in such a host of imperfectly sanctified eyes and ears. I was on the point, once or twice, of getting up and asking them all to go out for a few moments whilst I touched your hand for the first time.

I *saw* the play—oh yes, every stroke of it. There was no need to look at you. I felt your presence straining my heart all through.

Think of that, dear Ellen, even when you had that wicked, cruel, Indian-savageous, ugly, ridiculous plumage in your blessed hair to warn me that you have no heart. Ah, if only—well, nonsense! Good night, good night: I am a fool.

G. B. S.

CV: E. T. *to* G. B. S.

[*The Pinero play was The Princess and the Butterfly, produced at the St James's Theatre on 26 March.—Ellen Terry was wrong in thinking that Shaw would not like her in Sans-Gêne. Writing of her "apparent condescension to a vulgar part" he says: "There are a few people in the world with sufficient vitality and strength of character to get to close quarters with uncommon people, quite independently of the drill which qualifies common people (whatever their rank) to figure in the retinue indispensable to the state of Kings and Ministers. And there are a few actresses, who are able to interpret such exceptional people, because they are exceptional hemselves. Miss Terry is such an exceptional actress, and there the whole vonder of the business begins and ends."*]

Wᴀɴᴛ you to *"come nearer"* to me last night? Why of course I did. Yet I'm not sure, for I felt *very* near you. There were you, nd tucked into my bodice was a letter brought down to meet me at he Theatre (for I was in town all day looking after things for Sans-Gêne) A letter from you, which I could not read until I went to bed at ight. Yes, but I think I did want just to touch you, to put my hand n your arm (your coat sleeve!) and enjoy some of the things with you. For one thing Carlotta Addison's beautiful voice.) Well my dear, you ave the very strangest young, quick expression I ever knew on a 2 egged thing, and are you not a very ᴍɪɴx? and a very Duck too?

Wouldn't it have been funny if we had chanced to be next one an-ther? Perhaps it will be so at Pinero's play on Monday. That absurd hing on my head was not mine! A girl stuck it in my hair just as I was carting. "Ugly," yes. But why "cruel" and "wicked"?

I've been alternate days, rehearsing Sans-Gêne, and burying my head n blankets! I'm more sick of S. G. than the blankets. Never have I had uch a tiresome task. Words—words—words! How I shall bore the eople. What's the good of sending you a copy of the play? I think I'm little handicapped by knowing you wont like me in it, because I cant et it out of my head. The vulgarity I shall go for is the vulgarity (?) f ʙʀᴜᴛᴀʟ ɴᴀᴛᴜʀᴀʟɴᴇss, for the more I read the part the more I love the oman. I know her well, a big Frenchwoman who was once my servant nd will for ever serve me (altho' I could not keep her with the other ervants). When I'm ill, she takes me up in her arms (I'm no feather!!) nd puts me to bed, and washes me all over, and mothers me well again, I have time. She's no fit company for "Ladies" and "Gentlemen" of the eighton-Burgoyne stamp, but I'm just fond of her. A little of her goes long way however, and there's too much of Catherine, Madame S-Gêne, or one evening. I thought last night a little *brutal nature* would be a efreshment, for the 2 women in Jones's Play were irritating, werent they?

Oh, I'll let you off now, my poor dear. Wasnt Wyndham bright? (At he end.) In his old (young) days he could have played some of *your* arts. *Dorking!* and I am at *Leatherhead!*

I kiss you in the middle of your forehead for I am

Your ᴇʟʟᴇɴ

127

CVI: E. T. *to* G. B. S.

[Shaw's article on Meredith on Comedy appeared in The Saturday Review for 27 March 1897.]

27 March 1897.
22 Barkston Gardens,
Earls Court, S. W.

A̲LL you say in the Review about my darling George Meredith's view about play-goers is splendid. Our "Common nonsense"! Of cours one *knows* you are right.

Tell me. Is it true that little Alfred Beit has bought The Saturday? think he is such a nice little fellow considering his disadvantage in being possessed of millions.

Bless you my dear, very old friend.

I love you.

Your E. T.

Did *you* ever see the advance of spring in Italy? I have. I'm so unreason able. I am longing for that again.

CVII: G. B. S. *to* E. T.

[The New Century Theatre followed the example of its predecessor the In dependent Theatre (founded in 1891) in choosing a play by Ibsen for it opening performance. This was John Gabriel Borkman. The productio was severely criticized by Shaw in The Saturday Review in May of th year: "It is highly honourable to the pioneers of the drama that they ar poor; but in art what poverty can do only unhandsomely and stingily should not do at all."]

9 April 1897

O̲H ELLEN, dear Ellen, give up that unimportant Sans-Gêne and com and pet me, console me, tell me you have loved me at odd mo ments. I have been working sixteen hours a day at work that nobod should ever touch after lunch, and the sight of somebody more exhauste than yourself will do you good. I had to read You Never Can Tell t the Haymarket company today—two hours and forty minutes—it's to long: I shall have to spoil it to suit the fashionable dinner hour. Ol there's been no end of work about everything, from breakfast to thre next morning, and not a word, not a look, from Ellen. And I shall hav to swear that there was never anything so enchanting as her Sans-Gên and that those who have only seen Réjane little know etc. etc. etc. etc. and that Sardou is this that and the other, whilst all the time I am as sore as a beaten carpet, and never want to enter a theatre again and dont want you to act in any plays but mine—dont want you to act at all. Want you to come and hide with me somewhere and nurse me back into full life and villainy again.

And you—you think you have a terrible business in hand when it might as well be Penelope in The Area Belle, or Nance Oldfield, for any trouble it will give you. You'll do it on your head, and on my heart.

They havent invited me this time. "Miss Terry's strict orders, and Mr Bernard Shaw was not to be admitted." But I'll set The Saturday Review at them tomorrow and extort my seat by the majesty of the press. Or if you dont want me to be there I'll go away to the country if you'll come too. There must be an understudy available. I am growing impatient of the stage: it keeps a row of footlights between us.

Have you seen the prospectus of the New Century Theatre? You will see about it in The Saturday—but I forgot: you have given up reading it, fickle, faithless wretch that you are: I have only asked you for five minutes of your regard and you've cut me off with three. I am going to hit out with my usual treachery at this folly of collecting money for our Janets and Elizabeths to give matinées with and calling that the New Drama. We must get up a big subscription and make H. I. give a certain number of performances for it, or, if he wont, George Alexander.

Dont tell me you're tired: you are not half so tired as I am, nor so lonely nor so sore. *Dont* go to the Lyceum: stay at home and write to me: what does a first night matter? What is their silly curiosity to my heart's need?

No: I shall only bore you. Success attend you, heaped up and overflowing, whatever you play, whatever you do. You may chop off all my fingers and toes for a necklace, and have my heart as a locket if you will only say that you like them better than diamonds.

CVIII: E. T. *to* G. B. S.

[Edward:Edward Godwin, architect, archæologist, and artist. The father of Ellen Terry's children, Edith and Gordon Craig. The Bancrofts' production of The Merchant of Venice at the old Prince of Wales's Theatre in 1875 (in which Ellen Terry first played Portia) was Godwin's work. Sir Herbert Tree wrote in 1900 that it was the "first production in which the modern spirit of stage management asserted itself." Godwin's influence on

Irving's productions of Shakespear and Tennyson is referred to in Gordon Craig's Henry Irving.]

10 April 1897

A ND are you so tired? Tired-er than I? but you are a pet to write to me to-day. I was thinking of you this morning, before the light came (what greater proof that I am what they call "in love" with you!) and hoping you had written, and you had! I'm glad you are not coming to-night for I'm utterly tired out and unstrung. Over a month rehearsing a comic part and no "laughs" to cheer the dreary path of conviction that one is quite wrong in every act and every scene and every speech. My poor dear you will be going through with something of the kind soon at the Haymarket. A long dress-rehearsal yesterday morning and last night. Do you *mean* it that they have not sent you seats for to-night? Then come instead on Thursday or Friday next, and I'll send you just the seat or seats you want. What was the matter with Réjane's Sans-Gêne? Was it not admirable? I cant remember bits, but I know the whole thing appeared to me to be excellent. I only saw it the first night it was done in London, but then she had had hundreds of nights' practice in the part, and I liked her very much.

For the moment I *hate theatres*. Edy's a devil. She says I'm going to be so bad in this part. I think it is probably true, but for me to be such a fool as to care so much that I cant sleep! I pine for Hampton Court Gardens on a *week* day. It is so stately and slow and quiet and orderly. That was where I first invited you to an outing! I was in America, and oh, how wondrously lovely Hampton Court seemed from afar! You see I knew the place with Edward, and Edy and Ted, and the remembrance is sweeter than any other thought.

I am going to do my best to-night with a rush, and dash it all!

Yours with all my heart,

E. T.

CIX: G. B. S. *to* E. T.

[*Madame Sans-Gêne, an adaptation by J. Comyns Carr of the play by Sardou and Moreau in which Réjane had made a great success, was produced at the Lyceum on 10 April 1897.—Winifred Emery: the "leading lady" at the Haymarket, where You Never Can Tell was about to be put into rehearsal. Dolly, one of Mrs Clandon's flippant and garrulous twins, was the part which had attracted her.*]

130

I'VE been there, I've been there! (I calculate that you are reading this after the performance, though I'm writing before it.) I offered Hurst his choice of two methods of admission for me—one the usual stall for The Saturday Review, the other a hatchet and revolver plied by myself. He capitulated and gave me the stall, but said it was very hard on the governor to have the likes of me representing the papers when everyone knew it was only Miss Terry I came to see. You want laughs—you shall have them—the welkin shall shiver at my hee-haws, if only you dont soften my heart and give me strange pains in my inside, as you always do.

Well, what a tremendous success it has been, hasn't it? All thrown away on Sardou—might have been Shaw.

I have just learnt the result of my reading the play to the Haymarket Co. Just what I expected—Dolly precipitately abandoned and Gloria pounced on by the leading lady. I am to be played by everybody but my Ellen, who is too busy with Sar—where is my type-writer? I am impatient for Saturday's revenge. Oh play *me,* Ellen, *me,* ME, ME, ME, ME, ME, not Sardou or another. Now go and have a blessed sleep after it all.

G. B. S.

CX: E. T. *to* G. B. S.

[*Miss Millard: Evelyn Millard, who appeared in many of George Alexander's productions at the St James's Theatre from 1894 to 1896. She made a great success as Princess Flavia in The Prisoner of Zenda. Writing of Irving's Napoleon in Sans-Gêne in The Saturday Review Shaw says that "he produces the illusion of the Emperor behind the part."*]

WELL, *that's* over and Henry was splendid. I wont swear they heard all he said, but if he didn't speak as plainly as Terriss would have spoken, at least he didn't act as Terriss would have acted. If my part were half the length I should be pleased, but I kept my head and I dont think outsiders guessed I was working like mad even to do that. You were *not* there, were you? Now be a sweet and dont come before next Friday or Saturday. I'd sooner you didnt come for a fortnight; you told me once to have a "point of view" and stick to it. Whether right or wrong, to stick to it, and that's all I've done in regard to this part. After trying 3 or 4 ways I didnt believe in, thinking it would be best to meet what folk would say, I've gone straight for the only way I see clearly, and be dashed to everybody!

Oh, who will play Dolly now? What was Miss Millard going to play? Get Edy a chance some day with you. That's the way to make me adore you in any blessed way you will, even to the "walking on" in any of Ibsen's plays, or not writing to you, or in consenting to meet you, and for sure disgracing my years by plunging into love again, and then you could enjoy my foolishness and have a hearty laugh. Edy is a surprising person, but the only way in which she can surprise *me* is by *not* coming to the front! I love to have her with me at the Lyceum and in some ways for her own sake that is the best place for her, but she'll never get a chance of distinguishing herself there, and she can, and must, and will. Will you trust her with some good part? Some-day, and soon? Either a "lark" of a character, or a good what they call "heavy" part.

Oh I'm tired to-day, and so are *you* by now! When do you go to Boxhill? Ted has a wee cottage at Thames Ditton now. I *must* be off there soon for a day or so.

Yours my charming darling, E. T.

CXI: G. B. S. *to* E. T.

[*Eva Moore: both she and her sister Decima (whose early successes were won in musical pieces) were well known to English playgoers at this period. Eva married H. V. Esmond, actor and dramatist, and their daughter Jill is now (1931) among the most promising of our younger actresses.—Winifred Emery had refused to play Gloria in You Never Can Tell because Gloria's first entrance is a silent one. She enters and sits down without a word; and the play proceeds for some time without any reference to her. This, says Shaw, "was against all custom, all tradition, and apparently all respect for the actress's position." When Shaw read the play Miss Emery realized that this was a new device to give extraordinary effectiveness to Gloria's first words, and she immediately passed the scrap of paper to her husband (Cyril Maude) as described.*]

12 April 1897.
Lotus. Tower Hill, Dorking

I HAVE taken to running down here between the rehearsals of You Never Can Tell. Miss Millard was offered the part of Gloria, it being arranged then that Winifred Emery was to play Dolly. But Miss Millard refused it—I dont know why. Immediately after that came the reading of the play by the author. Miss Winifred was present on the occasion, and very soon began to prick up her ears. Presently she wrote "I shall play Gloria" on a scrap of paper and passed it to Cyril Maude. This settled the question of Gloria and left Dolly for Eva Moore, who is engaged at the theatre and will do very well. We rehearsed the first act today. Oh, if only they *wouldnt* act. They are tolerable until they begin that; but then—! Well, their sorrows have only begun, poor things. They think me a very harmless author so far. Wait until I begin silently and unobtrusively to get on their nerves a little.

I shall devote all my Saturday article to Sans-Gêne. It's a dreadfully bad play in many ways. Can you do nothing with that prince of dunderheads, Lefebvre? He spoils your business most hideously—cant give you a single line right. Can you not insist on his at least telling you about the divorce in such a tone as to give some color to your anxiety lest he should be giving in about it. He should deliberately fool you for the pleasure of getting a demonstration out of you—should rather grumblingly explain the disadvantages of Sans Gênism and put it to you as a reasonable woman whether he can be expected to stick to you under the circumstances. Instead of that the idiot declaims as if he were waving his wounded honor like a banner. His make-up is utterly wrong—like Laertes imitating Hamlet. He should be a burly, bullfighter, quartermaster sort of non-commissioned officer on promotion.

H. I. is amusing as the old stage hand making a part out of nothing —a Gladstonian sort of performance, and very clever. His play with his right hand—lifting it from the shoulder and shaking it with all the joints loose at every word—is exactly that of Jaurés, the French Socialist, a tremendous speaker.

Edy ought to have a lot more work now to complete her apprenticeship; but where is it to be had except on tour in South America? She has a remarkably beautiful voice, and is very clever and capable; but she is too sane to be a hysterical leading lady and too young for heavy parts of any value. Altogether very hard to fit, which shews that she ought to plunge into the rough and tumble of the business and fit herself to everything except the sort of thing that would spoil her voice. Nothing would please me better than to find an opening for her; but my apparent "influence" in such matters is just like yours: an invisible set of chains. If only she had nobody to help her she would get on fast enough; but with a secure position at the Lyceum, Ellen Terry for a mother, Bernard

133

Shaw for a friendly critic and a dozen other overwhelming chances, what prospect has she? It's like trying to win a swimming race with ten life belts on.

I must fly to catch my train. When do you come to Thames Ditton?

G. B. S.

CXII: E. T. *to* G. B. S.

14 April 1897

M ANY thanks for your words about Edy. I fear I didnt make my meaning plain if you think I want you to "find an opening for her." No, but I suppose you usually "cast" your own plays, and I want you only to MENTION Edith Craig as being fit for this or that ever-so-small-a-part.

So you *were* there, at the Lyceum, the first night! I'm sorry. It cant be helped, however. I'm sure you grieved, dearest judicious one! But do "have it out"—get rid of your feeling against me in the Review next Saturday. If you really belaboured me I'd think there was still some hope of my playing the part properly in time to come. I've *got* to play it, you know! It is hard work and they all think it is so easy. I'm wondering who will play the mother in You Never Can Tell! Little Eva Moore for Dolly will do very nicely. I'd love to see you at rehearsal! No answer please to this. My eyes are wrong again, because of all the horrid lights.

Be happy at Dorking, sweetheart.

E. T.

CXIII: G. B. S. *to* E. T.

[In the notice of Sans-Gêne in The Saturday Review Shaw complains, as he complains in this letter, that the translation is much too literary. "Catherine does not speak like a woman of the people . . . except when she is helping herself out with ready-made locutions in the manner of Sancho Panza. After a long speech consisting of a bundle of rich locutions padded with forced mistakes in grammar she will say 'That was my object,' or some similarly impossible. piece of Ciceronian eloquence."—Edith Craig played Prossy in Candida when the Independent Theatre took the play on tour in July 1897, and also in the first London production by the Stage Society in 1900 (see Letters CLVII and CCXLIV).—Dorothea Baird, who made her name as an actress when she appeared as Trilby with Beerbohm Tree at the Haymarket in 1895, married H. B. Irving, Henry's elder son, usually called Harry Irving, in 1896. She has retired from the stage.]

Y ou are making a most unnecessary fuss over your ridiculous Sans-
Gêne. There's nothing in the *execution* of that part that presents any
difficulty to you beyond the mere labor of it. Once you understand it
you have jumped out of the gulf that lies between it and Nan in Good
for Nothing, or anything else that you could do on your head. As a
matter of fact you played it very well, knocking off the exact shade of
every phase to perfection; but why shouldn't you? No doubt you'll do it
more comfortably to yourself when you are no longer afraid of fluffing;
but it wont make a penn'orth of difference to the public. I suppose it was
you who fluffed in the prologue (quite early in it); but the impression
conveyed was that Mackintosh was the offender. I suppose you didnt
give him his cue, and he waited long enough to be detected before he
made up his mind that he was not going to get it.

On the book, which arrived so dilapidated that I have had to patch
the outside page to prevent total disintegration, I have nothing to say
that you have not anticipated. The cut on page 17 is a mistake: Lefebvre's
ferocity needs the reminder of the stab to make it plausible. On p. 26 "La
Guinard" should be "La Guimard": at least there was a famous dancer
then called Madeleine Guimard, who was so thin that they compared her
dance between two satyrs to two dogs fighting for a bone. On p. 28 it is, of
course, impossible to say "Do you suppose that I walk with my head down-
wards, like a turnip," but you might very well say, "Well, do you suppose
I walk on my head." On p. 35 "That was my object," (Oh Comyns Carr,
Comyns Carr!!!) is absurd: it should be "I meant her to." At the foot
of p. 37 "What for?" is the best phrase, I think. On 41 it is too literary to
say *"a true man,* who has," etc. etc., but *"who* dare not" etc. I suggest "a
true man, with the right to ruin himself for her sake, but not to ruin
her for his own." Also, by saying "you will go now and not come back"
you throw away a point. I have scribbled an amendment at the foot of
the page. However, the part is not in the words, or in Sardou's play:
both are only a pretext for the real character to be embodied by you.

By the way, shouldn't Neipperg be pronounced Nyperg, not Nee-
perg? Or is it misprinted? My recollection of the spelling is Neipperg.

So you would like to see me at rehearsals. Well, you soon shall. The
Man of Destiny is due this year: there is no penalty for breach of the
agreement: consequently H. I. is on his honor. The scenes at the Hay-

market are not on the surface, but in the recesses of the hearts of the unhappy company. I sit there and stare at them. I get up and prowl. I sit somewhere else, but always with a dreadful patience and dreadful attention. It is useless to correct more than one speech per person per day; for I find that the result of my interposition—consisting of saying the thing as it ought to be said—(Heaven knows what my way of doing it may sound like to them!)—is invariably to paralyse them for five minutes, during which they are not only quite off their part, but utterly incapable of expressing any meaning whatever. So far we have only gone over the busy funny scenes repeatedly: all the big scenes for Gloria and so on are yet before us. Maude and Brandon Thomas will succeed no matter how they take their parts: that is all I can see at present. What is a Lyceum rehearsal like? Does H. I. work out all that business (see Sans-Gêne blank pages) at home, or does the prompter take it down as it turns up and works out in rehearsing?

Did I say "find an opening for Edy"? I apologize, I withdraw. I abase myself—you wretch: that was precisely what you ordered me to keep my eyes open for. She wants an opening ten times more than if she had no mother. Do you remember—or did you ever hear of—the obscurity of Mozart's son? An amiable man, a clever musician, an excellent player; but hopelessly extinguished by his father's reputation. How could any man do what was expected from Mozart's son? Not Mozart himself even. Look at Siegfried Wagner. Ellen Terry's daugther! Awful! Is Ted anything of a comedian? *I* want comedians.

Suppose this You Never Can Tell succeeds sufficiently to make it practically certain that a dozen matinées of a new cheap play by me would pay their way. Well, get somebody to finance a dozen matinées of Candida for Janet on condition that Ted plays Eugene and Edy Prossy. I told the Independent Theatre people that I'd let them do it if they could bank £1000. Or let them buy a fit-up and play Arms and the Man and You Never Can Tell in the provinces (I have *all* the British rights of Arms and all but eleven No. 1 towns for You Never Can Tell). Or let H. B. Irving and Ted, Dorothea Baird and Edy start a Next Generation theatre and play Othello and Iago, Emilia and Desdemona, on alternate nights. Or let them make up a nice little repertory and go round the world with it. That's the way to get trained now.

It's no use: I have nothing sensible to suggest. Teddy, though hypersensitized (got it that time!) and petulated by more luxury than was good for him in the way of a mammy, seems highly and nervously intelligent. He wants ten years of stern adversity— not domestic squabble— to solidify him. Pity he's married: why should he be a breeder of sinners?

What a Good Friday we're having! Rain, wind, cold, skating on all the ponds, icicles hanging from the eaves and George Bernard the shepherd blowing his nail.

When are you coming into this neighborhood? I can bike over to Thames Ditton—if only I dare. Dont let us break the spell, *do* let us break the spell, dont, do, dont, do, dont, do, dont—I resolved to let the end of the line decide it like Gretchen's flower, and it has decided nothing.

Cut out the Neipperg business from Sans-Gêne altogether, and there will be time to play The Man of Destiny before it.

G. B. S.

P. S. They're going to elect me to the St Pancras Vestry (more public work) and I'm spending Easter on a Fabian Tract—Employers' Liability. That's why I am so prosaic.

[*In the following narrative, contributed by Shaw, as much light is thrown on the case Shaw v. Irving, Ellen Terry intervening, as can be thrown, now that the defendant and intervener are dead. Evidence that of the three parties Irving was the one to whom the affair seemed of the least importance is forthcoming in a passage in one of Ellen Terry's letters in May 1897 (CXXV):"The fact is he [that is Irving] dont think the whole affair matters much."*]

The situation now takes a turn for the worse through a misunderstanding which prevents the ensuing letters from telling their own story clearly.

Up to this moment Ellen Terry believes that she could bring her two friends together through a triumphant production at the Lyceum of The Man of Destiny, described by Shaw himself as a bravura piece for two histrionic virtuosos. She knew that she could play the Strange Lady easily, and that Irving would be a superb Napoleon. She had actually brought Irving to a point at which he himself suggested the possibility of combining it into a single programme with the German play submitted to him by Grundy.

Suddenly her hopes were dashed by an irreconcilable quarrel between Shaw and Irving arising out of his criticism of Richard III in The Saturday Review. Irving believed that this unlucky article was a thinly veiled accusation of drunkenness on the stage. It contained such phrases as "He was not, as it seemed to me, answering his helm satisfactorily; and he was occasionally out of temper with his own nervous condition" and "He made some odd slips in the text, notably by substituting 'you' for 'I.' "

Now it is clear from the letters that follow that Shaw was entirely innocent of the construction which was put on these remarks. He assumes that Irving's displeasure is provoked by the criticism of Olivia in which, harping on his ancient grudge against stock companies (the reader will recollect his preface to this volume) he had said, in effect, that it was a relief to get rid of Irving for once at a Lyceum performance. In any case Shaw, not being a man of insinuation and hints and stabs in the back, would, if he had thought that Irving was drunk, have said so unequivocally, or said nothing.

For some time the misunderstanding was complete. When Irving suddenly turned down The Man of Destiny Shaw could see no other reason for this step and the manner of its announcement than that he had failed to deliver the favorable notices tacitly purchased by the formal acceptance of his play for production at the Lyceum. On this assumption he remonstrated vigorously, assenting to the withdrawal of the play, but urging that it must be done later on in such a way as to prevent the press and the public from connecting it with his criticisms. Irving, with modest unwisdom, called to his aid his devoted literary henchman L. F. Austin, who figures in Ellen Terry's Memoirs as endearing himself to the Lyceum Theatre by his *jeux d' esprit*. Austin drafted a sarcastic letter the tone of which may be guessed from the two scraps quoted by Ellen Terry in Letter CXXII. Shaw, roused by this, refused to accept letters from Austin over Irving's signature; and, demanding with characteristic arrogance what Irving thought would happen to his henchman if G. B. S. were to condescend to take him on in a literary encounter, insisted on an authentic answer from Irving himself.

He could not have given his antagonist sounder advice. Shortly after Irving's death, his son Laurence wrote to Shaw: "Out of his [Henry Irving's] possessions we have unearthed a number of letters written by him to his father, Mr Samuel Brodribb, packed closely into a little cigar box: they are very simple and affectionate; and in them his memory is sufficiently documented for me." When Shaw got his authentic answer from Irving, it was not affectionate; but it was simple and genuine. Irving refused to manufacture any explanation of his rejection of The Man of Destiny and just unaffectedly begged Shaw to let him alone.

However welcome the breach was to the two men, to Ellen Terry it was something of a blow: a good play thrown away because two men were quarrelling about nothing. If her interests and sympathies had been less wide, and her professional side less unambitious and unselfish, she might have brought them both to heel by mere violence of self-assertion. But then she would not have been Ellen Terry. As it was, she was "out" with Irving for the first time in the correspondence.

The reader will now be able to follow the course of the letters without sharing the misunderstandings under which they were written.

CXIV: G. B. S. *to* E. T.

17 April 1897

DEAREST ELLEN,

L OOK out for squalls. I have just received from Stoker a cool official intimation that Sir H. has changed his mind about producing The Man of Destiny. My answer goes by the same post as this card. I am in ecstasies. I have been spoiling for a row; and now I have Mansfield to fight with one hand, and H. I. with the other. Hooray! Kiss me good speed; and I'll toss them all about the stage as Cinquevalli tosses oranges and dinner plates.

By the way—no, not by the way, but mainly and chiefly and all importantly—are your eyes really bad again? I hope not from the very depths of me.

G. B. S.

P. S. Dont bother about The Man of Destiny. Watch the fun and chuckle. Leave them to me. Hahah ! ! !

CXV: E. T. *to* G. B. S.

April 1897

O H DEAR oh dear, My Dear, this vexes me very much. My friends to fight! And I love both of them, and want each to win. Henry has been much vexed lately (I only learned this last evening) by what he calls "your attacks" upon him in The Saturday Review, the Olivia article especially annoying him. For the life of me I cannot realize how it feels, the *pain* for a thing of the kind. (I cant express myself, but please try to understand what I mean.)

Your letter card was my first information of the play having been sent back. A quarter of an hour after H. came in and told me he was "going" (!) to send it back to you— "because" of this, that and the other reason. I said I believed he had another reason than that. For instance

139

that "S-Gêne was in for a long run, and that the 2 plays could not go to-gether." But he would not "own up." I believe he was ashamed and I felt strangely powerfully sorry for him. I cant bear that he should be ashamed. I didnt bother him about details then, for we both had to play our parts decently before a good many hundred, but my heart was beating fast all the while. However he and I are going for a long drive this afternoon, and he shall tell me all then. My chief desire in the affair is that *he* plays the part, for it's a part to play! For both your sakes I desire this.

I dont know why, but for the first time in all my long long life I am most frightfully dis-spirited. Oh God, how frightful it is. This last week I've had real courage, to consent to live, being out of love with life. The first time! Nobody sees it, except my dresser at the theatre, and I dont speak to her of how I feel, for it would make her ill. She has dressed me for 20 years and has survived, and to be ungrateful to her now! So I speak to you (or I'd burst) and you are not to "take notice," but the speaking will lighten me, perhaps, and I know that you will forgive me my selfishness.

Dont quarrel with H. That would add to my unhappiness. I kiss you on the tip of your innocent nose and *remain*—etc., etc. ("Remains" would be best I think.)

Please take me upstairs and read me by yourself.

CXVI: G. B. S. *to* E. T.

21 April 1897

THIS is at heart a tragic business, Ellen; but we cannot help it. My only anxiety is lest you should become involved in it. Of course I knew all about it: a good surgeon knows when his knife touches a nerve; and a good critic knows the same with his pen. There was a terrible thing in that Olivia notice—not, as everybody thinks, my saying that Vezin's vicar was the better of the two, or that your Olivia was better without him, but that it was a relief to get rid of him for a moment at the Lyceum. It was not so brutal as that; but as he does not understand critical points, and treats all intellectual positions as mere matters of feeling, he probably took it in that way and was hurt by it; and he will perhaps think it unfeeling of you not to be angry with me for saying it. So be kind to him, and if he is clever enough to tell you on that afternoon drive— as I should in his place—that he is giving up the play because he is ealous of me about you, take his part and console him: it is when a man is too much hurt to do the perfectly magnanimous thing that he most needs standing by.

As for me I promise not to quarrel. I'll fight if I have to; but that is quite a different thing: it makes no bad blood—clears it away, in fact. The worst of the business is that it has gone far beyond our control. The announcements have been made, and taken up so far that on the first night of Cymbeline (was it?) his speech was interrupted by some one calling out "What about Shaw's play?" and my friends promptly remonstrated with me for employing people to advertize me in this shameless fashion. So the papers will want to know why the play has been dropped; and what explanation is there but the true one? I have told him (via Stoker) that he must stand to his bargain or break faith, there being no penalty clause in the agreement to secure an honorable retreat; and that is the beginning, middle, and end of the situation. If he withdraws from his pledge on no other ground (transparent excuses apart) than that his acceptance has made no difference in my criticisms, then the obvious conclusion is that he meant to buy me. Besides, it is the only sign that the public has had of any rapprochement between the Lyceum and the younger school; and he will find that he cannot deal with me quite as he used to with Frank Marshall and the rest. Not from any malice of mine, mind: believe me that is the danger of me, that I am not likely to put myself in the wrong with you standing between us, or indeed *anyhow,* because I rather like him and—but enough about the business. Dont be anxious. I'll behave nicely and nothing particular will happen. I cant begin another sheet because I have my article to write and nothing to write about. And my news—oh, the rehearsals!—I could tell you pages of my sufferings. Sans Gêne alas! will make you unhappy because it has none of the water of life in it: it's only mechanical reaction: dont be cast down. Give me only till the rehearsals are going smoothly and I'll make the sun shine somehow. I shall be in town tomorrow.

G. B. S.

CXVII: E. T. *to* G. B. S.

22 April 1897

DEAR Fellow, to promise not to quarrel. A little fight does not matter much, tho' I'd rather not look on, as I'm weak headed and should merely see *right on both sides* and no need of a fight.

Yes. He spoke to me when we were driving, and with a treacherous memory and no facts at hand I did not dispute something he told me as reason for his anger. I looked up your Olivia article however when I got home, and can find no proof that you ever suggested indirectly that his emotion on the stage was stimulated artificially.

You *never* said it I know. Last night I said to him, "I just long for you to play a REAL Napoleon—and here it is!" I prayed him not to be a "fool" and a "silly-billy" and was rather horrid to him; and then I gave him a nice little kiss and left him.

Forgive all this, when you are surely too busy to spare a moment. H. is not jealous of me. I remember he once said: "The best proof of my love for you is that I am not jealous of you." (Of course you understand he meant "jealous of the public liking me!") He astounded me by saying that. As if one *could* be jealous of such a paltry having! As if one *could* do anything but give and give if one had even a little bit of true love! Ah, he makes me tired and sad and hopeless sometimes, and I do expect always the best from him. I nearly killed myself yesterday on my tricycle, and it has done me good.

CXVIII: E. T. *to* G. B. S.

[In spite of Ellen Terry's very wise advice Shaw withdrew his comedy from the Haymarket, to the great relief of the managers, after a couple of weeks' rehearsing; and as Ellen Terry foresaw, several years elapsed before he at last established himself as a London playwright under the famous Vedrenne-Granville-Barker management at the Court Theatre, an avowedly new departure in theatrical policy. The catastrophe at the Haymarket, of which there is an amusing description, evidently written by Shaw himself, in Cyril Maude's History of the Haymarket Theatre, seems to have been inevitable. Though the play, You Never Can Tell, was written for the occasion as a potboiler, and proved to be an infallible one later on, the London theatre at that date was so completely isolated from the social movements and changes in which Shaw was fiercely active that it could make nothing of his work. Even its purely theatrical qualities were so little felt that after the reading of the play two experienced members of the Haymarket company threw up their parts as ineffective and impossible. "No laughs and no exits" was the verdict of one of them. The breach thus made between the Shavian drama and the normal commercial theatre was never really healed, notwithstanding the sensational success of Pygmalion under Tree's management at His Majesty's Theatre in 1913. Shaw's experience at the Lyceum and Haymarket convinced him that the "normal commercial theatre" had no use for him nor he for it. His apparently perverse

throwing away of the few chances it offered him was part of a policy which was on the whole justified by subsequent events.]

24 April 1897

I'LL find your Richard III article and read it up. Dont let anything stop that comedy at the Haymarket. You have written a crowd of splendid plays. Now let some of 'em *be acted*. Kate Bishop should be far better than Miss C. (I've not seen Kate for about 20 years. She was young then, handsome, and had a splendid figure.) Of course the gentleman is a duffer. (Poor dear you, I'm sorry for you.) Edward G. Craig is not a duffer but would be too young for *that* part. Is Arthur Playfair free? Or I'll look up some name but Do Not let anything put that play off for I'm your loving old friend and I KNOW it will hurt your success.

E. T.

CXIX: G. B. S. *to* E. T.

[*The first performance in England of John Gabriel Borkman was given at the old Strand Theatre on 3 May 1897. Elizabeth Robins, Mrs (now Lady) Tree, and J. Martin (now Sir John Harvey) were in the cast.*]

4 May 1897

WHY dont you write me sometimes, you wretch? This weather! makes the birds sing incessantly, but not a note can it get out of you.

Here's a pretty instalment of the wrath to come. Yesterday evening, at Fitzroy Square, comes the inevitable interviewer with a cutting from the Daily News (evidently inspired) stating that Sir H. I. had sent me back my play to teach me better manners. Thereupon the smartest of the New Journalism editors scents a duel, and wants me to return H. I's fire in his paper. Not being able to tell the man that such a display of my famous marksmanship, though highly delightful to the public, would get me into trouble with my Ellen, I had to shuffle, and finally declined to say anything for publication except that the play had *not* been returned to me and that the agreement to perform could not be broken without a breach of faith impossible to the high contracting parties. So they had to be content with that for the present. What is going to happen?

Mansfield's coming over—not to act, though, as far as I know.

Saw Edy yesterday at Borkman.

G. B. S.

CXX: E. T. to G. B. S.

9 May 1897

H. AND I are out! A little bit. For he dont tell me things about you, because he's vexed always with people who wont agree always and entirely with everything he says, and although I try not to aggravate him by actually *saying* so, I dont agree with him about you, and he knows it. Have you written to him I wonder? Has he written to you? I never *ask* him things.

So you *publish* your Plays first! I'm sorry. What names you will be called for 2 of 'em at least! Henry last night mentioned quite casually ("accidently-on-purpose" perhaps—you never can tell!) that a certain play we were speaking of at the moment would "go" so well with The Man of Destiny. But I have learned from Henry's own instruction to let him talk, and hold my tongue. He said no more and left me wondering what was in his mind. Darling boy I tumbled out of my tricycle the other day and it shook me pretty badly and that is the chief reason for my not writing to you all this while. My Stars and Stripes! how stiff my whole right side is, even now. How is Miss P. T.? Shall I lend her my grandchild who is staying all alone with me? It seems greedy to have the treat all to myself.

Yours and yours and yours,

E. T.

CXXI: G. B. S. *to* E. T.

11 May 1897

ON GETTING down here I was much alarmed by your telegram, as my one anxiety in this business is to avoid entangling you in the warfare. I do most strictly and peremptorily entreat you not to touch it in any way, or, if you do, to take a part entirely sympathetic to H. I. He is heavily overweighted in the contest, and is making one mistake after another in trying to get out of a position into which he has wedged himself hopelessly. If he had come to me and said, "Look here: I want to get out of doing this play; and I want at the same time to express my intense irritation at your expense," I should have cheerfully found a way out for him and drafted him a letter to write to me which would have given him the keenest satisfaction. But he does not know me or trust me or like me well enough for that. And that is why you can do nothing with him just now. It is utterly impossible that he should understand me as you understand me. Do you remember that even you, when you knew no more about me than H. I. does now, and when you had to write to me about that Italian girl (what became of her?), thought me a disagreeable and *wounding* person. It has taken me about fifty thousand love letters since that to convince you that I am only a brute nor'-nor'-west; and H. I. hasn't had any love letters, and is precisely under the same impression of my malevolence as you were under then. Anything that you say in my favor, far from convincing him, will only strike him as an act of treachery to himself. Do not be anxious—do not, at all events, betray the least anxiety. When two men fight, they find out one another's value wonderfully quickly; and the mild tussle now in progress is quite sufficient to educate Henry on the subject of Bernard better than the most tactful special pleading on your part. At present he has less respect for me than I have for myself; and I have more respect for him than he has for himself. He has been trying to trifle with me; and he does not know that what has brought him up standing in that is the firm grip of a friendly hand, and not an attempt to trip him up. He sent for Austin *because* he knew that Austin could not afford to tell him that he has no case, and would teach him a literary thrust or two at me. All that is nothing to the purpose; and he knows by this time that I know what it is worth. Dont let it disturb you for a moment; sit quiet and wait patiently; I shall get what I deserve, depend on it; and he *shant;* so you need not be anxious about him.

Oh that tricycle, that tricycle! I told you that it was a dangerous contrivance; but you *would* have it that it was safe because it stands by itself like a perambulator when you're not on it. If you had been biking you would simply have jumped off and sworn at that old woman instead of nearly killing her and yourself as well. And if you *did* get a toss, you would ride it off in a mile or two. You should see the appalling accidents we have all lived through here—we four, Webb, Beatrice (Mrs W.) Miss P. T. and myself. On trikes we'd have been slain. No room for more. Write to *me:* dont talk to H. I.

G. B. S.

CXXII: E. T. *to* G. B. S.

[J. F. R.: Johnston Forbes-Robertson.—Mrs P.: Mrs Patrick Campbell, whose Ophelia in a revival of Hamlet in October 1897 seemed to Shaw finally to "settle in her favour the question of her right to the very important place assigned to her in Mr Forbes-Robertson's enterprise."—The German play by Voss Irving had acquired was Schuldig.—The "wee one": Ellen Terry's

11 May 1897

WELL, well! Henry told me all about the affair last evening, and now I have the opportunity of again reading his letter to you. "Be gentle" you say "with H." I am *always* gentle with him. Better for him if all these years I had acted being something else. It would take too long, and too clever, to tell you the why, but I've spoiled him! I was born meek. (Ugh.) His "policy of silence" was merely trying to get out of extra trouble, in writing. I do assure you it is *I* all along who wished so hard for the play. He never wishes for anything much outside his own individual effort. I admire him for it, and I hate him for it, that he appreciates NOTHING and NOBODY. You have to poke a play under his nose and read it, and speak of it, and act bits of it, and trouble about it (or rather about his part in it) until you are fagged out, before he'll look at it, and then it takes him a long time to see any good there. But he's worth every trouble, for when once he takes a thing up there's no one like him in mastering the whole affair.

"Gentle!" He wants a good slapping, but *you* must not do that, and *I* wont. I think I'm tired and too indifferent now. It makes me cry to know it, but I'm a patient person.

Now. If J. F. R. does Napoleon he'll not get half out of it that Henry would. On the other hand, Mrs P. is young and lovely and would do the Lady *well enough*. (But it is Nap. who is the Play.) Dont be a dear Idiot, and let anyone do that part but Henry. The position is simply this. Henry finding this Sans-Gêne "a big go" knows he couldnt do your little play just yet awhile. Being "in a temper" with you, he pretends to me that he wont play it (for he said so flatly once) but in fact it isnt "WONT." It's "CANT." Only you, not being a Manager, dont understand "cant" in dealing with a theatre and a public. Sometimes, in the Saturday you speak just like an amateur on the subject of conduction of a theatre (Forgive me darling) Often, when you dont get a letter from me it is because I've written reams to you on this subject and not being able to express myself properly have burnt the effusions in merciful pity towards you. Henry always blunders in the same manner when he *will* talk of the "Art of Music"—or of Painting and I cant explain to him, but at least I often *stop* him. At least I know I dont know, but then I

146

know he doesnt know. **Oh, heavens! You'll read me no more. You'll love me no more.** I disgrace myself when I *will* write.

When H. read me his letter to you last evening I screamed with laughter when he came to "callous to the feelings of others," and "lost the consciousness of vulgarity." Remember those paragraphs were none of his. This, of course, you understand since you are not a born fool. Now let Henry do the play when he can. The time will come *I* think, sooner than he reckons for.

We have a German play by Voss done splendidly by Mr Grundy. (We have had it for a long time.) Now he doesnt want to tell you this (WHY God knows) but he wants to make a perfect bill by playing Guilty and The Man of Destiny together. You can never make H. I. hurry, and in the end the result has always been a gain all round. You must trust him, and in business you *can,* because your interests and his are wrapped up together, combined, and he knows *quite well* what is best for himself. Scarcely ever goes wrong on this. Good-bye, I'm off to the Zoo, to give my weenie one a sight of the birds there, and by degrees of the Lions and Tigers! But *not yet.* She feeds my bull-finch but my cat and dog terrify her. The red flag in her face at the sight of them! So tender, so tremulous, but she trusts me so. The wee face in the bed next room to mine, every night when I come home, enraptures me. I hurry back, pelting, melting! How I'll miss her when they take her home. I keep on thinking she's mine!

Yours sweetheart,

E. T.

CXXIII: G. B. S. *to* E. T.

12 May 1897

OH MY dear, dear, dearest Ellen, I'm beaten. Forgive me! but your Henry is not a hero off the stage; and now that everything is ready to my hand for his discomfiture I find that I cannot bring myself to do any of the things I might do. He proposed originally that we should deal with one another "as two men of honor." Alas! that is not what a man of honor usually says; but I disregarded that ungenerous reflection and trusted him—or rather I gave him the power to behave like a confidence-trick man if he liked, which he has accordingly done, not because he is exactly a rogue, but because his self-absorption makes him as incapable as a baby of suffering the slightest cross without petu-

147

lance, or understanding obligations and treaties. I have tried to make the best of him; but there is no best: I have suddenly given him up; and now it's all over.

All that about his managerial plans is nonsense. I foresaw it all; and though he fought hard not to be tied to production this year, he finally undertook it in full view of all his arrangements. There has been no change: the accident only prevented Richard III from running uninterruptedly up to Sans-Gêne. He did not fail in his contract with Sardou, because Sardou did not deal with him "as between two men of honor." Even now he has returned the play without returning my agreement, the counterpart of which, though I should have had it for stamping within fourteen days, has *never* been sent to me. I have telegraphed to him for it. I am sorry about the Strange Lady; but I will have nothing to do with him now, least of all anything in which you are involved. It is a pity; for his bill of Shaw and Grundy could easily have been arranged if he had asked me to make any ultimate date moveable to the end of a run if necessary. But it is better as it is; he would have behaved like a baby sooner or later; and *I* shouldnt have spoiled him. There is no use in wasting the play: J. F. R. and Mrs Pat may as well do it as nobody; but I shall trouble myself no more about the theatre. I dont care, and never did care who plays Napoleon (it was written for Mansfield); but I should have liked you to play the Strange Lady; and since your infant has put a stop to that, it may be played by Mrs Pat's dresser for all I care.

Vengeance I leave to Destiny. You remember about Beaconsfield's plan? I am sorry to have lost my regard for him. Mind! You must not take his part now: I declare him unworthy of my Ellen.

G. B. S.

CXXIV: G. B. S. *to* E. T.

[*Hare: Sir John Hare, a great figure in the English Theatre for 50 years and more. (First appearance 1864.) On 22 May 1897, he re-appeared in London, after a long absence in America, in a revival of Pinero's The Hobby Horse.*]

13 May 1897

THERE ought to be in to-day's Daily Mail or Star or some such paper an interview with me. My uncertainty arises from the fact that instead of doing the business myself directly, I have used it to give a chance to a young journalist in whom I am interested. I wrote the dialogue of the interview and gave it to him, telling him to fill in the scenery and business, and giving him the names of a few papers which have applied to me for information. I told him to get it in today (Saturday) at latest; and I think The Daily Mail is the most likely choice for him to make. But the railway station is two miles off and I am full of work; so I must wait until the afternoon to discover what has happened. I go up to town to see Hare's reentry at the Court, back to-morrow morning, up on Monday to the Globe and Adelphi and so on.

You will find nothing quarrelsome in the interview: we all come out of it with haloes of glory round our heads. The management of it being in my hands I of course play H. off the stage; but I dress him well and allow him to make a point or two. I promised you not to quarrel, and I wont: besides, were I to let the public see that I have private reasons for destroying him, I never could criticise him again without suspicion of partiality. But that shall not save him: no, by all that is Inevitable, he shall lag superfluous and perish miserably from the profession he has disgraced. You made two pencil marks—just two—in that copy of The Man of Destiny, and when I saw them the sky blackened over his brainless head. Your career has been sacrificed to the egotism of a fool: he has warmed his wretched hands callously at the embers of nearly twenty of your priceless years; and now they will flame up, scorch his eyes, burn off his rum bathed hair, and finally consume him.

Yes. I know he has a play of Grundy's. He assured me with his finest manner that the statements to the effect that he had plays on his shelves were false. He tries to hide himself from himself with a rampart of lies; and he got behind it to hide himself from me. That was why he became an actor,—to escape from himself. You became an actress to realize yourself. Hence it is that all his performances have to be accepted subject to the initial drawback that they are utterly incredible and impossible, whilst you, even when you act badly, are a human reality to begin with. Oh Ellen, Ellen, this infinitesimal actor-nothingness whimpers over the things I have said of him! But if he knew the things I have *not* said, he would shudder and die.

Nevertheless you shall play for me yet; but not with him, not with him, not with him.

G. B. S.

CXXV: E. T. *to* G. B. S.

I CANT take things back (or I would)—for it's always so sweet to remember the sweets. I'd like to say "I hate you and detest you"—but then I'd "remember" THAT *too*. Well, you are quite stupid after all and *not* so unlike other people. You should have given in and said, "Take the play and do it when you can. You'll do it better than anyone else, and *nurse* it better than anyone else." Dont pity H. He thinks he has quite got the best of it in the recent altercation. The fact is he dont think the whole thing matters much. I do, and I'm angry with you. I keep out of the affair as you tell me to.—What I cared for more than for you or H.—or the parts, was THE PLAY—and NOW—well go your ways—

Oh my darling you are the horridest old—

E. T.

CXXVI: G. B. S. *to* E. T.

[Lilian Vavasour: the heroine of Tom Taylor's play New Men and Old Acres. In the original production the part, written for Ellen Terry, was played by Mrs (now Dame Madge) Kendal. On the revival at the old Court Theatre in 1876, under John Hare's management, Ellen Terry made a great success in it.]

16 May 1897

D AMN the play, dearest Ellen, I dont care two straws about *that*. And with you, to you, I shall be just like other people. Therefore I heap execrations on his infamous head, whilst in The Daily Mail it is "one gentleman to another." I do not pity him. "Tear-falling pity dwells not in this eye," least of all for my detested rival. I know that he thinks he has done well because he has done meanly, and for that I would pity him, only the thought comes that the crafty wrinkle in his overrated countenance which years of such base exultation have graven there may have been touched by Ellen's lips; and then I stretch my maddened hands to clutch the lightning. Also I know he thinks it does not matter, but at that I laugh. In 1888 John Morley thought that the Fabian Society did not matter; and as the Liberal party felt towards the Fabian Society, so the Lyceum felt later on towards the Ibsenites.

Yes, it would have been so nice of me to give him my friendship

and trust *again,* in order to prove to you that I give them to every foolish person who doesnt want them, and that therefore they are not worth
your having. I grant you he would nurse the play better (longer) than
anyone else, like a Lapland mother, who *never* weans her boys. He would
have nursed it, the selfish villain, until your grandchild was old enough
to come and laugh at you in that opera-bouffe hussar's uniform. Do you
know that I asked him to make it follow Imogen because you can with
perfect dignity put on a man's dress in a Shakespearean play, and immediately after that nobody would mind your doing it again, whereas to
do it without any such preparation in a silly little play like The Man of
Destiny would look like a mere romp. But his ineffable pigheadedness
could take in no idea that did not concern himself; and even on his own
account it did not occur to him that my jealousy of your dignity might
have its counterfoil for him in an objection to his age. That is the
aggravating thing about it: you *ought* to be too old for the part, if you
are really as old as you boast of being in all the books of reference,
whereas he, who equally ought to be able to carry off Napoleon's years
still, never looks under fifty except when he is playing Lear.

Oh, you thought I couldn't be spiteful, madam, and small, and petty,
but I *can.* Ha! Ha! Everybody said it to me when I told them it was
the young Napoleon. "Good God!" they shrieked, "do you remember
his Romeo? It's imPOSSible!" and nobody ever dreamt that you played
Mamilius in the year 1822 to Edmund Kean's Leontes, or that I fell in
love with Lilian Vavasour at the old Court in 1862. And you, *you,* YOU
tell me I should have taken your play to this idiot and said "Do it when
you can." Ah Ellen, Ellen, when you see two considerations in my head,
there are never less than twenty there. You have contracted your conceptions to suit *his* head—that narrow little cutlet of a forehead that
peers and guesses at my Temple of Reason. You should live here, where
we have to stretch our foreheads like concertinas to grapple even with
one another's small talk.

I have promised to join a cycling party, and they shriek for me.

Are you coming to The Wild Duck tomorrow?

Of course you've seen The Daily Mail, but I send you a copy to
make sure.

Ever dearest, be beautiful and happy, for ever and ever out of abun-
dance of life.

G. B. S.

P. S. Did he shew you *my* letters to him, as well as his to me? Ha ha-a-a-a-a-a!

CXXVII: G. B. S. *to* E. T.

[Mrs Warren's Profession was withheld from the English stage for thirty years by the Censorship, which could not, however, prevent its publication in 1898. It was first performed by the Stage Society (privately at the Lyric Club) in 1902. The first public performance in England was at Birmingham in July 1925. Mr Macdona in conjunction with Mr Arthur Bourchier put it on for a run at the Strand Theatre in March 1926 (86 performances).—The production of Antony and Cleopatra referred to was under the auspices of the Independent Theatre at the Olympic Theatre on the 24th of May. Janet Achurch played Cleopatra.—Othello was produced by Wilson Barrett at the Lyric Theatre on the 22nd. Shaw criticized these last two productions in The Saturday Review.]

24 May 1897

COME, what new infidelity is this?—How long am I to be deserted? I have not had a line these three months. Who is my rival? Is it Henry, or that stupid Cooper, or the grandchild? Or are you angry? Or tired of me? Well, remember that you have not *quite* exhausted me: there is one play, the best of them all, which you havent seen (Mrs Warren's Profession), and which I am preparing for the printer. Throw this disagreeable dog a bone, and you shall have a proof as soon as it is set up—I mean a printer's proof. I do not want to give any of that volume to the public until it has gone to you first. That is sentimental; but I have a headache after Antony & Cleopatra (Oh Lord!) and yet must turn out again to see Othello. One touch of your finger on my forehead would cure me; but of course you choose this moment to desert me. Miss P. T. has found me out: she tells me that I am "the most self-centred man she ever met." Just at present I am Ellen-centred; but the sun is hidden by clouds of silence. Well, I must wait. I suppose you will get tired of him, whoever he is; and then you will be sorry you starved me.

Did you see a wild article in a new paper called The Comet declaring that Wilson Barrett is the greatest of English actors who is kept back by a dastardly press conspiracy organised by H. I.? Oh my head! I must away to my stall of torment, unconsoled. Cruel Ellen. Poor

G. B. S.

P. S. I return to Dorking to-morrow. Up on Wednesday afternoon **for** the VESTRY!

CXXVIII: E. T. *to* G. B. S.

25 May 1897

WELL, I must say you are a funny boy. I wrote you last, and getting no answer to my meandering scrawl, I thought you were too busy for just a little while to pay any attention to your Ellen, or any sich like trash, and I was waiting with patience (?) for your sure-to-come answer. "Sure to come," 'cos in the letter I asked you to do something, and you always do what I ask you, and for anyone, I'm sure, what you can. By this token you will send me Mrs Warren's Profession (I've been told it is quite unfit for publication). Yes I saw The Comet. Heavens what common, what vulgar stuff! But no harm done to Henry since they didnt *praise* him. My poor Henry! That at least was spared him. No you have no rivals. You see I have no lovers, only loves, and I have as many of those as I want, and you are the only one I dont benefit! You do things for me. I do things for them.

So you are "self-centred"? You'd be wobbly I suppose if you were not. But everyone is alike. It's only, "but oh, the *difference to me!"*

I'm in bed, pretty ill. Rosy is at my back with a wee table, and we are going to partake of a meal together. The sunny beam she is! She is shrieking with pleasure when we "pretend" waiters, and animals, and things.

With a cool gentle kiss this warm day I say farewell my sweet.

CXXIX: G. B. S. *to* E. T.

[*Shaw had recently become a member of the old Vestry of St Pancras, now the Borough Council. He retired in 1903.*]

28 May 1897

No ILL! A thousand ills. I never see my Ellen; I hardly ever hear from my Ellen; when she writes to me she does not post her letters: at all events she reproaches me with not answering letters I never got, and not doing things she asked me to do in petitions which never reached me. That is 999 ills; and the other is that what with the preparation of the plays for publication and the ever returning Saturday windmill sail that strikes me down before I have stumbled to my knees after the last blow, and the Fabian with its two weekly committees, and now on top of it all the Vestry with *its* two committees, and the Webbs' great new treatise on Democracy which I have to help in revising, I cannot even write to you because I am afraid of boring you with the beaten-out fag end of my brains—because I cant feel my heart in my pen then. Of course it is all right: it is good for me to be worked to the last inch whilst I last; and I love the reality of the Vestry and its dustcarts and H'less orators after the silly visionary fashion-ridden theatres; but the machine, Shaw, is not quite perfect yet: just now I am worried because I have forgotten something, left something undone, something unsatisfied, and that is YOU and nothing else. And yet if it would be a blessed thing to have you, it is the next blessedest thing to want you—better than being hard and hellish, as I now am for longer and longer stretches because I have not time or opportunity to exercise my heart.

I cant send Mrs Warren yet because it isnt printed. Miss P. T. has learnt to typewrite and is making me a typed copy from my original almost defaced scrawl; and this copy I am revising and filling in with business for the printer. It's much my best play; but it makes my blood run cold: I can hardly bear the most appalling bits of it. Ah, when I wrote that, I *had* some nerve. And yet it's only three or four years ago—five at most.

I have written *such* a nasty article for to-morrow—nasty for Henry, nasty for Janet, nasty for Wilson Barrett. I've used Janet and H. I. as bolsters to bang one another with, recalling the old days when H. didnt know how to do the grand style, and comparing Janet in Cleopatra to him.

I go back to Dorking tomorrow morning by the 10.30 train. Had to come up tonight for the Fabian. Must come up again on Monday for a Vestry committee—Princess Dinner Fund—a ghastly, wicked, wasteful folly. But these things will give my letter a dry taste. If only I could bring you down with me. There's nobody there but Mrs Webb, Miss P. T., Beatrice Creighton (Bishop of London's daughter), Webb and myself. Alas! *four* too many. I wonder what you would think of our life—our eternal political shop; our mornings of dogged writing, all in separate rooms; our ravenous plain meals; our bicycling; the Webbs' incorrigible spooning over their industrial and political science; Miss P. T., Irish, shrewd and green eyed, finding everything "very interesting"; myself always tired and careworn, and always supposed to be "writing to Ellen." You'd die of it all in three hours, I'm afraid. Oh, I wish, I wish—

G. B. S.

CXXX: E. T. *to* G. B. S.

29 May 1897

Dᴏɴᴛ write to me for a month, and then only if you want to. I can see you are busied to death (and a little worried I think!). Dont trouble to send me Mrs Warren. Dont trouble for me at all. I know what it is like to feel like a bit of leather. "Hard and hellish" as you say, and to want nothing is the worst state of all states. I shall not write to you, but think of you most days, every day (Pooh pooh! It sounds like a love letter), and be wishing you well all the while. Evidently two of my scrawls have "gone wrong." There was nothing particular in 'em. I only asked you to read a fragment of a play I have to do for a "Charity," but I dont ask you now. My need has passed, and I've promised to do it. A Vestryman! *You!* You will glory in it.

I shant write for a month, not even then if I think—

Dont give me a thought. I'm happy enough and quite satisfied. You are a dear old kind fellow, as well as everything else.

Good-night. It's morning, but Good-night.

ᴇ. ᴛ.

CXXXI: E. T. *to* G. B. S.

7 June 1897

Cᴜʀɪᴏᴜs. I couldnt open your letter for ever so long. Opened the rest of my batch and answered them, but I *looked* only at yours for over three hours. Sir, the mislaid scrawls I wrote you were sent to Lotus, and not to Fitzroy Square. Therefore the new servant is not to blame. I said I would not write for a month because I detected signs of polite boredom on your part. Thinking how dense I had been not to perceive it before, I generously determined to give you a holiday. Oh, you darling wretch, how ungrateful you are!

Well when they have all married you—but there, I remember how once before you "drew" me to show you my heart, you horrid darling, and I wont say a word about marrying, or giving in marriage. I wonder what you think of your Mother now you have time to note her. So "affection" never reached you by way of your family. I wonder how this is. It would be a frightful loss if it were my case. I'm *very* fond of all

155

my people, and a few of 'em are fond of me, but the loving back again never has mattered much to me, altho' now, oddly enough I am very much touched by some affection that has come me-ward, and feel inclined to "go in" by way of a change for that sort of thing. I took Edy to the races and was interested in noting how little she appeared to care for it all. When I was her age I enjoyed things terribly. Even now the drive over the Down made me feel drunk, tho' I could not care for anything else except the horses.

Good-bye, my sweet. People seem to talk to you or me a good deal! Quite amusing.

Oh yes, I know I lose a lot by the "shutting you out" as you call it, *but you gain,* and I love you enough to wish that.

With a kiss on the middle of the inside of your hand I leave you. Dont be worried.

CXXXII: G. B. S. *to* E. T.

[The "innocent friend" referred to is Sir Emery Walker. He and Cobden-Sanderson controlled the famous Doves Press, one of the private presses inspired by William Morris which had an important influence on book production in England.]

11 June 1897

Again in the train—joggle, joggle—night— third class—after a Fabian meeting—on my right Webb—on my left—no matter.

I GOT a frantic notion at the Comedy Theatre the other afternoon that you were in the house. I thought there was a Lyceum party in a box because I met Cooper in the corridor. Cooper is quite a pretty, amiable-looking, chubby fellow off the stage, with a complexion as charming as wig paste. Perhaps it *is* wig paste. Why cant he be taught to act? Has he NO intelligence?

Well, it was a false alarm: you were not there. I havent seen you for so long that I have half a mind to accept my invitation to the Siddons Memorial unveiling. Oh, why isnt it the St Pancras Vestry instead of the Paddington?—I'd make a speech and drive Henry mad. An innocent friend of mine met him at dinner the other day and said cheerfully, "When are we going to have Mr Shaw's play?" H. observed that I was a clever person but disrespectful to dignitaries; and my friend hastened to say that he was a great friend of mine, whereupon H. said to himself,

156

"Dive, thoughts, down to my soul," and changed the subject. The other day a man said to me "Irving was drunk in Richard." "How do you know?" says I. "I had it from his son," says he. Such are our children, Ellen. I dont know which of the two young rascals it was, but both of them probably inherit enough of their parent's impishness to be unable to resist the joke of giving him away, with or without good grounds.

The first moral lesson I can remember as a tiny child was the lesson of teetotalism, instilled by my father, a futile person you would have thought him. One night, when I was still about as tall as his boots, he took me out for a walk. In the course of it I conceived a monstrous, incredible suspicion. When I got home I stole to my mother and in an awestruck whisper said to her, "Mamma, I think Papa's drunk." She turned away with impatient disgust and said "When is he ever anything else?" I have never believed in anything since: then the scoffer began: then was sown the seed which so annoys Henry when it comes up in my articles. Oh, a devil of a childhood, Ellen, rich only in dreams, frightful and loveless in realities. And still I have to dream of my Ellen and never touch her. Well, let them unveil Mrs Siddons; but beware that another actress too is not unveiled that day—snatched from the platform, borne from the despairing Henry and the shrieking vestry away into the land of dreams, over the plains of heaven, to my home, wherever that may be.

Oh Ellen, Ellen, Murray Carson is going to do that play at Croydon on the 28th; and the Strange Lady will be a strange lady indeed, (12th June, 1897). Who she will be I know not—care not. I am powerless: one must not behave like a child. But I hope it will fail, ludicrously, hideously, horribly. Stay, no, I hope the lady will fail as she deserves to, and that Carson may succeed so magnificently that he will be made a Jubilee baronet—not a miserable knight.

Wonder could Edy do the Strange Lady!

Lord, what a supernal night it was last night in the train and coming home. A ten inch moon, a limelight sky, nightingales, everything wonderful. Today the same clearness and an Italian heat. For the first time for months, I've loafed—read scraps of things—done nothing. I'm tired in all my bones. I finished the revision of Mrs Warren yesterday. And now I *must* do some work. But to sustain me in it—keep on loving me (if you ever did) O my Ellenest—love me hard, love me soft, and deep, and sweet, and for ever and ever and ever.

G. B. S.

14 June 1897

> The midnight train which gets to Dorking
> at 1 a.m. Stopping just now, but will joggle
> like mad presently.

D o you read these joggled scrawls, I wonder. I think of your poor eyes
and resolve to tear up what I have written. Then I look at the
ghostly country and the beautiful night, and I cannot bring myself to
read a miserable book: I must talk to you: nowhere else, no time else,
can we be so perfectly alone. Yes, as you guess, Ellen, I am having a
bad attack of you just at present. I am restless; and a man's restlessness
always means a woman; and my restlessness means Ellen. And your
conduct is often shocking. Today I was wandering somewhere, thinking
busily about what I supposed to be high human concerns when I glanced
at a shop window, and there you were—oh disgraceful and abandoned—
in your 3rd Act Sans-Gêne dress—a mere waistband, laughing wickedly
and saying maliciously: "Look here, restless one, at what you are really
thinking about." How can you look Window and Grove's camera in the
face with such thoughts in your head and almost nothing on. You are
worse than Lilith, Adam's first wife.

Oh fie, fie, let me get away from this stuff, which you have been
listening to all your life, and despise—though indeed, dearest Ellen, these
silly longings stir up great waves of tenderness in which there is no
guile. You were right about my letters; only it is not boredom, but ex-
haustion. That is the worst of letters: I must say something: I cant in
pen and ink rest these bruised brains in your lap and unburden my heart
with inarticulate cries. When I can think, when I can write, then my
ideas fly like stones: you can never be sure that one of them will not
hurt you. My very love gets knit into an infernal intellectual fabric that
wounds when I mean it to caress; and when I am tired and foolish I am
flat and apparently bored. Sometimes that happens to my articles; and
then I am terrified indeed, and must work fiercely to remedy it. When
you complain, I am terrified another way, thinking that the end has
come, for I have only one thing to say to you, and it must get tedious
sooner or later. I am particularly tedious at present in this midnight
solitary journey, wanting to sleep, and yet to sleep with you. Only do you
know what the consequences would be? Well, about to-morrow at noon
when the sun would be warm and the birds in full song you would

feel an irresistible impulse to fly into the woods. And there, to your great astonishment and scandal, you would be *confined* of a baby that would immediately spread a pair of wings and fly, and before you could rise to catch it it would be followed by another and another and another— hundreds of them, and they would finally catch you up and fly away with you to some heavenly country where they would grow into strong sweetheart sons with whom, in defiance of the prayerbook, you would found a divine race. Would you not like to be the mother of your own grandchildren? If you were my mother—but I have a lot of things to say and we are at Redhill already.

I shall find a letter from you when I get back to Lotus, shall I not? Reigate we are at now; and it is a quarter to one. In ten minutes, Dorking station; in seventeen minutes thereafter, Lotus, and a letter. Only a letter, perhaps not even that. O Ellen, what will you say when the Recording Angel asks you why none of your sins have my name to them?

What, no letter! not even this morning. Oh very good, madam, *ve*-ry good. Sorry I troubled you, I'm sure. Busy these times, no doubt. Of course: dont mention it. Where are my vestry papers? Nothing like prosaic local work—yes: I'll do an interview with "The St Pancras Lon- doner" about the dust destructor and the contractor system. After all, it is in the morning that one has one's wits about one. At night, fatigue and late hours and joggling trains upset a man and make him drivel. Still, there is such a thing as common politeness; and to leave most important letters from a vestryman unanswered, unnoticed—well, no matter.

G. B. S.

CXXXIV: E. T. *to* G. B. S.

[*Mr C.: Murray Carson. His features were, like those of many actors, su- perficially Napoleonic.—The "frock" is the Empire Court dress worn by Ellen Terry in the third act of Madame Sans-Gêne.*]

17 June 1897

M Y FROCK low in the bodice? You surely cannot mean it. You are not so squeamish. Mr C. has decided upon his Strange Lady— and it is not Edy. Mr C. by the way should be Napoleon to the life for SOME reasons. (That wont assure his being able to *act* the part.)

Ah, my sweet, that picture of the little boy making the terrible dis- covery that his Father was drunk presses on my memory. I see it and feel it most uncomfortably, and worse, the Mother saying it! Do you think the clear sight of children is *true* sight? I dont think it is. Did you catch sight of me last night going by the midnight train to Leatherhead? I didnt see you, but the Moon and the Glory and the Love.

E. T.

CXXXV: E. T. *to* G. B. S.

[*We shall never know what Shaw said about "the charwoman." His own surmise is that having been moved by a photograph of the famous French washerwoman which had the sex appeal proper to the part he pretended to reproach Ellen Terry for condescending to enchantments within the reach of a charwoman. Howbeit, his letter was evidently in the "unpleasant" category, and its literary excellence did not save it from destruction.*]

19 June 1897

YES, FOR a moment sometimes I think you *are* "intolerable." But I couldnt set it down against you, for of course you dont mean it. Then there's the point of view. For instance it's the oddest thing to me who find the gentlest expression of my tenderness in kissing the soft palm of my Baby's hand, that you should think of it in quite a different way. Then again what you say about the charwoman is horrible (and for a moment makes me loathe you and everyone else) but it's only "horrible" because it's the charwoman. "M. or N. as the case may be." But I'm used to being laughed at by most of my women friends for my "wrong (?) views." I cannot think differently. However, I seldom talk on sacred subjects. Forgive me. Thank you for wanting to help Edy. I say, isnt it a joke? I'm ill again, downright exhausted and, for the moment, worn out. The last week I've dragged myself through that long long part, and toppled down when it was Curtain on Thursday night. I'm *such* a willing horse! But I cant act again for a few days. Poor Henry!

Well, you two will marry. I've no settled opinions on such a subject, and I warn EVEN YOU not to express any, for you may chance to eat your words.

Anyhow I am yours always the same.

L–N.

CXXXVI: E. T. *to* G. B. S.

[*This letter is a reply to one from Shaw which is missing, and parts of it, unintelligible without the key of his, have been omitted.*]

THANK you for your letter. I am too ill to write but a few words. Down again, and unable to act, until Monday. Just too bad when the Lyceum is crammed. I've lost my voice. It fatigued itself away! I'm useless, to Henry, or anybody.

How, where, can I hear about The Man of Destiny at Croydon? To think it has been done (probably *done!*) and I know nothing.

Is marriage such a wicked business. . . .

I wonder what you think could be substituted, for the woman's sake I mean, and the children's. I know you see their perplexing difficulties. But marriage is even worse for the man than the woman.

"Bear with your brutality"? Well you see, I like you as you are. Ought not I, and all of us, to have *the brute?* Well, whether we ought to or not, we all *have!* And I respect it in myself.

E. T.

CXXXVII: G. B. S. *to* E. T.

[*This letter is incomplete, and the date is missing, but it is obviously an answer to Letter CXXXVI.*]

[Not dated. Assigned to July 1897.]

. . . Is IT not curious that the one thing not forgivable in an actor is *being* the part instead of playing it? Duse plays La Femme de Claude with an impossible perfection, and yet never touches the creature with the tips of her fingers.

. . . Nothing annoys me more than the want of self-respect in the English people in artistic matters which makes them believe that French acting is necessarily better than English. I must let fly in the Saturday about it. The other day a poor lady who had enjoyed Sans-Gêne at the Lyceum and was duly ashamed of herself pleaded for you most pathetically. "*Of course* she's not Réjane; but," etc., etc., etc. She had observed a difference, and preferred you, but took it for granted that her preference was the shameful penalty of her English simplicity and ignorance. I sometimes lay people in ashes who go on like this. You are, on a moderate computation, about sixty times as good an actress as Réjane, especially in grip and technique; but all that goes for nothing against the assumption that Paris, the least artistic place in the universe, is the centre of all art, especially stage art.

I am rambling frightfully: in another moment I shall tear this up in a rage. When I am tired and out of sorts I cant finish a speech or a letter: I drag on mechanically repeating the dullest things. The reason is that I want to say tender things to you and *wont* go away until I say them; and yet *cant* say them because my soul is shrouded in mists and my heart clogged. If you would just touch the spring it would all flow fast enough; but you prefer to desert me and remain obstinately at a distance.

What will happen about marriage is probably this. As soon as it is realized that people are learning how to do without it, it will be considerably modified, as in America, by a great extension of divorce. The English will never abolish marriage. They never abolish things; but they circumvent them more unscrupulously than any other nation. At present it is far better for two people who do not mean to devote themselves to a regular domestic, nursery career, to maintain a clandestine connection than to run the risks of marriage. But if the divorce laws were so extended that a marriage could be dissolved as easily as a business partnership, then everybody would marry even if they only contemplated a year's association: in fact most marriages would be "only for a year, mind," and would last a lifetime. In that way we shall have more marriages than ever through the virtual abolition of marriage by divorce. Divorce is the Achilles heel of marriage. But at present the old system has the support of women because they are not economically independent of men. If you earned your living by keeping a man's house for him and bearing and bringing up his children you would feel strongly the life-and-death importance to you of an iron law and a fierce public opinion to guarantee you against being dropped and turned out of doors when he was tired of you personally. Marriage is not the man's hold on the woman, but the woman's on the man, and she will hold on to it like grim death until, like you, she gets paid for her work. At present she's an amateur, and does everything as badly as most amateurs.

And now I *must* stop. I suppose you are not coming to Croydon tomorrow to see the last of The Man of Destiny?

G. B. S.

CXXXVIII: G. B. S. *to* E. T.

2 July 1897

No, i'm not altogether sorry you are ill, for when you are well you dont care for anybody (that's the glory of health—its iron-heartedness) but when you are ill, you become foolish, and love me. Heaven send you continual bad health, my dearest Ellen, so that you may lie at home writing to me, instead of making love to Napoleon and that stupid Lyceum audience.

Dont trouble about The Man of Destiny. *All* plays are thrown away on the stage: do you think even *that* piece would not be as much a secret between you and me as it is now if it were played for a thousand nights at the Lyceum or the Théâtre Français? It might have forced my Strange Lady to be no longer strange to me if it had been rehearsed; but then that plan was baffled. The matter concerned me no further. Words cannot express my indifference to all this external business at Croydon. If I could stay away to-morrow without seeming to slight the company, it would not occur to me to go. As to H. I. (of *him* you are thinking I know), serve him right. If all this theatre business mattered I should say that he had thrown *you* away, a blacker crime than the throwing of 50,000,000,000,000 Men of Destiny. But you also cannot be thrown away. A few people know, though none of them know as well as I do. Dearest love: send me one throb of your heart whilst it is still tender with illness. It will be hard again on Monday; so be quick, quick, quick.

G. BERNARD SHAW

CXXXIX: E. T. *to* G. B. S.

3 July 1897

'A THROB of my heart!" Why you dear little stupid you know I havent such a thing about me, at least if I told you I had, you'd laugh and deny it. I wonder will my half century (due in February) finish me up entirely! And end the "throb" I *do* still feel at a sound, or, most of all, at a touch. A woman spoke to me to-day in the woods at Coombe where *I* had been wandering for an hour with a book, and where *she* had slept all night, and her voice, the misery in it, I can never forget it! I gave her a drive in my shandry-dan! And she thought it so fine, but my stars! she *was* dirty. Tears and dust had made a pretty mess of her poor face. She looked quite nice when she'd had a nice 'wash and a brush up." Her VOICE however needed no washing. It was too, too beautiful. I tried to make her sing to me, in the wood, but she thought I was cracked and was almost frightened to drive with me. She asked me my name and I said it was Nellie *Shaw Wardell*. She has indigestion by now. She *did* eat! and so did I!

Where were we? At "throbs," wasnt it? I only feel sort of misty-kind about *you,* and a gently warming-all-over-sensation-of-pleasure when I see your writing, and know that "by and by," upstairs, I'm going to enjoy you, all to myself, lingeringly and word by word. The woman's voice made my heart "throb," or rather stand still, and so would the touch of . . . but I fly from "throbs" in these days. It is not becoming. It's absurd.

Darling, you are very kind to me. Now dont write again for awhile. I appreciate you and what you do for me very well, but take the time in which you'd be writing to me and rest in it instead. Do nothing for nobody, or rather do that for me! *Rest,* for I know you are tired.

Oh, I am very much yours

E. T.

CXL: G. B. S. *to* E. T.

[Written after a suburban performance of The Man of Destiny *at the Grand Theatre Croydon. The first presentation was on the first of July. The name in the cast which means most to the playgoer to-day (1931) is that of Horace Hodges who played the innkeeper. He is, I believe, the only surviving member. One of our most accomplished and fascinating actors, he is so racily English that it is hard to believe he was credible as an elderly Italian.]*

4 July 1897

O H LORD, Ellen, I've been to see The Man of Destiny. It's just as well perhaps; for I should perhaps have thought, if I hadnt seen it, that my noble brothers the critics were cutting it up, whereas I now boil with indignation at their corrupt friendliness. Picture to yourself the worst you ever feared for it; raise that worst to nightmare absurdity and horror; multiply it by ten; and then imagine even that result ruined by an attack of utter panic on the part of the company in which each made the other's speeches when he (or she) could think of anything to say at all, and then you will have some faint guess of what it was like. I was only seen to smile twice and that was when a rowdy little kitten, fluffy but disreputable, appeared in the vineyard and was chivied by the innkeeper, and when it subsequently revenged itself by unexpectedly walking on again at one of Napoleon's most Marengoesque moments and staring at him as if it could not understand how a man could go on in a way that no sane cat would dream of.

But it is not the blundering and incompetence that makes me feel criminal at these performances. As long as people are really *trying* (and they were really trying with pitiable sincerity last night) I have an enormous patience with them. The dreadful thing is the impossibility to them of getting on terms of real intimacy and enjoyment with my stuff. I can compare the effect to nothing but that made by our Italian opera people twenty years ago when they first tried Wagner, and had a theory that his music was very wonderful and strange and important and original, but could not for the life of them catch the melody or follow the harmony of it. The sub-lieutenant understood vaguely that he had a comic part; but he *could* not be comic, though ordinarily he is an arrant clown. Once when by pure accident he hit on the right delivery of a line, the instantaneous response from the bewildered and miserable house both excited and disconcerted him. The applause at the end—half good-nature to the actors, half a perplexed tribute to my reputation—was like a groan: it was more pathetic by far than a vigorous hooting would have been. There was something insane and ghastly about the business; for since the dialogue does not consist of obvious jokes (which must either come off or be perceptibly muffed) but has, apart from its comedy, as continuous a grammatical sense as any blue-book, it sounded at once serious and inexplicable, like a dream-play. Fortunately the audience was humble in its agony, and mutely respected Napoleon for saying things it could not understand. It would even make a mouselike attempt to shew its appreciation now and then, but each time it shrunk back lest it should be taking seriously something that was perhaps one of my dazzling jokes. An agonizing experience for the author, Ellen, but an intensely interesting one for the critic.

As to your health, what you dont realize is, that the playing-every-night system is only possible for *routine* acting. You are a frightfully strong woman; and you have been a good deal spared by the superficiality, discontinuity and ready-madeness of the Portia-Beatrice business at the Lyceum. But even Shakespear cant be played every night with impunity. If you had really played that headless man scene in Cymbeline every night at full pitch you would either have broken down in the second week, or else have been by this time a mere wreck, capable of being set to work only by coarsening ruinous stimulants. Duse does not attempt to play every night. Salvini in America resolutely refused to play more than four times a week, even when money was raining in. Barry Sullivan, a strictly temperate man, persisted in playing every night, with Charles Surface or Don Felix for resting parts; but he at last degenerated frightfully and had a shower of paralytic strokes. Sarah Bernhardt, though she has reduced her business to the most mechanical routine possible, is a worn out hack tragedienne, almost as terrible of aspect as ———. I have seen a good deal myself of the touring platform man (and woman), the Trade Union organizer, the Socialist, Temperance and Salvation apostles who speak almost every night. It is a ruinous business always: the only people who can keep it up with impunity are the easy phlegmatic ones who amble through it in a quite unexciting way. For instance, Howe could, I imagine, have played twice a day for a hundred years without turning a hair: I never saw him flurried except one night as Flamborough in Olivia at the Lyceum, when he happened to be very drunk indeed. Now you are not that sort of person: you lay hold of your part with a tremendous nervous grip. It is not seen on the stage, because you come on with a grip ready fixed; but when you recite, you have to come on the platform just as Ellen Terry (with, oh, what bamboozling tricks and manners!), and then, when you attack the inevitable "Stay gaoler, stay," a critic can see the clutch taking place, like the stringing of a bow. Well, at that rate it is useless to plan out hundreds of consecutive nights of Sans Gêne: you cant do it. With H. I. it is quite different: he has no grip at all, comparatively, just as he has no voice, and therefore doesnt lose it. The condition in which he works is a somnambulistic one: he hypnotises himself into a sort of dreamy energy, and is intoxicated by the humming of his words in his nose. Besides, he escapes the terrible fatigue of thought and intellectual self-consciousness, through having no brains. Wyndham *has* brains; but he, too, has found the somnambulistic method and the artificial voice. All that they need to get into the vein is a particular sort of dinner. But they pay the penalty too: they get older and muzzier and dreamier; and their flashes of genius become more delirious and shortwinded as they go on. Wyndham has been pulled up by something like a stroke on the stage. Now you have none of their reliefs and resources. Try the dinner system, and long before it has made you fat and coarse (forgive these blasphemies, dear Ellen) and destroyed your delicacy and charm, the degeneration will present itself to you as *illness* and inability to act, and stop you. What is happening to you now is Nature's forcible interference to prevent you from killing yourself with over-work; and I rejoice in it. I dont want you to play every night; and if H. I. were wise he would prepare for the time when he will have either to stop or to keep the Lyceum open to at least its expenses for two or three nights a week with *drama* alone, independently of himself and you. There's a sermon for you. Now I promise not to write again until my book is a little more advanced.

G. B. S.

CXLI: E. T *to* G. B. S.

[*Alma Murray was at one time a member of Irving's company. She first achieved a reputation as a tragic actress in 1886 when she played Beatrice in the single performance of Shelley's The Cenci, given by the Shelley Society in defiance of the Lord Chamberlain's ban (now withdrawn). She also distinguished herself in performances of Colombe's Birthday and other plays by Robert Browning. Shaw wrote the part of Raina in Arms and the Man for her, and insisted on her being engaged to create it in the first production in 1894. He still considers her the best of all his Rainas.*]

10 July 1897

Now I wonder do you really mean you think that nice little woman Alma Murray a good actress? I love you, I long to find the least little bit of "good actress" in everybody, anybody, but did you see her play Rosalind? I am just curious, that's all. Again: *"She* (Réjane) is supported by an EXCELLENT COMPANY!" That is too-oo wildly funny, for anyone not to see your joke, who has seen "the Company." But some people have not, and to mislead them like that! Oh you bad darling! Except Réjane herself, it is a grotesquely bad company, and if you dont know it I shall never know one scrap of you.

Your E. T.

CXLII: G. B. S. *to* E. T.

[*"Master Laurence's play": Laurence Irving's Peter the Great.—"The Haymarket play": Haymarket seems to be a slip. It is in a notice of a play at Her Majesty's Theatre (Mlle de Belleisle) that Shaw dissects Ellen Terry's methods (Dramatic Opinions and Essays).*]

11 July 1897

(Beginning of first attempt)

OH MOST presumptuous, how do you know—you, who never go to the theatre? If you leave this world without knowing me, you will be sent back after a million years of unspeakable purgatory, to accomplish that destiny; for there will always be some lonely Adam looking at the world amid millions of blind creatures stumbling about through their dreams, and cursing him when they trip over his foot, and you were made different to other women in order that you might be that lonely Adam's Eve.

167

(Beginning of second attempt)

Iɴʜᴜᴍᴀɴ Ellen! I tried twice to answer your letter; and both times you led me into an extra Saturday article. Why do you suppose I run from time to time to rest this weary head in your lap? To water my dry soul at the fountain of life, not to explain to you why Réjane's company is excellent or why Alma Murray has my good word.

14 July 1897

(Final attempt)

Iᴛ ꜱᴇʀᴠᴇꜱ you right: why do you overwork me with your critical con- undrums. It has ended in my writing a Saturday article about you and your methods under cover of noticing the Haymarket play. A more fearful dissection and demonstration of your methods has never been penned. By the way, I ought to see Portia before I correct the proof. But the Lyceum would fall on my head, and bury me with the fainting Stoker and the prostrate Henry if I presented myself.

Send me along Master Laurence's play if you like. If I steal the plot my version will be so Shawified that nobody will recognize it; and if I have anything critical to say about it you can say it as from yourself. Even if he finds out he wont mind: people always like to be read. If H. does not produce it, the Independent Theatre is always there to fall back on.

Talking of that, Charrington is taking out a Doll's House tour; and he's going to try Candida on the provincial dog. He wants somebody who can play Prossy (a character in Candida which you forget, probably) and Mrs Linden in the Ibsen play. I suggested Edy. Would she go, do you think? It will be a pretty miserable tour—start at Aberdeen, after 12 hours travelling; but she might pick up something from Charrington; and Janet would keep her in gossip for a twelvemonth to come.

(TURN OVER)

Now that you *have* turned over, I dont know that I have anything to say that will bear writing down. I am at present scudding close reefed before a gale. Oh why wont women be content to leave their stars in the heavens and not want to tear them down and hang them around their necks with a gold ring! Why does their pleasure turn to pain and their love to hate without their knowing that it has happened? I will put an end to it all by marrying. Do you know a reasonably healthy woman of about sixty, accustomed to plain vegetarian cookery, and able to read and write enough to forward letters when her husband is away, but otherwise uneducated? Must be plain featured, and of an easy, unjealous temperament. No relatives, if possible. Must not be a lady. One who has never been in a theatre preferred. Separate rooms.

This soirée is a nuisance. Only one woman invited me to the dinner (Janet) and I made her invite the editor of the Chronicle instead, after first dazzling the committee by about fifteen shillings' worth of effusive telegraphed regrets from Lord Dufferin. She who invited me to the soirée frightened me by getting into a sort of heart paroxysm on Monday after the opera because I foolishly pointed out to her (without the least malice—even with the tenderest regret) that she was beginning to dislike me, and not a word have I heard since, in spite of my message of enquiry. Can you give me the address of the nearest monastery? Your deliberately getting ill tonight (I had fully intended to carry you away off H.'s arm and leave him staring in the midst of the distinguished ones) is the last straw.

G. B. S.

CXLIII: E. T. *to* G. B. S.

[*The reference is to Laurence Irving's play Peter the Great*]

14 July 1897

A NOTHER breakdown! Could not act last night altho' I got as far as putting on "my things." Then the good-natured Gertrude Kingston took pity on me, and just *would not let* me act. No play-acting for me to-night, no "Jubilee Dinner," nor even "Soirée"—nothing but my bed and absolute quiet to be able to struggle with Portia to-morrow. Lordy—Lordy.

I write to tell you that the 2nd Irving boy has written a wonderful play (and if his Father doesnt act it "I give him up," as they say)! There's no doubt the boy is a born-ready-made-genius and there's an end of him. I am *quite sure* you will like the play. Five acts, fresh, original, powerful, grim, amusing. I *would* like you to read it—but I suppose I must not send it you to read—There is a small part for me in it, a very big part for Henry, and . . .

[*The rest of the letter is missing*]

CXLIV: G. B. S. *to* E. T.

[The reference to The Saturday Review is explained in the note to Letter CXLII. One of the "things" thrown at Ellen Terry in the article is: "She added what she learned in the studio to what she had already learned on the stage so successfully that when I first saw her in Hamlet, it was exactly as if the powers of a beautiful picture of Ophelia had been extended to speaking and singing."]

16 July 1894

A secret! Good: we must paragraph it at once; and H. I. must confirm the rumor by announcing it from the stage on the last night of the season. I saw Laurence at the Dinner-Soirée; but as I dont know him I did not speak to him. But I told everybody that he had written a magnificent play, which was the right thing to do for him under the circumstances. I made the acquaintance of Ted, who won my heart with great ease, though I have no doubt he made abundant fun of me with the other Heavenly Twin when my back was turned.

Your last autograph letter not only got delayed in posting, but lost half of itself on the way. I only got the last sheet, beginning in the middle of a sentence. A cruel robbery.

I have always said that there are only two really sympathetic women in London—yourself and Dorothy Tennant (Mrs. Stanley). Dorothy is the more sympathetic of the twain; for she has just *rested* me by getting me all alone and talking to me for an hour and a half. This should be an example to selfish people who shut themselves up and get ill all by themselves. I suppose I maynt go to Winchelsea. I am almost dying for a little sea air. However, hasten away to rest and health, with my heart's blessing.

If there really is a part for you in Laurence's play, send it to me and I'll study it for you and save you a lot of trouble. Ask his leave if you like.

Tomorrow you will open the Saturday with dread and shut it with shrieks of indignation. Used Mrs Charles Kean to throw things at you!

G. B. S.

P. S. Dont tire yourself by trying to write to me—at least not more than five or six pages.

[*Edith Craig at Shaw's suggestion had been engaged by Mr and Mrs Charrington (Janet Achurch) to play Prossy in Candida, and Mrs Linden in The Doll's House on tour.—The italics in this letter are Ellen Terry's.*]

20 July 1897

E DY is going to have a very difficult job of it with Mrs Linden, because Janet is so loathingly sick of rehearsing it with new Lindens that she wants Edy to get through with only one rehearsal. And the effort of swallowing all those words will be bad for Prossy. However, we must make the best of it.

The only difficulty about Prossy will be the usual difficulty—want of muscle in the enunciation of the words. When people intend to play the piano in public, they play scales for several hours a day for years. A pupil of Leschititsky (Paderewski's master) comes before the public with steel fingers, which give a quite peculiar quality and penetration even to pianissimo notes. *An actress should practise her alphabet in just the same way, and come before the public able to drive a nail up to the head with one touch of a consonant. For want of this athleticism, people get driven to slow intonings, and woolly execution.* Now for Prossy I want extreme snap in the execution: every consonant should have a ten pound gun hammer spring in it, also great rapidity and certainty of articulation. Of course Edy has not got all that yet; but I shall get more of it out of her than she dreams of troubling herself for at present. *Young people dont realize what a tremendous deal of work it takes to make a very small effect.* But she starts with a good deal in hand that one looks in vain for elsewhere. Her expression is, if anything, too expressive normally, like Forbes-Robertson's. *Her voice is quite her own. But she needs to work and use her head a good deal; for she is like a boy in her youth and virginity, and cannot fall back on "emotional effects"* which are really only the incontinences of a hysterical and sexually abandoned woman, but which pull a great many worthless and stupid actresses through leading parts of vulgar drama. *So she will—fortunately for herself—get nothing cheap.* I have told her that if I can do anything for her in the way of going over the part with her I will make time to do it. But probably she will not be able to make time for it. Still, if it can be done, I will fit myself into it somehow. A rehearsal (at Queen's Gate Hall) takes three hours. We begin at 11 to-morrow and should get finished a little after 2. I can put off writing the Saturday article (not yet begun, alas!) until the evening. Consequently, since you go to bed (dont you?) in the afternoon, I could lunch in the neighborhood and call at Barkston Gardens from half past three to half past five, if that would be any use. A couple of policemen on the stairs would be sufficient to prevent my attempting to see you by force. I do not see how she could call here without dislocating her day too frightfully. I have not proposed this to her, because she may feel—and be right in feeling—that she had better be satisfied with what she can pick up at rehearsal, and have all the rest of the time to herself. Just find out what she thinks; and if she wants a private rehearsal, propose my coming round as above, as a brilliant idea of your own. I can "hear her" over Mrs Linden if she likes, when my hand is in. If I can do anything else or anything more, say what; and I'll do it. But dont let her suppose that I doubt her perfect ability to look after herself. Far be such presumption from my mind!

How are you?

In haste, ever dearest Ellen,

your

G. B. S.

CXLVI: E. T. to G. B. S.

26 July 1897

I'VE BEEN too frightfully on the verge of breaking down to write at all. But I think I *did* tell you of Laurence's play? I'm off now to my Winchelsea, and am too ill to say more than thank you all over for all your little kindnesses to Edy. I've known of them between her words. I feel queerly about her going away to work without being able to hover around, but I think it may be best for her. How do you, my sweet? When I'm rested I've to answer some of the things you have said lately to me. Meanwhile thank you about my Edy.

L. N.

CXLVII: G. B. S. *to* E. T.

[*The play Irving had "ordered" from Robert Hichens and H. D. Traill was The Medicine Man, produced at the Lyceum in May 1898.—De Reszke: Jean de Reszke, the great Polish tenor (1850-1925) who from 1888 to 1900 sang every year at Covent Garden. In the great parts of Wagner, such as Walther, Tristan, and Siegfried, he was unrivalled, throwing new light upon the music by his wonderful power of interpreting the dramatic side, without loss of vocal purity. Shaw adds: "He could not however be induced to sing them in public, until I, at the height of my vogue as a musical critic, stung him to the attempt by contemptuously refusing to sign an address to him on the ground that a tenor who had never sung Siegfried could not be regarded as a serious artist. He was an example of my dictum that all the singers who know how to sing have been taught by their mothers."*]

27 July 1897

THE Candida people are off to Aberdeen at last; and I have struck Saturday work for a month or two; so now I have nothing to do but get my seven plays through the press; write the prefaces to the two volumes; read the proof sheets of the Webbs' great book Industrial Democracy (doesnt it sound succulent?) answer two years' arrears of letters; and write a play and a few articles and Fabian tracts or so before October. Holiday times, dearest Ellen, holiday times!

Johnston F. R. is in tribulation over his Hamlet. He turned up here the other day beating his breast, and wanting to know whether I couldnt write a nicer third act for The Devil's Disciple, since Cleopatra was not ready for Campellpatra. I wrote him out a lovely cast for Hamlet, including Teddy as Osric (if Edward Craig Esquire will so far condescend). Will you, however, give Ted this hint. Courtenay Thorpe lately played the Ghost, and made a hit in it. I put him down for it in my suggested cast; but I sincerely hope that F. R. wont take the suggestion, because it is (or may be) important to me to have Thorpe free for Candida. In that case, Ted, with his pathetic voice, might play the Ghost himself, if Thorpe has broken the tradition sufficiently to make the notion acceptable. At all events, put it into Ted's head that it is a possible thing; so that if he gets chatting with F. R. or anyone else in the affair, he may say that his three parts are Hamlet (of course), the Ghost, and Osric.

I am certain I could make Hamlet a success by having it played as Shakespear meant it. H. I. makes it a sentimental affair of his own; and this generation has consequently never seen the real thing. However, I am afraid F. R. will do the usual dreary business in the old way, and play the bass clarinet for four hours on end, with disastrous results. Lord! how I could make that play jump along at the Lyceum if I were manager. I'd make short work of that everlasting "room in the castle." You should have the most beautiful old English garden to go mad in, with the flowers to pluck fresh from the bushes, and a trout stream of the streamiest and ripplingest to drown yourself in. I'd make such a scene of "How all occasions do inform against me!"—Hamlet in his traveling furs on a heath like a polar desert, and Fortinbras and his men "going

173

to their graves like beds"—as should never be forgotten. I'd make lightning and thunder (comedy and tragedy) of the second and third acts: the people should say they had never seen such a play before. I'd—but no matter.

I was at the opera last night—Tristan. O Ellen, Ellen, Ellen, think of it! De Reszke, at 48, playing his *second* season of Tristan, to a perfectly crazy house, and cursing himself in his old age for not doing what I told him years ago when I cannonaded the Opera and himself just as I now cannonade the Lyceum and Henry. And now Henry capitulates and orders a play from the musical critic of The World (my successor Hichens) and Traill. In a year or two or three, you and he will be doing what I have told you, and saying, like De Reszke, "Why, oh why didnt we realize the godlike wisdom of this extraordinary man before!"

You need not be anxious about Edy: she will take care of herself and of the rest very efficiently. She has inherited your social powers and would be worth £20 a week in the company even if she didnt act at all. And she has lots of acting in her, though she has been much neglected technically by an unnatural mother. Charrington began, as usual, with the most elaborate and ingenious theories of what she must be (founded on masterly surveys of the Terry character, the Lyceum art, and her father's nature) but she bowled him out in no time, and it ended in his being so glad to have her in the company that if he were not by nature a hopelessly monogamic person, and so violent a partisan of his wife that he would be furiously jealous on her account if any other woman infringed her rights to his exclusive devotion, Heaven knows what might not happen. Edy made all the difference in the world in the comfort of the rehearsals: there was no strain in them for me. I am afraid I got on her nerves and hampered her—I always do, for I sit there apparently intently and sufferingly watching the most agonising maltreatment of my piece when I am really taking things quite easily—but she never failed in tact for a moment; and I positively have not a notion whether she thinks that all the tales from the Haymarket fell leagues short of the horrible reality, or whether she thinks me the most innocuously amiable ass of an author who was ever laughed at by a company. Similarly, I havent the ghost of a notion of what she really thinks of Thorpe or Janet or Charrington, although she is perfectly easy and unguarded and spontaneous in her ways. So you may leave her to herself with perfect tranquillity: she's the only member of the company that needs no looking after.

She is of course a little too young for Mrs Linden; but I am firmly persuaded that I could make her play it miles better in six rehearsals than it has ever been played before. Probably she will be the best on record as it is. She only wants to be shewn a few trumpery little tricks—mostly turns of the head and other methods of escape from perpetual profile—to get on capitally. Then she says "Ah'll" for "I'll" occasionally without a pang of remorse; but it's so pretty in effect that not for worlds would I call her attention to it. It is like her aunt Marion's trick of saying "doant," which is Irish for "dont," and much better than "downt."

I suppose I am going to Wales on Friday. My address there will be The Argoed, Penallt, Monmouth.

Are you reviving with the ozone?

G. B. S.

CXLVIII: E. T. to G. B. S.

["No—not that one": the reference is to Anna Held, the American revue star, famous for her audacity in the nineties.]

28 July 1897
Tower Cottage,
Winchelsea, Sussex

IN WALES are you? I wonder sometimes if you get all the pleasure (that's a poor word) out of the open that I do. Oh, the sweet smells of the freshness.

I drove down here with Anna Held! No—not that one, but a German lady, an old friend of mine, who just loved the drive. When I reached here, to my amazement there was Henry! A troop of girls came with me from London on their bicycles, so there were seven females to dinner that evening, and only one Henry! They are all gone now however but Miss Held, and she sits in one hammock and I lie in another and silence between us most of the time, thank goodness!

I miss my Edy every minute of the time. However, I know she is happy; and it is good for her to feel the struggle of life alone for awhile. She has always thought it so easy, and it's time she knew some of the little difficulties. She is splendidly resourceful in *big* happenings, and displays great character, but she must make acquaintance with the small worries I suppose. This is Bank Holiday and I've sent the maids out in the carriage with the coachman for the entire day, and Anna and I will have a grand cold spread in the garden. That vulgar Hastings attracts the servants immensely. It is ten miles off and thither they have gone.

I wonder what you are doing? I am wondering something about *you two*. How I do think and think of it. I am inane. To be obsessed by a thought is the way of so many women, and I've always noted it and guarded against it for it is ruin.

You couldnt be dull, could you? So strange many clever people dont see the sun shines in the sky.

Have you been down to see Candida yet? I had no idea it was to be done yet awhile and was surprised to get a newspaper telling of it. (Thanks by the way for the newscutting you sent me.) Is Johnston Forbes-Robertson going to do the Devil? Are you going to alter the last act?

I'm told you are going to Leamington. True? Edy is dying to do the Housekeeper in Rosmersholm when it is played. She tells me, "Miss Achurch has been very nice to me about my parts." Edy with children is at her best, unselfish and devoted, so I'm delighted that little Nora (Charrington's and Janet's daughter) is about with her a good deal. I'm hoping they will all come near here, either Eastbourne or Brighton, for then I shall go there. Edy wont write to me of Candida but says she will *tell* me when we meet.

I'm going to sleep! (in the hammock—just where I am!) although it is 12—noon—

Cant keep my eyes open! (Generally cant keep 'em shut!)

Farewell, dearly beloved.

E. T.

CXLIX: E. T. *to* G. B. S.

[Mr Webb: not Sidney, but Philip Webb, the architect (see note to Letter LXXXIII).]

3 August 1897

O NE line. Altho' I always long for your letters and delight in 'em when they come, I remember this is your holiday, and crammed up with holiday tasks, so dont write.

I know you well enough to know you would reply to this morning's scrawl unless I let you off and told you not to.

I've nearly had a fit. Taking my first walk in the village this evening I looked up at our lovely church and, behold, a bright and shining NEW CLOCK was stuck upon its sweet old face. I could not believe my eyes. Can nothing be done to stop the brutes? The cruel sight has made my body ache all over. Impotent rage shakes me.

176

The beasts, the idiots! Just two new cogs would have put the old clock right. Your holiday! Oh Good Lord, forgive me! But where are the Architects? Where's Mr Webb?

Your convulsive

ELLEN

Dont write to me. DONT WRITE.

CL: G. B. S. *to* E. T.

[*"The Bo family"*: *Bo is Beatrice Webb who was always thus called by her relatives.*]

5 August 1897
The Argoed, Penallt,
Monmouth

JUST another line in the fresh morning before breakfast. If you have never been here it is no use describing this country to you. Dorking and Surrey are to it what Tottenham Court Road is to the 15th Century. You have not only all the ordinary naturalnesses and freshnesses of Nature; but a deliberate poetic beauty. The god who made this country was an artist: he moulded his hills so that their lines ran down into the valleys quite magically, and trimmed them with tufted woods so that not an acre *glares,* however warm the sun is. The fellow who turned out Dorking was a bank holiday tradesman in comparison.

It is a lovely morning, and from this lawn, 800 feet above the Wye, I can see away across it over the forest of Dean. There is not a cloud in the sky except a few toy white ones; and yet it is thundering away like mad, peal after peal, over eastward. And now they are just dropping a gauze over the horizon, and the tree under which I am sitting has shivered and sighed, as if it were catching cold. So perhaps we shall have some Rheingold effects presently.

Oh Lord, Ellen, I am so tired, even in the morning. I get out of bed so tired that I am in despair until I have braced myself with tubbing. When I sit down my back gets tired: when I jump up, I get giddy and have to catch hold of something to save myself from falling. Miss P. T. has brought down hammocks. Two days in one without a thought or a pen would re-establish me; but I havent the energy to fix them up. I can only rest myself by thinking that *you* are in a hammock, and writing to you.

Before I left town I got a letter from Charrington. He said that

Edy was too sympathetic for my notion of Prossy, but that a Terry couldnt be otherwise than sympathetic, and there was no use in trying to alter it. However, I am quite content with that account. I quite meant that the part should come out sympathetic *in spite of itself,* which is exactly what it seems to have done by his account. He is wrong about Edy. She can do a hard bit of character well enough: at least she did it in Pinero's whats-its-name? Bygones, is it? He said that Janet was very good in the scenes with Morrell in the second act (it was evident at rehearsal that she would be), but that in the great final speech she sat there articulating staccato, and religiously imitating my way of doing it until he could hardly hold himself back from getting up and stopping the play. Burgess, the comic father, was the success of the evening; and the drunken scene in the third act carried Aberdeen off its feet so that every exit was followed by a minute's uproarious applause. On the other hand, the poet was quite as misunderstood as he was in his own family, and this, Charrington says, was not Thorpe's fault, but Aberdeen's. He says nothing about himself.

They are to play the piece at Eastbourne and Bournemouth. See it if you can, and tell me about it; probably I shant see it at all, though there is some question of my going over to Leamington with Miss P. T. Excuse me one moment: she is calling me from her window. Tableau.

. . . .

Now I am all right. She threw me out two waterproof packets looking like Army Stores. I found a hammock in each and I have actually suspended them both from this tree, taking care to put one so high that nobody but myself will be able to get into it. And now I am swinging in that hammock, with your letter to answer, and Arms and the Man to prepare for the printer as soon as I feel disposed to work.

The tiredness, by the way, *is maladie du pays:* it is wearing off; and in a day or two I shall be sublime.

Well, as I was saying, that revelation of my self-centredness as a mere artistic machine was a shock; but now she says: "What a curious person you are!" or "What an utter brute you are!" as the humor takes her; and we live an irreproachable life in the bosom of the Bo family. By the way we have had one desertion. Graham Wallas has suddenly got engaged to a Miss Radford. They all succumb sooner or later: I alone remain (and will die) faithful to myself and Ellen.

Oh, I must do some work this morning. I have the proofs of Mrs Warren all but the last few pages. When they come I'll send you a spare set, and you must tell me what you think of it. By the way, that stupid old Widowers' Houses is not so bad as I thought. I've made it quite presentable with a little touching up. Did you see Archer's column of weary and disgusted vituperation of The Man of Destiny in *St Paul's?* I intended to send it to you, but I find I've left it in the pocket of a London coat. No news from Forbes. He'll never touch The D.'s D. unless he is drawn to it by **flat** play-bankruptcy. Mustn't begin another sheet. Ever—

G. B. S.

CLI: G. B. S. *to* E. T.

[*The letter from Ellen Terry criticizing the length of the speeches in Mrs Warren's Profession is missing.*]

10 August 1897

THAT's what they all want—a play in which pretty lies will make as much effect as awful truths. But it's impossible. You have seen all my plays now (except Widowers' Houses?). The hand is the same, the heart is the same (none at all), the brain is the same, the man is the same; but you see how different the play is when it grapples with life unconditionally.

You are wrong, believe me, about the long speeches. The easiest thing to do in public is a monologue. It is sheer want of practice that makes actors self-mistrustful when they are asked to deliver a speech or tell a story on the stage instead of asking or answering questions, or throwing sentences at one another's heads. Why does nobody ever fail as Hamlet? Because he has long speeches. Remember, the nation is trained to hear sermons. The real difficulty in that scene is not Mrs Warren's talking, but Vivie's listening. Bless you, I've made speeches hours long to casual wayfarers who could go away when they pleased; and they all stopped at least half an hour, though I am by no means as attractive a speaker as you are an actress. They would not have stood ten minutes of duologue. Do you know "Madame attend Monsieur"? It is virtually a monologue. Of course, a flimsy, unreal subject wont stand long speeches; but if you have the right stuff, the speeches cant be too long.

I have a lot of other things to say; but it is time to go to post. Imagine! I've been a week here, and I've only finished the second act of Arms and the Man (the revision for the printer). It is a stupendous job.

The Weekly Sun says that you have gone to Winchelsea, where you have a cottage, and that H. I. has gone to Somewherelse, where Mrs Pat has a cottage. Such is journalistic tact.

G. B. S.

CLII: E. T. *to* G. B. S.

26 August 1897
Albion Hotel,
Eastbourne

I WENT last night to the Theatre and enjoyed the Play (Doll's House) immensely. Janet played splendidly. They *all* played very cleverly. Edy was too young for Mrs Linden but her great repose was of service to Janet, contrasting well with the impetuosity of the others. I was just wrapped up in the play from beginning to end, and I think the audience was also. Janet's voice was admirable, and I like her last act now much better than when I saw it last. What a nice fellow Charles Charrington appears to be. I'm very happy about Edy being with them, and we have arranged she stays on, and does not return to the Lyceum. But oh, my friend, how I shall miss her!

I cant write to-day. I love you, and I'm going to see Candida tonight. Dont you envy me? I wish you were with me. I hope you are caring for the whole thing down there in Wales as much as ever. I wish I was there too. Oh dear, I'm getting so lazy. Dont want to go back to work, but I begin again 27th Sept. at Birmingham. Here's our tour list. Shall you be at any of the places by chance? If you be, be with me. Oh, this PEN. I miss you very much.

Farewell everywhere

E. T.

CLIII: E. T. *to* G. B. S.

[*Thorpe: Courtenay Thorpe, a member of the Charringtons' company at this time. He appeared in nearly all the first productions of Ibsen's plays in England. His unusual treatment of the part of the Ghost in Hamlet moved Shaw to write that "Courtenay Thorpe alone had a glimpse of the reason why Shakespear would not trust anyone else with it, and played it himself." Byron's Manfred was Thorpe's last creation. Ellen Terry's first paragraph here hits off his weakness exactly.*]

THAT work of art, Thorpe, haunts me! He does every part so cleverly. Helmer or Eugene, the more difficult the thing to be done the better he does it. But I cant think it right to show as clever as that. Must one *show* all "the tricks of the trade" to be understood by an audience?

Well, I've seen Candida, and it comes out on the stage even better than when one reads it. It is absorbingly interesting every second, and I long for it to be done in London. Even the audience understood it all. I dont see how anything so simple and direct could fail to be understood by the dullest. Only *one* thing struck me at the time as wrong. Towards quite the end of a play to say "Now let's sit down and talk the matter over." Several people took out their watches and some of them left to catch a train, or a drink! And it interrupted the attention of all of us who stayed. Of course you may think it unnecessary to mention such a trifle. I'm going to write to Janet about one or two trifling things in her acting, suggestions which she may care, or not care, to try over. She is a dear thing.

I was very happy being able to be with Edy. I know she was glad to have me here. I went for a drive with Janet and Mr Charrington (I like him) but was so ill when they came to supper in the evening I could scarce sit up. My eyes were dazed with the pain in my head. I'm well again now. It was the great excitement of seeing Candida. I was all right the night before!

Darlingest are you well? and happy enough? Where are you? When does your holiday end? Are you most of your time working? I guess you are!

I begin a drive of ten days on the first or second of September. We go 226 miles (to Aylesbury first) and amongst other wonderful places I go to Tewkesbury. I wonder I dont turn into an Angel there, I feel so nice, and as if I could fly. I'm reading now all the time of Russia.

Let me press you to a jelly now, for I must go.   Your ELLEN

CLIV: E. T. *to* G. B. S.

[*The first part of the letter refers to Forbes-Robertson's production of Hamlet, at the Lyceum. He took the theatre during Irving's vacation and autumn tour of the provinces.—"Peter": Laurence Irving's play Peter the Great.*]

I ONLY saw the last two scenes of the last act of Hamlet. I could never understand how Fortinbras could be left out, if the whole of what the play means is to be conveyed to the spectators. That beastly *Do-er,* coming in all swelling and victorious at the end of the play, makes me love more than ever the gentle dead Prince. I could not gather much on Saturday evening concerning the acting. I went in in the dark and heard whisperings that the people liked Johnston, and didnt like anything else, and I saw a very good Norse-like picture of Hamlet's death, heard Johnston's voice, and saw his poor dear face, worn to tatters, but now and again very beautiful. Pathetic fellow Johnston. I'm glad you are still in the fresh air. This London is lovely when one drives out as I did yesterday at 9 in the morning, but about noon a pall of heavy murkiness hangs over everything and it seems to crush in one's head. Edy came from Folkestone Sunday morning and yesterday went on to Nottingham. I would advise you to see Candida before producing it in London. If it is to be done, when is it to be done? A clever friend of mine said to me yesterday—"If Edy stays long with the Independent Theatre Company she will get dull, heavy, conceited, frowsy, trollopy, and *dirty!* In fact will look *moth-eaten!* And *no* one will see her act, because nobody goes to their Theatre." That's lively news for Edy's Mama, who is missing her all the while and for you who have a play there. I have a frightful cold and am stuck in bed to-day. I'll send Peter in a day or so. Oh, my muddled head. I think I'm fit for nothing. Look now! You and Miss P. T. live in a fine house in the country and I will "keep the Lodge"! And run out wet or shine and open the gates! And then sometimes you'll come to tea with me. I can make delicious griddle-cakes and jam, fruitfools and Hominy cakes. Send me my letter my very precious Bernie!

E. T.

CLV: E. T. to G. B. S.

N OW it made me very wild to be compelled to tear up your letter before at least I could "get it by heart"—but I *had* to, for there's gas about this hotel and an explosion would detain me on my journey.

Why do you write so? So silly. Not like you a bit, surely. And you know that sort of thing is well enough for me (nothing matters, I suppose, for *me*), but I dont believe you know the people you oughtnt to write to like that! And you'll get into trouble some day, and hurt some nice person very much. Why it even shakes me, just for one minute. Ah you stupid! But that's not you, I know, for you are a duck, of the best, and of the highest, and I love you. Whenever you have time to think, just throw your gratitude over Miss P. T. Make up your picture of life from material at hand, for God's sake, or you will miss it all. I see you working, working at those Plays. That's good, but dont forget to say thank you sometimes for the help and tending you are getting. Bless me, how impertinent, how stupid! As if I could think of anything you could neglect. Peter shall go to you next week. I'm beginning to like (at least to find rest with) "stupid" people. My brother-in-law, who is driving me through the country, is exceedingly—*quiet!* He is so very polite to me, and reads to me all evenings, and for the first time in my life I'm having all little things done for me, instead of doing all for myself and all others. Blessed dearest, farewell.

CLVI: E. T. *to* G. B. S.

[*The "new Hamlet": Johnston Forbes-Robertson*]

7 September 1897

D ONT you think you have been treating me rather ill lately? I know you are wildly busy, and that I told you not to write but bless my fur and whiskers I didnt *mean* it. You *know* it eases you to write to me! Where are you now? Have you found another comfy house in the same lovely spot? When do you expect to deliver your baby to the publishers? Are your labours over mayhap, and you "as well as can be expected"? I've had a wonderful time—stuck up high above the hedges and walls in that tandem cart. Do you know Tewkesbury? Do you like beech trees with their exquisite arms and legs? Were you ever in Lord Brownlow's Park in Hertfordshire where all may come and go? Do you like blackberry cheese? Do you love me?

I came back early yesterday from the country and (passing his door) went in and pulled the new Hamlet out of bed. Poor fellow. Hamlet's mother and young sisters and I cheered him up a bit. He looks sadly old for a young man. His poor long face! I assured him there was no part written in which he'd shine so brightly as in The Devil's Disciple. I'll ask him if he'd like to play it with me at a Matinée. Shall I?

Oh, you little dear thing, send me a word or two! With heaps of oughts and crosses (I mean hugs and kisses) I am your owniest own L. N.

CLVII: G. B. S. *to* E. T.

[*Julia: the jealous heroine of Shaw's second play* The Philanderer. *But Julia had an original. The lady whom he calls Julia was Mrs Jenny Patterson, who died in 1924. Her stormy intercourse with Shaw came to an end before the opening of his correspondence with Ellen Terry.—The play mentioned towards the end of the letter which had come into Shaw's head and driven* Cæsar and Cleopatra *out of it was* Pygmalion, *but he did not write it until 1912.*]

8 September 1897.
The Argoed, Penallt,
Monmouth

You cant imagine how it terrifies me to date a letter. It is incredible how the days fly past, like the telegraph poles on a railway journey. The 8th of September actually gone and still a whole four act play to be revised. And what a play! Oh! Ellen, Ellen, did you really read You Never Can Tell? *could* anyone read it? It maddens me. I'll have my revenge in the preface by offering it as a frightful example of the result of trying to write for the *théâtre de nos jours*.

Oh, I do not neglect "the material at hand." At my side people do not suffer from cold neglect: life is one long scene sometimes: at others it is as placid as possible. I make it a habit when I get restless over my work to seize the nearest woman and squeeze all the breath out of her stays. She does not feel neglected under these circumstances, nor is she much scandalized after the first few shocks. And when she does anything for me I always have a stock of fantastic complaints to make of it which are much more interesting than if I insulted her with delicate acknowledgements. It is not the small things that woman miss in me, but the big things. My pockets are always full of the small change of love-making; but it is magic money, not real money. Mrs Webb, who is a remarkably shrewd woman, explains her freedom from the fascination to which she sees all the others succumb by saying "You cannot fall in love with a sprite; and Shaw is a sprite in such matters, not a real person." Perhaps you can divine the truth in this: I am too lazy to explain it now, even if I understood it. It is certainly true: I am fond of women (or one in a thousand, say); but I am in earnest about quite other things. To most women one man and one lifetime make a world. I require whole populations and historical epochs to engage my interests seriously and make the writing machine (for that is what G. B. S. is) work at full speed and pressure: love is only diversion and recreation to me. Doubtless, dear Ellen, you've observed that you cant act things perfectly until you have got beyond them, and so have nothing to fear from them. That's why the women who fall in love with me worry me and torment me and make scenes (which they cant act) with me and suffer misery and destroy their health and beauty, whilst you, who could do without me as easily as I do without Julia (for instance) are my blessing and refuge, and really care more for *everybody* (including myself) than Julia cared for me. It is also, alas! why I act the lover so diabolically well that even the women who are clever enough to understand that such a person as myself might exist, cant bring themselves to believe that I am that person. My *impulses* are so prettily played— oh, you know: you wretch, you've done it often enough yourself.

Do you notice that this letter began on the 8th. Well, it's now the 14th, and that miserable play You Never Can Tell is not yet *half* ready. If only I could hurry it and still trust my work! For what I want to get at, you understand, is the preface, or rather the two prefaces. I am full of it, overripe and ready for it; and yet I must stick to this steady slow, slow, slow, SO slow testing and correcting and punctuating and recasting of mere trivialities. It is frightful, and I want to have my finger in the Webbs' work too; for they also are struggling against time with the completion of a huge task for which our three wits would be all too few. It's the trifles that eat up time. Have you never wished that you could keep a ghost to do that part of your work that is within the reach of ordinary intelligence and industry? Nonsense, 'tis bootless to exclaim!

I refuse to infer that you had fine weather for your drive. Here the fine weather has only begun. This house (oh, by the way, the address now is Moorcraft, Penallt, Monmouth) has a garden close and some charm about it, and life here is softer. The woodpeckers are hammering like leprechaun cobblers all round, and keeping me industrious by the sound. And then your letter has just arrived, and I perceive from it that your holiday has renewed the fountain of your youth. I sent you a hasty scrawl yesterday about Hamlet. I gave Forbes a description of what the end ought to be like. Fortinbras with a winged helmet and Hamlet carried off on the shields, with the "ordinance shot off within" just as the wily William planned it. Nisbett in The Times describes the scene almost in my own terms; so that my idea seems to have come off; so you see, madam, I am not a dreamer who doesnt understand the practical exigencies of the stage, and the sooner you send Peter along the better. I suppose F. R. couldnt afford the snow scene, with Fortinbras on the march and Hamlet in his travelling furs; so Henry can have a present of that. I saw his Hamlet once many years ago (the object of my visit being Ophelia). It was frightfully bad. He hadnt got hold of his classic style then: that began with Claude Melnotte, which I saw incidentally whilst I was looking at Pauline.

Are you going to do Peter on the road? You should. Think of how much anxiety it will save you if you have difficulties with the words settled before the first night in London. Mansfield produces The Devil's Disciple at the 5th Avenue Theatre on the 6th Oct., after an experiment or two with it in the provinces. Ah, if you only *would* play a matinée of it with Forbes, I would actually go to see it (a compliment I havent paid Candida). Besides, I would teach that rapscallionly flower girl of his something. Cæsar and Cleopatra has been driven clean out of my head by a play I want to write for them in which he shall be a west end gentleman and she an east end dona in an apron and three orange and red ostrich feathers.

I see you wont tell me anything about Prossy. It would be seething the kid in its mother's milk, I suppose; but still I do want to know in general terms whether my style of work fits her.

It is luncheon hour, and there's a visitor.

That letter would not have surprised anybody at the Hotel. Did you ever read Rejected Addresses? I only remember three lines from Lady Elizabeth Mugg:

> ...for who would not slavery hug,
>   to spend but one exquisite hour
>   in the arms of Elizabeth Mugg!

I should write the same about you if there were any rhyme to Ellen. I love you soulfully and bodyfully, properly and improperly, every way that a woman can be loved.

G. B. S.

CLVIII: E. T. *to* G. B. S.

[*Every autumn for many years Henry Irving with Ellen Terry and the whole Lyceum Company visited the chief provincial towns. This is the explanation of their being great figures in the England of their time, not merely stars of the London stage.*]

September 1897

So THAT'S what you are then? (You *must* be, if "Bo" who *knows* you says so.) A SPRITE. Months ago when you sent me a photograph of yourself by Mr Evans, I wrote *"A Sprite"* underneath it. It was one with the head turned round looking merry, and flashing. And now it appears Mrs Webb confirms what I thought.

Here I am in Wales. First time. Some of the people I've met here seem to be very gentle, and clever, and sly (sly, not shy)! I'm busy but I send you Peter. Please dont let other people read it, and send it back to me at Nottingham. I expect to be there the week after next (Oct. 4 to 9th) at the Theatre Royal.

A Banquet (Oh lor') yesterday and to-day I possess a beautiful scarlet and gold-bound tribute to my virtues, beauty, and talent. What a fool one feels, and how silly it all is, and how kind they all were! I sat there for 3 mortal hours, and thought a good deal about you, all the while they were talking and talking. I was thinking you were tired, and breaking your back over those commas and stops, and breaking your head. When will your labour pains be over and that babe be born into the world? Off on a bit of magic carpet would I go if I could, and wave my hands over your blessed head, touch your cerise (?) hair gently with my lips, whisper to you I was there, although invisible, that I love you tho' I could not show you how much (one never does!) and then skip back again on my carpet to—this place. Tho' I'd rather go to Edy.

Do you know the future movements of Charrington & Co? WHO is the Independent Theatre Company? They must be a *rich* Company. Yours, my Duck, ever and ever, E. T.

187

CLIX: E. T. *to* G. B. S.

27 September 1897.
The Plough & Harrow Hotel,
Edgbaston, Birmingham

Hog-dog why dont you write to me? That horrid baby of yours tires you out, I guess, but oh, I want two or three lines!

I begin play-acting to-night and dont want to, but would rather go to Gilbert's new play done for the first time tonight here. Holidays are mistakes. I always long to be "in love," to be dreaming, after a holiday. Life gets so soft and muzzy. Work hardens and alerts me. I shall become a vegetarian I think. I wonder do the Charringtons LIKE to play to empty houses? In these days let *anyone* take ONE play for a week to *anywhere,* even a big City, and they will effectually empty the houses. Now we have every seat gone for the coming week but it would not be so unless we what is called "forced the business" by playing more than one play. We do four, and the C's could easily do three or four with just the Company and scenery they already have. It's not "all alive" but a sleepy business and I'd like to shake them! Why dont you let them have You Never Can Tell? (You know you dont value it.)

I shall be late for rehearsal. Good-bye my poppet!

Your old lover,

E. T.

CLX: E. T. *to* G. B. S.

[*William Burges: designer, architect, and antiquary, 1827–81*]

1 October 1897.
The Plough & Harrow Hotel,
Edgbaston, Birmingham

Are you alive? Your neglect of L. N. is—well she sends you her *cuss,* not her kiss. And when you have finished your big book, and it is out, think of what will be said of it. "Indecent." "Madness." "Clever, no doubt, but all the more dangerous." I see Henry's face if he glances at Mrs W.'s Prof.! "Your friend Mr Pshaw." (He always says your name like that—*Pshaw!* It is so funny.)

Oh, and it was all so funny at Cardiff. The battle of Caste there! The "business man," the "country." The Tory disdain of the Cardiff Wesleyans. Then the Cardiff wives, the Welsh Militia. Real sport I tell you to hear all about it and observe a bit. You see I had no work there and went here and there for fun, and HAD it! Then little Lord Dumfries showed me all over the Castle, of which he knew nothing! (Altho' it's as good as his own.) And *I* chanced to know a lot, having made a complete set of tracings of all the decorative work in the Castle for William Burges who was a friend of mine.

Brute! Darling! Write.

CLXI: E. T. *to* G. B. S.

[*That "nice blue letter-card" is missing. I assume it was about the recent production of Hamlet at the Lyceum in which Mrs Patrick Campbell played Ophelia. Shaw writes in his notice in The Saturday Review: "Mrs Patrick Campbell, with that complacent audacity of hers which is so exasperating when she is doing the wrong thing, this time does the right thing by making Ophelia really mad ...... and the scene instead of being a pretty interlude coming in just when a little relief from the inky cloak is welcome, touches us with a chill of the blood that gives it its right tragic power and dramatic significance." Mrs Ebbsmith: Mrs Patrick Campbell first appeared in Pinero's The Notorious Mrs Ebbsmith at the Garrick Theatre in March 1895. There was no difference of opinion between Ellen Terry and Bernard Shaw about that performance. Her "just splendid" is endorsed by his "an irresistible projection of Mrs Campbell's personal genius, a projection which sweeps the play aside and imperiously becomes the play itself."*]

1 October 1897.
The Plough & Harrow Hotel,
Edgbaston, Birmingham

Rest, rest, poor dear! It's all right, I dont *want* to have a letter—to skin you! I had sent off my screed before your nice blue letter-card came to me. So you *are* in London. It was a pot-shot of mine directing there.

I *am* so sorry we dont like the same things. Quite honestly I'd love to like all you like, but Mrs Campbell as Ophelia I know I could not like. Dont be that kind of donkey to say, "Ah, yes, jealousy!" I admire Mrs P. C. as much as most people but I cannot like her Ophelia. If she plays that rightly then she played Mrs Ebbsmith wrongly, and Mrs E. was just splendid. The Saturday Review of to-morrow will, I expect, explain you. "To tea with her"? Why, yes. Why not? You shall come to *breakfast* with me!

189

I've just had the most extraordinary experience of my life. The awful thing is, I cant tell you. 'Cos paper and pen cant. No, THEY CANT: Oh, dont get headaches. They will distort everything. Finish you! I guess you had a "headache" when you were seeing Ophelia! (Well, I know I *know*.) It's because you work too hard, and what a foolish thing you are.

L. N.

CLXII: E. T. *to* G. B. S.

[*The Devil's Disciple was first performed in America on 1 October 1897, at Albany, and the next week was produced in New York by Richard Mans- field at the Fifth Avenue Theatre.*]

17 October 1897.
Queen's Hotel,
Leeds

Yes, I feel that the New York production is *solid*. One cant tell at first, but three weeks will about decide it, and I scream for pleasure for I love that play. Johnston F. R. will be obliged I should say to do just Hamlet and Hamlet only during his Lyceum stay, but after- wards? Will he go on a tour and prepare new things for a new London Theatre? Ah, you call me names! *"Fickle."* Why, you know they al- ways said so! And what "they" say must of course be true, but you like me for that, dont you? So inconvenient to you if I were constant. You know quite well, you wretch, I've kept from worrying you with my scrawls out of real good-natured thoughtfulness. How are you feeling now? Are all the commas, stops, and corrections finished with? Are you at something new in the way of a play? How *many* new? Never a play for your Ellen, oh no. I'm rather hating everything just at present and have had quite enough of doing without Edy. No work for me. No diversion. No fun. Tell me of something to read, something very light (for night) and something more absorbing. I dread feeling "dull," "blue," and I do believe it's coming on! Good Lord how funny! All the people (the Public) treat me just as if I were about 30. I'm not neglected. It is one fuss, one shout of approval, of me all along the route, and yet— Well, I've nothing to read. Perhaps it's *that*. Tell me (when you have a nice feeling me-ward, and can spare me some time) tell me what F. R. says about The D's Disciple.

As a vestryman does *Milk* come under your notice? The Lactometer is frustrated in these cheating days, but everywhere the wicked fraud goes on. I speak to the doctors in the villages. They *wont* up and complain, and *they know* what the adulteration of milk means for the children and women under their care. So many could live on milk alone. It is disgracefully dear too. If you can, send me an American paper about Mansfield.

Your E. T.

CLXIII: E. T. *to* G. B. S.

[*The production of The Devil's Disciple in New York had evidently stimulated interest in it in London.—Frohman: Charles Frohman, who was at this time the most influential theatre manager in America. Later he was concerned in many enterprises in London. He met his death on the* Lusitania *in 1915.—Drew: John Drew, the famous American actor, whose sister Georgie married Maurice Barrymore. Their children, John, Lionel, and Ethel, have all become eminent in their family's profession.*]

19 October 1897.
Sheffield

F ROHMAN is the best of those you name. He would produce it you say in London and with Drew. Well, I think that might be good. Oh, sweetheart, I am so tired to-day, tired and cross. I'd like to put my nose into somebody's neck and sleep for a month. I'm sick of fresh beds (or rather *un*fresh beds) once a week in these horrid cheating uncomfortable Hotels, and I cant *sleep*. I want to go home.

Frohman is good, I think. I wish you'd send me The Devil's Disciple.

Your own old L. N.

May I let Laurence I. read your W.'s Houses? Answer.

E. T.

CLXIV: E. T. *to* G. B. S.

[*Arms and the Man was the first Shaw play produced in America. The date was September 1894. The notices in the New York Press referred to are of The Devil's Disciple. As there was no revival of Arms and the Man in New York at this time the derogatory remark about it quoted by Ellen Terry must have occurred in a notice of The Devil's Disciple.*]

20 October 1897.
The Old King's Head Hotel,
Sheffield

W ELL!! Calling your Arms and the Man "a quaint and wheezy trifle."
Here are the newspaper cuttings. They are *silly*. I dont believe the writers understand it a bit! However they record how enthusiastically

the audience received your play and so there's some use in *that*. The New York Press is very vulgar, very low. The man knows you so well too when he says, "His spleen lies where his heart should be," etc.

I'm cold as a vegetable marrow. I think I must give up trying any more to act. If *only* I could be "in love." I cant go on acting like this. I could laugh out loud at times when they applaud me. The last three nights I've felt like frozen leather.

L. N.

CLXV: E. T. *to* G. B. S.

[The letters from Shaw referred to are unfortunately all missing. None from him between 8 September and 24 December 1897 can be traced.—Mr Richter: the famous conductor Hans Richter, who from the time of his first appearance in England in 1877, when he shared the duties of conductor with Wagner himself at a series of Wagner concerts at the Albert Hall, remained a prominent figure in our musical life until 1911. Shaw gave an interesting description of Wagner's restlessness at the Albert Hall Concerts in an article written on the occasion of Siegfried Wagner's first appearance in England as a conductor. In this note, as in others, allowance has been made for the possibility that as time goes on many of the distinguished people mentioned in these letters may become less well known than they are at the date of their publication.]

25 October 1897

I'M SORRY you are tired. Where's Miss P. T.? Believe me, the worst woman is better than the best man. Are you unselfish? If so, you are a rare bird. How I did laugh at you in a disgusting smoking carriage with the newspaper men! When I first met you I wanted to drive you about in the fresh air and that's what I still want. I dont want you to talk, just to sit there and enjoy the freshness with me and write, if you want to, and rest. Your horrid cold has gone now I hope. Poor thing why cant doctors arrest that sort of thing. It's so over-powering and frustrating. I raced round to see Mr Richter the other night in Sheffield and came in for some ravishing music. What a dear simple mannered creature R. is, to be sure. It made me very ill the next day. Music always does. Oh, I must get back your Widowers' Houses from Laurence. I beg your pardon for keeping it so long. It's highly diverting but—

Darlingest, good-night. I say farewell and press you to a jelly!

Your NELLEN.

Thank you all over for your letter. It's a horrid life this in the Province and your letters are the only—

CLXVI: E. T. *to* G. B. S.

1 November 1897.
The Grand Hotel,
Manchester

THIS is a filthy hole, my little heart, but even here the sun is shining, to-day at least! Did you ever see a beautifuller October? Oh, I can see Winchelsea in my mind's eye. The colour of it, and all the space in which to breathe. Of course I believe not in that Richard Mansfield nor in his fifty per cent. I should say that was all rubbish. But do you *expect* to gather figs from thistles? I am sticking at Henry day and night to do Ibsen, *just one* play. The Pretenders they all talk about is simply impossible, but An Enemy of The People or The Pillars of Society, just *one* play, to get about 50 nights out of it. Dont you advise it just now, or that will settle the whole business! H. *ought* to do something to please me; for I am just a sheep to play this Catherine for him (in Peter). If I were vainer I should think it might do me a lot of harm, but that's the way all actors talk, and to hear them disgusts me.

Do you remember what you said in your last note to me of Miss P. T.? Now you will not do anything of the sort. Oh, I'd like to PINCH you now and again. To *lard* you all over with pins, to——Nothing is devised finely cruel enough for you. (Now what rubbish.) I dont mean it, nor believe anything against my Bernard Shaw for I am his in all ways.

E. T.

P. S. When I get to Edinburgh I'm going to marry a man (and *Scotch* at that!) rich, and old. Then I butter the stairs, and wear a widow's cap next day!

CLXVII: E. T. *to* G. B. S.

3 November 1897

THE pretenders! You should hear him (H. I.) on the subject. Lord, Lord! how funny he is, as he tells of one person after another bounding into his rooms and excitedly roaring *"Pretenders!,"* until at last *he* got excited too, and all aflame, and (declining to join a gathering where extra superfine incense was to be burned before him) buried himself in the play full of hope and belief that here was the Play at last! And how he was left staring before him all through the night wondering was *he* or all his friends stark staring raving mad! *I* had only said one word on the subject, that he would play the Bishop to utter perfection. *That* fired him! Brand and Borkman are really the plays for us now, one thing and another considered. You see as long as we "go one better" than anybody else, what's the good of suggesting anyone knows better than he? Mr Richter brings his full orchestra for only one night in the week to Music-loving Provinces and we are in the same town with only 2 plays (Shakespear and Sardou) for the whole week, yet our place is over crammed each night wherever we go, and Wagner suffers considerably. You see Henry's is not a *losing cause.* Folk crowd around his banner, and he says he is a *do-er* and you are all *dreamers,* that the world is full of people (*he* says "Asses"!) who while watching the workers (and their success) ask, "Why is not the work done another way?" (Tho' he doesnt say it stupidly like that, of course.)

These hideous towns are killing me. I do so long for Thames- Ditton and the wee children. I could work until my last moment with *that* refreshment (or *some* refreshment) but I turn faint, if I starve. Nothing for the touch, nothing for the ear, nothing for the eye, not nothing for nothing! Only your stupid letters! I'll let you go (say thank you, L. N.!) and be off for a drive as far as I can go before I'm wanted for the matinée.

L. N.

CLXVIII: E. T. *to* G. B. S.

[Mrs Nettleship: the wife of the well-known animal painter. She was herself an artist, in dressmaking, and most of Ellen Terry's stage costumes were her work. "One of Mrs Nettle's greatest triumphs" Ellen Terry writes in her autobiography "was my Lady Macbeth dress. I am glad to think it is immortalized in Sargent's picture."—The name of the Scottish admirer, responsible for the rumour which had provoked Shaw's question "Is it all a joke?", is not known. But he brought out that curious side of Shaw's character, the Interfering Person and Amateur Solicitor. Shaw recalls that on reading this letter he at once wrote to Ellen Terry (the letter is missing) to warn her that her will would be cancelled by a marriage and that the consequences to her children might be serious unless she executed a new one immediately after the ceremony. This is what Ellen Terry means by "all these wise things for guarding me."—Apropos of the reference to Edith Craig the reader should be assured that those "folk" who thought she "cared for" her mother were right. To one as ebulliently expressive as Ellen Terry, her daughter's Cordelia-like abstention from the demonstrations of admiration and affection lavished on her by adoring friends of both sexes must often have caused pain. Later in their lives that shyness which often exists between parents and children disappeared and the friendship between

Ellen Terry and Edy became more intimate. It outlasted all Ellen Terry's other friendships, and was the chief consolation of her old age. "Edy" was the last name her lips pronounced in the hour of her death.—Laurence: Laurence Irving, Henry Irving's younger son, whom Ellen Terry was getting to know well through the rehearsals of Peter the Great.]

4 November 1897.
Palace Hotel,
Edinburgh

You say "Or is it all a joke?" Well, I cant see a *"joke"* in it anyhow, from any point of view, but, marry? Who on earth in their senses ever thought of such a thing? Not I.

Sometimes if Edy is away and I know Ted's heart is full enough of his wife and that crowd of children, and Henry is full enough of his work, I feel as if I'd like to go to one who would be full enough of me, if it only lasted for five minutes. But the feeling of loneliness (for that's what it is, *loneliness* mixed up with *jealousy,* ugh! detestable!) passes directly Edy turns up. I think she is the only one I was ever jealous about. Folk think she cares for me. I dont. I never plague her with my love, but oh, how she cuts my heart to ribbons sometimes, and very likely she doesnt intend to be unkind.

Arent you just a darling to trouble so for my sake to write me all these wise things for guarding me. Bless you. I kiss you all over for it.

In your letter you wrote a week ago, you said something about my marriage hurting Edy. Have you forgotten I *have* married, since Edy? I did it for her and for Ted. A mistake I know now, but no harm to her came of it, although no good.

How I have just longed to hear from you. *You* wrote last I know and now like a bountiful Bernie, and my most dearest and preciousest, you write again, full of lovely thought and care for another human being. I shall begin soon to think you have a little bit of real love for me. I've left my Scotsman behind in Glasgow. He's just the same, and he's hateful to me, altho' I admire and respect him from top to bottom, in and out, and all over. Only if he touched me I'd die.

P. S. Edy, Laurence and four others are lunching here, shouting at the top of their voices, all at the same time, whilst I am writing to Mrs Nettleship (and to you am scrawling the Lord knows what). Only I know I wish you were here.

E. T.

195

CLXIX: E. T. *to* G. B. S.

[Bourchier: Arthur Bourchier, one of the many actors who was attracted by The Devil's Disciple. In 1895 he had become lessee of the Royalty Theatre, his debut in actor-management. The reference to the "sleepiness" of touring companies is interesting in view of the opinion current now (1931) that they began to deteriorate after the war. Ellen Terry was never very sympathetic to complaints that actors and actresses in the lower ranks of the profession were ill-paid. She often said that many of them did not even earn their meagre salaries.—The opening lines refer to a bicycle accident (described in a Saturday Review article) in which Shaw's face was cut by a stone and sewn up by a Doctor Findlates of Edgware who refused to accept a fee.]

17 November 1897.
The Palace Hotel,
Edinburgh

You poor thing! Your face must be feeling so stiff and uncomfortable, and the *colour* of you! How absurd to make me laugh all the while I was feeling so sorry for you, but praise be blest the hurt is superficial and none of those blessed bones broken! You would not have the heart to speak against doctors if you knew as much of them personally as I do. The comfort their little knowledge brings to mothers who love and must leave their children, and to children who love their mothers. Some doctors go to sleep! That's all there is against 'em.

Fancy *Bourchier* as a Devil! Your play should have a solid "innings" in London and then be sent a-touring with conscientious people who will not go to sleep, but keep up honestly to good work. The wretched lot they are most of 'em. I go around and take a peep at these touring companies. They are all asleep, dishonest, meanly dishonest. I have got several of the girls in our Sans-Gêne Company engagements for Christmas, in these big towns as we go around. But I've cautioned them that if they go to sleep they will become pickpockets! One girl will get as much as £3 per week and "extra" for Matinées. I think she has to speak three lines! She is *fairly* pretty, and speaks FAIRLY well. The engagement will last for three months and she will be able to save about £2 every week, yet that girl will go to sleep over her work like the rest of them. Such an unthrifty lot. They are all so healthy too! Quite able to work, and play, and save. They will only get drivelling. Sweetheart, *please* dont write on dark blue paper with pale ink! Farewell. Be good.

E. T.

CLXX: E. T. *to* G. B. S.

[*Bellew-Potter: Kyrle Bellew and Mrs Brown-Potter who had been asso-ciated in management (touring India, China, Australia, and America) since 1887, offered Edith Craig a part in their production of Charlotte Corday, which took place at the Adelphi Theatre in January 1898.—The part of Alexis in Laurence Irving's play Peter the Great was played by Robert Taber.—Fussie: Henry Irving's fox-terrier.—Mr Byles: afterwards Sir William Byles, a famous editor of The Bradford Observer. Lady Byles, who survives him, is a notably able woman. Her kindness as a hostess was affectionately remembered by Shaw as well as by Ellen Terry.*]

1 December 1897.
Bradford

SWEETKIN, dont you think you have been treating me shamefully? Or is it *I* who have been neglecting *you?* Anyhow I forgive you, only dont do it again. You "want a mistress?" What rubbish! I want "a master," but I say to myself as I say to you, "What rubbish." We must do without these luxuries. There's so much work, so little time.

You dont mean to tell me you have scarred your face all over by that bicycle accident? How dunderheaded you must be. You should have broken your *left* arm, protecting your face. I wish sometimes I could break *my* arms. This Tour time I write 30 letters a day. Every letter I get asks me to do something, generally something I cant do. The letters must be answered. Edy is a wretch who hates writing, and has no conscience to help me. Then, too, Henry being away, there are many extra things for me to do in the theatre. I shall be delighted to get back home. Edy as the mistress of Marat-Bellew! Amusing, I should say. Edy contemplates touring with Bellew-Potter. Dont say anything about it please, but I'll be glad to be home and looking after things. I should like to start up a London offer for the damsel.

Yes, as you say, Courtenay Thorpe is not normal. That's it exactly and that is why he would have been the very best for our Alexis. Neither Alexis nor Peter is normal. Poor Henry has lost his doggie, and he was almost as fond of him as of one of his rehearsals and will miss him, for there are many rehearsals but only one fat Fussie. He lost his voice also. You see he *will* go to every doctor, and do everything they all tell him! Cant understand how it is he is alive! I would not add *my* rubbish to The Morning Post in re: Stage as a Profession. I wonder you didnt write more, or less. The cry is started every year. It's all so silly.

I sat yesterday in a chair you sat in, and Mr and Mrs Byles are nice people and their room was full of folk who seemed all pleasant and I enjoyed myself. I generally do the very few times I go among people. I like the way Mrs Byles carries her head. She has distinction and a sweet voice. What is your voice like I wonder? You sang so *very* small that day I was eavesdropping at the Lyceum office door. I am very well, a little tired but Peter will be my rock. How do you. Bless you.

CLXXI: E. T. *to* G. B. S.

[Ellen Terry had now returned from the Lyceum Company's autumn tour, and was rehearsing Peter the Great.—Gabriele d'Annunzio's Sogno d'un mattina di Primavera (a play in one act) had recently been produced in Italian by Duse and in French by Bernhardt. One of the English versions sent to Ellen Terry was by me. I hope it was the "good" one, not the "bad." It seemed fairly good when, many years later, it was produced at the Birmingham Repertory Theatre, with Gwen Ffrangcon-Davies in Duse's part. I remember coming up from Oxford and delivering a beautifully bound copy of the manuscript at the stage-door of the Lyceum, with "Please give this to Miss Terry at once. It is very important." "Important to you, or important to her?" Barry, the imposing Lyceum stage-door keeper, enquired sardonically.]

23 December 1897

I'M NIGH dead from my anxiety about this play, but hush! Your finger on your lip I pray. New actors. I'm not well. Unkind! Did I not write when you first started your holiday and tell you all about a *good* version and a *bad* version I had received of D'Annunzio's "Spring" play. It is of no use for the English stage. (Although D'Annunzio is a great little fellow.) I read all that was said about Duse in the part. She's not likely to play it again.

I should like to read Miss P. T.'s version of the thing, when Peter is out. I *live* (or nearly *die!*) in the theatre now, until the 1st Jan. Send me a scrap now and again (in pity, for I have no joy) unless you too are rushed at this moment.

Your ELLEN

CLXXII: G. B. S. *to* E. T.

[Annunzio: so Shaw writes Gabriele d'Annunzio's name in the original of this letter.—The Caledonian Hotel has since been converted into flats, and one is the home of J. M. Barrie. Shaw lived opposite at 10 Adelphi Terrace

for many years after his marriage to Miss Payne-Townshend.—William Terriss was murdered at the stage-door of the Adelphi in December 1897 (see note to Letter CLXXIII).—Waring: Herbert Waring. He made his mark by playing Helmer to Janet Achurch's Nora in her literally epoch-making production of A Doll's House in 1889. For many years he was a member of George Alexander's company at the St James's. He played Captain Ardale in The Second Mrs Tanqueray, and Michael in The Prisoner of Zenda. At the date of this letter he was appearing with William Gillette in Secret Service. He is still on the stage. A recent performance of note was his Polonius in John Barrymore's London production of Hamlet.]

24 December 1897.
29 Fitzroy Square, W.

Now I swear that you never mentioned Annunzio's name to me in your life. I believe you have multitudes of lovers, and in writing to them you forget which is which. However, it dont matter if you've read the play: Miss P. T.'s version is only a translation. Only, if you get very tired of the Lyceum, and the Savoy, you can go round to 10 Adelphi Terrace (door round the corner, opposite the Caledonian Hotel, with a lamp inscribed "London School of Economics") and get a cup of tea and an hour's rest on pretense of calling about a reputed version of the Spring Morning's Dream. Miss P. T. is a restful person, plain, green-eyed, very ladylike, completely demoralized by contact with my ideas, independent and unencumbered, and not so plain either when you are in her confidence. So whenever you want to run away and hide, probably the last place you will be sought for in is the London School of Economics and Political Science. She will be pretty curious about you, not only on the usual grounds of your celebrity, but because she has discovered that "work" and "important business" on my part sometimes means writing long letters to you. (N. B. She doesnt know that I have mentioned her Annunzio project to you.)

My calculations are quite put out by the unforseen extinction of Terriss. I was scheming to get the D's D. produced with him in the part and Jessie Millward as Judith. The alternative was a Waring-Bourchier combination—Bourchier to play Burgoyne. And now Terriss is only a name and a batch of lies in the newspapers, and Waring goes to the Adelphi in his place. However, Waring may need stronger plays than Terriss, who was a play in himself; so perhaps Jessie may play Judith yet. If I invest the author's fees from the New York run in County Council stock

I shall have £20 a year for my old age. They run to £850. I roll in gold. I am a man of wealth and consideration. I will take a theatre presently, and engage Henry for eccentric comedy.

I cannot understand why you didnt get Laurence or Courtenay Thorpe to play Alexis instead of importing an American.

And now prithee, dear Ellen, what is to be done for you to-morrow and the day after, with no post? On the 28th I go down to Shakespearland (address care of Sir G. O. Trevelyan Bt., M. P.—I suppose that is correct—Welcombe, Stratford on Avon—however, it doesnt matter as you wont have time to write to me and I'll have to write to you) for a few days. I am casting about for some deadly means of provoking Henry to strike me off the press list, so that I may astonish him by a magnificent notice of the play without having seen it.

The Playgoers Club always want to get me to attend their annual dinner and respond to the toast of The Press. This time they urge that as Sir Henry Irving is going to respond for the drama, I cannot refuse. The prospect of blighting the traitor's oratory is too tempting: I *have accepted,* ha! ha! so let him tremble. My whole speech will not be about "my dear friend, Miss Ellen Terry." That is, unless she buys mercy for him in the meantime by letting me kiss the tip of her little finger.

G. B. S.

CLXXIII: E. T. *to* G. B. S.

[*Jessie M.: Miss Millward, Terriss's leading lady at the Adelphi, who had the terrible shock of witnessing his murder. She was a member of the Lyceum Company for many years, playing among other parts Hero in Much Ado About Nothing in 1882. Ellen Terry's objection to Terriss's nickname "Breezy Bill" is shared by her son Gordon Craig, who writes in his Henry Irving: "They called him 'Breezy Bill' but he was a much deeper, nobler character than that sort of nickname conveys."*]

26 December 1897.
22 Barkston Gardens,
Earls Court, S. W.

Now darling dont be naughty! You *know* I wrote to you all about that Play of Duse's. It was when you first went off for your holiday. By the way I remember now there were at least 3 letters of mine miscarried and I asked you at the time why I had not heard in answer to some of my questions. The D. D. would be best *now* I think with Wyndham who would I should say revel in the part. . . . Poor Willie

Terriss, I'll miss him. That calling him "Breezy Bill" always annoyed me. So vulgar and so very stupid to call him that. Poor Jessie M!

I envy you leaving London for Shakespear land. I've so little to do in Peter, but that boy Laurence wont let me leave the stage for a moment. I'm going to make the best of the situation and take some rest during the run of Peter, and now and again play a few Matinées if Henry will let me, for my friends. You are going to Sir George Trevelyan's? I knew him a little when I was a girl years ago. I fancy he admired my sister Kate very much, as an actress, in those old young days. So you are getting rich? You wont care for that. How about your book? I shall go and see Miss P. T. (some day) and say I asked Mr B. S. if the report that she had a version of the D'Annunzio Play was true. If you worry (or try to worry) Henry, I must end our long and close friendship. He is ill, and what would I not do to better him?

All one's eggs in one basket is a wretched business dont you think? I charge thee Cromwell, fling away *Ambition*. You have none, have you? With some of my precious love all warm towards you.

I am E. T.

CLXXIV: G. B. S. *to* E. T.

[*The pantomime mentioned was The Babes in the Wood at Drury Lane 27 December 1897.—Violet: Violet Vanbrugh, eldest daughter of the late Rev. Prebendary Barnes of Exeter. She married Arthur Bourchier. She and her sister Irene Vanbrugh are still well known to English playgoers. Violet played Anne Boleyn in Irving's production of Henry VIII in 1892, and understudied Ellen Terry as Cordelia in King Lear and as Rosamund in Becket.—Arthur Bourchier produced an adaptation of Divorçons, called The Queen's Proctor, at the Royalty Theatre in November 1896. "Ibsen will have his due." Shaw wrote that month in The Saturday Review, so he noticed Little Eyolf, not The Queen's Proctor.*]

27 December 1897.
29 Fitzroy Square, W.

PITY me, Ellen: I am going to the pantomime. However, it might have been worse. Barrett might have invited me to the Garrick; but happily he didn't; so I shall get off with Drury Lane.

Do you mean to say that Wyndham should play the D's D. himself? It would be impossible: he's too old; and he has not the peculiar fascination. But he would be admirable as the husband: it would suit him to a hair's breadth. Are you quite sure that you are up to date about the

Bourchiers? Five years ago, when Violet was a *seconda donna* at the Lyceum, and he half amateur, half farceur, I should have agreed; but now things are altered. Bourchier is not only a very clever and effective comedian but his physical power and completeness give him a large range: he can play light and heavy, gallant and ridiculous, normal and eccentric. Violet, who has just sent me (and probably you) her portrait on a Xmas card with the very latest Parisian blouse on, has also developed into a personality of the first striking rank. Their adaptation of Divorçons, whatever else it was, was certainly not underplayed: there has been nothing like it since the Kendals in A Scrap of Paper. The woman's part in the D's D. would not suit her; but she could do it without disaster; and there can be no doubt about Bourchier's making a good—even a very imposing—Burgoyne. I put their merits strongly because I know how extraordinarily the landscape changes from five years to five years. That pair will cut a figure, I assure you. And B. is no such bad diplomatist either. Did you appreciate his noble tribute to H. I. in the Morning Post correspondence, which meant: "Good people: you think Sir H. I. is still the colossally rich man of business. You're wrong: he has lost money: he's only a nobly poor artist: hip, hip, hurrah for his fine qualities; and let us hope that the Lyceum is not really on its last legs."? Further, he has slipped in front of all the rest whilst they were explaining to one another what an amateur and booby he was. Keep your eye on that ménage, Ellen: you underrate it. Or am I an ass?

I should like to get the piece on at the Adelphi with Waring in order to secure Jessie's part for her. H. I. scored nobly by standing by her at the funeral: had it been his funeral, Lady Irving would have been in the position of Mrs Terris; and you would have been—probably taking a nice drive through Richmond Park with me, or perhaps with that villain you persuaded me you were going to marry the other day. Jessie must have been consoled a little; for she adores H. I. and always reserved his claims, as an intellectual prince, before Terriss's, greatly to William's indignation; for he knew that Henry was intellectually an impostor, nothing like so hardheaded as himself.

I must break off to catch the post. I go to Welcombe tomorrow afternoon. Dont break off your friendship with Henry on my account: I'll let him alone, under compulsion. What a nasty letter this is, isnt it? No matter: my heart is true to Ellen, and even to Ellen's wicked friends for her sake.

G. B. S.

CLXXV: E. T. *to* G. B. S.

[*The B's: Mr and Mrs Arthur Bourchier (Violet Vanbrugh). Jessie: Miss Millward. Mrs T.: Mrs Terriss. Billy: William Terriss. Boo: Mrs Rumball, who lived with Ellen Terry for many years, looked after her house, and relieved her as far as she could from domestic cares. A faithful and devoted "watch-dog."*]

28 December 1897.
22 Barkston Gardens,
Earls Court, S. W.

WELL, I should try them (the B's) in your play by all means. If they are what you think them the play will get its chance and certainly the actors will get *their* chance with your play. But I note you say Burgoyne! He's quite a side issue with the dazzling Devil alongside. Waring would score. Poor little Jessie. I went to see her the night before the funeral. She seemed so wee and crumpled up. I hope she will get good work. She will need help now.

I daresay Mrs T. was satisfied in getting the Queen's compensation message (again through that poor man H. I. whose whole time could be taken up in doing such trifles by the thousand). I want to get a house a little way out of London and move my family "for good and all" during the next 2 years.

Boo goes every year into Norfolk for two months. She used to alone. Now I have to send some-one with her, and send to fetch her back, and soon I'm sure she will not be able to move at all! So before that comes I should like us to get into fresh air. Edy loves being away from London and so do I, so the plan will suit us all. Do you know of a place? I wrote to poor Billy about it only 3 weeks ago. He spoke of Windsor. I should be obliged to have 2 rooms in London either at a Hotel near the theatre or in some quiet street close by. I went to review the Adelphi yesterday. It appeared to me to be stuffy and not over-clean! Miss P. T. would know. Oh, for some simple clean wooden-furnished Inn, fresh, with *one* luxury, a good clean sweet bed. I've a mind to turn landlady. My house is at least the *cleanest* in London. No velvets and stuffs, only washable cotton. I'm crazy on the subject of clean-and-sweet around me. Edy and I could have 2 beds in one room, 2 latchkeys, one living-room and go out o' doors for food. We should very seldom stay in town the night, only when (as now) rehearsals are going on night and day. Now I'm going for a few days to the Savoy. It's so expensive, but *clean,* and Edy loves it. She comes and goes to me.

Oh, Heavens! What a screed!

Take a hurried New Year's hug and I'll leave you, my Poppet.

Your NELLEN

CLXXVI: G. B. S. *to* E. T.

31 December 1897.
Welcombe,
Stratford on Avon

THIS is how I break my promises to write to you by every post. The moment I get away to the country, there is nothing to stop my work; and it accordingly becomes incessant. This is a gigantic house, with sixteen hall doors, rooms that no man has ever counted, a conservatory like the Crystal Palace, 76 bath rooms, and 1300 miles of corridor, with every door the exact counterpart of every other door, so that we have to crumble bread as we walk, like the child in the fairy story, to find our way back to the eating room. By a violent effort, a corner of the place has been made humanly habitable; and in this corner now dwell Trevelyan junior (our host), the Webbs, the Reeveses (Reeves is Agent General for New Zealand, where he was a shining light of the Fabian Ministry which set our variety of Socialism on foot there), and myself. I correct proofs of the plays, and read up the subject of Peter. When I set aside an hour to write to you, they drag me off to bicycle to Warwick, or to go to Stratford and scatter innumerable sixpences on the relics of the immortal William. I return tomorrow afternoon, having written you only one letter.

I really dont like the notion of your pretending to be Catherine I! You see, she had one talent and one accomplishment. She could get round people; and she could act. Just like you! And she never cared a straw for anybody. I wonder is that like you! When she found she could cure Peter's headaches, and beg off his victims, she set up in the business; and when anybody was condemned to be impaled, or knouted, or beheaded, he or she promptly retained the Empress as intercessor at a handsome fee; so that she made no end of money out of her mercy, the quality of which was carefully strained. It dropped like the gentle dew of a showerbath when you paid her to pull the string. When Peter had her lover chopped up, and took her for a nice drive round the scaffold, she contemplated the spectacle like the Cheshire cat, smiling. When he put the poor fellow's head in a bottle of brandy, and set it on her bedroom mantelpiece, she hung her pads on it, quite unruffled. When Peter died (shouldnt be at all surprised if she poisoned him) she dragged Eudoxia, who had survived two martyrdoms, out of her convent and flung her into a dungeon, a fact which disposes of Laurence's pretty romance—really taken from her conduct towards the Queen of Prussia, whom she wanted to get round. When she was rid of Peter, she made one glorious plunge into unlimited brandy and impropriety, and had such a roaring time of it that she killed herself inside of two years. And now, by the infinite irony of fate, she is to be revived again in the person of my Ellen, and I am to pretend to like it.

I was to have written to you last night; but they made me read The Devil's Disciple instead. The nervous effort of firing off those three acts all in one breath of course undid all my holiday. When I went to bed I dreamt that I had to play an important part with Forbes-Robertson in a drama which I didnt know. It was necessary—I dont know why—that I should bluff it out at all hazards, and improvise my part. Whilst I was remonstrating about it, F. R.'s call came, and he bounded on the stage (a street, with a great tower and a harbor at the end—all real, not scenery) and I had to follow and begin. My first utterance, delivered from the top of the tower to him as he stood below on the quay, made him shriek with laughter; and I was anticipating utter disaster when I noticed that nobody was listening to us, and then the dream changed.

Yes: the curse of London is its dirt. Also its lack of *light*. (The Agent General, snoring on the sofa, is going to wake—yes: there he goes.) My much ridiculed Jaegerism is an attempt at cleanliness and porousness: I want my body to breathe. I have long resigned myself to dust and dirt and squalor in external matters: if seven maids with seven mops swept my den for half a century they would make no impression on it; but I always have the window wide open night and day; I shun cotton and linen and all fibrous fabrics that collect odors, as far as my person is concerned; and I never eat dead—oh, I forgot; you do. Shame! Now I must get back to my work. Choose that new house with a nice gate lodge or gamekeeper's cottage, communicating by a secret passage with the best bedroom. I'll find a tenant for it. Success tomorrow, oh ever dearest, for you and even for him. I cant write; I am too Ellen-hungry.

G. B. S.

CLXXVII: G. B. S. *to* E. T.

[*The reference in the first paragraph is to Shaw's Saturday Review article on Laurence Irving's Peter the Great, produced at the Lyceum on New Year's Day 1898. Shaw reviewed the play from the book. He did not see it per-*

formed until Henry Irving had relinquished the title-part to his son.—In May 1898 Shaw resigned from The Saturday Review and was succeeded by Max Beerbohm. This is also the year he married Miss Payne-Townshend, who can be identified as the secretary referred to in this letter.—Shorter: Clement Shorter, later editor of The Sphere.—Cissy: probably Cecilia (Cissie) Loftus, who was in London at this time giving her famous imitations of actors and actresses at various music-halls.]

3 January 1898.
29 Fitzroy Square, W.

THERE *that's* done. A much better notice, though I say it that shouldnt, than any of those written by the men who saw the play. The son must not be made to suffer for the childishness of the father.

I have had a bad time of it. Duty is duty; and as tickets sometimes come the night before a performance, or even later, I had to come up from Stratford, knowing perfectly well that it was useless, and lose my Sunday in the country. The journey and the change back to the London air upset me: and the escape from seeing Peter turned into Louis XI was a poor consolation for being robbed of my half yearly glimpse of Ellen. I sat up till two writing letters furiously. In the morning I rushed to Adelphi Terrace, and dictated the first half of an article on Peter to my secretary. Then I began to get a headache. It got worse and worse: I had to go to supper at Shorter's (Illustrated London News Editor &c.), where they kept pressing me to eat a steaming frowsy turkey and mince pies. I coudnt eat anything and at last fled. Lord! how I wanted to lie down in the fog and die! By a fearful effort and struggle I postponed my collapse until I was able to collapse into bed, leaving my clothes on the floor. I swooned rather than slept for eleven hours, believing all the time that the blankets were a huge square building of which I was the foundation. This morning the papers were full of pictures of you in breeches, with your heels on the table. My secretary came; and I dictated the second half of the article (you may order Sir Henry Irving's funeral for twelve on Saturday). After lunch came a commission for two days hard work on a review of Webb's book. I rushed off and got the book, in charge of my secretary. At four we got to Adelphi Terrace, where I lay like a log whilst the faithful secretary petted me and rubbed the bicycle gash in my cheek with vaseline in the hope that diligent massage may rub it out and restore my ancient beauty. Then I came home; and the secretary went to the Lyceum, where they had refused her a first night seat, to her great indignation, as she is rightly incredulous as to any impossibilities existing for a person with her income. And now the head-ache and prostration are ending and my vigor is coming back, all the better for a rest.

Did you see the nice things about you in The Morning Post? The critic is Spenser Wilkinson, who writes books and articles about foreign policy and the army and that sort of thing—a man much wider and abler than the average dramatic critic.

By the way, dont, I strictly charge you, say anything to anybody—Laurence or anyone else—about my not having seen Peter, until after the Saturday appears. It is much better for Laurence that he should have the article all to himself. Later on I will buy a seat and tell you all about the performance privately. This is the moment to play up for Laurence, and not for the Lyceum which has had its innings and made its name already. I'm glad you have a light, restful part: it will give you time to write to me. I got your message on Cissy's envelope. Cissy is one of your most promising understudies in my affections. Is she as nice all through as she is on top?

G. B. S.

CLXXVIII: E. T. *to* G. B. S.

5 January 1898.
22 Barkston Gardens,
Earls Court, S. W.

THANK you for troubling to write and tell me, but I quite understood you might have seen the Play in many ways besides the way-o'-me, altho' I told Laurence I was going to send it you. It's very good of Miss P. T. to be pleased with me as C. Do you know I have about 30 lines! My second dress is an outrageous one. I take it Catherine put on all her fine "togs" to call upon the minx beloved by Alexis, even her crown, to go out into the storm. I wear (fur inside) a man's huge coat of skin only, Henry's boots, and a fur cap. To my amusement, nobody has laughed at my enormous hoops! They are outrageous, but I fancy people just think me merely fat! During my *"waits,"* I think I'll go to all the pantomimes!

How ill you seem to have been, and for how very short a time, thanks, I fancy, to Miss T.

The house I shall try to get half an hour from London will be only as big as the Lodge to most big houses.

I've rheumatism in my knee! And my heart is cold, and "I wish I was dead"! No I dont!

I love you a little and no one else (except Edy) even a little!
Where's your book of plays?

NELLEN

CLXXIX: G. B. S. *to* E. T.

5 January 1898.
29 Fitzroy Square, W.

S HUT up your purse, tight, or else give me all your money to keep for you. No secrecy is necessary with regard to Edward Aveling. His exploits as a borrower have grown into a Homeric legend. He has his good points, has Edward: for instance, he does not deny his faiths, and will nail his atheism and socialism to the masthead incorruptibly enough. But he is incorrigible when women or money or the fulfilment of his engagements (especially prepaid ones) are in question. You write to him as follows—"Dear Dr Aveling: You must excuse me; but I know a great many people, among them some of your old friends of the National Secularist Society and the Socialist League, and some of your pupils. Dont ask me for any money. Yours sincerely, Ellen Terry." He will understand. If the application takes the form of a post-dated cheque, dont cash it. If you would like to try a few references, consult Mrs Besant, John Mackinnon Robertson, George Standring, or the spirits of Bradlaugh and William Morris. Or come to see me, and I'll tell you all about him. Just walk into a room where we are all assembled, and say, in a cautious tentative way, "What sort of fellow is Dr Aveling?", and you will bring down the house with a shriek of laughter, and a shout of "How much have you lent him?"

Did you ever see him? He is always at the Lyceum on first nights, at the back of the dress circle. His wife, Karl Marx's youngest daughter, is a clever woman. For some years past he has been behaving well, because Marx's friend Engels left Eleanor £9,000. But the other day he tried the old familiar postdated cheque on Sidney Webb—in vain. And then, I suppose, he tried you. Must I really not tell anyone? If you only knew how utterly your delicacy is wasted! . . .

. . . The worry is all reaction after the parturition of Peter. The best thing for the knee is kissage; for the heart, careful wrapping round by the arms of a rather tall man, with, if possible, a red beard.

The book of plays still creeps through the press. Oh those proofs, those proofs! Imagine going through a play again and again, scanning the commas, and sticking in words to make the printing look decent—to get the rivers of white out of it!

I never stop working now. I get no exercise. My digestion is beginning simply to stop. Oh, when you see me at last, you will be sorry that you did not bite me off and swallow me when I was young and beautiful.

G. B. S.

CLXXX: E. T. *to* G. B. S.

[*Ethel Barrymore played Euphrosyne in Peter the Great; Ben Webster played Kikine. Ellen Terry here mentions a weakness of hers to which some of her colleagues were less indulgent than her loving public*].

10 January 1898.
Lyceum Theatre

I F YOU only had seen how disgracefully I have been behaving, laughing on the stage and AT MYSELF! We were all convulsed, Ethel Barrymore, Mr Webster, myself and the audience!

It was abominable. I wish someone had hissed me, tho' I fear I should have laughed the more!

What you wrote was too splendid. I've not seen Laurence yet. Poor H. is almost voiceless tonight and I fear wont act on Monday. Do send me a wire when you are going to be in front. Please.

I'm nursing two of Ted's babies at home. So I'm happy. A real old hen.

Your

E. T.

CLXXXI: E. T. *to* G. B. S.

[*Laurence Irving's "promise" was broken when the* Empress of Ireland *sank in the St Lawrence in 1914. Like all strong positive characters who have not been on the stage and "through the mill" from childhood (like Ellen Terry, for example) he had great difficulty in subduing himself "like the dyer's hand" when he gave up diplomacy, for which he had been educated, and resolved to become an actor instead, as it was clear that his inherited position in the theatre was much more favorable than his chances at the Foreign Office. He had his father's distinction and perserverance, with the general knowledge and culture his father had missed, but physically he was the son of his Irish mother. His portrait would look perfectly in place in the National Portrait Gallery of Ireland. He was well "in the movement," playing Dr Relling in Ibsen's* Wild Duck, *and the hunter in* When We Dead Awaken, *besides producing* The Pretenders. *He was never mediocre: when he acted badly he acted very badly: when well, so well that his friends hoped he might succeed ultimately to his father's position as head of the theatre in England.*]

209

Laurence Irving's engagement to the irresistibly pretty Ethel Barry-
more, who played Euphrosyne in Peter the Great, did not last long. He mar-
ried an English actress Mabel Hackney who was drowned with him. She
succeeded Ellen Terry as Henry Irving's leading lady in 1903, and after-
wards occupied the same position in her husband's company, 1904–14.]

13 January 1898.
22 Barkston Gardens,
Earls Court, S. W.

THEY told me last night just as I was leaving the theatre that you
had been in front. You unkind wretch! Well, what about my boy
Laurence? I think as an actor, too, he shows every promise. He didnt do
his best last night, for he was thinking of something else than this work.
The young man went and engaged himself the night before to Euphrosyne, after having been refused by Her Highness about half a dozen
times. I'd like to bang them both, although I fear it is through me the
affair has come about.

Did you notice how ill I was last night? If Peter Pater had been there,
I should have stayed in bed at home, but he knows I wont leave whilst
he is away at Brighton. I have an influenza cold just as you described it
when the fit was on you, and I am senseless. Why didn't I see you?
Two of Ted's children are staying with me, and as they arrived with fearful colds I've got one of them with me in my room.

Wont you tell me you'll have a spare hour next week, day or night
(of course any time) and will come up here and meet Laurence who
(before his engagement) asked me again and again to contrive it. Your
approbation makes him simmer!

Your ghastly ill

ELLEN

CLXXXII: G. B. S. *to* E. T.

13 January 1898.
29 Fitzroy Square, W.

WHAT! gobbled up by Barrymore? I give him up: I have wasted my
article. Quite useless to make any appointment to meet him now:
he has other fish to fry. Satty Fairchild wanted me to allow her to send
Barrymore to call on me. I morosely refused, being surfeited with American geniuses; but Ethel took the law into her own hands, and made my
acquaintance summarily one evening at the Haymarket Theatre. Lau-

rence has no sort of business to tie himself up like that: he has entered on a career which means not being grown up until forty and hardly mature then. How does he know what he will like in 1910, except that it will be something very different to what he likes now? No man should marry until he knows what he is going to be. However, let's hope she may turn out a treasure.

Of course his acting was very bad. As author of the piece, he tried to do everything that he wanted Peter to do, instead of, like a cunning old actor, simply picking out what he himself *could* do. Besides, he couldnt do anything. He kept driving at it as hard as he could in a highly commendable way; and there is no doubt that if he sticks at it he will begin to shape soon, and end as a very creditable artist and perhaps something more; but at present Peter is quite beyond him. Even if he had the skill and solidity, he is too young: the notion of his being Alexis' father was absurd on the face of it.

There is something disabling in this weather. I could do nothing this morning. I did not detect anything wrong with you: you seemed in excellent spirits. I was under your nose in the middle front row stall. I sent Miss P. T. to buy the seats: she said they could give her nothing but either back or front row; so, said she, "I chose the front, to give you a good look at your Ellen!"

G. B. S.

CLXXXIII: E. T. *to* G. B. S.

18 January 1898.
22 Barkston Gardens,
Earls Court, S. W.

M^{Y B— B—,} Everyone is ill. Are you well? I have been ghastly this last week, almost insane some hours from neuralgia in the palate! My face felt bulging out! But everything passes. I fortunately thought of that, and laughed. They thought me hysterical from pain!

Is it next Sunday you and Henry speak at the Playgoers' Club? I must go if so. Tell me. Henry is so nice to me lately that I'm convinced he has a new "flame" (he is always nicer then, which I think is to his credit). Tell me of next Sunday and how I'm to set about going.

Your old
E. T.

CLXXXIV: G. B. S. *to* E. T.

For heaven's sake, my dearest darling Ellen, dont tell me such frightful things about yourself. What new and horrible invention is "neuralgia in the palate"?—it goes right down into my entrails. Neuralgia means generally insufficient nourishment, except when it's constitutional, and is an alternative to gout or asthma or fits. Probably you dont take enough bodily exercise to sharpen your assimilative powers. You had better take my arm and let me walk you round the streets for a mile or two every day. Miss P. T. used to have neuralgia a good deal: she now hasnt much of it. When she walked with me she used to stop in five minutes and get palpitations and say I must not walk like an express train. Now she hooks on and steeplechases with me without turning a hair. The Webbs are going away in March for a tour round the world which I cant afford. They want her to go. If she does, she will be away for about a year, just time enough for a new love affair. Would you mind taking me on a short lease—my novelty would last very nearly all the time? You cant think what delightful agony it is to be in love with me: my genius for hurting women is extraordinary; and I always do it with the best intentions.

No, bless you, not next Sunday—not until the 13th February.

Nothing will happen. I hate after-dinner speaking, and will not waste eloquence on a half-drunk dinner party. I will simply fire off any half dozen sentences that occur to me at the moment. Hare will burn the midnight oil for weeks preparing his reply. Henry will call in Austin, Stoker and all the rest of them to prepare an oration full of extensive classical learning and profound philosophy. And the whole speechifying business will be as dull and silly as it can be. Dont dream of coming: you'll be bored and headached to distraction. But if you like, I'll get them to invite you as a guest. I'm sure they'd be delighted. Now to bed.

G. B. S.

CLXXXV: E. T. *to* G. B. S.

[The play referred to must have been Marie Corelli's The Sorrows of Satan. Lewis Waller played Satan.]

[Not dated. Assigned to end of January 1898.]

22 Barkston Gardens,
Earls Court, S. W.

WELL, well. If that wasnt the funniest play we saw together last night! I saw all your, so charmingly disguised, yawns during (and between) the acts. I only saw 2 acts. From a dull dinner party I escaped to a duller play, and nearly plumped into your arms! For I was asked to sit in the front row of the stalls, and declined since I was alone. You have the "youngest" look I ever saw on any animal's face except Fussy's! I should like to go about with you for you are so quiet, with pauses, in your chatter.

That PLAY! The presumption of the whole thing! The bit of the Corsican Brothers! The bit of the Lyceum Faust and Arthur, etc., etc. Now was Waller good? No answer needed.

Yours, my sweet,
E.

CLXXXVI: G. B. S. *to* E. T.

[See note to Letter CLXXXVII for what Shaw meant by "Your Tabers and Rockmans," etc.—A Story of Waterloo by A. Conan Doyle was first produced by Irving in May 1895, and frequently revived. The public did not, like Shaw, think it "silly." His criticism of it in The Saturday Review, headed Mr Irving takes Paregoric, was mainly a comparison of the praise given to Irving for what was to him a very easy feat with the indifference often shown to his really difficult and subtle achievements.—Mr (afterwards Sir Laurence) Alma Tadema designed the scenery and costumes for Tree's production of Julius Cæsar. "The real hero of the revival is Mr Tadema." (G. B. S. in The Saturday Review.)]

29 January 1898

OH ELLEN, Ellen, what a week! nay, a fortnight! Three first nights, two County Council election meetings, four Vestry committees, one Fabian Committee, a pamphlet to write about the Southwark police business (just completed), an adaptation of a novel to make to secure the dramatic rights for an ancient revolutionary comrade (feminine Nihilist), the Julius Cæsar article, and one frightful headache. There's a program for you, with the perpetual proofs of the book omitted. And now, instead of petting me, you bully me for not writing to you. I cant help it: I've even lost the post: but I will bike over to Barkston and drop this in the letterbox. Then I will sit down on the steps and sob: and your

213

skirt will sweep up my tears (beware of rheumatism!) when you come home.

I see that Peter is coming off, and that H. I. is going to fall back on that silly old Story of Waterloo as a first piece to The Bells. This is heaven's vengeance on him for assassinating the Strange Lady. Alma Tadema has struck up Julius Cæsar most magnificently for Tree. Curious chap, Beerbohm! You remember how unparallellellellellelledly I went for his Falstaff, and how Archer wrote a special article in his defence? Well, now he shuts Archer out from his Cæsar first night and makes much of me. Just as huffy as Henry, apparently: and yet he gives Waller and McLeay as big a chance as himself in the production. That's where Tree is dangerous: he surrounds himself with counter-attractions and lets them play him off the stage to their heart's content as long as he takes the money at the doors. Good policy, Ellen: look to it. Your Tabers and Rockmans and Julia Arthurs and Barrymores are all very well; but you dont catch Alexander and Tree and Co depending on them. You want fresh flowers in the basket.

I make myself disagreeable in this fashion because I sometimes have flashes of anxiety about you. A theatre can lose money at such a frightful rate that Henry, who, with all his crafty instinct, has no brains and is as much behind the times now as Pinwell's and Fred Walker's and Mason's pictures are (I always call them the Lyceum school) might quite easily lose all his money. And the next step, naturally, would be to lose all yours as well. I wish you'd give it to Sidney Webb to keep.

I must drop the pen now. Miss P. T. sails with the Webbs on the 23rd March. What about the 24th?

G. B. S.

CLXXXVII: E. T. to G. B. S.

[*This reply to Shaw's criticism of Irving's company, and of his managerial policy, is amplified in Gordon Craig's Henry Irving.—Julia Arthur, a Canadian by birth, began her career in America with Daniel Bandmann. She made her first appearance in England at the Lyceum in 1895. She was a member of Irving's company until 1897.—Robert Taber, also a recruit from the American stage, subsequently went into management in London, and produced Laurence Irving's Bonnie Dundee.—Ray Rockman played Eudoxia in Peter the Great.—Franklin McLeay was at this time at His Majesty's Theatre, playing Cassius in Julius Cæsar.—The allusion in the last paragraph is to Irving's approaching production of The Medicine Man by H. D. Traill and Robert Hichens.—Violet: Violet Vanbrugh (Mrs Arthur*

Bourchier).—Miss Kingston: Gertrude Kingston, a clever comedy actress who played Lady Cicely Waynflete in the revival of Captain Brassbound's Conversion at the Little Theatre in 1912. In 1913 she played Catherine II in Great Catherine, which Shaw wrote specially for her. He had previously induced the Vedrenne-Barker management to offer her the part of Helen of Troy in the Trojan Women of Euripides, which was perhaps her finest achievement.—Alec: Sir George Alexander.]

31 January 1898

O H DEAR, oh dear! I must sit up to write you a line.
First of all thank you for writing altho' you must not do it again when you are so tired. I'm sorry I didnt guess at the reason for your silence.

My dear friend, you should know the receipts at the various Theatres before you question H.'s policy. Our "Tabers, Rockmans, Julia Arthurs and Barrymores" you say are all well enough, but you dont catch Alec or Beerbohm depending on them. Each one of them comes to us for less money than the rest of the Managers would have given them. As for Julia Arthur, Alexander thinks there's none like her!

Do you think *Waller* an inspired or inspiriting actor? Oh Lor' a mussy! Mr McLeay is a trifle better than our Mr Clarence Hague. You think Tree "lets the rest of his company play him off the stage"! I'd like you to see what is written on his heart upon that subject. And then "Tree takes the money at the doors." We thought we didnt do at all well with Sans-Gêne during last season, but we did far far and far away better than any other Theatre in London during that dreadful Jubilee time. To start with, our Theatre holds so much more money. At a benefit of mine I had it at its fullest and got £430. The St James's and Haymarket hold when full about half that sum. By the way I wish people would understand that what is called "a benefit" of some leading person in a theatre is merely part of the business arrangement with the Manager. A matter simply concerning those two persons. I used to give away nearly the whole house to folk who could not afford to see me often act. I have told H. the last 3 years I would not take a benefit. He scarcely said thank you! However I'm soon going to take a benefit and (for the first time) ask my fellow players to act for me, and then I'm going to give the whole lump sum away. Such fun! Peter has brought us the very thinnest audiences.

When you have time I would love to have your advice about what I am to do. I dont want to mention it to anyone; for it would be unfair

215

for everyone to know beforehand about the new play by Traill and Hichens (I'm nearly asleep and am fogged). My part in it is just drivel. In the nineteenth century only a child of fourteen could express herself as I have to. If I'm not in a play at the Lyceum it does a good deal to harm that play. If I play this part it will "harm" me, inasmuch as I shall be simply ridiculous! Violet I think will be in it. Miss Kingston too I fancy. 1 wish I knew what to do. Indeed, indeed I'm not vain, and just thinking of myself in the affair. But I do play such a big slice in the Lyceum Plays with the people and it is so silly of H. not to see this. His part is very long but I dont think good. Dont trouble about me until you have pause.

CLXXXVIII: G. B. S. *to* E. T.

[*The Masqueraders, one of Henry Arthur Jones's most successful plays, was produced at the St James's Theatre in 1894.—The reader should not be misled by the dialectical skill of this letter into assuming that the Lyceum "revolutionized" on the lines suggested by Shaw would necessarily have been a better theatre than the one Irving made of it. It is also a question of opinion whether Ellen Terry was "stupid" in not admiring Lewis Waller's acting. He was a great popular favourite. Girl playgoers formed a society known as the "K. O. W." (Keen-on-Wallerites).*]

3 February 1898.
29 Fitzroy Square, W.

I F I dont write to you I shall die; if I make another stroke with a pen I shall go mad. Oh Ellen, I am the world's pack-horse; and it beats my lean ribs unmercifully.

Listen to me. I know all about those theatres, just as you do. But when I am preaching to you about the effect on the public I take them from the public point of view. From that point of view, Tree owns Her Majesty's Theatre, empties the payboxes into his own pockets, and magnanimously makes as much of Waller as Sir Henry Irving makes of Laurence. I also know that the Lyceum is a larger theatre than the St James's, though the St James's holds much more than half £430 (i. e. £215) if I am not mistaken. (I was told something about the Masqueraders returns which gave me the impression that it holds upwards of £300.) But remember that that largeness of the Lyceum makes the actors look small, and that to produce an impression of as good acting as the Criterion, you would need twice as good actors. Instead of that, you have worse actors—dull people who produce an effect of being repressed and not allowed to act, and Americans who come cheap to get the Lyceum hallmark. Henry is an execrable manager in this way: he takes an intense interest in his productions and rehearsals, but none in his people. The result is that people who can do nothing at the Lyceum suddenly blossom into life when they leave it; whereas Wilson Barrett comes with a horde of novices, not worth thirty shillings a week, and not only makes them play as if they were all geniuses, but sows a big harvest of good feeling towards himself among them. The attraction at the Lyceum begins and ends with H. I. and E. T.: nothing can get over the awful fact that when, after that unlucky first night of Richard, you were both disabled, the company could not draw enough to pay for the gas. Now people get tired of everything; and the younger generation is knocking at the door. And here are you, oh stupid old Ellen, talking of "Mr Bolster Waller," as if the public thought that of him. Waller, ever since he played Hotspur, has never had a reverse until he tried Brutus, which is beyond anybody on the stage. He is *ten* times as good as the very best man you have supporting Henry at the Lyceum; and the public think him thirty times as good, small blame to 'em. He has authority, self-respect, dignity, and often brilliancy: you do not see him dodging about the stage with one eye on "the governor." McLeay, who has nothing yet but intensity and keenness, also plays as if the house belonged to him. If you engaged the pair at the Lyceum, they would probably end by telling Henry bluntly that if he could not arrange his effects without keeping them standing about doing nothing, he must cut them. (Oh G O D: do you remember that tent scene in King Lear, when he kept you waiting in an impossible pose for five minutes between "I will not swear" and "these are my hands"?) He has no idea of the play, no idea of the other people: he is hypnotised with his own effect, and sacrifices everything and everybody else to it. Give him his fair share of a play— force him to concert his business so as to avoid interruptions and waits on the part of the others—and you would revolutionize the Lyceum.

Now why do I say all these nasty things? Because, if you once realize that the sacrifice of the other parts is not a conscious, malicious, jealous, direct act of his, but an inevitable condition of his methods and effects, you will see that you, too, must be sacrificed. That he is not crudely jealous is shewn by the fact that he has no objection to your success in Sans-Gêne and Nance Oldfield, where, since he is not on the stage, your playing does not interfere with his. But the moment he is there, he cannot work out his slow, labored, self-absorbed stage conceptions unless you wait for him and play to him. This is a frightful handicap for you. Increase it by a bad part and the task becomes impossible. If you have a bad part in the Hichens play, and H. a very long one, it will not run much longer than Peter, unless it contains some catching novelty. But I cant advise you unless I see the play.

Oh dear: this letter was to console me; and what a letter it has been! All my wretched tired brains, and my uncomforted heart still aching. And I know so well that this sort of thing makes you hate me!

G. B. S.

CLXXXIX: E. T. *to* G. B. S.

9 February 1898

I ONLY returned from Paris last evening in time for my work, and was too done up to write you a line.

It would be very nice to go *anywhere* with Miss P. T. but I quaver, I fear, I tremble when I'm told there are to be 500 men and probably most of 'em smoking!

No. I've no courage when it comes to the point and I'll drive to Thames Ditton to Teddy and Co. through the delicious Richmond Park on Sunday and not go to the Playgoers' Club. It was dear of you though to trouble for me and I thank you and thank you.

I took Edy to Paris (or rather she took me!), and left her with some nice friends. Leaving London on Saturday, I had a good time on Sunday and Monday in Paris and saw three plays. I send you my tired love, which is a nice restful thing for a man to have.

Your

L. N.

P. S. Isnt it sad poor Laurence I's play comes off so soon? But dont you think he has compensations?

CXC: E. T. *to* G. B. S.

[Ellen Terry's enquiry at the beginning of this letter refers to Mrs Aria, a well-known London journalist whose friendship with Irving began about this date. Her sister Mrs Frankau ("Frank Danby"), a talented novelist, had introduced her casually to Shaw, who was thus enabled to report to Ellen Terry that as far as he could judge from his slight acquaintance she was "a good sort" (see Letter CXCI in which Ellen Terry quotes this testimonial). In her book My Sentimental Self Mrs Aria gives us every reason for thinking Shaw's tribute was well deserved. It is clear that her friend-

218

ship did much to solace Irving's later and less fortunate years. His will,
in which he left all his property to be divided equally between his sons and
Mrs Aria was a brave and simple gesture of gratitude to a woman whose
devotion was quite disinterested.]

18 February 1898

BUT WHO is Mrs A? I only know she is "a journalist" and "a friend" of
H. I.'s. I never set eyes on her and she has no idea I know of her.
(This is fun, and would be better fun, if I knew something about her.)
If you know her personally dont "give away" that I know of her existence.

Are you "a blackmailer," my precious? (This question has nothing
to do with Mrs A.) Someone speaking at my elbow the other day and
hearing me singing your admirabilities, said "G. B. S. is a charming
fellow certainly. Pity he's a blackmailer." (The "charming" was meant
to be ironical.) I was writing in a girl's book at the time, and I set down
"Oh, what a lie!" as a quotation from Peter the Great. But I thought
I would ask you first if you were a blackmailer before I gave the lie direct.
I am annoyed with myself to find how vexed I can be by chatterers. I
must be getting old, tho' I'm only 50 in a few days, and I dont feel a day
older than 200.

Laurence tells me you were entirely delightful on Sunday. I wish
I had heard you. "So rapid in his delivery." I've been quite ill. Because
of not hearing from you. But I dont want to, if you dont want to write.

Ever your E.T.

CXCI: E. T. to G. B. S.

[*"Austin the Terrible": Alfred Austin, Poet Laureate.—The subject of The*
Saturday Review article referred to in the postscript was George Alexander's
production of As You Like It at the St James's, in which Julia Neilson
("J") played Rosalind.]

26 February 1898

"THE entire population of Florence (or Italy) harassing and slaugh-
tering birds" is not a comforting thing to read about just as you
are going to bed! Yet Austin the Terrible writes so from Italy. Can it
be true? I hope Florence, or Italy, will not tar and feather our own pocket
Laureate! Thank you for answering my questions about Mrs A. I'm glad
to hear she is a "good sort" . . .

Please read my dear Laurence's Godefroi and Yolande. Shall I send
you the book? Or perhaps it has been sent you? I wish you could read
my part in the new play, but as it is "an original play," I suppose it must

not be read by outsiders? Get it, if you can, from somebody other than me. I die to have your opinion.

I have been trying to be a vegetarian and am suffering tortures of indigestion!

Arent the days lovely just now with the flicker of golden sunshine? It is the only thing I am feeling any enjoyment in just now.

Your

E. T.

You contrived so well to-day in the Saturday R. to be bitter-sweet. J. never "does herself justice."

CXCII: E. T. *to* G. B. S.

12 March 1898

No, it was not your turn but I joy'd to see the fair Roman hand, the dear fist. Why dont you go off to Rome with Miss P. T. to-day? I wish I could. Arent we Britons slaves?

I cant write to you, cant feel, cant think. I work and work but am ill and hate it all. Edy has been in Paris for a month, enjoying everything. (Her chief companion there has been Richard-Harding Davis.) She has been busy there, making a useful illustrated prompt book of Cyrano de Bergerac for Henry, who paid her £8 for it. She had great fun in the doing it and it will be very useful to Henry. Henry was very naughty about Mr Charrington and the Election, but he is naughty all along the road lately, and I shall have to propose we give each other up.

Edy is now in Manchester. I suppose you know it. I am so glad your book is passed for press. Congratulations.

Cant see. My head is so full of ache. The Merchant of Venice last night drew one of the biggest houses we have ever played to!

Now could I "drink hot blood." (Oh, filthy! no I couldnt.) But oh, I'm tired out. You, half dead, will spring up again, but I shall go whole dead very soon.

Good-bye

Your

E. T.

CXCIII: E. T. *to* G. B. S.

[*"The Page": an illustrated journal published by Gordon Craig. His first woodcuts appeared in it.*]

(S TUPID! I wish you would not write to me as if you thought me as big a donkey as all that! This "Ellen hunger" stuff I've laughed at long enough.) Perhaps Farren's age would tell against him in a new part. Macklin has refused his part in our "mysterious new play," so I dare say he will be eligible for the D's D. I must read up Anderson.

That rascal Edy is a superb story teller, yes, but you must take much salt with the joke she serves up to you. Didnt I send you The Page? Well, well! Yet I despatched nearly one hundred copies, N. E. S. and West.

Now *do* have plenty of rehearsals. Where will the rehearsals take place? Dont trouble to answer this until you want to know something I can tell you. I'm just as much in love with you as ever.

ELLEN

CXCIV: E. T. *to* G. B. S.

[*Fussy was "interred with honour" in the dogs' cemetery, Hyde Park.— Irene: Irene Vanbrugh. Pinero's Trelawny of The Wells in which she played the title-part was produced at the Court Theatre on 20 January 1898. "It has touched me more than anything else Mr Pinero has ever written." (G. B. S. in The Saturday Review.)—Lena: Miss Lena Ashwell.—Farren: William Farren, the third actor of the name. One of his most successful performances was given in The Doctor's Dilemma as Sir Patrick Cullen, the old-fashioned physician.*]

28 March 1898

I T IS not only "that part" my precious which occupies me, but the affairs of all my friends appear to have got into hopeless muddles all together and I'm wanted by all of 'em, and all at the same moment! I never now seem to belong to myself. You are rather intelligent and I leave you the above to untwist.

Waring for the D. D. Well, he will be Waring. Though why should I object; for anyhow I want the play to be presented.

Yes, Lena is the best I think for the woman—(you and I seldom agree about a "cast.") Farren would be very good for Anderson. A difficult part.

I saw Irene as Rose Trelawny last night and thought she was quite admirable. A young girl like that to study gradation as she has done in this part is now-a-days singular.

The Webbs and Miss P. T. away! That's good for them, and for you all. Thanks, Edy is quite clear as to any "rights," and all rights of her own. She would drive me mad, if *anyone* could, for I'm always after, in her trail, clearing up for her and I never seem to be able to finish! However, a labour of love should be pleasant labour, and one day I will rest I suppose, for Fussy always struck me as being as anxious about his master as I am about my child, and *he* is resting now. (In Hyde Park if you please, as a swell dog!)

Now *you* shall rest from me, my patient precious. Let me know when the rehearsals for the D. D. begin, and *where,* for go in now and again to watch them, I must. In the shrouded front of the house no-one would see me, and I should love it so.

Your ELLEN

I have received Cyranos by the gross! Never was a Play so much translated. I think W. S. Gilbert could do it best. But best of all would be—! (Guess!)

CXCV: E. T. *to* G. B. S.

[*Dorothy Irving: Dorothea Baird, who married H. B. Irving, Henry Irving's elder son. She made her first hit as Trilby.—"A Hanbury": there were two Hanburys, Lily and Hilda. Lily was a dark beauty of the type which appeals to the Jewish taste, then as now very influential in the London theatre, and seldom appreciative of distinctively British types.—The "new play" in rehearsal at the Lyceum was The Medicine Man, the last Lyceum production Shaw criticized in The Saturday Review. It was Irving's last great mistake; and Shaw rubbed it in mercilessly. He wrote of Ellen Terry's performance (4 May 1898): "She put forth all her enchantments and so beglamoured the play act by act that she forced the audience to accept Sylvia as a witching and lovely creation of high literary drama. The very anguish the effort caused her heightened the effect."*]

9 April 1898

WHY, my sweetheart, you surely cant think I can afford a holiday amongst my children just now! No. They have gone to Southwold and I am here with one friend and 2 servants, having taken the cottage for a month. I fear though when I go back to rehearsals on Tuesday it will be difficult to get back here any more! But I *am* enjoying these few days spite of this detestable Sylvia (my part in the new play). Now just attend to me. If you can spare the time to read it, I shall send you the play right or wrong, and get you to read it for me as my adviser. For I dont see how to get through with it, try my hardest. Dorothy

Irving should do it, or Marion my sister (who would play it sincerely) or Mary Moore. I ask you not to speak of this to anyone.

If this thing is a success I believe I'll give it all up, sell my possessions, try to get back some of the money I've lent, and live on £3 per week as I did for some number of years in the days gone by with Edward. Of course your D's-D should be out in May. Then it could run until the end of July. Would that suit you? That Essie surely should be played by a little wan, slight, pale thing who could be caught up in the arms of Dick. Did you say a Hanbury! Do, *do* let me read your play again. I have no copy of it, remember.

Will you glance over my play for me? or cant you for lack of time? Much love to you, my precious, from your E. T.

There is quite a proper-sized house at Hampton Court I perhaps may take and give up Barkston G.

CXCVI: E. T. *to* G. B. S.

11 April 1898

M<small>Y DEAR</small>, I'm sending you a copy of this month's The Page. Will you read Edy's (first) lines, To Robin (Ted's boy of 2½ years) I think they are good, very, especially the third st nza. It is a *word picture* of the queer little boy. I'm Edy's Mother and I so fear I dont know the people I adore. Tell me, are the lines good? You always can tell me the truth. Edy is back for a week in London so I go back tomorrow. I'm much better for my few days' rest here (Thames Ditton) Edy wants to go to South Africa with Mrs Potter. I *do* wish someone would hasten and offer her (Edy) a *London* engagement. It is *so* bad for her to be far from me for a long time. Commend her to someone in London if you love me a scrap.

Your E. T.

CXCVII: E. T. *to* G. B. S.

13 April 1898

[*Lily: Lily Hanbury.*]

I<small>DONT</small> often cry, now-a-days, quietly and softly like this, but your letter touched me and broke me up. Thank you for it. I believe you are quite right all through. As to Edy becoming an actress, I feel sure she can become something better than the best actress in the world. The difference between Edy in Manchester and Edy in Africa (oh, my heart is in my boots as I realize it) is this. If she is in any real difficulty she always sends to me, or comes to me, and we pick up her ends together. But when she is in Africa! Oh Lord, whom will she go to? And if she is ill too, she gets better quicker with me than with anybody. It's not jealous thought, all this. (I'm "made that way," with no inside Hell) and if someone would go to her and forgetting self for ever so short a time (as I'm able to do, just because I love her) then she would be healed, but there is not very much love wasting about, and folk like Edy dont get it just at the right moment. However, I know I am too anxious. I shall let her go. She is only sorry to leave me; else she delights in going. I wish I were going with her. You are most dear and kind to decide me for myself. Thank you and thank you for all your trouble. I think I'll get out of this big house, and get rid of most of my possessions. When you hear of an old house (of a fair modest size, just as they used to build houses) tell me of it and I'll take it, if it is out of the dust of London about 15 miles.

Do you think Theatre Managers think about, or dread "Spies"? There appears to me to be so much light on everybody's life in a theatre now-a-days that there's nothing left unknown! I'm afraid you dont mean it about my Winchelsea cottage? But the key is yours, and every inch of the place yours, if you care to go to it. All the fruit trees are in blossom now I know, and the wee place is wonderland for the next month. Also Ted's cottage (mine for a month) is yours. Now I *do* think you would find *that* scrap of a place quite practical for your present use. Anyhow wheel down one day and go in, and over it. Do, Do! No one is there, and the enclosed card will get you the key to open the cottage. I am quite set up by my few days' rest in the fresh air and the quiet. I wish you would go at once. You'd get quite well. Anyhow, go and see it some fine afternoon or morning and give the key back to Mrs. Hopson the caretaker. (I wonder have you read me as far as this?) Lily is beautiful and sweet and kind I should think but I tell her she is silly to make such faces. The making faces is not an accident with our young actresses. It is because they are "pretending" all the while, the silly silly things.

Your "first kiss of spring," for me? Thank you, sweetheart. I will take it gratefully, on paper: it comforts me— like the Cocoa! Thank you for making me soft enough to cry.

Your loving

E. T.

CXCVIII: E. T. *to* G. B. S.

[*This letter seems to refer to an article by William Archer on Gilbert and Shaw.—The "big book": Plays Pleasant and Unpleasant first published this year.—The "absurd part" Irving was rehearsing was that of Tregenna (a doctor with hypnotic powers) in The Medicine Man.*]

23 April 1898

"**A** PSYCHOLOGICAL woman tamer!"

You and Gilbert put together!

That's odd. I dont understand that clever Gilbert's fun. When it appears in print it seems to me to have been made below somewhere, fashioned with great perplexity, in agony and bloody sweat, a copy taken, carefully punctuated, and at last sent up a little chilled, and chilling!

Your fun comes spouting out, "all alive oh." All sparkle. Young, strong. It catches hold of one, shakes one, wakes one! And however devilish you may choose to try to appear, in the end you are all heavenly! I knew of all your pains before your big book came out, but as I read (each night) the result appears to me MIGHTY, and effortless. I wish I were as clever as Archer. I grudge his being able to write of you, although Gilbert and Shaw—!

It "lunatics" me to watch Henry at these rehearsals. Hours and hours of loving care over this twaddle! He just *adores* his absurd part.

Are you well my precious? Cant get my words into my memory!

Your old sweetheart.

CXCIX: E. T. *to* G. B. S.

[*"You have hurt your foot." This proved serious. Shaw had been overworking for so long that a breakdown had become inevitable. Its first effect was the development of a trifling injury caused by a too tightly laced shoe into an abscess with necrosis of the bone, involving two operations. He was on crutches for eighteen months.—The "Kate" mentioned is Kate Terry (Mrs Arthur Lewis), who in April 1898 made her re-appearance on the stage which she had left in 1867 to be married. Writing of her performance in The Master (by Stuart Ogilvie) Shaw says: "She apparently began, in point of skill and practice, just where she had left off years ago, without a trace of rust."—"Julia" had long passed out of Shaw's life, but Ellen Terry, to whom she was only a name dropped once in a letter, did not know this.*]

NEVERTHELESS "I wish I were as clever as Archer." You have hurt your foot! Oh, my sweetheart, I'm sorry. How the —why the—what the—? (By the way please dont let Julia see the rubbish I talk to you. I dont mind Miss P. T. much!)

Farewell now. I too must go to Kate. Poor dear old Kate! I'll hold a wager she has stopped exactly where she left off 30 years ago! Lord! it was conventional, it was artificial, but she looked so sweet in those days. She doubts nothing, but I fear her throat, and some other things. Why, I shall see you tonight! Perhaps go forward and offer you my arm! I'd love to!

Your

E. T.

CC: E. T. *to* G. B. S.

[*Mabel: Mabel Terry-Lewis, Kate Terry's daughter. She made her stage debut in* A Pair of Spectacles *in 1895, but had played in only one other London production when she appeared with her mother and John Hare in* The Master. *Shaw, in his notice of the play in* The Saturday Review, *says: "She played between her mother and Mr. Hare without being technically outclassed. . . . She has walked on to the stage with a knowledge of her business, and a delicacy in its execution, to which most of our younger leading ladies seem no nearer than when they first blundered on the boards in a maze of millinery and professional ignorance." She has since had a very successful career, interrupted for a time by her marriage in 1904. She played Gloria Clandon in the first performance of* You Never Can Tell.]

25 April 1898

WHAT a play! "Same old game"! Stupid, vulgar, stupid! I *couldnt* believe it was Kate! No. Mabel was Kate. And Kate was strange to me! And I could scarcely bear it all. I was in a box just above dear you; kept back and out of sight until, not finding you anywhere just at the end of the 3rd Act I leaned over for a moment, and a few of my pit admirers catching sight of me began to make noises so I bobbed back again, but I did see you, DUCK! I do want to know how you are. I'm afraid about that foot. Do tell Miss P. T. to come back and look after it, or somebody. (Your Mother probably would be best of all.) Now dont neglect it. I do wish I knew what the Doctor says about it. What Doctor saw it? Tell me. Goodbye, you pathetic old thing.

E. T.

CCI: G. B. S. *to* E. T.

[*An article appeared in The Saturday Review on 14 May under the title
G. B. S. Vivisected which explains what was wrong with the "patient": "A
few weeks ago one of my feet, which had borne me without complaining for
forty years, struck work. . . . After The Medicine Man at the Lyceum, the
foot got into such a condition that it literally had to be looked into." (See
note to Letter CXCIX.)*]

15 May 1898.
29 Fitzroy Square, W.

PATIENT much worse, in consequence of repeated and bitter disappointments after each postal delivery. Fatal results expected if nothing arrives to-morrow.

Ten letters written and four visitors received; so there has been no sparing. Square full of pretty bonnets, tears, flowers and fruit.

"But what are vernal joys to me?
Where thou art not, no spring can be."

G. B. S.

CCII: E. T. *to* G. B. S.

17 May 1898

TO RECEIVE four visitors and write ten letters is enough to kill any man, but of course *you* survive for, as I knew all along, you never were a man. Dearest silly-billy, I feel sure you are getting better, but I daresay you'll upset the apple cart by such behaviour. I shall not add to the tears you get, nor to the fruit and flowers. Yes! if you get buttercups and daisies (or a Willow Garland) *they* will be from me!

I'll write you a few lines if you promise to give me nothing back. Exert yourself to write to the other "nine hundred" but make me a speciality, please. Your

ELLEN

CCIII: E. T. *to* G. B. S.

[*Bernard Shaw and Charlotte Frances Payne-Townshend were married on
1 June 1898.*]

1 June 1898

How splendid! What intrepidity to make such a courageous bid for happiness. Into it you both go! Eyes wide open!

An example to the world, and may all the gods have you in their keeping.

ELLEN TERRY

CCIV: E. T. *to* G. B. S.

22 June 1898.
22 Barkston Gardens,
Earls Court, S. W.

DEAR MR G. B. S.,

A RENT you *naughty* to give so much anxiety to your friends? I cant speak of it and I've no scrap of news which could possibly interest you, and I'm sorry, since I'm told you kindly said you would like to hear from me. Last Sunday and the Sunday before that, Edy and I were to have gone to Witley. That's close by where you are now staying, isnt it? But I was too tired, and Edy after travelling all around chose to stay with me. I fancy if I had come upon you unawares and seen you with crutches (YOU!) the tears that never will come would have escaped at last and I should have felt better. Surrey isnt much of a place as regards water, I remember. Always wanted it to complete the view!

London is dusty, and London is dull, but *you* are in heaven, in the open, and on a hill. I would change with you spite of the crutches! However, Friday 1st July I finish at my workshop, and Saturday the 2nd July I start for Boulogne with Edy for a few days AIR!

Get well, get well.

Yours ever,

ELLEN TERRY

And Burne-Jones is dead.

CCV: E. T. *to* G. B. S.

[*Ellen Terry was rehearsing for a tour of the Provinces with Frank Cooper. She played Desdemona in Othello and Pauline in The Lady of Lyons on this tour. It has been said that this was a new departure, but in the early days of her partnership with Irving, she toured the Provinces with Charles Kelly (Charles Wardell, her second husband). Still, there is a sentence in her next letter (CCVI) which suggests that she is not happy about her position at the Lyceum.*]

12 August 1898

"Sing all a green willow must be my garland
Sing willow willow willow."

W RAPPED up in my part you see of course! But I'm sorry, sorry about your foot. Another operation? Horrible! I'm sorry. No, I'm not "in difficulties" if you mean about money. I've plenty for others, if they want it. They *dont* (not excessively). I'm tired, not ill. "The cure" nearly killed me (at Harrogate) but I'm recovering from the cure.

Bless you and those you love.

ELLEN

But I dont want to write to you.

CCVI: E. T. *to* G. B. S.

20 August 1898.
22 Barkston Gardens,
Earls Court, S. W.

BERNARD,

I THANK you for your letter and advice regarding Othello. The only reason for my doing it is that I've nothing in the way of any interesting part to look forward to, for the next three years (which will I suppose see the end of me) and these two, Desdemona and Pauline, are easy, as I've done them before.

Nothing "serious" has happened. I am not in difficulties, and you are a kind creature to be a wee bit anxious on my account.

I'm grieved to think of you as still disabled, but you would never have taken a proper holiday unless you had been brought low, and so I see your lucky fate in all these accidents and can almost congratulate Charlotte upon the aid she has received from Providence in trying to take care of you.

I send much love to you both always.

E. T.

Henry in hurting his poor knee, was saved from a frightful breakdown. The enforced rest was submitted to by the patient and philosophical gentleman.

CCVII: E. T. *to* G. B. S.

[*The reader will find answers to the questions Ellen Terry asks about* You Never Can Tell *in the note to Letter CXVIII.*]

6 November 1898.
Liverpool

WILL you tell me why Bernard Shaw's play You Never Can Tell was rehearsed and then "left"?

Whilst Henry remains so ill something must be done. Amongst the plays we have by us there is none with any particular part for me in it, which under present circumstances is rather unfortunate. Nothing can be written in the short time we have before us. You know Cyril Maude I fancy. Would *he* say Shaw was an "impossible man" to do business with, I wonder? Why was that Play half begun and not well done?! That puzzles me. If he (M) would tell me, of course Shaw should never know the telling! Where is the Cleopatra Play? Is that settled on Mrs Campbell? Something must be done and amongst other things in my head and heart there is Bernard and his Plays. Ask your wife to be sweet to me and to write instead of you, or the sight of the well known handwriting will induce me to write again, and it's oh, oh, oh, I've no time to call my own. It all belongs to the sick man in Glasgow.

But I should like to know:—

i. About Cyril Maude, his conduct *in re* your Play.
ii. About Cleopatra.
iii. About you and yours.
iv. ⸻

I want to know nothing more.

E. T.

I hope the dear arms and legs and things are intact.

CCVIII: E. T. *to* G. B. S.

18 November 1898.
The Grand Hotel,
Manchester

I DONT think you are serious about your "perhaps losing a toe"! A ghastly joke anyhow and I hope you may keep all ten until the end of the book. By the same post your letter came by I oddly enough heard news of a friend of mine losing hers! But it's the second toe she has chopped off, the poor child. She seems getting used to it! Affairs are shaping to no shape. Thank you for your suggestions, altho' all the Plays you mentioned had occurred to me, especially a very pretty production of She Stoops to Conquer. The Ale house, the Settles, the quiet old fustiness, the pretty quaintness, have always been attractive to me. Meanwhile I'm laid up in bed the last fortnight just blooming on the stage for 3 hours daily and withering all the rest of the time. However I venture out on Sunday if it is a pretty day. How fine that you have a nice new house at Haslemere. May Charlotte and Bernard find peace within its doors.

Many thanks for your letter. Henry slowly, surely makes progress towards normal naughtiness.

I was far too ill to travel to Glasgow as I had intended last Sunday.

You see I must keep on! We have very good houses here. At Bradford it was a dreadful business.

Blessings on you and yours.

Yours always the same,

E. T.

CCIX: E. T. *to* G. B. S.

[*The "work" Ellen Terry began on the 30th of this January was the provincial tour with Frank Cooper. She returned to the Lyceum for Irving's production of Robespierre in April.*]

15 January 1899

WHERE is the Play? I do want something to read. I'm going out to a dinner party this evening because I have nothing to read. I begin (as if I werent always working!) *work* again on the 30th. Nothing new in the way of Plays. Horrid, but I thought it best to jog along awhile and pay my bills until I saw light ahead, something settled. For if one *jogs* one *pays* and if one *pays* one may be able to flash out and do something in a little while. And so I am working all the while.

[*Here follows a list of the places to be visited during her tour*]

Then further afield after Easter if I'm not wanted for Robespierre by then. (Such a part for me!) If H. were not in the dumps just now I'd "see him further" before I'd do it! It is reported that a subscription was gotten up to send Henry down to Bournemouth! Not quite so bad as that. (I'm so cold I cant even hold my pen. *Inward* cold.) I hope you and your wife are peaceful and busy and that Mr and Mrs Webb were satisfied with their travels and that you will send Cleopatra and Cæsar along this minute. Not a good enough part for Mrs P. C.?

E. T.

CCX: E. T. *to* G. B. S.

[*Edith Craig made all the dresses for the Lyceum production of Robespierre.*]

THERE's nothing left of me to "attend to you"! I'm dead. A dulled thing from keeping on, on, on, at work when a holiday (if only for a week) is necessary. If only I could lose my voice, or some slight and manifest ill come to me to lay me up in bed. (Anyone could play my part) I do go to your part of the world on Sunday, but not to you. Some friends have a dear cottage at Witley and Edy and I were going last Sunday but found ourselves so dead beat we put off our visit until next Sunday week.

Yes, my dear old Kate would playact again if only they'd offer her an engagement. She is rather high priced. I'll try to see her today and give her a bit of "sound advice." Her "return to the stage" is "serious" enough, for she says nobody wants her!

You Dear I'm glad you are being taken care of, and that that pathetic foot of yours is better.

My love is all over the house you are living in.

E. T.

Edy's work (crowds of dresses at nothing a piece and all excellent) turned out splendidly on Saturday. She is a tremendous organiser, and a first-rate worker. She's a duck!

CCXI: G. B. S. to E. T.

[Hermann Vezin played Dr Primrose in the revival of Olivia at the Lyceum in January 1897. His Vicar was in Shaw's opinion more credible and Goldsmithian, more of a vicar and less of a prince of the church, than Irving's.—Alma Murray: (see note to Letter CXLI).—Eleanor Calhoun: a gorgeous Southern American brunette who achieved considerable success on the London stage in the nineties. She married a foreign Prince and crusaded with him on behalf of some new religion.—Yorke Stephens played Bluntschli in the first performance of Arms and the Man and Valentine in the first performance of You Never Can Tell.—Kate Phillips, a very finished broad comedian of the 19th century manner, played Cerisette in The Dead Heart at the Lyceum in 1889, and appeared there frequently until 1894. She applied the old method with success to the part of Gina in The Wild Duck.— Marion Terry took up the part of Audrie Lesdon in Henry Arthur Jones's play Michael and His Lost Angel when Mrs Patrick Campbell, for whom the author had written it, relinquished it just before the date announced for the production (1896).—Carr: J. Comyns Carr.—Ugo Biondi: a "quick-change" music-hall artist.—Tod Sloan: the American jockey who intro-

20 April 1899.
Blen-Cathra, Hindhead,
Haslemere

IF THOU canst come to Witley, Ellen, thou canst come to Hindhead and to me: 't is but five miles further. Sidney Webb is coming on Saturday: otherwise I would say come next Sunday and bring Edy; but as we have only two spare beds, Edy would have to sleep with Webb or I with you. I should prefer the latter arrangement; but I feel bound to offer you the alternative of coming alone, or coming with Edy some other Sunday, or letting us send a trap to Witley to bring you both to lunch or tea next Sunday week, or, in short, anything you please. If you go anyotherwhither, you will be made to talk and flash and coruscate and tire yourself. Here I will do the talking, and you can do just as you like—stay in bed all the time if you prefer it. I know what rest means: most other people, never having worked, dont.

As to Kate, she will have to face the steady prejudice against people who can act, and who are not voluptuous Jewesses. But there is a great want of somebody to play matronly parts. They used to tell me that Rose Leclerq's terms were "frightfully stiff," and as she got them readily enough (whatever they were—I dont know the figure) as soon as she got to be the "fashionable exponent" of such parts, I should imagine that if Kate made one or two appearances in that line she would be able thereafter to get more than anybody else would for it. And after all, she will not have to climb down in point of terms as Lily Hanbury (for instance) would if she left the stage and came back to it to play matrons; for when Kate was a leading lady salaries did not run to modern figures. Imagine Charles Kean's or Fechter's face if she had asked £100 a week and 2 per cent, which somebody told me was Mrs Pat's living wage in the heyday of her Tanqueradiance! If she becomes the indispensable *grande dame* of the modern fashionable play, she will surely be able to stand out for £25 or £30 a week by dint of reckless dressing and diamonding, and make a greater compliment of taking it than she used to make of playing lead for £20. But she oughtnt to begin by asking £30 or even £25. I dare not try to remember what Mrs Calvert, who is a stupendous comedian, played for in Arms and the Man in order to get her foot in. However, I really talk at random about these things: I know very little about them,

233

except that £5 a week and constant work would be better for 99% of the profession than the present high salaries and scarce engagements. Look at all the very capable, willing, experienced, fairly attractive people there are about: Hermann Vezin, Alma Murray, Eleanor Calhoun, Yorke Stephens, Kate Phillips, etc., etc., etc. In the course of my four years of dramatic criticism, I saw them about twice, except Kate Phillips, whom I saw perhaps four or five times. Marion, a tolerably familiar figure whilst Carr was at the Comedy, practically vanished afterwards, except for chancing to get Henry Arthur Jones out of his scrape with Mrs Pat. Ask them their salaries. £20 a week *and upwards*. Ask them their incomes! Sometimes it must have been under £100 a year as far as London was their market. And I, meanwhile, glad to do far more difficult and exhausting work in the very front rank of my profession for £6 a week (my salary on the Saturday). But my £6 a week meant £312 a year. I do not want to grind down salaries: I always say "Take as big a salary as you can get; but dont confuse asking for a salary with getting it." Half the mischief lies in their ridiculous and ignorant sense of dignity. They will not take less than So and So—as if you were to say "I will not take less than Ugo Biondi or Tod Sloan." Good Lord, when I think of the German actresses and prima donnas, with their three-pound-ten costumes, and their provincial little salaries and their pensions to look forward to. I wonder our unfortunate people have not the sense to envy them. A German actress will make herself as ugly as Satan for the sake of the play, or as dowdy, or as old. Dare any English actress to do such a thing? She is always hanging on by her eyebrows, whereas the German is comfortably seated in a solid, permanent, broadbottomed engagement. The moral of all this which you have heard pretty often, is that Kate should try to ascertain what she is commercially worth instead of insisting on what her dignity demands. That silly play at the Globe was worse than useless to her: anybody else would have done as well. Mrs Clandon is better than that, at all events.

Now shall I tell you how to get a rest at the theatre, drive all worry from your brain, and be perfectly light of heart and happy, though in bodily agony. Sprain your ankle. I did it again on Monday—for the third time—frightfully—the bad foot; and I can guarantee the effect. I have been immoveable ever since. The pain has stopped now; but the foot looks perfectly AWFUL.

Henry Arthur Jones is coming on Saturday for half the day. Wont

234

you be persuaded to let Edy play your part that night (a splendid chance for her) and come from Saturday to Monday?

Finally will you do an act of charity to a depressed sick woman, and send Cæsar and Cleopatra off to

Lady Grey

Falloden

Chathill

Northumberland.

She has been hard hit by influenza and will only consent to live on condition of having one of my plays to read.

Ever blessed and dearest; the longer one lives, the more one values you.

CCXII: G. B. S. *to* E. T.

[*Max: Max Beerbohm, who had succeeded Shaw as dramatic critic of The Saturday Review.—Tallien: the part Laurence Irving played in Robespierre.—Miss Jeff: Maud Jeffries, Wilson Barrett's leading lady for many years. She married in 1904, and retired from the stage in 1906.— Mansfield's refusal to play Cæsar provoked Shaw's retort: "Farewell, Pompey" and ended their relation as actor and author.*]

30 April 1899.

Blen-Cathra, Hindhead,

Haslemere, Surrey

MISS TERRY,

I T IS extremely ill natured of you not to write to me.

Did you send C & C to Lady Grey?

Forbes-Robertson has given up Cæsar. "Cant run the risk of such a heavy production." Is going on tour next Sept. instead of opening a new theatre—wants the last act of the Devil's Disciple altered into an English victory. I have cut him off without a shilling.

By the way, is there any truth in what Max says about Laurence's Tallien? Laurence would make rather a good Devil's Disciple, wouldnt he?

What's to be done with Cæsar now? You and H. I. or Wilson Barrett and Miss Jeff? Mansfield funks it also and wants another D's D; so the American rights are available.

Glad you have such a good day for Witley, though you *are* too uppish to notice my entreaties for one little glimpse of you.

G. B. S.

I have a book called Actors of the Century, with a lot of portraits, especially one of you dated about 1824 (?) with your hair like this.* I suppose you've seen it. G. B. S.

CCXIII: E. T. *to* G. B. S.

[*"The Play": Captain Brassbound's Conversion. Shaw's first title for it was The Witch of Atlas (see Letter CCXIV).*]

31 May 1899.
Lyceum Theatre

I AM all attention "Bernie."

1. Will you send me the first act of "the Play"? (*What* Play? if you mean a Play for me all depends upon whether I like it, or dont like it. I'm pretty nearly sure to, but——!)

2. H. I. I let him read your C & C. He will never play anything of yours. I feel sure of that now. For he could have done *wonder*s with that Play if he had done it. (There was no need for him to be hampered with me as Cleopatra, for I took unquestioningly your reply to my question about the part, altho' I dont believe the public would have thought with you. That's not my *vanity,* not a bit of it.)

3. Well Henry will never produce a play by you. In America we only do Robespierre, Merchant of Venice and The Bells. I am engaged to go to America and go I will, *must!* It's a pity, but—

4. When I come back I shall probably be *quite* a year younger, and if H. I. gives me only half a fair good part, I shall play it, but if a part is offered me like the kind of thing I did (or didnt!) in Peter the Great, Medicine Man, or Robespierre I shall "refuse to act" (for the first time in my life) and give it all up and come and settle quietly in a place like this (Laleham) and perhaps act sometimes, on occasions when I could fit in better than another. I should never say good-bye. Just leave off.

5. I am not likely to act with "Mr" Cooper or any other particular "Mr."

6. I would like very much to hear that the poor dear foot is better, the whole person of "G. B. S.," and that Mrs "G. B. S." is therefore better also.

Attention, dear Bernie. Send along that finished first Act, please, so I may have an interest in it as it develops—E. T.

* A rough sketch in the original letter.

CCXIV: G. B. S. *to* E. T.

[Nelly Farren was the star of the burlesques at the old Gaiety in the eighties.
Her benefit took place at Drury Lane in 1896. The programme included
the "Mad scene" from Hamlet. This was Ellen Terry's last appearance as
Ophelia. She writes in The Story of My Life: "When I played the mad
scene for Nelly Farren's benefit, and took farewell of the part for ever, I
was just damnable!*" Yet Gordon Craig dedicates a number of The Page,*
published shortly afterwards, to "The Divine Ophelia of Drury Lane."—
The allusion to Wilson Barrett is not to be taken seriously. He was anath-
ema at the Lyceum, and a threat to offer him a play was one of Shaw's
stock jokes.]

1 June 1899.
Blen-Cathra, Hindhead,
Haslemere

I T IS useless for you to attempt to assert yourself against ME. It is true
that all depends on whether you like the play; but as it depends on
me whether you will like it or not, that does not advance you an inch.

It may be that H. I. will never play anything of mine. It is quite
certain that, except through you, he will never get the chance. In sub-
mitting like a lamb to the necessity of tolerating him in your play, I have
made a sacrifice of the most heroic kind. But the play will be quite
practicable without him.

I quite endorse the trip to America: it did you ever so much good
before. But the point is, do you seriously propose to go back there without H. I. on your own account? As I take it from your letter that you
dont, I may let Mansfield have the Witch of Atlas (provisional title, as
it represents you travelling in the Atlas mountains) if he wants it.

But now comes the difficult part of the business. If H. I. wont produce
the play, you must either produce it yourself with Somebody (Cooper
or another) as the Brigand of the Atlas, or else it must be produced by
Wilson Barrett with you as his leading lady. If you produce it yourself,
it mustnt be with your own money: I darent run the risk of ruining you
and reducing you to taking a Nelly Farren benefit. A transfer to
another management would not be practicable, as you would find when
you came to the point: the public couldnt bear it. A Lyceum season during
H. I.'s absence would be the only practicable alternative; and I have my
doubts as to whether that would prove very practicable either. The horrible truth is that unless H. I. produces the play, you will find an overwhelming weight of convenience and comfort on the side of reading

237

the play for your private amusement and letting it alone as far as acting it is concerned. Then I shall have to fall back on Mrs Kendal, who is the only other person who could touch the part. You see I see everything ten miles ahead. Most people do not see a barricade until they knock against it. I, being very clever, see it before I take the turning.

I really dont doubt that you are right about Cleopatra. With a line or two altered, and the third act struck bodily out (because it makes the play too long), and my brains in H. I.'s head, the public would take it with rapture. None the less, I could not honestly have said anything but what I did say. Besides, how do I know how old you look? Do you suppose I can tell your appearance from your handwriting? And then, I dont want you to do Cleopatra. She is an animal—a bad lot. Yours is a beneficent personality.

Cant send the first act in its present state. It's neither separable nor readable.

I can walk three miles now without crutches. Where is Laleham? May I come and see you there? I might *read* you the first act.

G. B. S.

CCXV: E. T. *to* G. B. S.

[The straits of the Lyceum were public by this time. In 1898 the theatre over which Henry Irving had ruled as absolute monarch had been turned into the Lyceum Limited Liability Company. This step only precipitated the end by making it more difficult for Irving to obtain credit. He finally showed his sense of what it had done for him by putting his own shares in the fire.]

24 June 1899

I DONT think I like you. Yes I do, but you are just "a silly-billy." Satty wrote you a line for me at the Theatre last night. Am I not to see your newest Play? You see, I go away a-touring very soon, and am meanwhile very busy preparing for it with an entirely new (entirely "cheap and nasty") Company. And *I'm not* dead yet but if the weather turns hot again, that will finish me! So let me see something of the Play, rough and anyhow, before I die.

ELEANORA ALICIA

Henry has promised me something good on my return to London "if he can possibly contrive it," because I told him after America I would rather not act unless there was something good. You see it's "a *Company*" now, at the Lyceum, not H. I.

238

CCXVI: E. T. *to* G. B. S.

[*The Witch of Atlas: Captain Brassbound's Conversion (see Letter CCXIV).*]

27 June 1899

WE GO on playing "as per contract" for a hundred performances at the Lyceum, and that will bring us to about the first week in August. Then I have a holiday! (Praise the gods!) and begin play-acting again in the Provinces on September 11th until Friday 9th October. The next day (Saturday) we start for America, and shall be away until the middle of March.

However, I do want to see the first Act of The Witch of Atlas, when it is decipherable. I wont send any more boring notes about it. Only please remember

ELLEN

Satty is in Westminster among the other monuments.

I've bought a cottage just outside Robin Hood Gate, in Kingston Vale. A nice cheap cottage, £265 "all told." Shall only spend a few pounds in having the drains put right, and no expensive thing in the place, except very comfortable beds. Everything else of wood, and the curtains cotton. Then when I'm not able to be in it I can without any fuss send down a couple of poor girls or women from the Theatre and that does their health and spirits a heap of good. There's a wee garden and such a quiet look-out at the back over a private part of Richmond Park.

CCXVII: G. B. S. *to* E. T.

[*Miss Dickens: the typist who still has the privilege of doing Shaw's work.*]

7 July 1899.
Blen-Cathra, Hindhead,
Haslemere, Surrey

FINISHED, finished, dear Ellen, and on the whole not so bad as I feared. And yet, alas! not finished; for now I have to go over it to get the business right, which will take many grievous brain-racking days. And then further delay whilst Charlotte deciphers my wretched notebooks and makes a typewritten draft, with such unprofessional speed as her housekeeping and wifely cares allow. After that a final revision of the draft; and then Miss Dickens; and then, at last, you. But the main point is that the play now exists, though I died to-morrow, and cannot be unmade save by unlucky fire.

It is a shocking leading lady business, after all; but then, *such* a leading lady! All the other characters are the merest doormats for her. The wretched leading man has nothing in the last act but ignominious dumbness and ridicule until the final scene, in which he gets a consolation prize.

We had a real open air As You Like It in the woods yesterday. It nearly drove me mad. They had white soup plates full of roses to represent footlights (without which it would not have been real acting, of course); the foresters wore faded silk tights (also indispensable to true art); and there was a cottage piano to accompany Amiens in a new setting of Blow, Blow, in the style of Blumenthal. I sang "Damn, damn" between my teeth all the time. Incarnadined fools!

I think you will have to christen the play yourself: I havent yet invented a name for it.

Two months work, with some £60 worth of journalism stolen out of the middle of it.

And yet you think I do not love you: you do *not* believe each word I say.

G. B. S.

CCXVIII: E. T. *to* G. B. S.

10 July 1899.
Lyceum Theatre

WHAT about that half witted girl? Did she kill her sister? *If* she did, did she understand? Should she be *hanged*? (Why *no*, of course not.) There's a petition at the office of the Daily Mail for her pardon. (!) Shall I go and sign it, to help? I never did such a thing, and perhaps ought to have done so long ago and many times. Say yes or no. Please!

Yours, E. T.

P. S. I dont think that Play of yours will do for me at all! You suggest it is a *one part Play!* I loathe that sort of thing. Why cant the printing and such like trash be done by electricity, in a flash. I leave London for Harrogate and Ilkley almost directly. However, you can forward the Play, cant you? E. T.

H ow outrageous that I should ask you questions which take up long
time to answer. You forge ahead so steadily and are so full of
wisdom, I cant help asking your advice. We fools do so much mischief
not knowing what we do. (1) I dont believe a word you say. (2) I implicitly believe you and know that you know. Now *both* those sentences
are true.

I'm much obliged to you for telling me about poor Mary Ansell.
"Capital Punishment" always seemed to me to be horrible and ridiculous.

I suppose they believe all the publicity and disgrace will act on the
minds of others and keep them from sending "poisoned cakes"! etc.,
etc.? Poor Mary Ansell.

Nobody can tell you but Charlotte what your girl in the Play should
wear when she is travelling in Morocco. I dont like the play one bit. Only
one woman in it? How *ugly* it will look, and there will not be a penny
in it. Miss Rehan was in London a few days since, staying with friends.
Now she has gone North. She is a dear woman.

Satty dwells with Edy Craig at 15 Barton St. Westminster when
she is at home, but she isnt at home now. Nobody ever is, nowadays!
That's why I want to leave off working. I want to be at home now, always. I hope, I hope that I can see a copy of your play before I go right
away (*ever* so rough a copy). We close at the Lyceum on the 29th. I am
slaving at rehearsals for Amber Heart so as to make up the number
of performances we have contracted to play (100 performances). Then
I go straight off to Ilkley for *one* week to get rested before going the
following 2 weeks to that blessed Harrogate. Then another week at Ilkley
and then—Birmingham! And, then—(see enclosed lively list). Blessings
on you. E. T.

I know nothing of the Humanitarian League. On a P. C. say where I
can read about it and send something—E.

CCXX: G. B. S. *to* E. T.

[*Ada Rehan never acted in England after Daly's death, but she continued to
tour in the United States until 1906. Shaw had no use for Daly, whose
methods of producing Shakespear he often held up to ridicule in The Saturday Review, but he was a great admirer of Ada Rehan. In his notice of*

14 July 1899

THERE is no reasonable doubt that the play will be in your hands before the 29th. I have quite finished the first act; and Charlotte is toiling after me as fast as she can on the typewriter. As we intend to leave this place in the first week in August (a big move after all this time) we are desperately aware of the necessity for getting the Play clean off our hands well before that time. At present it is proposed to go to some hole in Cornwall named Cadgwith, to sea-bathe my weak ankle. Then round the Mediterranean in an Orient steamer as far as Athens and back. I submit to this mainly because the steamer calls at Tangier. I want to see a Moorish town, as the Witch of Atlas scene is laid in Mogador, except the second act, which is in the mountains.

What about copyrighting the play? Shall I do that at Bayswater in the usual way? or would it amuse you to do it at the Lyceum or on tour? Decide this just as you like, as I shirk all the Bayswater trouble by appealing to Florence Farr to take it off my hands.

The play will not be so ugly as an English play would be without women's dresses. There are Arabs and pirates, Sheikhs and Cadis and so on, with views of the Atlantic Ocean. I intended at first to introduce some young tourists; but it would have lengthened the play and scattered the interest. Even a part for Edy was impossible. But you will pull it through: I count you as six good women's parts, all well acted, and all beautiful. Remember that the Devil's Disciple had *practically* only one woman in it.

I see that the Rehan's engagment at Drury Lane is off, in consequence of the devil having claimed his servant Daly.

The Witch of Atlas ought to be done in a small theatre to get the best effect out of it. Here is the speaking cast—Lady Cicely Waynflete; Sir Howard Hallam, her brother-in-law, a judge (old); Clement Hallam, alias Black Paquito, alias Captain Brassbound (hero); Leslie Rankin, a Missionary; the Cadi of Kintafi; the Sheikh Sidi el Assif (very handsome); Captain Hamlin Kearney of the United States cruiser Santiago; Felix Drinkwater, a Hooligan follower of Brassbound, etc., etc., etc.

That is a little to go on with.

242

Remember that you can hear the whole play at any moment by allowing the author to read it to you, and to kiss you at least once at the end.

G. B. S.

CCXXI: G. B. S. *to* E. T.

[Fuller-Mellish: the son of a distinguished Victorian actress Rose Leclercq. He first joined the Lyceum Company in 1884, left it, and returned for a few years about this time.—Welch: James Welch (see note to Letter CCLIII).— Louie Freear: a diminutive comedian who excelled in Cockney parts. She gave a striking performance of Puck in Tree's production of A Midsummer Night's Dream in 1900.]

1 August 1899.
Blen-Cathra, Hindhead

AFTER much title-searching, I have resolved to give that play (which you seem to have thrown into your waste-paper basket with the other tragedies when it arrived last Friday morning) the ugly but arresting name Captain Brassbound's Conversion. I did my best to make Lady Cicely a "title part," but could find nothing better than The Angel in the Atlas or some such silliness. Besides, when I publish my next volume, which will contain the Devil's Disciple, Cæsar and Cleopatra, and Captain B, I will call it Three Plays for Puritans. Captain B's Conversion has a blatant Puritan sound in it.

I presume you have left town. We should have been out of this and away to the seaside this week but for a Saturday to Monday visitor, who seized the opportunity to have a quiet little attack of DIPHTHERIA! We are all in quarantine in consequence. The patient cannot be moved until the end of next week; so we shall be here until the 15th or 17th.

Archer was down here last Sunday week. He says the critics wont like my damned ostentation of intellectual superiority, but begs me most earnestly to give the play a chance, by waiting at least two years for somebody to produce it before publishing it, and not infuriating all the managers by entering into personal negotiations with them. He vented his sense of years of suffering from your first-night imperfections by saying "She'll never learn it." He suggested H. B. Irving for Brassbound —not a bad idea if it could be managed. Drinkwater is a difficulty: he must be a genuine comedian, not merely an actor who can imitate cockney—(Fuller Mellish)—but the real thing, a creature with tears in him. Dan Leno would probably undertake it for not more than twice your

243

salary. Welch could do it if he could cocknify himself enough. It requires a male Louie Freear. The other parts are easy enough, except that Sir Ahrd Ellam (Howard Hallam) must be gentleman enough to be dignified when he is crusty.

However, there's your play—Ellen's play. My conscience was so burdened with the infamy of having written plays for other people about whom I dont care a straw (thank my stars they cant act them) and made no play for you, that it had to be done. Now it *is* done—the only thing on earth in my power to do for you. And now no more plays—at least no more practicable ones. None at all, indeed, for some time to come: it is time to do something more in Shaw-philosophy, in politics and sociology. Your author, dear Ellen, must be more than a common dramatist.

By the way, what are your wishes concerning the press? Shall I say nothing and leave everything of that sort to you; or shall I start an epidemic of paragraphs to the effect that I have written a play expressly for you? One way is to give a copywriting performance (what about *that,* eh?) and send round copies of the program to the critics and paragraphists. That is what I generally do. But it is quite easy to let it alone, though the fact of the play being written is sure to leak out: the question is, do you want your name connected with it?

G. B. S.

CCXXII: E. T. *to* G. B. S.

[*Ellen Terry was at first disappointed in Captain Brassbound's Conversion as this letter plainly shows. Later, when she became more familiar with the play, her opinion of it changed. It is a question, however, whether her original conviction that it was not the sort of play for her and not as fine in itself as the other plays by Shaw she mentions was altogether unsound. Shaw adds that she might have reminded him of his own words (Letter CXXXVII): "Is it not curious that the one thing not forgivable in an actor is being* the part instead of playing it?" *But she did not at first realize, and was perhaps never able to realize, that Lady Cicely Wayneflete was herself.*]

3 August 1899

No one but Shaw could have written the last Play Cap. B's Conversion (?) but it's not the sort of play for me in the least. The three I think finest are Arms and the Man, Mrs Warren's Profession, and the Cleopatra thing.

I couldnt do this one, and I believe it would never do for the stage. The two parts, the man and woman, are right; but that *bore* Drink-water! Mrs Pat for Lady C! I couldnt do it. Mrs Potter would revel in the part, but it is surely for Mrs Pat. *Not* for me. Some day, spite of your saying you wont, you'll be pushed by everything within you to write more Plays and then (I'll be grown up *then* certainly!) perhaps one will fit me.

I just enjoyed the reading it up to the hilt, and Sir Howard especially delighted me, and Lady C! but the expressions: "There's not a penny in it"—"More fitted for the closet than the stage," occur to one when one has finished it. Also, after reading it comes a great refreshment to the tired spirit, but it would not be so when it was acted! (And it would not *"Act* well.") Shall I send it back to you? Or may I keep it with some of the others for a while longer? Satty is at Haslemere I fancy. I'm just starting for Harrogate and I envy you going to see for the first time the wondrous white city Tangiers. All white, all white, and single, simple. I'm nigh dead. Work and heat. My address by next Sunday will be Prince of Wales Hotel, Harrogate. Edy is at Bath.

Yours, E. T.

My love to Mr Archer. Doesnt know anything about it! I mean about my memory. I acted to please Henry when I was frightfully ill (1st night Robespierre) and now it's a proverb about my not learning my parts.

CCXXIII: G. B. S. *to* E. T.

[*Robson: Frederick Robson, who took London by storm in the fifties. After his appearance in a burlesque of The Merchant of Venice at the Olympic, the critic of The Times pronounced him to be the greatest actor seen on the stage since Edmund Kean. He drank madly and died in 1864 at the age of 43. He was a low comedian, playing the commonest routine of vulgar drollery, yet he made an indelible impression on all who saw him by sudden moments of tragic passion and intense characterization. Irving, however, was right in dismissing as silly the notion that Robson could have kept on the level of his brief explosions long enough to qualify himself for the rank claimed for him by The Times.*]

(until the 25th)
Blen-Cathra, Hindhead.
4 August 1899

A<small>LAS</small>! dear Ellen, is it really so? Then I can do nothing for you. I honestly thought that Lady Cicely would fit you like a glove, that I had sacrificed everything to make the play go effectively from second to second, even that Drinkwater was a tragi-comic figure worthy of Robson. And now you tell me it is a play for the closet, and that Lady Cicely would suit Mrs P. C.—all of which proves that either I am mad, or you are mad, or else there is an impassable gulf between my drama and your drama.

I wont suggest it to Mrs Pat, because I am now quite convinced that she would consider herself born to play it, just as you want to play Cleopatra. No: it is clear that I have nothing to do with the theatre of to-day: I must educate a new generation with my pen from childhood up—audience, actors and all, and leave them my plays to murder after I am cremated. Captain B. shall not be profaned by the stage: I will publish it presently with the D's D and Cæsar, and preach a nice sermon in the preface.

And so farewell our project—all fancy, like most projects. Send me back the script when you are done with it: I will send you the printed volume when it is ready.

Silly Ellen!

G. B. S.

CCXXIV: E. T. *to* G. B. S.

6 August 1899.
Harrogate

I <small>DONT</small> want to play Cleopatra particularly, but I particularly wanted the Play to be produced with the Henry-Irving-Lyceum-advantages! And when all is said and done, and *I* am nearly done, yet I should be your safest card for the part. I'm not so vain as you think me. Of course you never *really* meant Lady Cicely for me—but to be published along with other Plays. For delight I'd soonest act your Mrs Warren and Cleopatra. For money I'd choose your You Never Can Tell, The Devil's D, and Candida—(properly acted). And so, and so, I am not to—

Too tired to write, but shall be very well soon.

Yours "<small>SILLY ELLEN</small>"

CCXXV: G. B. S. *to* E. T.

[*The description of the part of Lady Cicely in this letter is a remarkable example of Shaw's skill in morally limelighting his parts to tempt the imagination of his actresses, but is this the part he wrote? In letter CCXXXVI Ellen Terry records the impression produced on her daughter by the copyrighting performance of Brassbound that Shaw thought Lady Cicely one sort of woman and wrote another. He says that he "simply exploited her wonderful personality theatrically and invited her without a qualm of delicacy to become his accomplice."*]

8 August 1899.
Blen-Cathra, Hindhead

OH YOU lie, Ellen, you lie: never was there a part so deeply written for a woman as this for you, silly, self-unconscious, will o' the wisp beglamoured child actress as you still are. It is like offering the play to Kate. "Sir, I do this sort of thing. Take it to some ordinary leading lady—I believe there is a person named Campbell, or is it Kendal?— whom it might suit. My line is romantic tragedy, supported by Mr Fechter. Your offering it to me shews a complete misunderstanding of my rank as an artist. I expected something better from you. Classic language at least instead of this vulgar colloquialism; but—but no matter. Good morning."

Lyceum advantages! Havent you had enough of them yet? You talk to me, ME, of this ogre's den into which your talent has been thrown and eaten. Go then, wretch, and get Comyns Carr and Calmour to write you some nice new part with a name like the latest hairwash, and be as romantic and picturesque as you please, and bury what reality there is in Ellen under ten tons more of tomfoolery.

Listen to me, woman with no religion. Send to your library for two books of travel in Africa: one Miss Kingsley's (have you met her?) and the other H. M. Stanley's. Compare the brave woman, with her commonsense and good will, with the wild-beast man, with his elephant rifle, and his atmosphere of dread and murder, breaking his way by mad selfish assassination out of the difficulties created by his own cowardice. Think of all that has been rising up under your eyes in Europe for years past, Bismarck worship, Stanley worship, Dr Jim worship, and now at last Kitchener worship with dead enemies dug up and mutilated. Think also on the law—the gallows, penal servitude, hysterical clamoring for the lash, more cowardice masquerading as "resolute government," "law and order" and the like. Well, how have you felt about things? Have you had any real belief in the heroism of the filibuster? Have you had any sympathy with the punishments of the judge? Have you found in your own life and your own small affairs no better way, no more instructive heart wisdom, no warrant for trusting to the good side of people instead of terrorizing the bad side of them. I—poor idiot!—thought the distinction of Ellen Terry was that she had this heart wisdom, and managed her own little world as Tolstoy would have our Chamberlains and Balfours and German Emperors and Kitcheners and Lord Chief Justices and other slaves of false ideas and imaginary fears manage Europe. I accordingly give you a play in which you stand in the very place where Imperialism is most believed to be necessary, on the border line where the European meets the fanatical African, with judge on the one hand, and indomitable adventurer-filibuster on the other, said I. A-F. pushing forward "civilization" in the shape of rifles and pistols in the hands of Hooligans, aristocratic *mauvais sujets* and stupid drifters. I try to shew these men gaining a sense of courage and resolution from continual contact with and defiance of their own fears. I try to shew you fearing nobody and managing them all as Daniel managed the lions, not by cunning—above all, not by even a momentary appeal to Cleopatra's stand-by, their passions—but by simple moral superiority. It is a world-wide situation, and one totally incomprehensible to Cleopatras of all sorts and periods. (Cleopatra would have waited to guess which of the two men was going to beat the other, and then tried to seduce him, after which, as in the case of Antony and Cæsar, she would have found that she had guessed wrong.) Here then is your portrait painted on a map of the world— and you prefer Sargent's Lady Macbeth! Here you get far beyond Candida, with her boy and her parson, and her suspicion of trading a little on the softness of her contours—and you want to get back to Cleopatra! Here is a part which dominates a play because the character it represents dominates the world—and you think it might do for Mrs P. C.! The wretched Hooligan who gives the final touch by turning from the navy, the bench, and all the powers and principalities, to Ellen, in his extremity—"they dassent do it if you tell 'em not"—is dull to you. In every other play I have ever written—even in Candida—I have prostituted the actress more or less by making the interest in her partly a sexual interest: only the *man* in the Devil's Disciple draws clear of it. In Lady Cicely I have done without this, and gained a greater fascination by it. And you are disappointed.

Oh, wretch, wretch, wretch! It is true that the record of the play as a book written by me for you is worth a thousand Lyceum successes; but its publication with "Repudiated by Miss Ellen Terry as unworthy of her professional eminence" across it—do you think I intended that? And do you think I regard you as a person needing to be arranged with sphinxes and limelights to be relished by a luxurious public? Oh Ellen, Ellen, Ellen, Ellen. This is the end of everything.

G. B. S.

CCXXVI: E. T. *to* G. B. S.

9 August 1899

IF YOU wanted to make me weep on a nice morning and feel quite miserable you have done it. You have gotten your "want"! I'm not in the least Kate-ish, or rather not like the absurd Kate you have drawn, and the best of the fun is (tho' where "the *fun*" comes in the Lord knows)—the horridness of it all is, that all the time I think exactly as you do! So where is the fuss? And why do you pitch into me so and make me feel quite ill just as I'm going for a ride. (I shant go now.) Of course I know it's *me* all the while. My fault. I dont know what I wrote to you, but what I wanted to say particularly (amongst a good many things) was *two things:*

1. The part of Lady C. as I should act it would not be thought by the audience to be acting at all and wouldnt satisfy them.

2. I *wanted* to satisfy them. Else they wouldnt come in numbers and I wanted them to come. (It's all past now) and I wanted to make money for your sake, you stupid, much more than for my own.
Of course you say you "dont want it" and all that, but *I* wanted the people to come in flocks, in droves, to see your play and me together.

The placing it (your scene) in the white City was so fascinating I held my breath when I began to read it, and I loved the whole thing to the end (except "Drinkwater" who bored me dreadfully), and now you fall out with me for it—What is the good of words to me? Half an hour ago I was so quiet and merry and then comes your letter and you talk to me of the brute donkey *STANLEY!* And as if that were not enough to upset any calm and quiet peacefullness in a woman, you also are unkind between every line of your dear blessed letter.

I hate it.

I was getting well, and now I shall be ill again—and all you!

249

Oh, poor Charlotte! (This is a *joke!* Go to! You are just as thick-headed as I am.)

ELLEN

CCXXVII: E. T. *to* G. B. S.

20 August 1899.
Wells House,
Ilkley, Yorkshire

I HAVE put it straight and nicely to Henry that if I fall ill in America he can act on quite well without me in Robespierre, but if he should fall ill *I* cant get on with only the Merchant of Venice. I propose a Play which gives all the rest of us good parts. Can be *"produced"* quite easily by Laurence and me. Would not cost much. Modern but also picturesque. A first rate Play and a sure success in America. At present I've not said it is yours! I've asked him will he read it? Or better still, let Laurence read it? Now what do you think of all this? The Casting of the Play would of course have to be within our means. Within the Company we'd take with us. How about this?

Rankin	Charles Dodsworth
Sir Howard H.	C. Garry
Drinkwater	—?

(Lord, how difficult it is without a commonplace useful catalogue of the characters to get through with work of this kind.) Cant bother just at this moment. However, of those we have in hand, Laurence Irving would have to do Brassbound, and he'd *revel* in it! and do it very well, spite of not possessing "nostrils large and strained." (But he could *act* that!) A very good *Rankin* I think could be found in Charles Dodsworth. *Drinkwater* is difficult (as Mellish has left us). *Sir Howard* could be well done by a Mr Garry. *The Kid,* a good-looking boy we have in the Company. Sidi El Assif, The Cadi Osman and all the rest could be done splendidly.

I hope your poor body bears you stiffly up upon your journey, and that you and C. are well and darling. Couldnt write until now. Have had a sharp attack of flu. In bed only 4 days, but am precious weak now. I look quite nice—pale and almost what they call "interesting." My maid has read a Play to me 2 or 3 times through lately. "She would never dream the part of Lady C. was like me." She is a very nice girl devoted, respectful, and self-respecting. She goes nearly everywhere with me the last 6 years or more. Well, we were amongst a lot of very old, very poor houses going over them a week ago, and now and again when I was speaking with the poor people who crowded around me, I caught a peculiar expression on her face: "Much amused at something," I thought. Yesterday at Bolton Abbey I suddenly found myself amongst a swarm of "fine" ladies and gentlemen—"smart" I *should* say. Again the expression on that girl's face! *"Why?"* I asked this morning. Then bursting with suppressed laughter she said: "Oh, I'm very sorry. Excuse me, but Lady Cicely is *so* like you!" (She is quite out of any of my private affairs.) "She gets her way in *everything—just like you!*" I cant understand it. *I* think I'm always horribly rough.

Now please answer:—

(1) My I let Henry or the boy read the Play?

(2) If H. sees the sense and advantage of the arrangement would you let *him* have the play? Or let *me* have the play?

I see no chance of playing anything when I come back, unless I am given a bad part in the new production, in which case I should rest a while and then start a tour, or a London smallish theatre on my own account. Some folk, without selling a play right out, take 5% on the gross receipts and the play returns to the author after a few months—some stipulated time. If I could do this play either in London or the Provinces I should like that arrangement. In America everything is of course different. Cornwall is too relaxing for me. But kind Kornwall, do my friend good. E. T.

CCXXVIII: G. B. S. *to* E. T.

22 August 1899.
Ruan Minor, Cornwall

Your letter makes me shriek with laughter, though I am in the worst of tempers. "Straight and nicely," you say, you have put it to Henry. And then you explain that the straightness consists in keeping him in the dark as to the authorship! Oh Ellen, Ellen!

First, of course, you must let the murder out. The strongest reason from *his* business point of view against the American proposal is one of which he will have not the faintest suspicion: namely, that the production of a play by ME on his tour would be such an important event that his absence from the cast would produce exactly the same impression as it would at the Lyceum. If he is wise (which he isnt) he will either have nothing whatever to do with me or else make a feature of me rather larger than his own reverberative nose.

As to the cast, the main difficulty is **Drinkwater**. I am afraid that Laurence, as you say, *would* revel in Brassbound: if he only wouldnt revel he would be a tolerable actor. But the inevitable contrast the American press would draw between his Brassbound and Mansfield's Dick Dudgeon would probably do him some good. Mellish couldnt have done Drinkwater. It's not a question of dialect, but of farcical tragedy. *Who* are you taking out with you? You must have Gobbos and people of that sort. If I had a list of the company, I could tell ever so much better.

Let me see what your questions are.

1. May you let Henry or the boy read the Play? Certainly: anybody you please.

2. If H. sees the sense and advantage of the arrangement, would I let *him* have the play? Hm! In the first place, he wont, probably. But *if*, IF, IF he does? Well, yes—on certain terms. You say that "some folk, without selling a play right out, take 5% on the gross receipts." *I* take 10%; and I should want that for America, for the Lyceum, and for seven or eight choice places in the provinces and suburbs. Henry doesnt go to the 5% places: it's not worth his eminent while. On the other hand, I dont ask for any advance; so that if the play fails, his loss will be much less than mine. Probably I should ask for a crushing penalty for non-production if London is proposed; as I have had enough of trusting to Henry's good faith, and know that he will break his word if I annoy him (which is extremely likely) whereas he knows that he can depend on me. Further, I will not give him exclusive rights except during the period of your leading-ladyship: indeed, I will not give him any exclusive rights as against you, although—but these details are premature: if anything comes of it I can steam-roller Stoker on the subject.

Finally, you ask me will I let you have the play? I have been considering about that; and it seems to me that I might give you a license to perform it for the rest of your natural life in the United Kingdom under your own management on condition that you always play Lady Cicely, and that you pay me—I must get this clearer—5% on the gross receipts when there is no more than £100 in the house, 7½% when there is more than £100 and no more than £150 and 10% when there is more than £150. Thus if you took £100 you would give me £5: if you took £100.1.0 you would give me £7.10.0: £150, £11.15.0: £150.1.0, £15: £200, £20: £300, £30, etc., etc. By "under your own management" I mean when you are not playing for a salary, but paying the expenses and taking the receipts. Consequently this would not apply to the Lyceum; but I could put in a clause licensing you also to play under the management of Sir Henry Irving, he taking part in the performance except in case of illness, for 10%. By extending this clause to the forthcoming American tour, the contingency of a production there would be covered.

But observe, the license will be only for the United Kingdom and not for America; and it will not be an *exclusive* license except for the first 2 or 3 years. My reason for the first stinginess is that if you dont do the Play this time on the tour, you will probably never play it in America at all and in that case I should lose a large sum without benefiting you unless I could give complete rights to an American Manager. For the second my reason is obvious. You will live about thirty years after your retirement from the stage; and though you will to your last hour have the right to play Lady Cicely when you please, there is no reason why the other geniuses should not have a turn at it too in the meantime if they want to.

These terms are neither particularly generous nor particularly grasping. Do not forget that they considerably modify the advisability of your suggestions as to America and H. I., as far as your interests are concerned. And do not commit yourself to anybody—Laurence or anyone else. H. B. would do the part better—he is much graver. Put all the disagreeable part of the business, if there is any, on the author. I am an excellent Mr Jorkins.

G. B. S.

CCXXIX: E. T. *to* G.B.S.

[*Miss Milton: Maud Milton, who had been a member of the Lyceum Company since 1892. Among other parts she played Regan in King Lear, Jeannette in The Lyons Mail, Jessica in The Merchant of Venice, and Mrs Primrose in Olivia. Her last appearances were made in America.—Ellen Terry's preference for Laurence Irving and Shaw's for his elder brother "H. B." meant only that Shaw did not as yet know the very likeable Laurence personally and was influenced only by the fact that Harry's development as an actor had been far quicker.*]

27 August 1899

I'M GLAD my scrawl made you "laugh." *Your* letter made my head spin, when I came to the "per-cent-y" page. However after a few days rest after studying your letter I see quite plainly your plan is quite fair.

We should gain in *all* ways, together, or lose in all ways together. You and I, or H. and you. But a letter from him today makes me almost decide *not* to let him read the play. (Not until I go up to town at least and read it to him. I know it very well by now—and delight in it) This is what he says. *"I will read with pleasure"*—(how I hate that *"with pleasure"*! E. T.)—*"the Play you speak of—but not for America. If we are either of us ill there, Laurence and Miss Milton will be at hand and Robespierre will still go on"* (Will it? E. T.) *"For there will be but little time to spare for we must push on with a new Play for our opening at the Lyceum in March."* (He doesnt say which of two Plays I know of, but they are both just simply idiotic. E. T.)

Now my plan is to go up and read him the Play and propose *that* as my desire for the reopening.

If he doesnt "see it," I shall be sorry, but *my* sight is rather queer lately and I fear *I* cannot *"see it"* (!) in regard to aiding and abetting him by acting in the Play he is thinking about for March. I was guilty in joining with him in that dreadful Medicine Man, but I shall be obliged to leave off acting at the Lyceum if anything more of the kind is imminent. I dont think for a minute he would play Brassbound—but oh, if only he will clear up his fogs and see well just for an hour, then he will play it, and produce the Play in March. If not—and if I leave the Lyceum for a while—I'd like to do it in a first class London theatre first and afterwards go with it to America. Certainly not for more than "two or three years" as you say. To have "the right" to play parts for ever is absurd! If Olivia were my Play I should like to be on the watch from now, and give it (prize-like!) to the most promising young actress (to be handed on again by her as a present to the next generation, and so forth). Do you really like H. B. better than Laurence? Laurence has many more faults but—H. B. is so modern, slangy of speech it seems to me, and oh, how old he is compared with *my* Irving boy.

I'll know more in a week and write. I'll tell Henry of the freshness, the picturesqueness, the delicious fun and sweetness of the Play before he hears it.

E. T.

CCXXX: E. T. *to* G. B. S.

17 September 1899

Dear G. B. S.:—Your best card under the circumstances is *Ada Rehan!* I can decide no plans for myself until I know H. I.'s and he has not yet read the play he has announced he will produce upon his return to the Lyceum. The play, as it stood, was simply *frightful* and I for one refused absolutely to have anything to do with it. (For obvious reasons my saying this must remain between us two.) Now it is being altered and if the thing turns out a better article (?), I have promised Henry I will act in it. And so, until I see that Play I can do nothing.

Remember Lady C in my hands is worth a great deal more to you than if Ada or (I think) anybody else played the part, but as you say it ought to be done at once, I am tongue-tied in the matter. You have crowds, stacks of other wonderful Plays. Why cant you let this particular Brassbound bide a while? Do you understand that I "cannot speak"? Yet I've had a frightful fortnight of work, rehearsing all day until I nearly gave way. But the worst is past now and I've a month of mere "playacting" before me—and then America!

My wish would be, to rest a little while upon my return from America, and then do Capn. B's Conversion at—the Garrick perhaps, and then go with it to America. It's not a question of "breaking with H. I." If the Charles IX thing is too bad for me to have anything to do with, I could go somewhere with a fine Play and again go to the Lyceum when there was something decent for me to do! It is all different now. The Lyceum is a "Company" and H. I. (and they) would be very glad to have me back again if I *did* go away for a while. You are so wrong in your apprehensions about H. I., my dear, dear G. B. When I've more time I must send you back a letter of yours, the last but one to me, and remark upon your words between the lines, but I cannot now. After a railway journey I am dazed. I have not let any *man* yet see your Play. Meanwhile I love it more and more. The last bit grows tragic-er and tragic-er as I see it before me. Only I can do that bit properly, and the touch where Lady C. speaks to B. of Gordon! Nor Ada nor another! Still, I do suppose *she* is your best card under the circumstances.

CCXXXI: G. B. S. *to* E. T.

13 September 1899.
Ruan Minor, Cornwall

THOU DEAR ELLEN,

I RETURN to London by tomorrow night's train, arriving on Friday morning. On the 21st I sail away and can do nothing for six weeks, nor can any effective business communication be kept up with me. In the meantime the play is not copyrighted; and as to America I have only a casual remark of yours that you might take the play there at some future time. Now you must give your inconstant mind more strenuously to this for a moment. Do you realize that these American rights are worth about £2,500 to me, argent comptant, and that if you ask me to keep them for you, and then dont use them, you may possibly deprive me of it altogether, and certainly deprive me of the interest on it for several years. Do you understand? Two thousand five hundred solid golden sovereigns. I shouldnt mind if the result of my losing them was that you would get them; but you wouldnt: they would be simply annihilated—wasted.

Ask your conscience in the small hours of the night whether there is any serious likelihood of your going to America next winter with a company of your own, and without Henry, who will then have to take somebody else if he also goes to America next year. If you can say to the conscience, "Yes: Henry isnt going next year; and I am; and I have fully made up my mind to book the dates or otherwise arrange the business this next tour," then I think you may commit yourself, always bearing in mind that if Henry is not in America he will be somewhere else and must replace you. If you cant say this, then cry off the American part of the plan, and leave half the globe to Ada Rehan.

I worry you about this purposely. It is important for yourself that you should get this business settled soon. The English production can wait as long as you like; but America is my lever to force you into action. Besides, a horrible misfortune has happened to me—a money trouble. I have succeeded through the death of my uncle to a family estate in Ireland—a miserable relic of former county splendor, all mortgages and poor relations. I am not sure that I shall not repudiate it. What with this and a letter just received from America (proposing, among other things, a production of Mrs Warren's Profession) I feel for the moment quite avaricious. My blessed uncle had not paid even his servants' wages for ten years, and had borrowed every farthing he could. I shall have to pay his debts because I am inheriting the privilege of paying the interest on half a dozen Carlow mortgages. And this is the moment at which you propose to throw my thousands into the Atlantic.

Now as to the copyrighting. Will you do that for me, or shall I get it done at Bayswater by Florence Farr? If you will, you must arrange with the manager a fortnight ahead at whose house you will be playing as he must send a copy of the play and a cheque for two guineas (both of which I will send you) to the Licenser, G. A. Redford

Lord Chamberlain's Office, St James's Palace. Redford is not bound to license at less than a fortnight's notice. I have the parts all ready, and can send them to the theatre selected for the ceremony, addressed to you.

Dont do this unless it would be a piece of fun for you and your friends in the company. I can get it done without any trouble here. But one way or another it must be arranged for before I leave for the Bay of Biscay O.

I see an announcement that the Lyceum will reopen with a play on the Massacre of St Bartholomew. Are you to be Marguerite de Valois or Catherine de Medici?

Now proceed to think, Ellen. Remember, it is a money question. Remember that I am a most mean man about money, and will throw it in your teeth for ever after if you dont make a heap of it for me. Breaking loose from the Lyceum means a great deal. And I dont think you can, without great generalship, elope with my play and keep your place at the Lyceum at the same time.

Forgive this confused letter: we are packing, or rather Charlotte is, bearing malice the while against me for writing letters instead of helping her. G. B. S.

CCXXXII: E. T. *to* G. B. S.

18 September 1899

I WROTE you last night and not having your letter at hand and forgetting you were going to London, I addressed my letter to Cornwall! What a—donkey! Yes, please. Let *me* at least have the copyrighting performance done at Manchester or at Liverpool. Dodsworth played Launcelot Gobbo last Friday and was very funny in it. And I'm glad, as he is *my* prize packet at the Lyceum. Now he can do Drinkwater, for he looked a half made up bit of goods as Launcelot strangely like Leno. I will enclose a list of the rest of the Cast and we will read it and have great fun. I shall have to ask Henry this morning I suppose for his "permission" for his Company to do this for *"my"* Play! I'll then wire you.

If I do the Play in England I think I'd prefer having the American rights as well. And Ada would like the same arrangements, I fancy, should she get the American rights. But as I have told you in the letter gone to Cornwall I can settle nothing until I have seen the Charles IX play, which will be read to me in Liverpool. I should not in the least care in which of the two countries I first played the piece. I think America would be best, for you have had greater "success" there in your produced plays. But *you* should decide. I *do* hope the part for me in Charles IX will be very bad. The whole Play was *awful* when I read it more than a year ago, but it has been entirely re-arranged and re-written and I have promised Henry I'll do it if it is good, fairly good. How *can* a bad play be made good! I'll write again shortly, and *shorter!!*

E. T.

P. S. I have H.'s permission about the reading. So, Manchester—or Liverpool. E.

CCXXXIII: G. B. S. *to* E.T.

[*Malcolm Watson: critic and dramatist. For many years he contributed a weekly column headed Drama of the Day to The Daily Telegraph.—The ridiculous copyrighting ceremony described in this letter was abolished by the Copyright Act of 1911.—The Charles IX play faded out of the Lyceum arrangements, and may be presumed to have justified Ellen Terry's opinion of it.*]

19 September 1899.
10 Adelphi Terrace, W. C.

E LLEN: you are utterly incorrigible. I dont believe you have the faintest real intention of doing that play either in England or America. However, perhaps the Cornwall letter is more explicit: it hasnt come yet.

Now as to the copyrighting performance, which I must leave entirely in your hands. (This is a brute of a typewriter.) I send you a copy of the play, and a set of parts to read from. Send the copy of the play, with the enclosed cheque for two guineas, to the manager of the theatre at which the reading will take place; and ask him to send both of them to The Examiner of Plays, Lord Chamberlain's Office, St James's Palace, London, S. W. with a request for a license, which will be sent in the course of a fortnight. Of course, Sir H. I., as a manager, can apply if that is more convenient (unless he objects) as when the license is once issued, it does not matter in the least in whose theatre or where the performance takes place. Do this straight away.

For the performance itself you will need an ordinary poster, giving the cast, prices, day, hour, and everything as usual. This must be posted up outside the theatre during the performance in such a way that anybody passing along the street can see, if he reads it, that there is a performance going on, and that he can see it by paying at the door. This

258

is the most essential part of the business, as without it the performance is not a public one and therefore of no validity. Lest this should result in a crowded house, admission to all parts of the theatre must be One Guinea. Somebody (one person will be enough) must pay a guinea and come in: and a box office return of that guinea must be solemnly made out and preserved as evidence. The play must be performed (read from the parts will do) to that single representative of the public and as many more people as you like to give tickets to; and that is all.

However, though this is what you MUST do, there is a little more that you *may* do, if you think fit. If you want the performance paragraphed, either to advertise the fact of its existence and its patronage by you, or to give your prize packets a little show in the papers, get a program printed as well as the poster—an ordinary program in the same form as those you use at night; and send a copy to all the dramatic critics and to all the papers.

BUT if you do this you must put on the program "This is the only performance of the play in England prior to its production by Miss Ellen Terry." Without that—which will start a devil of a gossip—all the papers would conclude and announce that the play had been accepted and was to be produced by H. I. This would be most particularly awkward in view of the fact that the really frightful and unpardonable part of my row with him over The Man of Destiny was caused by his setting his henchmen to circulate a paragraph stating that all that had happened about that play was that I had sent in a piece in the usual course and had it rejected. I resented this attack with an energy which simply stood Henry, Stoker, and Austin on their heads in a row; and it was that episode, in which I shewed about as much sense of Sir Henry's dignity as a mad bull might have done if he had put on his Mephistopheles costume and ordered it out of its field, that made all further negotiations for ever impossible between us. So unless the program can be so worded as to make any misunderstanding of that sort quite unreasonable, it had better not be resorted to. In deciding, be governed entirely by whether you wish to prepare the public mind for a venture of your own in management away from the Lyceum. If you dont want to suggest that, have no program.

Keep the performance strictly secret until it is over. When Candida was copyrighted at South Shields, the Daily News published nearly a column of a horribly garbled account of it by somebody who got wind of it, and paid one guinea to earn two. Of course, if you prefer it, you can make the reading an extra good one, and invite Malcolm Watson and all the critics to come and see it.

After the performance, send me (*a*) a copy of the poster (*b*) the box office return of the guinea, (*c*) a copy of the program—if any, and (*d*) the printer's bill, which I will liquidate, with any other cash expenses that may be incurred. If Sir Henry chooses to play Brassbound for half salary, he must reduce his terms for the week to five pounds, as I will go no further than fifty shillings for a leading man.

Your Cornwall letter will come tomorrow probably. Until then, I will content myself with saying that if you play in Charles IX, you will end your days at the Lyceum, and that I have serious thoughts of limiting your license to the expiration of your next birthday but one. Something must be done to hurry you.

Murray Carson wants me to let him do The Devil's Disciple at Kennington, where he has been flourishing as Richard III with much éclat.

Remember, I sail on Thursday morning. I enclose you a list of the places at which letters can reach me.

The script for Redford and the parts will go by parcels post tomorrow. Too late to send them tonight.

See page 15 Act II for a few words added to one of Sir Howard's speeches. You had better write it into your own copy.

G. B. S.

CCXXXIV: E. T. *to* G. B. S.

2 October 1899.
23 Ducie Street,
Manchester

WHY, what a donkey I was not to take advantage of your words in one of your letters. You said you had money to pay away at once. *Then* I ought to have said "Dear Mr Shaw, here is £500. I want the entire rights of your Brassbound, and if you dont think £500 is fair, then you must tell me what else (and *less* than you would perhaps stipulate for because of your getting the *immediate* advantage of the money!)." Of course that's what I ought to have said. And I *do* say it *now!* Isnt that what they call "driving a bargain"? Shall I send a cheque by return for the five hundred or will you wait for me a little while longer? Yesterday in travelling from Glasgow to this place I heard the first Act of the new (Lyceum) play. So far I see no possible chance of my playing Marguerite de Valois. The part (I will say naught of the Play) is a wretched one, but I must wait and hear the end, for I told H.

I. I would do so. I said yesterday "If it goes on like *this* of course it would be impossible" but he says the whole play is Marguerite's later on! I take that with a pinch of salt! And a bad play it would be if it were true! I've studied Lady C. now, and am *transported*. The tragic end I go over and over again and just ———— *see it*. A triumph for us both. I love the whole thing and am certain I could do it.

Pray send me a line at once and send me leave to have the Play *all* for my very own. It's a lovely day here and Manchester is beautiful! You see I chance to feel well: let me play Drinkwater! "Let me play the Lion"!!

Your ELLEN

CCXXXV: G. B. S. *to* E. T.

[*A letter from Ellen Terry at the end of September seems to be missing. There is no reference to Irving's arrangements with Tennyson in any of her letters about the Brassbound business.—The play by Henry Arthur Jones referred to is The Manœuvres of Jane, produced at the Haymarket Theatre in 1898.*]

3 October 1899.
Somewhere between Villefranche and Syracuse.
S.S. *Lusitania*

EVER CHERISHED ELLEN,

THIS is a brute of a place, morally hideous, physically only pretty-pretty. Would it were Spitzbergen! I was born to bite the north wind, not to soak in this lukewarm Reckitt's blue purlieu of gamblers.

What you say about Henry's disgust at my exorbitant terms makes me conscious that you ought to have an agent to drive your bargain for you. You have signed nothing and paid nothing; so you are still free. Will you put yourself into Henry's hands, or Stoker's, or anybody who will get the last farthing for you out of the bargain. I should prefer Henry; for what I should do is to drive him to the wall, compel him to give me my utmost pound of flesh, and then offer you your choice between his bargain and my original one. Still, there may be something that I am overlooking that should be secured in your interest; so perhaps it would be as well to put yourself in some hands less blindly egotistical than mine, however excellent my intentions may be towards you.

However, Henry's Tennysonian instance is worth considering, as T. was by no means a soft person in business. If Henry paid him a sum in advance and guaranteed him a fixed sum per week during the run of the play, then the arrangement may have been on the whole a handsome one, especially for an author who had absolutely no alternative, since for Tennyson it was a case of the Lyceum or nowhere (except perhaps Daly). But a percentage with an advance and guarantee is a very different matter to a percentage without either. Suppose, for example, I were to say you shall pay me so many hundred pounds on the delivery of the MS., and so many hundred more if the play is not produced by a certain date, and in addition guarantee me a run of six weeks, a minimum fee per week during the run (heads I win, tails you lose)! Henry's indignation would be justified, although the bargain would not be at all unprecedented. But when the author takes the risk of getting practically nothing in case of failure, it is quite another pair of shoes. Look at it from my point of view. I have put three months' hard professional work into the play, and only finished it in that time by a *tour de force* and by taking things otherwise very easily indeed at a horrifying rate of domestic expenditure. I then have to wait for my chance—only a chance—of getting paid for that work. You may produce the play in one year, two years, sometime, never—most likely never, because of the difficulty of your breaking with H. I. I take that risk, though I would bind H. I. himself in chains of gold to produce within a given time or pay penalties. When you do produce it, you will probably, like Murray Carson, try an experiment in the suburbs or provinces, on sharing terms. If this *ballon d'essai* collapses, you will lose your share of the cost of a cheap experiment; and I shall lose my work, coming out with absolutely nothing but the disgrace of failure. These conditions are so hard on the author (as such things go) that nobody of any standing would look at them for a moment as a mere matter of business. But have I exacted any *unusual* percentages to compensate me (generous creature!) for taking them?

Well, do you remember Oscar Wilde's sliding scale with Alexander, as disclosed in the bankruptcy proceedings? It went up to 15% for full houses; and Wilde got substantial advances. The agreement at the Haymarket for You Never Can Tell was for 10% on all receipts—no sliding scale, but 10 all through. Waring agreed to the same for The Devil's Disciple when there was a question of his playing it. For Kennington I am taking half Murray Carson's share of the profits on a license to the end of this month only. The 5, 7½, 10 sliding scale which I suggest for you is the ordinary provincial arrangement, and is the one I made with Florence Farr for Arms and the Man when I was unknown as a dramatic author, and bound to make matters as friendly as possible for her. If you look at a number of The Author, you will see that the customary fees for dramatists are stated there as from 5 to 15%.

Henry Arthur Jones tried a new plan at the Haymarket for Jane. It was agreed that the expenses should be put at £800 a week; and he took one third of everything over this, Harrison and Maude taking the other two thirds.

You will see by these examples that Henry's stupendous ignorance of everything connected with the drama is responsible for his remarks. At the same time, I should rather like to know what terms Sardou exacted for Robespierre.

Now let me shew you the other side of the business—the actor's side of it. Every farthing that is made out of Captain Brassbound will be made by a fresh stroke of labor on your part. You may be tired; you may be ill; you may be prostrated by grief; the play may become detestable to you by repetition. No matter: you will have to turn out and go through your part every time. Meanwhile I lie on my back and do nothing but tax the fruits of your hard work. Think of poor Mansfield for instance with The Devil's Disciple. He has drawn by bodily labor £25,000 from the American public by pounding away through it night after night. And I have had £2,500 of it without adding a stroke to the original work—about a couple of months' pastime—of writing it. And if I get £2,500 more, which seems likely enough, I shall still go on as hungrily as if I had never been paid a farthing. It is the old Socialistic difficulty, you see. An author, once he has hammered out a play, treats it as a landlord treats his land or a capitalist his investment: he lends it out at usury, and sweats the actual worker. However, there is an end to all things, even copyright. In forty years, or six years after my death, whichever period be the longer, the copyright will lapse; and then anybody may play Lady Cicely for nothing just as you play Portia. It is not a fair way of securing the author's living any more than it is fair that a charwoman should get eighteen shillings for a much harder week than ever Patti got £500 for; but it is the way we authorize at present. And its iniquities —literally its inequities—are the real secret of the rebellion of the actor— the protests of Henry. But I take a grim delight in exploiting Henry. He protests against the dramatists' shortlived toll; but at County Council elections and the like he takes the side of the ground landlord and contractor. And, as entrepreneur and manager, he does not see that what I do to him he does to the carpenter and checktaker. Ask him, and he will tell you that he is generous to his dependents. So am I: I take 10% when I might exact 15.

Now enough of political economy, which I inflict on you only to educate you as a manageress. To be immediately practical, there is one thing rather lacking between us; and that is a stamped agreement. However, keep my letters and depend on them for the present. The only danger you run is my death, and the subsequent disposal of the play by my executors to the highest bidder. I thought over this before I started on this tour; but as my successors would be Charlotte or my mother or Lucy (my sister) you would probably have less trouble with them than with me; so there is no great urgency in the matter. But before you make any engagements in the affair you must stir me up to give you explicit powers.

I have received the first night notices of the D.'s D., and a telegram from Carson about the West End; but I await further developments, as a first night sensation is invariable with me and does not afford the faintest presumption of a success. Arms and the Man had the wildest first night I ever saw; but it never drew £30 afterwards. I hope, however, the D.'s D. will come off solidly, as its success will make that of Capt. B. as certain as anything theatrical can be.

I'm full of remorse for your dear eyes when I look at this handwriting. The ship *will* joggle.

I've forgotten to bring your itinerary, so must send this to Earls Court. G. B. S.

CCXXXVI: E. T. *to* G. B. S.

[*Ellen Terry gave a copyright performance of Captain Brassbound's Conversion at Liverpool before sailing for America for her last tour there with Irving.*]

11 October 1899.
Liverpool

Capn. B's Conversion

I ENCLOSE
(1) Copy of the Poster
(2) Copy " " Programme
(3) Box office return of the Guinea!
(4) Cash expenses: two shillings! !

One part of the reading was perfectly done, by a **Mr W. Lugg.** A very tall white-haired, young-faced man, but the sparkle in the eye, the pleased-with-himself-and-everybody-else look, the smartness, the American accent, everything was truly refreshing. Drinkwater, the *really* cleverest in the

action, was missed. Laurence was surprisingly good. Tyars was—*Tyars!*
And bad at that! I gave him the part to read in a spirit of fun, thought it
would please him so to be a *Sir* Somebody! Sidi was good. (*Looked* so
well.) Marzo was good. They all loathe Lady Cicely. A "tremendous
humbug." "Arch" (!) "Detestable woman," etc., etc. I said "It's because
I read it wrong," but Edy who was in front, absorbed, and loving the
play, says I could not read the lines other than I did, but that it seemed
to her you *thought* your Lady C. *one* sort of woman and have *written*
another. Conveyed another idea. She doesnt think Lady C. is shown to
be either very clever or humorous, or vital, and certainly not "of great
humanity." I should have to get you to know more about Lady C.'s *inside*
before I did her! (Or did for her!)

Everyone loved the Play. Brassbound and Drinkwater are two overwhelming parts. Do you fancy Brassbound as looking like Mr Gillette—
in Secret Service—in exterior?

I'm rehearsing, and in my other time frightfully busy. No forwarder
in knowledge of future plans. On the Boat perhaps H. I. will *divulge!*
He is worried now and I cant bear to push him. We all enjoyed doing
your play immensely. H. I. never came near the place! Horrid of him.

CCXXXVII: G. B. S. *to* E. T.

12 October 1899.
S. S. *Lusitania*

GOOD God, Ellen, the Grecian Archipelago! Cant you see it in your
mind's eye, a group of exquisite islands in a turquoise setting?
Ugh! Cold, storm, sleety grey, pitching and rolling, misery, headaches,
horrors of universal belchings! A moment's respite in the Dardanelles
enables me to write to you: soon we shall be in the sea of Marmora,
reputed, as I learn for the first time, the coldest and windiest in the
world.

However, I am at least quit of Athens, with its stupid classic Acropolis
and smashed pillars. Charlotte, who *will* cultivate French acting and
thinks the Comédie Française the most perfect thing on earth, insisted
on my going to hear that bellowing donkey, Mounet Sully, as Othello.
Good Lord! The 4th act ended at 12.30; the fifth began punctually at one.
Poor Moony Silly grinned like a fairy queen in a fifth rate pantomime
and howled like a newsboy. Shakespear won the third act triumphantly;
and Moony got the credit of it. A horrible experience.

At Athens the best thing was your letter. Also a most aggravating telegram asking me what about the American rights—the very question I have been vainly asking you for a month past. However, there is no hurry about them now, since it is too late to do anything for this winter. So I will keep them for you until your return from your American tour, in the course of which you must try to arrange a Lady Cicely tour for 1900, on the understanding that the author's fees are to be the same as for England when *you* pay them. If Frohman or any other speculator pays them, they will be 10% all through, as for Mansfield.

Your offer of £500 for the entire rights of Brassbound shews a commendable wakening up on your part to your business responsibilities; but I wont take it, because it is far too little if the play succeeds, and far too much if it fails. Henry buys impossible plays from critics in that way, to bribe them. The fact is, if the play fails, I shall get nothing; but if it succeeds I fully intend you to make £5,000 for me before it is exhausted.

Marguerite de Valois was supposed some forty years ago to be a romantic person because she was a *femme galante.* As a matter of fact she was a beauty when she was a girl; but she ate too much and drank too much and soon became a ridiculous fat over-rouged creature at whom everybody laughed. No really able dramatist could make a heroine of her. A play about her might appeal to Henry, who has never read anything since he read Ainsworth's novels in his boyhood (that is, if he ever read any books at all); but it wont appeal to the public unless it is a very strong and quite unhistorical play—which of course it quite possibly may be.

I am inundated with notices of The Devil's Disciple, but cannot make out whether it was anything more than a first night Shaw firework. You ought to get Edy or somebody to go on some off night (not Saturday) in the second week, to see whether there is anybody in the house. But bless me! it is too late: the fortnight will be over before this reaches you. It is very important for you to know the real state of affairs; for if the D.'s D. (third act) is not only tolerated but popular, the battle is won for Lady Cicely.

Do not be anxious about the rights of Brassbound. I cannot do better than have you play it everywhere if you will. But I know the difficulties that will arise as to your getting free from the Lyceum; and I am not yet convinced that you will be able to do it at all. On the whole, if H. can induce you to postpone Lady C. for Marguerite, there seems no reason why he should not repeat that exploit *ad infinitum*. He is a crafty scoundrel, and an expert in hanging up plays that he does not want to do or let anyone else do. If I think he is going to outwit you, I shall write you a letter stating that the play is going to the Haymarket to be Lady Babbied into popularity there with Maude as the judge. And if that fails to rescue you I shall carry out the threat and devote the rest of my life to destroying H.'s prestige with my pen. So there! Ugh! Here's the Sea of Marmora! Farewell across the Atlantic. G. B. S.

CCXXXVIII: G. B. S. *to* E. T.

[*Redford: G. A. Redford, the official Examiner of Plays for licensing by the Lord Chamberlain. His refusal to license Tolstoy's Powers of Darkness, Ibsen's Ghosts, Brieux's Les Avariés, Shaw's Mrs Warren's Profession, Press Cuttings, and The Shewing Up of Blanco Posnet made him specially obnoxious to the advance guard of the drama. He was a well-meaning but (for the purposes of his office) extaordinarily stupid man.*]

13 October 1899.
Constantinople.
S. S. *Lusitania*

MY DEAR ELLEN,

YOUR Liverpool manager, on hearing from the Lord Chamberlain's office that he might perform Brassbound and that his cheque (mine) had come safely to hand, promptly replied that he knew nothing about it and had never sent any play or any cheque. Whereupon Redford very civilly writes to Fitzroy Square for an explanation, but of course gets none, as I am at the other end of Europe. I am writing to him by this post, and hope that no hitch was made as to the performance by the mistake. I suppose you forgot to warn the manager, and he couldnt conceive that a play by me could have any reference to Sir Henry Irving's tour.

We are just now at anchor in the Golden Horn, and Constantinople smells—oh, how it smells! Yet it looks rather well by moonlight; but I am too tired, after a day spent shuffling about the mosques in ridiculous overshoes, to write more. Besides, you'll get my other letter by this same post.

ever and ever
G. B. S.

CCXXXIX: E. T. *to* G. B. S.

[The war: the South African War]

(Dictated)

28 January 1900.
Boody House,
Toledo, O.

MY DEAR MR BERNIE,

I HAVE been thinking of you every day for the last fortnight, for I'm sure you must be thinking that I am behaving very badly to you. It seems so, I know. But it's only "Seems"! Until a few days since I couldnt see beyond my nose into the immediate future. Now there's a glimmer of light ahead and I can see plainly enough.

So far, my little maid—a secretary-cook-dressmaker-house-maid, (where she began 6 years ago). But now it is next day 29 January. My headache has passed away and I'll write to you my own self.

This is the situation!

My intention (nearly fixed) had been to finish this present tour with H., go back to the Lyceum with him, play there until the Theatre closed in July, and never again to act with H. After a good rest, I should then have announced "a farewell tour" on my own account and hoped to reap, with about two years' work, enough Corn to provide against a Famine in my old age. (And for my children. I feed them all the while, I assure you. *Not* I hope *"over-*feed" them, but I believe in a good generous diet for the growing body and brain of the young, and so all along I have not *"stenched"* (!) them, as my gardener boy said. He meant *stinted!*)

In these two years my intention was to provide myself with two or three new plays and re-prepare three old ones and with these 6 to go around the English provinces and through some American and Canadian cities, just saving all the money possible, and then, if I lived through it—which I probably should (I'm so tough)—do my best to become a dear old Frump in an arm chair in one of my pretty cottages, and teach Ted's youngest babes to be rather useful and not to trouble about little things.

Now, however my plans are somewhat shattered, for H. is wanting to arrange an autumn tour here, and asks me to come too. A tour of six months beginning next October. This, if I agree to it, will probably see me through most of the rest of my working life! This beastly Robespierre is what they call "a Boom" over here, and we carry it on for a long time. As it has turned out I see quite well he could have come out here this time without me! I told him so yesterday. My very tiny part could have been played well enough by a £10 per week actress. It scarcely counts in the play. However he wants me to come again. *And,* looking at the situation all around, I think I shall come!

To begin with, my head aches too often for me not to consider the chances of my breaking *up* (!) under the pressure of anxious times, of times of enterprise. If I did break down the younger people would soon make ducks and drakes of the very moderate sum I have got together by close steady work. I rather dread poverty. My needs are very few: but oh, if I could never help anyone with that *useful stuff,* "golden ointment," when they were gashed and slashed, in need, it would come very hard to me. The six months tour would bring me about——. I have noted the sum. It is not usually made with ease!

Do you apprehend my situation now? Do you call me "a money-grubber"? A weak, unenterprising, silly fool? An ass? I have not the time, nor the ability, to show you the ins and outs of the whole affair. I appear to be of strange *use* to H., and I have always thought to be *useful, really* useful to any one person *is* rather fine and satisfactory. Now if I come back to America in October I can no longer hope that you will keep Brassbound for me! Must I give it up? Do you think me dishonest to have philandered so long about the dear play and now tell you this long rigmarole? Is the prospect for the autumn of 1901 too far off for you, and for me (as a grandmother)? Must it go to another?

Write me a dear letter, and dont be hard on me! Have you read about this Dramatic Syndicate business in America? A nice fellow (Norman Hapgood of New York) is being slated (by the D. Syndicate, I rather think!) for what he writes about the unfairness of the arrangement. Mr Frohman, who holds the whole American theatre in his hand, is treating *us* exceeding well, but surely the whole affair is *un*-fair! Isnt it, my dear righter-of-the-wrong?

If my play, *your* play, *our* play, Brassbound, goes to another I should like Mrs Minnie Maddern Fiske to have it! She is a very clever, very nice woman, and has suffered greatly by the Syndicate game. Altho' as I write, I am told she has either gone over, or is going over, to the stronger side. A little while ago, I know, she could neither get a decent theatre to act in, nor buy a play of any worth. "All along o' 'the Syndicate.'" She would play Lady C. splendidly, and would be glad enough to get the Play. If I came over here alone (I mean without H.) if Frohman were "running" H. and wanted to keep me out of it all, he could!

I dont think he would, for of course H. would not wish it so (not so unfair as that), and altho' I dont know Frohman at all well, still he is not a pretty fellow at all I believe.

Oh my dear friend, how I must tire you with my words—words—words! To conclude: Write me a word about what I am to do in re *the Play*—Capn. B.'s Conversion.

I'm very fairly well and look *very* well. My hair is getting nicely grey (lively for Lady C.!), and it is becoming! The climate is to blame for that, not worry. What's the *use* of worrying? I meet some very nice and pleasant and good people in most of the places I visit and am just looking forward to the next minute and not beyond it! The war—and the disgrace of it (beef-headed Buller's doings)—this is the only subject which excites me and makes me want to kill, Kill, KILL! I often think of you, and hope that your Charlotte is well and very happy, that your poor leg is less brittle, and your brain as unclouded as ever, and your heart as fresh. I wonder are you reading the new Tolstoy. (Resurrection.) Dear Gentleman, farewell. Give me news of you and yours, and forgive this terrible scrawl.

ELLEN

I must ask you to be careful and keep this private as it concerns H.'s business affairs. E. T.

CCXL: G. B. S. *to* E. T.

[*The Stage Society referred to in this letter has managed to survive for 30 years. Besides You Never Can Tell it has produced the following plays by Shaw: Candida, for the first time in London (July 1900); Captain Brassbound's Conversion (December 1900); Mrs Warren's Profession (January 1902); Man and Superman (May 1905); Augustus Does His Bit (1917).— Dolmetsch concert: Arnold Dolmetsch, a high authority on old music and the pioneer of the movement for performing it on the instruments for which it was composed. He was able to prove that the harpsichord and clavichord ought never to have been allowed to become obsolete, not only by restoring fine specimens of the work of old craftsmen, but by making these instruments himself and exhibiting their capacities at his concerts of old music. He was at this time giving these concerts in his house in Bayley Street, Bloomsbury. He now has a workshop at Haslemere, Surrey, and gives annual festivals there.*]

Very well, dear Ellen: we cry off Brassbound. I have always foreseen, and foretold to you, that when it came to the point, you would find it practically impossible to detach yourself from the Lyceum. And apart from the business reasons, the breaking up of an old partnership like yours and H. I.'s is not a thing to be done except on extreme occasion. It was my feeling concerning this that made me so very determined not to let you interfere in the Man of Destiny squabble. I wrote Brassbound for you merely for the sake of writing it for you, without any faith in your ever being able to produce it, knowing that the existence of the play would strengthen your hold of H. I. (by making you independent of him if you chose to abandon his ship) and thereby make it doubly certain that he would not let you go for want of asking you to stay —and obviously if he really wants you to stay, stay you must. Consequently I am in no way disappointed or surprised: destiny has fulfilled itself exactly as I foresaw it would if affairs took their normal course.

You are quite right to return to America for the winter tour. I never go into a theatre now; but the gossip is that business is very bad, the war being apparently unfavorable to it. To throw away a certain £2,400 for the chance of losing that sum and worrying your life out with a new part and a new theatre would be madness. No sane friend, as *was* a friend, could advise you to act otherwise than you are acting.

Only, I want you to face the fact that this means that you are not going to do Brassbound at all—never, world without end. The reasons which prevent your doing it now will be stronger in 1901. I told you that if you accepted the St Bartholomew part, that would virtually cast the die, as the same position would inevitably recur at the beginning of every fresh season, and at each recurrence you would make the same choice. So now for one of my celebrated *volte faces*. I hold on pretty hard until the stars declare themselves against me, and then I always give up and try something else with a promptitude which seems cynical and unfeeling to the slow witted Englishman who only tells himself his misfortunes by degrees. And now I recognize that you and I can never be associated as author and player—that you will remain Olivia, and that Lady Cicely is some young creature in short skirts at a High School at this moment. I have pitched so many dreams out of the window that one more or less makes little difference. In fact, by this time I take a certain Satanic delight in doing it and noting how little it hurts me. So out of the window you go, my dear Ellen; and off goes the play to my agents as in the market for the highest bidder. Mrs Maddie Minnern Fiske shall have it unless somebody else offers sixpence more.

At least that is what I will do when I have time. But I am so full of serious work just now that I have hardly any time for bothering about these plays.

The agitation against the syndicate is all nonsense: it is just the same as the wail of the small shopkeeper when you go to the Stores or to Shoolbred's. It is quite true that the syndicate deals mostly in machine made melodramas and farcical comedies that are not even machine made; but that is because the public (meaning the shop-girls mostly) want them. The reason Mrs Maddie couldnt get any plays was that she wanted the same plays as the syndicate. If she had wanted better ones, she could have got them just as you did.

The Stage Society, a sort of Sunday night Independent Theatre started by an energetic Fabian, did You Never Can Tell the other day. Performance might have been worse. At any rate we shall hear no more now about its being a bad stage play. I was ashamed of its tricks and laughs and popularities. It would make a great hit at the Lyceum with Henry as the Waiter.

This Stage Society, by the way, is catching on in its little coterie-theatre way. The announcement of You Never Can Tell brought in three hundred members at two guineas each like a shot. What do you think of that? Edy seems to be a member: she was at the last performance. Met her also at a Dolmetsch concert, immediately after a report had appeared in the papers here describing you as having harangued a crowd in your nightdress from the windows of a burning hotel, exhorting them to be calm, and being finally carried down the fire-escape by Henry (in pyjamas) amid tremendous cheering.

Emery Walker, an old Morris-circle friend of mine, wants me to meet H. B. Irving at his house (at H. B.'s instance). Now I should put H. B. on to Brassbound like a shot if I could see Dorothea as Lady Cicely. But I dont: do you?

Do not excite yourself about the war: it is quite the usual thing. Charlotte's brother-in-law (Colonel Hugh Cholmondeley) has gone out with the City Imperial Volunteers. Cholmondeley took them out on Wimbledon Commons to see them ride; and presently the common was strewn in all directions with the Dismounted Infantry. They had mostly learnt their manège at Mawgit [Margate] or on Empstead Eath. Poor devils!

The above named Emery Walker once met H. I. at dinner. H. I. had me on his nerves at that time, and complained to E. W. that I had a disagreeable lack of reverence for persons in dignified positions. Walker hastily remarked that I was a special friend of his; and the subject dropped before further blood was shed.

Oh my dear Ellen, now that I have thrown you out of the window, I am fain to go and sweep you up gently and put you together again. But that would be weakness.

G. B. S.

P. S. You dont give me any address; so I must send this to the next theatre on your itinerary. Chicago is a comparatively enlightened town; my plays get good houses there. Mansfield revived Arms and the Man for a night in New York last month. It was still alive enough to draw $1000.

CCXLI: E. T. *to* G. B. S.

8 February 1900.
Planters Hotel,
St Louis, U. S. A.

H ENRY's plans are altered, and I write at once to tell you this, before I begin to think over my own plans. Instead of coming back here next October, the trip is to be put off for a year. I fancy his engagement with the Lyceum Syndicate is for 5 years. At the end of that time he would be able to take a farewell tour *alone,* that is to say without *sharing* with a Directing Company.

Please, under these new circumstances, think for me a bit and I will think also. I am of course obliged to carry through my share of the plan to appear with H. the end of May, for June and July, at the Lyceum.

This place, St Louis, suggests that the wild and woolly West is wilder and woolly-er than ever. A man was "held up" in the street last night for 10 cents! The Police are all "in" with the roughs and toughs, and in the *Society* column it is announced that "Mrs Otis will hold a *Welsh Rarebit,* in honor of her niece Miss Maimie Otis."

The Board of Health warns all against drinking the water without boiling; and the streets are over one's feet in slush and mud. And yet I love the country! So many *nicer* happenings, than nasty. But you see I have red baize laid down for *me* from England all through America and back again! They spoiled me. Oh, I could be homesick tho' if I "let myself go." No good yet awhile.

Yours

E. T.

CCXLII: E. T. *to* G. B. S.

24 March 1900

I AM *rushed* too much for a sick woman.

Yes, Minnie certainly *is* at loggerheads with the Frohman Syndicate. *That* I fear is a fact. She plays everything well, however, and—— oh, I dont care for anything. I'm disgusted at my not *weakness* but *strength* in sticking on with folk who wont "play fair." I want only *that*. I never say one word, and never look disgusted nor show contempt. It's all too late, but I am deeply furious (inwardly) that all my desire for Brassbound is all of no use! A man solid for *HIMSELF* is like the Boer Kopje land. There's no impression made upon him by anything outside of him! There's a true stolid *innocence* and *ignorance* of anything and everything going on outside the HIM. It's amusing and frustrating. I'd like to know if you are well nowadays. You and C. I've been very ill. Am very well now. E. T.

CCXLIII: E. T. *to* G. B. S.

[Andromache was later on produced by the Stage Society]

13 June 1900.
22 Barkston Gardens

I HAVE bought Gilbert Murray's Andromache. I read it the second day I was in England. It's fine—but I will have nothing to do with the Lyceum plans for the future. Only refuse to act in too, too bad a play. What is it you say? "Do something for Fame." How funny! If only I could get a little rested! I'd do something for *fun,* for just love of the doing it, but there can be no sport for me until I get some rest. I had a nice time last evening at Mr Dolmetsch's little Bayley Street house. I was positively rested enough to enjoy it—having stayed in bed all day on purpose. Pity me on Saturday. *Olivia* "at my time of life." It is the *audience* I pity, for I feel quite young all the time I am playing in a young part, but they wont know how young I feel if I cant *look* young. This is scrawled in a cab on my way to rehearsal. Will you give me an Automobile Hansom? I want one. It's *so* ugly, but one is there in a flash—and then I could live in the country and work in town. Any more plays? I hear Candida is to be done on the July Sunday (I like Mrs Warren better). Are the dear legs (that look like a hairpin!) all well again now? Where (in what printed thing) are you writing now?

E. T.

CCXLIV: E. T. *to* G. B. S.

[*The Stage Society produced* Candida *for the first time in London on 1 July 1900, and Edith Craig played Prossy as she had in the original production by the Independent Theatre in the Provinces.—Gordon Craig's production of Purcell's* Dido and Æneas *in May was an important event in the history of the theatre, but at the time this was not realized.—J. F. Runciman was the music critic of* The Saturday Review.]

4 July 1900

MY DEAR BERNIE,

How was Edy's behaviour as the typewriter last Sunday? I could not be there to see. Have you heard anything, I wonder, of the doing of the "Purcell Operatic Society"? Ted had a big finger in the performance of Dido last May and if the thing could be seen for a week at least at the proper place, at the proper time, exactly as it was seen in May at Hampstead, I should feel inclined to back it in a substantial manner and I know two others who would follow suit. Mr Saturday Review is a funny man. *Runciman*, isnt it? I wish you would advise me on the Purcell question. Since my children are very enthusiastic and hot over it, I dont want to be cold, but I lack knowledge: help me a little, please!

E. T.

CCXLV: G. B. S. *to* E. T.

[*Purcell's* Dido and Æneas *was first performed at Mr Josiah Priest's boarding-school at Chelsea, between 1688 and 1690. Mr Barclay Squire, the author of the article on Purcell in Grove's Dictionary, says that "in dramatic directness, characterisation, adaptation of means to ends, feeling for climax, as well as actual beauty, the opera is as much alive in the 20th century as are any of Gluck's." Shaw attributes his coolness about the work and this notable production of it by Gordon Craig to the fact that it was no novelty to him, as it was always chosen for performances by Purcell enthusiasts, though* King Arthur *and* The Faery Queen, "much bigger and more brilliant works, could alone have effectively revived Purcell's vogue, as the performances at Cambridge under Cyril Rootham subsequently proved."— The italics in this letter are Ellen Terry's.*]

4 July 1900.
10 Adelphi Terrace, W. C.

O NLY time for two words about business, though I have been longing to write to you for weeks. But I am crazy with work over The Devil's Disciple, half printer, half Forbes-Robertson.

Dido has been done for the first and only time since its original production at the girl's school on quite a number of occasions within my recollection. Nothing more can be done with it than they did at Hampstead (*not that I was there;* but I know the work). It might be repeated at Blackheath, Ealing, Brixton etc. etc., on the same scale; but if Ted wants you to take Covent Garden for it, dont. There is a very devoted little Purcell public clustering round Dolmetsch, whom Runciman (can I mediate with him in any way, by the by: I know him?) writes up very properly; but it is a very tiny public; and what your phrase "substantial backing" suggests to me is quite out of the question. Tell me exactly what is proposed, and I will tell you exactly what I know as to its chances. Meanwhile, hold your hand, and love me as much as you can.

G. B. S.

CCXLVI: G. B. S. *to* E. T.

[*The play Forbes-Robertson was rehearsing was The Devil's Disciple.— E. W. Garden: an experienced comedian who made his first appearance in the days of the old stock companies at Nottingham in 1864.*]

10 July 1900.
10 Adelphi Terrace, W. C.

I N MY haste I left your last letter only half answered.

Edy pulled off the typist successfully—how, I dont exactly know. I believe she actually worked at it when it came to the point. The first impression she produces (professionally) on an author is that she is incapable of application, and lends a hand on the stage out of sheer good nature, to help a lame dog over a stile. At the rehearsals, she so utterly failed to express any indignation or surprise when she was called a liar by the poet, that we concluded that she had no moral sense, and had heard the same remark from you every day of her life since her birth. All she had to say was "Oh!", but she could only say "O," without any note of exclamation. "I'm saying it as loud as I can," she would observe, in reply to the agonized remonstrances of the author. She came to Adelphi Terrace for private instruction, and made a most agreeable impression on Charlotte, but received none whatever concerning the part from Charlotte's unfortunate husband. However, when the night came, nervousness, or something that produced grip, seized her; and the audience was delighted. So was I, as she was pleasanter than the real Prossy, and kept the scene with the poet far nicer than she (the real one) could have done.

What have you done about Dido? I am afraid my advice was rather confused and inconclusive. What I meant to convey was, shortly, that Dido is musical and not theatrical business. The difference is that with music each performance must pay for itself, the money at the door paying all the performers and the rent, and leaving a surplus; whereas with theatre business, you invest a heap of money, and only get it back in the course of a run. Moral: Do not back Dido for a run; but if a performance costing £80 can be given in a hall holding £100, then the thing will pay if the hall is full, and if it isnt, it wont. Dido *might* fill a hall: the thing is not impossible that's all I can say.

I am nearly dead with work because of the wiliness of Forbes-Robertson. I usually rely on my bad character to get me kept away from rehearsals; but Forbes politely begged me to *conduct* the first rehearsals and settle the business, besides reading the play. Of course the result is that everything goes on castors: at each rehearsal we take one act, and go through it twice. It goes without a hitch, and we are off in two hours to lunch, remarking, if you please, that the play is *quite easy*. And they think that since I only have to prepare an act at a time, it is holiday work for me, whereas with the Vestry, the Fabian, the printers (American and English) and a thousand other things, I am working like mad sixteen hours a day. Such is life—*my* life.

The only dreadful thing is that as far as I can ascertain there are only two men in the country who can act. Of course I have had to give them the two little parts (the sergeant and the silly brother) because these are comic and character parts; and you *must* have acting for comedy and character, whereas the big serious sympathetic parts take care of themselves with a little coaching. But imagine the feelings of a competent old professional, longing to play the big part and able to do it, when the author gives it to a goodhearted young duffer and puts him the (c. o. p.) into a mere bit of clowning. I experience agonies of remorse every time I meet E. W. Garden's eye: I long to atone by writing him a curtain raiser all to himself. Will you come and see us some day? I enclose a portrait of my latest love meeting me by moonlight alone.

G. B. S.

CCXLVII: G. B. S. *to* E. T.

28 October 1900.
10 Adelphi Terrace, W. C.

DEAR MISS TERRY,

MAY I presume on a correspondence which passed between us several years ago so far as to ask your advice in the following matter.

A play of mine entitled Captain Brassbound's Conversion is to be performed privately by the Stage Society, probably under the new title Ellen Brassheart's Obduracy. It was written for a deserving actress employed in a subordinate capacity by an Ogre at one of our leading theatres. Neither my personal advances nor my play, however, made any impression on this insensible female; and now the question is, who is to play the part? The matter is urgent; and I shall have to appeal in desperation to Mrs Kendal as the only alternative supplying the requisite technical accomplishment, unless you will be good enough to suggest another way out of the difficulty.

You will be glad to hear that Mr Forbes-Robertson's tour with The Devil's Disciple, Hamlet, and Othello, has been—at least as far as the first named play is concerned (naturally I have not seen the returns from the others) a success. When Cæsar and Cleopatra is produced with the millions thus acquired, Mr Forbes-Robertson will take the position that belongs to him on the English stage; but he will be generous to old employers: the part of second gravedigger will ever be at the disposal of the Ogre.

On the occasion of my last visit to Mr F-R.'s study, I observed that a certain laurel-crowned portrait had disappeared, and that the place of honor was again occupied by the woman who jilted *me*.

I have the honor to be, dear Miss Terry,

Your obedient servant,
GEORGE BERNARD SHAW

CCXLVIII: E. T. *to* G. B. S.

2 November 1900

THE question is not of *Brassbound* but of *BEEF!*

"They say" that you have eaten a steak, "the Apostate Shaw." How much I should like to know the *truth* of the matter, the only matter which can concern me at this moment when I am on an uncomfortable bed in a poor Manchester lodging, and have been stuck there the last 2 weeks unable to act, unable to do anything but cough all day and all night. How the thought of you and *that steak* has worried me. "I'd like to know" (*American saying*).

I have not seen Henry since I got your letter. I fear he is greatly driven in consequence of my illness (*so aggravating!*) but on Sunday I can speak to him (for the last time) about Brassbound since you so Angel-like open up the subject again. I only see *one* way in which I (belonging to H. I. and "the Concern") could get a chance of doing the play. Henry doesnt like it. I adore it.

To save each other labour in America we used to arrange matters thus on Saturdays, when a double performance:

Matinée—Amber Heart	Nance Oldfield	E. T.
Evening—Bells	Waterloo	H. I.

Or sometimes it was:

Matinée—Amber Heart	E. T.	Waterloo	H. I.
Evening—The Bells	H. I.	Waterloo	H. I.

Now if I had the Matinée all to myself, well and good! For Brassbound need not be necessarily acted by Henry. But I see no possible reason why *you* should agree to this, altho' this is the only way I can imagine H. I. would let me play the part of Lady C.

Just tell me you will consent to B. being played only once a week and of course then I will play it, but you wont do this I feel sure. Besides there's Mrs Kendal who would play it as she plays all her parts, *finely,* and there's the Stage Society. (I have had half a dozen visitors in and out all the while I'm trying to write to you from my bed, and I can only "give it up.")

On Sunday I'll see Henry and give him another chance. I'll say *you* have given me another chance to have the play, and then I'll write to you. *You* meanwhile tell me if you consent that I should play Lady C. once a week. And, tell me too if you no longer are a vegetarian. I hope you are weller than I am, tho' I hope to be very well. E. T.

CCXLIX: G. B. S. *to* E. T.

3 November 1900.
10 Adelphi Terrace, W. C.

O ELLEN, Ellen, you have given me no address. "A poor Manchester lodging" only oppresses me (I know those Manchester lodgings): it does not enable me to reach you through the post in time for H. I. on

Sunday. The cough, too—but no matter: everybody has a cough now. It is the weather, I suppose. My mother has had to go to Margate, and as for me, I get fresh colds and sneezings every five minutes, and my gums ache, and my soul despairs, and my election to the Borough Council seems a sentence of hard labor (as it actually is).

The story about the steak is a weak invention of the enemy. Even Charlotte is beginning to doubt the necessity of cannibalism.

The Saturday arrangement as to Brassbound would not work, even if it were a reasonable proposal in other respects. The play, treated that way, would fail, probably. I dont care whether Henry likes the play or not: the quality of the play is my business, not his. If it is produced on his tour, he must play in it himself; and he must bind himself to produce it in London the next time he plays there. It must become the most important work he has in hand. I confer an enormous and undeserved favor on him by letting "the concern" have it for your sake.

But all this is hopeless and useless. I told you you would have to choose between Lady Cicely and Henry; and I foresaw that when it came to the point you would have no real choice in the matter. Only, when it comes to writing to Mrs Madge, it seems a pity that you cannot at least create the part, and shew a select few what they will lose when you go back to your Amber Hearts and Nance Oldfields and the like.

How could we two be such fools as to avoid meeting each other lest we should rub the bloom off our relations, and then enter into that most accursed of all relations, the professional relation? Why did I not rather spring on that foolish Lyceum stage, drag you bodily away, and ravish you a thousand times rather than write a play for you? For it has now become a mere money business and nothing else. Charlotte is entitled to half profits; and I am no longer free to give the play away, save on honourable conditions; and these stolen Saturday conditions are silly.

Oh, let us have done with it and never mention it again. I am for the highest bidder now. (Did you mention a sum, Mrs Brown Potter, Mrs Anybody—)

But never shall the Ogre be forgiven.

G. B. S.

CCL: E. T. *to* G. B. S.

[*"My farm": Small Hythe Place, Tenterden, Kent, a fine Tudor timbered house Ellen Terry had bought at Michaelmas (1900). When it was made habitable a few years later she spent every summer there, and after her retirement from the stage it was her favorite home. She died at Small*

Hythe, and shortly after her death a fund was started to purchase the house
as a memorial. The minimum sum needed to acquire and endow it has not
been reached at the time of this publication, but it has been adapted for the
purpose of a memorial museum by her daughter Edith Craig, and is shown
to visitors.]

7 November 1900.
35 Princes Avenue,
Liverpool

H ENRY says—but never mind what he says. (I cant much nowadays,
try how I will.) Of course the Saturday arrangement would not
work, so farewell Lady C. Ah, I feel so certain Henry just hates me! I
can only *guess* at it, for he is exactly the same sweet-mannered person
he was when "I felt so certain" Henry loved me! We have not met for
years now, except before other people, where my conduct exactly matches
his of course. All my own fault. It is *I* am changed, not he. It's all right,
but it has squeezed me up dreadfully, and after the long pause of illness,
I went back last night, weak and nervous, but looking well and acting
well, thank the Lord. Only for the first time not glad to go back to my
dear work.

I cant speak, you see, so it has been a very tough business. I'm better
now, and if I were not a *worm* I'd take my illness as an excuse to outsiders and leave all theatres, Henry, "and such like trash," behind me
and go and live on my farm, but all folk are better working hard, and
I know he wants me more than ever in the theatre so on I go. Now:
business.

I have the Acts and all the Parts of Brassbound all beautifully typed,
remember. Shall I tell my stupid-good-servants at home to send them to
me (so I see they are right) and *I* send them to *you?* Will Mrs Madge
play it? That would prevent its being acted by the Stage Society wouldnt
it? But who for Brassbound? Oh dear, oh dear! I and H. would have
been *perfect* in it. He riles me so (but nowadays I've learned from him
and never show I'm riled) when he says "Brassbound is like *a Comic
Opera*"! So stupid, and of course you know he is *not* stupid. Oh, by no
manner of means.

Now, am I to send you the MSS and the "Parts"? And am I to send
you money for having delayed the production of your play so long? It
only seems fair I should, it seems to me. If in doubt ask Charlotte! To
her my salaams and to you too.

E. T.

281

CCLI: G. B. S. *to* E. T.

NEWS this morning that the incontinent youth Johnston Forbes-Robertson is going to be led to the altar by his leading lady, Miss Gertrude Elliott. I foresaw it, and wanted to put a clause in our agreement against it. However, he might do worse. She is a nice American woman, and will mend his extensively broken heart for him.

No reply as yet from Mrs Madge. Let us hope that she will indignantly refuse to act on Sunday. My feeling about it is that I should like everybody to refuse, leaving me to beat you with a poker for your infamous desertion of me. Duse herself can be nothing to me in the part but your supplanter. You wretch, you! You faithless, lazy, trifling good-for-nothing! Were your gifts entrusted to you to endow you as Matron of The Concern? Damn the Concern!

Of course he hates you when you talk to him about me. Talk to him about himself: then he will love you, to your great alarm. I know what it is to be loved. Good heavens! You are a thousand times right to keep me out of reach of your petticoats. What people call love is impossible except as a joke (and even then one of the two is sure to turn serious) between two strangers meeting accidentally at an inn or in a forest path. Why, I dare not for my life's happiness make love to my own wife. A delusion, Ellen, all this love romance: that way madness lies.

You need not pay for detaining Brassbound. My allusion to Charlotte's interests was one of those brutalities which are useful in forcing people to attend to business. I get mischievous impulses of that sort occasionally. And I love the sordid side of business: the play of economic motive fascinates me.

I had a most tragic scene yesterday with the Charringtons, not having seen them since they played Candida at the Stage Society. They wanted to do matinées of it at the Comedy; and I said that Janet only pulled it through—wasnt the right woman for it at all, and that Charrington was grotesquely damnable as the parson, and should never play it again. Then the tempest raged round this heartless Eddystone. It was the more cruel because my marriage has cut me off a good deal from them. Janet said everything she could lay her tongue to: Charrington was cut to the soul: the Eddystone shone without a flicker until the exhausted ocean calmed itself and the sky shone again. But they sternly renounced their moral rights in the play, observing that now they had made it a success, no doubt other people would make money out of it. And so forth, the Eddystone, being a revolving light, merely winking. So you can now play Candida since you wont play Lady Cicely.

That is all the news, so far.

G. B. S.

CCLII: E. T. to G. B. S.

[*Captain Brassbound's Conversion was produced by the Stage Society at the Old Strand Theatre (pulled down in 1904) on 16 December 1900. Janet Achurch played Lady Cicely Waynflete, and Laurence Irving Captain Brassbound.*]

[Some time in December 1900.]

Newcastle

I WONDER is it true you are going to do Brassbound on December 16? So I am told. (If it had been *January 16,* I could have been there to see. This present tour ends on the 22nd of this month.) I dont think I shall be acting all the summer! Henry is very ill, and it is necessary now that he should obey "Doctor's orders" and go South. He is splendid, but he *must* give in, and he knows it. I shall probably carry out his arrangements for another Tour in February and March. I have my hands full now he's ill, as you would say if you could only see us. He is very good now and lets me do everything for him. However, I'm glad when he has a cross day now and again for then I know he is feeling better for the minute. In a few days people interested will know his plans. What's going to be *said* I dont quite know, but I do know he is very ill, and that a lot of hard work is before me. Then in the summer, rest I hope. Meanwhile with "thoughts and remembrance" I send you the Lord Chamberlain's license for Brassbound, as I conclude you may want it.

I heard lovely things about your Charlotte the other day, from a *man.* I send you both my love.

L. N.

Just starting for rosy Sheffield.

CCLIII: E. T. to G. B. S.

[*Mr Jimmy Welch: James Welch, an actor of rare talent, who became a favourite with the public in farcical comedies, but gave his best performances in plays by Ibsen, Shaw, and Maxim Gorki. He played Lickcheese in the first performance of Shaw's first play Widowers' Houses (1892) and the*

283

Waiter in the first performance of You Never Can Tell *(1899); but he re-*
fused the part of Drinkwater because he thought the passage in which the
poor little cockney hooligan breaks down over the threatened destruction of
his "library" of the old "penny numbers" which "formed his mind" was
too silly to be acted. Laurence Irving was at this time a member of his fa-
ther's company, and had to return from the Stage Society's rehearsals of
Brassbound to play in the Lyceum performances in the provinces at night.]

[Some time in December 1900.]
Sheffield

WHAT exciting news! Brassbound on the 16th and I *shall* be able to
see it. May I ask you to trouble to get me a box by any means,
rough or smooth? And Laurence is to be "Brassbound"! I'm very glad,
for many reasons. Who "Drinkwater"? Weedon Grossmith? Or Dan
Leno? Mr Jimmy Welch I hope.

There was doubt about H. I. going "on Tour" in February and
March. Now it is decided he will go, and rest during the summer.

Brassbound! I cant get away from the thought. If I get the box for
that night Edy and her friend and I and my friend can cram into it
and oh, shant we enjoy it all. I'm going off my head! Laurence must
be sure not to miss his train, and must be back in time to act here during
his rehearsals in town.

BRASSBOUND! Too, too bad that I am not Lady C. Really tho' you
might as well have let me have it for a couple of performances a week,
as do it on Sundays "for the Stage Society"! Sooner or later I know
I'll play Lady C.

I'm so enchanted that you and Laurence have met. I hope Charlotte
likes him. If you dont (both of you) like him now, you *must* in time.
He is unique.

CCLIV: E. T. *to* G. B. S.

[*The serious professional actress trained in a serious school speaks in this*
letter. "Some of us who derive from this school," her son Gordon Craig
writes in his Henry Irving, *"follow Irving anyhow in this. . . . We do better*
to err on the side of being even a trifle too serious about it all, rather than
not serious enough."—By "Captain" is meant Captain Kearney, the com-
mander of the American ship who presides over the court of enquiry on
Brassbound and his gang.]

284

7 December 1900.
Sheffield

A m I "ever serious about my plans"? Well *my* plans are bounded by another's plans outside mine, always, but *you!* How about *your* being "serious about your plans." To try to get together a company, rehearse and produce a play under a fortnight! I'm more serious in my plans than *that!*

Twelve careful rehearsals are needed for that play. One might *do* with 6 long very careful ones, but what *can* be the result of your present plans? If I were you I would at once announce Candida, or something else of yours (You Never Can Tell) for Sunday 16, and do Brassbound a few Sundays further on. . . . The thing might be given a *chance* of success by the right people being collected and rehearsed. (Our man Lugg was an admirable "Captain.")

I'm glad Charlotte likes Laurence. Yes, it's a "crool shime" this back and forwarding in trains but the young and tender can endure any physical discomfort.

Yes, Laurence does love his father. We both do, but oh Lord how he does try us!

I think I told you he (H. I.) had decided not to go on tour in February. Well, now he has changed his plans and *will* go. *How* much I do wish I could see your rehearsals of Brassbound. Edy was much struck by our absurd first (and only) rehearsal. She sat in the stalls and was spellbound and said it all "came out" (even in that rough rehearsal) better than in the reading. Dont stop to read this. Off, off and rehearse night and day the little time there is left, or better still concoct an excuse and postpone the play until 3rd or 4th week in January. . . .

Try to get—But of course you have studied the advertisements for names and will have to get anyone who will come, unless you *POST-PONE*. DO, DO, DO.

L. N.

CCLV: E. T. *to* G. B. S.

[*At the performance of Brassbound, two days after the letter following was written, Ellen Terry and Bernard Shaw met. (In Letter CCLVIII Ellen Terry refers to the meeting.) Fifteen months then passed before the correspondence was resumed, and in the twenty years following, which include three years when no letters at all were exchanged, it averages three letters a year. From these data the inference might reasonably be drawn that the disenchantment that Ellen Terry dreaded would be the result of a meeting with Shaw had actually occurred. Some readers will be the more tempted to draw it because of Ellen Terry's remark: "They say you could not bear me, when we met, that one time, under the stage." (See Letter CCLVIII.) But the following note by Shaw suggests that the meeting had nothing to do either with the subsequent slackening in the correspondence or with the change in the relations of the correspondents.]*

R EADERS with an eye for dates and a turn for statistics have perhaps already noted that the correspondence had slackened two years before the meeting. In 1896 the pair had written to one another every four days. In 1897 every three days. During these two years they must have written to one another to solace themselves in every spare moment. In 1898 they wrote every eleven or twelve days, on the old affectionate terms, but always on business as well as for fun. And in 1898 Shaw married, and was presumably no longer wholly dependent on Ellen Terry for his more intimate unbosomings. There was no breach between them, and never was any to the end; but the delicious flirtation changed insensibly into a friendship in which the relations became more those of actress to author, and amateur solicitor to unprotected female client, in spite of the fact that the consultations and negotiations were enlivened by the old loverlike talk.

This development was hastened by the crumbling of the Lyceum enterprise and the inevitable dissolution of the memorable partnership between Ellen Terry and Irving. This was not willed by either party. To the last Irving urged her to continue acting with him, and she would have done so most gladly if only he had been able to second his entreaties by offering her parts in which she could have maintained her position. But though the parts were there, they were in plays which to Irving did not seem to be plays at all. Ellen Terry has herself told us that when Ibsen's The Pretenders was recommended to him by one person after another, he wondered after having studied the play whether they were "mad" (Letter CLXVII). He was thus offering her a salary not to exercise her great talents, but to keep her famous name in the bill until she had lost her hold on the public; and this for many reasons she could not sanely fall in with. She saw that she must either launch out into management for herself, or else seek engagements from strange managements, leaving her safe moorings in the comfortable harbor where she had been happy and glorious for 24 years to venture into unchartered and stormy seas. Nobody with a scrap of imagination can suppose that she did this willingly or that Irving let her go willingly.

Meanwhile the star of Beerbohm Tree had risen in London. No actor less like Irving could be conceived, but he too had personality and overwhelming singleness of purpose, and the new theatre (Her Majesty's) he had built on the site of one of the great London opera-houses had supplanted the Lyceum as the centre of theatrical fashion. When the position at the Lyceum had become hopeless to those behind the scenes Tree offered Ellen Terry an engagement to play with Mrs (now Dame Madge) Kendal the two Merry Wives to his Falstaff in Shakespear's comedy. It must have cost her a great deal to accept this offer, and be accused as she was of deserting Irving.*

After a success in The Merry Wives as triumphant as any she had achieved in her Lyceum heyday, Ellen Terry rejoined Irving for a last tour in the Provinces. Then he shook the dust of the Lyceum off his feet and went to Drury Lane to appear there in a play written by Sardou "around " Dante's profile—and Irving's. There was no part in it which Ellen Terry could accept with dignity. Irving nevertheless pressed her to play in it, and it was her refusal that finally convinced him that their old association, so dear to yesterday's generation, was no longer possible.

[It ought to be added that this Dante season was not Irving's last in London. In 1905, the year of his death, he appeared again at Drury Lane in revivals of some of his old Lyceum productions. So playgoers who are middle-aged to-day (1931) may have seen him in parts he had created when a younger man, and was still able to play magnificently. He showed no signs in them of being "excessively tired and not at all himself." (Gordon Craig in Henry Irving.)

On the last night of this last London season (10 June 1905) Irving appeared as Corporal Brewster in Conan Doyle's A Story of Waterloo, and as Thomas Becket in Tennyson's Becket, shortened by the omission of the prologue. He received a wonderful ovation at the end of the performance. After he had taken an unprecedented number of calls, and made his customary speech of thanks in that manner which Max Beerbohm once likened to a Cardinal's when washing the beggarmen's feet on Holy Thursday, the fireproof curtain was lowered and the house lights turned out. But the audience re-

---

* Edith Craig tells me that the most important reason her mother had for feeling herself free to accept Tree's offer was that her position at the Lyceum had greatly changed. "When talking over business arrangements with Bram Stoker not long before the offer was made, my mother was told for the first time that another actress (Maude Fealey) had been engaged to play some of the parts she could no longer play owing to her age. My mother realized that she could not in these circumstances be of the same use to Irving."—C. St. J.

mained in the theatre, and for at least twenty minutes cheered and applauded with undiminished enthusiasm. Perhaps they had a premonition that if they could not shout that curtain up, they would never see Irving again. ... .

He was told of the demonstration as he was leaving the theatre, and returned to the stage. But the staff had gone, and a stage hand had to be fetched from a public-house nearby to raise the curtain. A London audience saw Irving for the last time in his "street clothes," and very fine he looked, I remember, in a long loose tweed overcoat, much the same colour as his abundant grey hair.

"I assure you this has taken me completely by surprise," he began, and he may have said this sardonically, for a new public had come along in 1905 which had rarely gone to see him act, but all I can remember is that he smiled benignly when he was interrupted by an excited Scottish admirer who bawled out: "And don't ye desairve it?"

Four months later Irving died suddenly in the hall of his hotel at Bradford within a few minutes of leaving the theatre. His last appearance of all, like his last appearance in London, was made in Becket. "What a heroic thing" Ellen Terry writes in her memoirs "was that last performance of Becket. . . . I am told by those who were acting with him that night (October 13 1905) that he was obviously suffering and dazed. But he went through it all as usual. The courteous little speech to the audience, the signing of a worrying boy's drawing at the stage door—all that he had done for years, he did faithfully to the end."

It is from Ellen Terry too that we know Irving died as he had wished to die. She relates that during a conversation between them at Wolverhampton, where she had gone to see him at the news of his serious illness in the spring of 1905, they spoke of "the end."

" 'And the end? How would you like that to come?'

" 'How would I like that to come?' He repeated my question lightly, yet meditatively. Then he was silent for some thirty seconds before he snapped his fingers . . . 'Like that!' "

14 December 1900.

Leeds

DEAR BERNARD SHAW,

Y ES, unfortunately Laurence is quite indispensable on Saturday evening. His part in the Lyons Mail is a long one, important in a most intricate 2nd act, and he plays it in an excruciatingly funny way. (Note that it is a *comic part!*) With all the good will in the world (if it were forthcoming!) I fear his father could not let him go.

Sunday so near! And Brassbound! Can scarcely believe it. I'm so excited, but ill and lifeless.

288

So many thanks for getting me the Box. What's mine is always Edy's, Edy says. I suppose she will remember to keep me a corner in her box! I should be glad to know where, what, who I am to pay for it? But please dont trouble. I'll find out somehow.

Poor old Laurence. I wish he could be let off. I'll find out whether it would be of any convenience to him to come straight to Barkston Gardens with his man ("the poor emmergrant") after a night journey: I'm sure I would be as eager as *any* mother to welcome him by day or night and feed him and take care of him: he is a dear fellow. I hope he'll not be ill. He is excited and fatigued. I think he wishes I was acting Lady C. with him. (Not a word to Janet please.) By the way if you'd like it best I will sit 'way back in Dress Circle, Pit or Gallery. Tell Edy.

Yours, E. T.

CCLVI: G. B. S. *to* E. T.

[Shaw reopens the correspondence, and it is clear from his letter that it had been suspended since December 1900. It is the only letter from him Ellen Terry asked and obtained permission to publish in The Story of My Life. It is printed on p. 320 of the first English edition published by Hutchinson in 1908. Ellen Terry told me when we were working on the book that she had "many other letters from Shaw somewhere." I urged her to produce them, and consider the inclusion, subject to Shaw's approval, of those she did not mind being published. But she put me off with the plea that she could not find them, adding one day that this did not matter, as "there are things in them about Henry which ought not to be published so soon after his death." —The allusion to Ellen Terry's wishing to play Martha is explained by the fact that in April 1902 Irving revived Faust at the Lyceum. Cissie Loftus played Ellen Terry's old part of Margaret.]

3 April 1902.
10 Adelphi Terrace, W. C.
Piccards Cottage, St Catherines,
Guildford, Surrey

M<small>R BERNARD SHAW</small>'s compliments to Miss Ellen Terry. Mr Bernard Shaw has been approached by Miss Langtry with a view to the immediate and splendid production of Captain Brassbound's Conversion at the Imperial Theatre.

Mr Bernard Shaw, with the last flash of a trampled out love, has repulsed Mrs Langtry with a petulance bordering on brutality.

Mr Bernard Shaw has been actuated in this ungentlemanly and unbusinesslike course by an angry desire to seize Miss Ellen Terry by the hair and make her play Lady Cicely.

Mr Bernard Shaw would be glad to know whether Miss Ellen Terry wishes to play Martha at the Lyceum instead.

Mr Bernard Shaw will go to the length of keeping a minor part open for Sir Henry Irving when Faust fails, if Miss Ellen Terry desires it.

Mr Bernard Shaw lives in daily fear of Mrs Langtry recovering sufficiently from her natural resentment of his ill manners to reopen the subject.

Mr Bernard Shaw begs Miss Ellen Terry to answer this letter.

Mr Bernard Shaw is looking for a new cottage or house in the country and wants advice on the subject.

Mr Bernard Shaw craves for the sight of Miss Ellen Terry's once familiar handwriting.

G. B. S.

CCLVII: E. T. *to* G. B. S.

[Mrs Langtry had built a beautiful new theatre in Westminister (the Imperial Theatre alluded to in Shaw's letter (CCLVI)) and had opened it with a production of The Royal Necklace, which had been a failure. Her second production Mademoiselle Mars (for which Edith Craig made the costumes) met with little more success. It was at the Imperial Theatre that Ellen Terry and Gordon Craig produced Ibsen's The Vikings (1903).—The cottage referred to in the postscript is Ellen Terry's at Winchelsea.]

5 April 1902

"MR BERNARD SHAW has been approached by Mrs Langtry"— Dont break her heart along with the rest but let her have the play. You write great plays and always ruin them with the first start off. You have no powers of selection. You know everything. You know nothing.

> You are a great man.
> You are "a silly Ass."
> You are a dear.
> You are a "worry."
> Poor Charlotte!*

(*That's envy, isnt it?)

Your ownest ELLEN

My love to Charlotte and her husband.

E. T.

Why not try this if you are looking out for a cottage? It is small enough for anything. An *open* place. Sea respectful distance of a mile. Makes no noise to be heard. Garden and Gardener. Apples and shells. Best time from June to September. I wonder would C. like it?

E. T.

CCLVIII: E. T. *to* G. B. S.

[*On this letter there is a note in Shaw's writing: "Wrote suggesting that she could get C. Frohman to produce Brassbound in London with H. B. Irving and then tour it in America."—Sardou's Dante was the last new play Irving produced. After its failure, he appeared only in revivals of past successes (see note to Letter CCLV).—"Under the stage": the stage referred to is the stage of the Strand Theatre where Brassbound was produced. In some of the inconvenient old London theatres there was no access to the dressing-rooms on the stage-level, and the actors had to go under it to reach them. It is probable that Ellen Terry was "en route" to the dressing-rooms to congratulate the players in Brassbound when she met the author "under the stage."*]

10 December 1902.

Imperial Hotel,

Clifton

OH, MY dear friend, I cannot answer your—*epistle,* for I cannot for the moment speak surely about my business plans. I've not pieced the puzzle together yet. Therefore your steps must not wait on my uncertain ones. I've wondered the last few days (at odd idle moments) what I could say to you, and I find (dash this wobbly pen) I can say nothing. Henry is pretending he is not furious with me, and that makes me feel a guilty wretch for refusing to speak a few lines in his old Dante.

Edy had a birthday yesterday and I could only reach her on the telephone when my eyes longed for her. My poor little dog has a big wound (the vain idiot fought a thing at least 50 times his own size). I'm very cold, and they say you could not bear me, when we met, that one time, under the stage.

Consider then my misery when I tell you of all these trials and believe me

A miserable sinner!

How is Charlotte? To her my love, and to you! But you cant abide me! And no wonder! Can I ever abide myself!

CCLIX: E. T. *to* G. B. S.

[*During her engagement at His Majesty's Theatre Ellen Terry continued to play in matinées at the Lyceum with Irving. She acted there for the last time on 19 July 1902, but went on a provincial tour with Irving as usual in the autumn.—George Lewis: Sir George Lewis, the head of Lewis and Lewis, a famous firm of solicitors, an old friend of Ellen Terry's.—Gordon Craig had recently produced Laurence Housman's miracle play Bethlehem.—Note that in this letter Ellen Terry first makes Shaw aware that her appreciation of Brassbound does not include any faith in its attractiveness to the large paying public.*]

18 December 1902

DEAR G. B. S. I have nothing settled about a theatre. I'm aching to settle something but everyone is so slow. You are a dear to bother about me. When I dont fly for Brassbound too! The fact is I dont care about playing an engagement at most of the theatres (altho' I'm going to fool about as Mistress Page for Tree for a month or so) and I dont want to take the risk of a theatre on my own shoulders. You say: "But I cant guarantee a financial success" with Brassbound. And, dear G. B. S., a financial success is all I want! Want to be certain of, I mean. I'm quite certain it would have every other success, and I believe this one as well, for my friends in the Public are not generally idiots!

I have saved for my old age, and spite of my children pressing me to risk it, I cannot. Altho' Mr Frohman will finance me in America, he plump says he doesnt hanker after doing it in England. I cant go about thumping a drum and asking to be Syndicated! Asking for people's money that shall benefit *me*. I cant ask for a shilling even at a Bazaar! I should have thought there were many who would like to— what they call "run" me! but they dont flock around and so I think I'll ask my good friend George Lewis if he knows of anyone who would like to make a fortune along o' me. I'll venture some, but not *all* my pennies. I dont care a fig about making money but I dont want to risk my savings. I'd like to include Brassbound in my list of plays, but at present I am hidebound. I cant move.

I've written tonight to ask Wyndham whether he would let me have his new theatre for 3 or 4 months if I want it. I'll speak to George Lewis.

I have new (!) "ralgia" or "ritis" or some such thing, and am (for the moment only, I hope) half daft with the pain in my head. Stupid isnt it? Ted's work in the Houseman play is good. I think you'd like it.

Yours,

E. T.

CCLX: G. B. S. *to* E. T.

[In April 1903 Ellen Terry had done what in December 1902 she had writ-ten to Shaw she did not want to do. She had "risked her savings" by going into management at the Imperial Theatre. Her first production was Ibsen's The Vikings, and when it failed to attract the public she put on a revival of Much Ado About Nothing, which was no more popular. Nevertheless this financially unfortunate season brought her compensations. She had the sat-isfaction of knowing that it had established the reputation of her son Gordon Craig as a producer of genius. We find Shaw (who was not in sympathy with the new movement in the theatre heralded by Craig's productions) ad-mitting in this letter that "nothing quite like it [the production of Much Ado About Nothing] has been done before," and one may add in 1931 that nothing quite like it has been done since. Although Craig has had many imi-tators, and has added a new word to the German language in "Craigische," what made the work he did at the Imperial Theatre, under his mother's man-agement, remarkable was the man, not the method. The reader will find in Craig's Henry Irving p. 158 his defence to the charge that he ignored Ibsen's stage directions and distorted some of his scenes.—Ellen Terry took Much Ado into the Provinces, but not The Vikings.—The "young man" who couldnt say the line of Claudio's quoted was Conway Tearle, a member of a famous old theatrical family, who subsequently became a successful film "star" in America.]

3 June 1903.

10 Adelphi Terrace, W. C.

I WENT to see Much Adoodle-do yesterday evening. It is a shocking bad play, and can only be saved by Dogberry picking it up at the end, when Beatrice and Benedick are worn out after the church scene. But Dogberry *cannot* pick it up unless he has his scene before the wedding, because without that the audience is unprepared for the ex-amination scene and does not find him out until too late. Why dont you believe me when I tell you these things? You believe everyone else; but nobody else tells you the truth.

You shouldnt fidget in the scene of the masks. In the other scenes it doesnt matter, because you are supposed to be provoking and inscrut-able and cant-tell-whether-you're-serious-or-not. But here you should be *demure* and *most sincere,* as if you were telling a dear friend what a dull fool the poor man is. In other respects your Beatrice is a rather creditable performance, considering that I didnt stage-manage it.

Why dont you tell that young man how to say "Silence is the perfect'st herald of joy"? A little fluttering flower of a line which he makes a turnip of.

As usual Ted has the best of it. I have never seen the church scene go before—didnt think it *could* go, in fact. He should have done something better with the monument scene or else left it alone altogether; but still, when all is said, nothing quite like it has been done before; and if only the extra people were trained dancers instead of athletic amateurs, and Asche were Dogberry with his first scene left in, and the choir were complete instead of having one twopenny tenor and no basses, and the stalls were abolished and replaced with a comfortable half crown parterre right up to the orchestra, why, something might be done with it all, especially if the public were born over again and born different, and the guillotine freely used in Trafalgar Square for a few months beforehand. But as it is I tell you for the thousandth time, do no more unless Ted finds the money as well as the scenery.

I am not very cheerful, am I? But I want to see you safe out of it. Are you going to take The Vikings and Much Ado into the provinces?

G. B. S.

CCLXI: G. B. S. *to* E. T.

[*The correspondence now jumps the whole year during which Ellen Terry's provincial tour had been followed by her return to His Majesty's Theatre to resume her part of Mrs Page in some special matinées of The Merry Wives. It reopens on a new situation which, through no fault of either Shaw's or Ellen Terry's put an end to the possibilities of artistic co-operation between the two. The Shavian drama, decisively ostracized by the fashionable theatres, found in the year 1904 a theatre and a management which, after a series of experimental afternoon performances became devoted to it, and almost entirely dependent on it for remunerative public support. "Granville Barker and the Court people" means the Royal Court Theatre in Sloane Square. The matinées of Candida were the beginning of the experiment. It was now Shaw's turn to offer Ellen Terry an engagement at his particular little Lyceum. Later on, when the experimental stage had been survived, and the Court Theatre had been visited by Royalty and had acquired an unquestionable prestige, the offer became worth her acceptance. But the effect on their professional relations was immediate in that from this time until Ellen Terry's retirement Shaw's entire activity as a playwright was occu-*

*pied in keeping the managements in which Harley Granville-Barker was
concerned supplied with suitable new plays, and that none of them were of
any use to Ellen Terry. Brassbound had no successor. The Court Theatre
stood between them as the Lyceum had done before.*]

12 June 1904.
10 Adelphi Terrace, W. C.

MY DEAR ELLEN,

I was on my way to call on you yesterday when I suddenly bethought
me that it was Saturday and that you were matinéeing.

As you have no doubt heard, Granville Barker and the Court people
gave half a dozen matinées of Candida, with Kate Rorke in the title
part. Result very satisfactory: heaps of press notices, all compliments
for the company, and a modest profit for Barker and the theatre, besides some thirty pounds or so fees for the author.

Naturally they want to try again—with Brassbound.

Now you see what I am driving at!

They will lose by Brassbound, because it is a *much* more expensive
play than Candida (the cheapest piece in the world). There will be
extras, the scenery, and costumes, and ten parts. The highly cultivated
audiences who came to Candida at the rate of from £60 to £80 each
matinée will not be sufficient to cover the larger expenses of Brassbound, much less give a profit. But the loss will not be great, and if
Lady Cicely hit the public at all, it might disappear altogether. The
theatre is to be redecorated in the autumn; and Brassbound would come
on in October, probably.

Now consider. Six matinées only would be announced and given.
No failure would be possible. The press notices would be much more
voluminous and interesting than the Lyceum ones ever were. Lady
Cicely would get no salary, of course. £25 and "find her own gowns"
is the sort of thing the Court runs to. But then she would lose nothing,
and she would be promoted from Shakespear and Ibsen to Shaw. What
do you think of it? Remember, I dare not ever let you do the play under
your own management at your own risk; and it is only in some such
way as at the Court that you will be engaged for the part, because no
regular management will touch my plays. Why should they? It was
written for you; and unless you do it at least once, posterity will
never forgive you: you will go down to all the ages as the woman who
made *"il gran' rifiuto,"* for there never was and never will be again
such a part written for any mortal. I stooped for your sake to do what

295

Shakespear did when he manufactured Rosalind. *He* gave her away
by flinging her at the public with a shout of "as *you* like it" (Pilate
washing his hands); but I will gravely offer this impossible quintessence
of Ellen as a real woman; and everybody will be delighted.

If you are too lazy to learn the part I will teach it to you speech
by speech until you can repeat it in your sleep. Would you like to talk
it over? If yes, shall I call on you or will you come here, say to lunch
on Wednesday on your way to the matinée, if there is a matinée? If
you will, let me have a line by return, with any instructions you may
wish given to our cook.

Your still faithful

G. B. S.

CCLXII: E. T. *to* G. B. S.

14 June 1904.

The Farm, Small Hythe,

Tenterden

MY DEAR G. B. S.,

FROM the 18th of August to Xmas I am disporting myself in the Provinces. The arrangements are made and there's an end. Else it would
have been pleasant to me to have played Cicely for a week for nothing, or at least next-to-nothing. (Having lost all the money I had, I
find it quite easy to do with next to nothing, unless money comes one's
way! As it generally chances to do with me.) Sir, I never was lazy.
Where is a fine part for a woman between 50 and 60? Please let me
study one. My eyes are much better nowadays, and I have learned to
rest better, and can get the words of a new part into my memory with
less difficulty.

It was refreshing to see your handwriting again. Thank you for
your letter. Why dont you and Charlotte balloon, or motor down here.
Food in the garden to suit you, and comfy beds in and out of doors,
at your service.

Edy is here. Did I tell you she is my right hand, and still growing
to be my left hand, and happy as a sandboy all the while? I fear to
be too happy in her—I try to be very quiet with it all. She has a cottage
of her own here and we visit each other every day!

Brassbound should not cost much. (I know all about that sort of
thing now.) Existing scenery, chosen well, and people who *are* the
characters! This can be cheap and not nasty. I'm in town next week
for 2 matinées at H. M. Theatre and then return here for some weeks.

ELLEN NORA

CCLXIII: G. B. S. *to* E. T.

[*The new play with which Shaw was "dashing ahead" was John Bull's Other Island—his first play written for the Court Theatre and the one which brought the Vedrenne-Barker management there decisively into fame and fashion. It was intended also for the Irish Literary Theatre (see note to Letter CCLXV).—The play by Barrie written for Ellen Terry was Alice-Sit-By-The-Fire. It was produced at the Duke of York's Theatre in 1905 under Charles Frohman's management.*]

26 July 1904.
The Old House, Harmer Green,
Welwyn

MADAM,

So you have got Barrie to write a new play for you. Very well. VERY well. But why, oh *why* didnt you make Frohman undertake the London production, and give you a nice salary and a percentage, with no anxiety, no risk, and nothing to do but walk to your dressing-room and wait there without a care for the respectful summons of the call boy? As it is, you have all the trouble and risk, and he comes in for the certainty—America being the certainty.

As for me, when I realized that you really and finally and honestly didnt believe in Brassbound, I at last did the irrevocable thing: I read it to Ada Rehan. Now she, too, had read Brassbound; and she, too, had discovered that it wasnt a play, that it *might* be something clever to read, but was not fit for the stage; that Lady Cicely's part was a small one and didnt dominate the play, etc., etc. And when she heard the play even badly read (I was not at my best or she would have expired with amazement) she was the most astonished lady as ever you could see in all your born days, mum. I told her I'd written it for you, and that your opinion was precisely as stated above; and she owned up nobly and said she was no better herself. "You know," says she, "the truth is, we were so accustomed to beautiful poetry in those days that we did not understand a real woman like that, and besides, it's so different when you *hear* it." In short, she must have it for England and for America and for all the world. Serve Ellen right, thought I: I hope she's proud of herself *now,* with her Vikings and her Beatrices and her Barries.

But alas! this stately Rehan is a most fiery, simple, sentimental, loyal, faithful soul; and now she dismisses Brassbound from her life as her bitterest disappointment because "we can never see things from the same

297

point of view," which means that she has found me out in two brutal and cynical crimes: first, that I actually want her to make terms with the syndicate which squeezed her dear dead teacher and manager Daly almost into bankruptcy, and second and worst, that my opinion of the said Daly as a manager for a woman of genius when Ibsen revolutions are taking place is hardly more flattering than my opinion of Henry Irving in the same capacity. She is simpler than you, and has not your literary genius; so that I am much more disagreeable and bewildering for her. Besides, your infamous treatment of me has soured my disposition; and I now see that the way to treat women is to parade the most utter disregard of their interests and their feelings.

And then I am dashing ahead with my new play and care for nothing else just at present.

This house is not Dr Webb's. We looked at that years ago (we hold his brother Philip its architect in very special esteem) but it was too big for us, and it's in a hole. This is a 16th or at latest 17th century house—a gem. Welwyn is 2 miles off: we are at Harmer Green, on the other side of the line and only half a mile from the station. Also at the top of the hill.

Will you *really* come? If so, name your day—except next Thursday. There is a 1.15 train from King's Cross in time for lunch. Charlotte says you wont; and I daresay she's right.

Your turned worm,

G. BERNARD SHAW

CCLXIV: E. T. *to* G. B. S.

[*A. R.: Ada Rehan.*—"*This farm*": *Small Hythe Place, Tenterden (see note to Letter CCL).*]

28 July 1904.

Small Hythe

I HAVE already done all you say is wise and best in my arrangements with B. about his play. The fact is he did it for me and F. bought it and engaged me. You ought to give A. R. your play. She would do great things with it. I *do* think it a fine play, but Lady C is not strong enough to act itself. Most of your things do. You ought to give away all your work as Tolstoy does, because you know no middle, reasonable course in your business arrangements, or so it appears to me. *I* am going to begin to be extortionate now, to try to make some money, and to keep a little for a trifle a week, and this farm for my old age.

CCLXV: G. B. S. to E. T.

[*The Irish Literary Theatre eventually had to relinquish John Bull's Other Island although it was written at the request of Mr W. B. Yeats as a patriotic contribution to its repertory. "Like most people who have asked me to write plays," Shaw says in the preface to the play, "Mr Yeats got rather more than he bargained for. . . . It was at that time beyond the resources of the New Abbey Theatre. . . . There was another reason for changing the destination of John Bull's Other Island. It was uncongenial to the whole spirit of the neo-Gallic movement, which is bent on creating a new Ireland after its own ideal, whereas my play is a very uncompromising presentment of the real old Ireland." How He Lied To Her Husband, the little play "thirty-five minutes long," has recently won wide notoriety as "Bernard Shaw's first talkie."—Daly: Arnold Daly who first sprang into fame as an actor by a production of Candida in New York. He lost his life there in a fire a few years ago.—The title of the story by Kipling is They. Shaw did actually try to persuade Kipling to write for the theatre, but without success.—Alec: the reference is to George Alexander, manager of the St James's Theatre.*]

9 September 1904.
Sitting on the sands at Chancery Ness

MY DEAREST ELLEN,

I HAVE lived a dog's life since last I heard from you; but to-morrow we leave this horrible place, at which we have had nothing but ignoble misfortunes, for Edinburgh, where we will look about for some pleasant beach to snatch a brief holiday on. I have finished a big play and a little one. The little one thirty-five minutes long, the big one about thirty-five years. Titles, respectively, How He Lied To Her Husband (pathos at which you cant help screaming laughing) and John Bull's Other Island (meaning Ireland), which is to be done at the Court and by the Irish Literary Theatre in Dublin, if the populace do not burn the theatre.

I had to work against time to get the thing finished, especially as I had to stop in the middle to write How He Lied for Daly, who wanted a curtain raiser for The Man of Destiny. But now it's gone to Miss Dickens; and I have a moment to breathe, which I accordingly employ in writing to you.

Have you seen the Kipling story in Scribner's, which I send you by this post? Wouldnt you like to play the blind woman? That is what I call genius: one forgives all the creature's schoolboy ruffianisms and vulgarities for his good things, of which this is one of the goodest. What a pity the thrilling turning point of it— when he feels the child's kiss in his palm, and then, seeing that there is no child there, *realizes* —is impossible on the stage! I wonder could I get him to try his hand at the theatre in his fine style—not his Lights that Failed and Limmacons and the like.

That is all right about Frohman buying Barrie's play and engaging you; but oh Ellen, Ellen, why didnt you announce this? Dont let it be done "under your management." Look at Mrs Pat, just gone to America with £308 a week! Everybody says, "What a woman! How the syndicates run after her!" Now if she were announced as having to go into management for herself as she does here, everybody would say "Poor woman! No manager will look at her!" You do not realize—at least I'll assume that you dont; for I always take it for granted that nobody knows anything but myself—that the day of the manager with his or her single theatre has passed by; and that now it is the syndicate with fifty theatres that controls the business of the English and American world; so that the great actress must no longer say "I have my own theatre," but, on the contrary, "I know nothing about theatres and nothing about business. Neither do I deal with actor-managers, who employ leading ladies: Trees, Alecs and Irvings. I simply *act,* on my own terms; and Mr Frohman or Mr Shubert or Mr Anybody representing a sufficiently big combination arranges everything for me. Mr Frohman has the honor of presenting Miss Ellen Terry: she has no occasion to present herself, like your Bernhardts and Campbells and Ashwells and other infinitesimal persons. In the case of the Barrie play you have actually hidden this ace of trumps under the table instead of playing it for all it is worth. That's because you dont trust *me.*

What is all this about my being extortionate and knowing no middle course in business? Who puts these notions into your head? I am not only the cheapest author in the market, but by far the most reasonable. I must not "cut prices," and try to get my plays acted by offering them cheap; but as a matter of fact I have never made a bargain by which a manager has lost. Of course they *say* they lose, because they never study their accounts, and always read Green Room Gossip. Forbes-Robertson told me that the fees on The Devil's Disciple in the provinces came out of the profits of Hamlet. "Shakespear paid your fees," he said. I went to the returns and found that his *average* takings for the D.'s D. up to that time had been £130 a night, sometimes of course under

£100 and sometimes over £200, but on the whole figuring out at £130 each performance, which, as you know, does not mean losing money when the author has not asked a farthing in advance, and the tour is on the cheapest scale (the cast was just barely good enough for Hamlet; and you know what *that* means), and the towns by no means all Number Ones. My real difficulty is that I cant get actors to think about business or to watch what really pays and what does not. They believe what the papers tell them; they lose, lose, lose again and again by doing the very thing that they have lost by invariably before; they want to buy plays for ever that they could have much cheaper by the job; they object to royalties and finally let the authors plant a profit sharing system on them which is much worse for them: in short, they do everything that is stupid, and hate people like me who force them to make bargains that are fair to themselves. I now always draw up the agreement myself and say sweetly: "Will you sign it, or would you like to argue about it for a couple of hours?" They sign.

Why have you led me into all this unprofitable twaddle? It was not for this that I began my letter, but for consolation, which you owe me after your perfidy about Brassbound, which, now that I am finally baffled, and must dazzle and fascinate the proud great Rehan, makes me openly furious, though I did not think about it whilst you were playing with me all those years. It was your revenge for my marriage, I believe. There! Or was it mere old-fashionedness: do you still doubt, and think that Lady C. would not act itself *with you in it*. Naturally, writing it for you, I did not mean it to act itself with a nobody in it.

You tell me I should give away my plays, as Tolstoy does. What would be the result? Does anybody play Tolstoy?

Suppose you put a notice in the Era this week to say that in future Miss E. T. will act without salary for anyone who asks her, what will happen? Why, you will never get another engagement. . . .

[*The rest of the letter is missing*]

CCLXVI: E. T. *to* G. B. S.

[*Ellen Terry writes from her new London home, a small early Georgian panelled house she had bought when she left Barkston Gardens. She lived here until 1921, when she was forced, owing to financial difficulties, to sell it and move into a flat. During the tour mentioned she played Beatrice, Portia, Nance Oldfield, Queen Katharine (in the Trial Scene from Henry VIII); and for the first time Kniertje in Heijerman's play The Good Hope (in an Eng-*

[Undated, but obviously from the
contents written late in 1904.]

215 King's Road,
Chelsea

I'M QUITE ashamed, dear friend, to appear to be so ungrateful to you, but I cant do everything I *can* do, let alone what I *cant!* (Riddle me, riddle-me-ree!) Have you forgotten you sent me a wondrously lovely story by Kipling? Thanks and thanks. I never loved him before for I admired him too much, but that story was the meltingest loveliest thing. The stage would be too rough for it I fear and I should fear to touch it. If I were thin I'd like to experiment with it, but I always feel so maternally fat, and happy-looking, enough to ruin anything delicate and azalea-like. The woman is exquisite. Forgive my not having said thank you for sending her to me.

I ended up my tour last night, at the Camden Theatre; and now I'm off to Winchelsea to rest and quietly study Alice Grey in Barrie's play. I'm very tired, but I have had an exceedingly pleasant 15 weeks' tour. Edy was with me (and she is splendid) and all the company very happy and agreeable people, and I made a lot of money, luckily! When I read of Tree's Shakespeare Tour I think I *am* lucky—but the best bit of fun lately for me has been getting over £22 for some of the theatrical charities by signing my name on those silly postcards. Hard work I tell you, to get £22 in three months when most people only sent me 6d! The money was worth it, I thought, so I signed with a will.

Candida! I must go and see it again before I leave the City. Mr Barker should be fine as the penny Poet. Are you still at Welwyn? Will you give my love to Charlotte. Will you give my love to yourself, for I am affectionately yours,

ELLEN

CCLXVII: E. T. *to* G. B. S.

23 August 1905.
Small Hythe, Tenterden,
Kent

DEAR G. B. S.,

I AM only just beginning to feel a wee bit rested and able to admire and delight in all this beautiful day. Do you know the joy of a canoe, on a Canal? I was there all yesterday with just Edy and a young lad, a friend of hers. The peace! the quiet! "O my" (as they say in America sometimes)! I hear you and Mistress Charlotte Chaw are in a heaven of a place. Arent we all horribly fortunate? Yours, and hers, E. T.

CCLXVIII: G. B. S. *to* E. T.

[*The arrangements for producing Brassbound in the spring of 1906 were now being made, the Court Theatre having won its spurs. Frederick Kerr, not Louis Calvert, was eventually chosen to play Captain Brassbound at the Court. He made his first appearance on the stage in New York in 1882 as Sir Toby in Lester Wallack's revival of The School for Scandal, and is still after a busy and successful career in the front rank of his profession. The career of Louis Calvert, the original Broadbent in John Bull's Other Island, is summarized in the note to Letter CII.*]

27 August 1905.
Derry, Rosscarbery,
Co. Cork

MY DEAR ELLEN,

Have you any views about the part of Brassbound? It lies practically between Calvert and Fred Kerr.

I am looking forward with malicious glee to the rehearsals. I shall have my revenge then. I will not leave a rag, not a wink, not a flippety-flop of that tiresome Ellen Terry who wouldnt do my play. I will shew London something it has not seen since the old Court days of New Men and Old Acres—and only saw the possibility of then. But the process will be a fearful one, braying in a mortar, boiling two or three skins off, passing through the fire. If you have tears, prepare, etc., etc.

G. B. S.

CCLXIX: E. T. *to* G. B. S.

30 August 1905.
Small Hythe, Tenterden,
Kent

For heaven's sake let it be—well *not* Calvert! That lazy-clever-get-out-of-all-blame-of-it, happy-go-lucky-easy, honest, "taking" man, would irritate me into a fever. He could not even *look* the part. (Neither can I. Of course I know that, so I say it "more in sorrow than in anger.") K. is very good in all I have seen him do and sometimes he is fatter (sometimes leaner) and then the drawing of his face *goes*. That would

303

be a pity for the last scene. For I think the two should suddenly look quite different for a few moments.

So you promise to lead me a life during the rehearsals! Well, I'm a mighty tame cat nowadays. Dont sit on me too hard. I'm old and feeble. But now I'm off for a motor spin. I've so few motor friends. Lena Ashwell is at Tonbridge near here and has one of her own! Splendid!

Yours E. T.

CCLXX: E. T. *to* G. B. S.

[The reference is to a translated article on Henry Irving by Shaw which appeared in Die Neue Freie Presse a few days after Irving's death. I am very fortunate in being able to give Shaw's account of the affair, which has frequently been misrepresented.]

Henry Irving died in harness on the 13th of October 1905 aged 67. Die Neue Freie Presse of Vienna asked me for an obituary which I wrote, with momentarily disturbing results. My article had first to be translated into German; and the translator either took it for granted that I always wrote maliciously, and chose his words accordingly, or else thought that a malicious article would be better relished by the Viennese public. Howsoever, the article in its German dress was malicious, and when it was immediately retranslated in the London press as such, the retranslation was more malicious than the translation. There was a terrible to-do about it: and Laurence Irving wrote: "My kindred, with the exception of my wife and myself, tell me you are a monstrous Yahoo for whom nothing but excommunication is fitting." I immediately printed the original English text of my article, and sent copies to all the leading papers in the country, placing it at their disposal as a free contribution. Unfortunately, in newspaperland a slander is interesting news, always welcomed by news-editors. An explanation that is baseless is disappointing and goes into the wastepaper basket: hence by the way the excellent French law that if a newspaper disparages a citizen it must willy-nilly publish his reply at equal length. No such law existing in Britain, only one newspaper, and that not a London one, inserted my authentic version.

But in any case my estimate of Irving would not have satisfied the great actor's admirers, many of whom hardly stopped "this side idolatry." Irving had splendidly maintained the social status of the theatre, and

304

greatly raised that of the actor, but he had done nothing for contemporary dramatic literature. For this the playwrights could not quite forgive him. Even Henry Arthur Jones, in an enthusiastic eulogy of Irving as a man and an actor, written in 1913, found unfinished at his death, and not published until this year (1931) had to reserve the point. When I was offered, rather reluctantly, a seat in the lantern of Westminster Abbey at Irving's funeral by George Alexander, I refused it on the public ground that Literature had no place at Irving's graveside.* Privately I was friendly enough, but in my public character I was inhuman. This most touching letter from Ellen Terry on the death of the great artist whose professional consort and intimate friend she had been for over twenty years is his most precious epitaph.

24 October 1905

Y ou never wrote the words they say you wrote, except when Henry was well, was at work and *fighting*. Then it was all right enough —fair. You never said it I'm sure when all his friends were sore and smarting. *You* don't add hyssop to the wounds. That would be *un*fair. I never knew you to do an unkind action, but heaps of lovely ones. *He* was prematurely old from constantly doing practical little goodnesses. Did he have faults? Yes! But of course *we* have none!

I'm far away in the North and have only just heard you were unkind. I dont believe that. I suppose time will bring me printed matter. When it comes I shall have no eyes to read with. I couldnt *cry* and something seemed to fix my eyes open and strain them. I feel badly. I'm sorry because I didnt do enough whilst I could, just a little longer. Of course I am glad for him, and I believe no one appreciated him much more than *you* did! I'm sure of it. My love to Charlotte, and you, for you wrote that a long while ago I'm sure. Tell me so.

Yours E. T.

CCLXXI: G. B. S. *to* E. T.

[*It is obvious that this was written before Ellen Terry's letter of the 24th had reached Shaw. His letter of the 28th is his answer to that.—Stephen Coleridge: younger son of the first Lord Coleridge, a famous judge, and a relative of the great poet. Stephen Coleridge was an intimate friend of Ellen*

* A strange statement in view of the fact that Irving produced play after play by Shakespear for some ten to fifteen years! Irving also did something for "contemporary dramatic literature" by producing plays by Tennyson.—C. St. J.

Terry's and for many years acted as her business adviser. He was by no means the only person who made "a fearful row" about the Vienna article.]

25 October 1905.
10 Adelphi Terrace

MY DEAR ELLEN,

A s THE fearful row made by Stephen Coleridge in the papers yesterday may have reached you, I send you a copy of my letter in to-day's Times.

Yours always,

G. B. S.

CCLXXII: G. B. S. *to* E. T.

28 October 1905.
10 Adelphi Terrace, W. C.

MY DEAR ELLEN,

B EYOND sending you that Times letter to prevent Coleridge making you loathe me, I did not like to intrude on you and Irving in this matter. But now that you have accorded me the privilege of knowing how you feel, just let me explain to you how hopeless it is to depend on the papers when really delicate and intimate matters are in question. In the now famous Vienna article (I believe you dont read German; so I dont send you a copy) I said—"The truth is, Irving was interested in nothing but himself; and the self in which he was interested was an imaginary self in an imaginary world. He lived in a dream." Now, first comes the German translator who gives this as "nur (only) ein imaginären Person in einer imaginären Pose." And next comes The Referee, The Pelican, etc., etc. translating from the German—not from the original article but from descriptions of it in other German papers—thus: "He was a narrow minded egoist, devoid of culture, and living on the dream of his own greatness."

Of course I told the truth about him on such matters as concerned his claim to Westminster Abbey; and part of that truth was necessarily sterner than the polite things that are said of small men at funerals in Brompton Cemetery. But when all is said, I seem to be the only journalist in England who really remembers him as he was, or ever knew him as he was—strength and weakness together.

Laurence, who is coming to lunch with me on Wednesday, says the family regard me as a most unmitigated Yahoo, and assures me, very Irvingesquely, that his father was so truly kindhearted that he would

306

willingly have paid my funeral expenses at any time. Such is the un-quenchable heart of youth.

Ever, dearest Ellen,

Your hardest hearted lover,

G. B. S.

CCLXXIII: E. T. *to* G. B. S.

[*Ellen Terry's reproach "indelicate" probably refers only to the haste with which Shaw came to bury Irving not to praise him. As to the general effect of his estimate of her comrade, she often said in later years that she thought it less harmful to Irving's memory than the unintelligent eulogies poured out after his death by his admirers.*]

1 November 1905.

Edinburgh

WELL, it was just stupid in you, that's all—and that's enough I should say for *you*. I cant understand how one without gross food in him, who takes no wine to befuddle his wits, can have been so indelicate. Nothing is expected of *me,* or of most of us, but of you I expect every-thing.

A doctor has gotten hold of me and planted a *nurse* here! Heavens! a Keeper! She wont let me write, nor read, and I've only skimmed through your words. I cant help wanting to burn you, but all my im-pulse is bad and wrong. I've no head and my heart is rotten.

ELLEN

CCLXXIV: G. B. S. *to* E. T.

[*Teddy: Edward Gordon Craig. Shaw's picturesque Cæsar and Cleopatra had been accepted for production at the Lessing Theatre in Berlin, and Shaw, glad to be able to please Ellen Terry and at the same time avail himself of the genius her son had revealed in staging The Vikings, made it a condition that his play should be produced by Gordon Craig, who was accordingly retained for the occasion. Shaw adds this note:*

Unfortunately Gordon Craig had taken with him from the Lyceum the tradition that Shaw was an author of no importance whilst Shaw's estimate of his own dimensions was comparatively astronomical. The Lessing Theatre insisted on delivery of the producer's designs by a fixed date: Gordon Craig explicitly refused to be bound by the limits of time and space. The only design forthcoming after a long delay was

307

a vague pencil memorandum on a half sheet of paper. The Lessing management, made desperate by stress of date, sent this sketch to the author and asked him to use his supposed influence with the producer to hurry up matters, or else to release the theatre from the obligation to wait. An ultimatum was then sent to the artist, who replied by stipulating that he must be placed in complete control, with freedom to do as he thought best with the play without regard to the views of the author. On this the negotiations broke down. The breach was a pity; for Shaw was the only English playwright who cared enough for Craig's work to try to enlist his co-operation.

[*Major Barbara was first produced at the Court Theatre on 28 November 1905.—Alice-Sit-By-The-Fire was still running at the Duke of York's Theatre where it had been produced on 1 April.*]

25 November 1905.
10 Adelphi Terrace, W. C.

MY DEAR ELLEN,

IT APPEARS now that Kerr will be available for Brassbound. Unless you contradict me I shall assume that you prefer him to the available alternatives.

You must allow me to teach you the part of Lady C. What I dread is that you will set your nurses and young ladies to read it to you, so that it will get into your head all wrong. You will then be forced to try to learn it by main force through your eyes, and ruin your nerves and wreck your happiness. You can learn it as easily as a child learns hush-a-bye-baby if only you hear it *rightly* read to you. But that can only be done by another Ellen Terry or by me.

I came to see you at the theatre because I *must* accustom myself to meet you. At present, "old as I am, for ladies' love unfit," something wild happens inside me; and I have to look on gasping for breath whilst an artificial G. B. S. talks to an equally artificial Miss Terry, the two minuetting on the carpet while we stagger in the immensities. I took Barker with me to chaperone me. By the way, that young man is a genius—a cold-hearted Italian devil, but a noble soul all the same.

I did not succeed in making you understand about the Irving article; but now comes my revenge. Die Neue Freie Presse, delighted with G. B. S. on Irving, now asks for G. B. S. on Ellen Terry; and as Teddy is delaying my Cæsar and Cleopatra very badly in Berlin (he is to do the scenery) I shall say yes, and immortalize you.

I think Brassbound will be better understood after Major Barbara, a frankly religious play in which the most effective scene is the conversion of a rough by a Salvation girl.

I think Alice a horrid part; and I am more than ever bent on shewing the people something nobler in you than that. I like Barrie and his work; but someday a demon in the shape of Alice will sit by the fire in hell and poke up the flames in which he is consuming.

G. B. S.

CCLXXV: E. T. *to* G. B. S.

[An apology for not being able to attend a rehearsal of Brassbound which was produced at the Court Theatre (under the Vedrenne-Barker management) on 20 March 1906.]

22 February 1906.

215 King's Road,

Chelsea

(In bed!)

I'M *so* sorry. I could not let you know this morning, so the doctor telephoned to the Court. Indeed I could not come. Frantic from pain in eyes and head. The last hour I'm better. I'll come to-morrow 11 o'clock, if I can crawl. I'm so sorry. Thinking of you all there made me worse. I'll come to-morrow.

E. T.

CCLXXVI: G. B. S. *to* E. T.

[Ellen Terry was born on 27 February 1848, so this was her 58th birthday. Readers may be surprised that there are no congratulations from Shaw, but he was utterly insensible to all such occasions, they having been abolished in his family in his childhood as nuisances. One of his early journalistic exploits he tells me was the invention of a Society for the Abolition of Christmas. When invited to celebrate the birthday of Shakespear at Stratford-on-Avon, he replied: "Why should I celebrate Shakespear's birthday? I do not even celebrate my own."]

27 February 1906.

10 Adelphi Terrace, W. C.

MY DEAR ELLEN,

REMORSE! Remorse! You got it [the headache] from me. Nurse yourself well and let Cicely go hang. I can do quite well with your understudy until you are able to work again quite comfort-

309

ably. They are all ten years behind you in their knowledge of the play; and your absence will do no harm whilst I am getting the business into shape.

Take a week—a fortnight, if you need it. You need not be anxious: what you have at stake is not success or failure, but only the difference between scoring 99 and scoring 100.

Behave as if you were more precious than many plays, which is the truth.

Yours ever,

G. B. S.

CCLXXVII: G. B. S. *to* E. T.

[*The three postcards below, all written on the same date, refer to words in Lady Cicely's part. All actors miss certain words repeatedly at rehearsal, and postcards were Shaw's pet cure.*]

14 March 1906

a) Have you ever thought of the GRANDEUR of wickedness?

Grand! That's the word. Something grandly wicked. Not very wicked not dreadfully wicked, not shocking wicked, but

GRANDLY WICKED.

GRANDIOSO

SOMETHING Grandly WICKED to their enemies.

b) If you take a man and pay him £500 a year, and HAVE—

Ah, that's it.

Beautiful Phrase! Happy expression! "And HAVE policemen and courts and laws and juries etc."

Just think of it!

HAVE policemen and courts and laws and juries to DRIVE him into it. HAVE! Ah! *Have!*

c) *That's what English people are like, Captain Kearney.*

Yes, positively.

That's what English people are like.

No use your contradicting it, Captain Kearney. I tell you THAT'S what English people are like.

CCLXXVIII: G. B. S. *to* E. T.

[*Written four days before the performance of Brassbound.—Carew: James Carew, an American actor, born in Indiana, who made his first appearance on the London stage in 1905 with Maxine Elliott in Her Own Way. He played Hector Malone in Man and Superman at the Court in October that year, and rejoined the Vedrenne-Barker company in the spring of 1906 to play Captain Kearney, the American naval officer, in Brassbound. In 1907, when Ellen Terry went to America on a tour under Frohman's management, James Carew accompanied her as her leading man playing Captain Brassbound, and Geert in The Good Hope. Their marriage took place at Pittsburg (22 March 1907) during this tour. An unofficial separation was the sequel to this romance. Thenceforth they seldom met, though there was unspoiled good will on both sides. Ellen Terry spent the last 20 years of her life literally in single blessedness, having been adored by many men, and always having come back to herself in the end. Not a man was present when she passed out of this world.*]

16 March 1906

MY DEAREST ELLEN,

Remember that the way to prevent the first act from flattening out from over-rehearsal and the familiarity which breeds contempt, is to work up three passages.

1. Oh that is so nice of you, Mr Rankin (more pounce).
2. I dont want an escort (fearful fuss) and
   Oh how nice of him Mr Rankin (sunburst after rain).
3. Both the remonstrances with Howard for punishing people, "I wont have this poor man trampled on" etc. should be very indignant.

The only other point of importance is that you look 25; and I love you; and I am furiously jealous of Carew, with whom you fell in love at first sight.

I tell thee, scorner of these whitening hairs—but no matter.

You will be most ausserordentlich good in the part. I never realized how well I did that job until I saw you rehearse.

G. B. S.

CCLXXIX: E. T. *to* G. B. S.

[*"Try, try again" as she might, Ellen Terry could not play Lady Cicely as she thought Shaw thought the part ought to be played. He may have made her feel that he was never satisfied. If so, we have his own assurance that she was completely mistaken. The mistake arose from that saintly humility the reader must by now have discovered to be one of her most precious qualities. An actress of fifty years' experience, reckoned by many a genius, she still feels she has much to learn.—"More for painting": Shaw has been painted by many artists, including Sir John Lavery, Augustus John, Neville Lytton, John Collier, Sir William Rothenstein, Lady Lavery, and Nellie Heath. He went this year (1906) to Paris and spent a month sitting to Rodin for a bust. There are two busts and a bronze mask of Shaw in the Rodin Museum in Paris, all three different from the one modelled from life. Prince Paul Troubetskoy also did two busts, one of which is in the Tate Gallery and the other in the foyer of the Theatre Guild in New York. The same sculptor has made a full length life size statue of Shaw, and charming statuette with the figure seated. Another bust is by the American sculptor Davidson. Shaw's friend H. G. Wells certainly had some ground for his complaint that "it is impossible to move without coming up against Shaw in effigy."*

18 April 1906.
215 King's Road,
Chelsea

GENTLE SHEPHERD,

Y ou are a faithful heroic DEAR! You try to keep up your illusions about me, about my acting, altho' you know all the while—

Well, thank you for your this morning's letter of directions re Lady Cicely. I am going to have a good practice in the part whilst you are away and I hope you will think I'm better when you come back.

If I were Rodin I should marble you into Pan. I worship Pan, and he has never "had his likeness taken," as they say, by anyone to my satisfaction. Sir Ned Burne-Jones came nearest to it, in his Pan and Psyche, and I love the picture, the tender face of Pan, the tender lines of the body of Psyche. Exquisite! You and Rodin! I envy you both, and I do hope Charlotte is having the splendidness of it all. What long lovely peaceful times you will all have during the sittings! He will catch the *gleam* of you and the result should be fine, but I think you are more for painting than marble.

I wonder will this reach you! It comes to wish you a good time, to assure you I am going to "try, try again" at Lady Cicely, and to bring you my affection.

ELLEN

CCLXXX: E. T. *to* G. B. S.

[*Ellen Terry's jubilee to which she alludes was celebrated by a star matinée at Drury Lane and by a public dinner at which the Rt Hon. Winston*

Churchill presided (June 1906). A testimonial fund was opened in The Tribune (a Liberal morning journal, long extinct) to which the public subscribed generously. The fund would probably have reached a much larger figure, however, if it had been organized by a paper with a wider circulation than the infant Tribune.]

5 May 1906
215 King's Road,
Chelsea

DEAREST G. B. S.,

I THINK we are nearly all of us going astray in your play, some way or another. Wont you come one evening and give us a gentle chiding? Or a whack! I dont do it "on purpose" but I'm sure to have gone wrong, and should be tremendously obliged by corrections from you, if you will spare the time. Besides dont I want to see you? And hear you tell whether or no you liked it all in Paris. I am very miserable (for me) just now, and it's not kind for you (and Charlotte too!) to turn your back on me. Although it's a nice long gentle line-y back, I'd sooner see your face. Worried by dirty London streets, and jubilees and things, I tore off into the country, 8 o'clock last Sunday morning, and I entered into heaven. The blue-bells were a carpet in the woods, and the fields a mass of cowslips, and the hedges full of primroses. I revelled in it all. Exquisite excitement. I got some sleep too, and wanted it.

Yours E. T.

CCLXXXI: G. B. S. *to* E. T.

[*This letter is longer than it appears here. Much of it, about business at the Court Theatre, is of no interest now.*]

27 May 1906.
Harmer Green, Welwyn

MY DEAR DEAREST ELLEN,

You are all right. Ada Rehan is coming to see you play: she is due in England on the 2nd June.

G. B. S.

CCLXXXII: E. T. *to* G. B. S.

[*Ada: Ada Rehan.—In December 1906 Ellen Terry went on her first American tour "on her own," under the direction of Charles Frohman (see note to Letter CCLXXVIII). Her repertory consisted of Captain Brassbound's Conversion, The Good Hope, and Nance Oldfield. Before she left England she appeared as Hermione in The Winter's Tale at His Majesty's.*]

313

11 July 1906.
Tors Hotel,
Lynmouth

ADA WAS there, and we didnt know it? Now that wasnt fair. The poor
dear. She is in a better place in Cumberland. Yes, I understood
Brassbound had been arranged for, for me in America by you and
Charles Frohman, who takes me over. Between the two of us I'm afraid
he will not make very much by the transaction, for it would be a grand
mistake to play Brassbound in one of the *big* American theatres. I think
my engagement is all right for *me*. It is only for about 3 months and if
I find out I cant do matinée performances I need not. I have found C.
F. always very considerate and fair, not to say generous. I'll trust him not
to overwork me. We go to all the *best* Cities only, and I only travel by
night once. Thank you for writing "big" for me. Of course you are a
Dear. My eyes are much better thank you. I daresay I shant come back
from America, but settle there, in the Earth, 6 ft. x 2 ft.

Do you know this place, this Lynmouth? *Grand!* You and Charlotte
ought to sample it. Exmoor is so much more bracing than Dartmoor. I
can only have about 3 weeks rest; for rehearsals of The Winter's Tale
begin on the 7th of August. I wish I were not going to do it, for the late
jubilations have nearly killed me.

Shall you never want me to play anything of yours again? I fear B.
didnt do well. Good-night, good friend. I am tired and dull. They called
me to-night "the life and soul of the party" (of 16) and I felt all the while
suicidal! Too many people about.

Yours, E. T.

CCLXXXIII: E. T. *to* G. B. S.

[*"Your play"*: The Doctor's Dilemma *which had been produced at the Court
Theatre on 20 November. The allusion to Shaw's "preaching against marriage" is the more interesting because at this time Ellen Terry was considering marrying again.*]

28 November 1906.
Small Hythe, Tenterden,
Kent

OH, I *was*, I *was*, I *was* interested, amused, *thrilled* sitting at your play
the other day. I want to see it again soon. It is mighty pleasant
down here, and I drive about wet or shine in an open "shay," eat fish

and vegetables (Heaps in the garden! Jolly! Do you like Salsify?) make curtains and do heaps of needle work jobs in the evenings, and the days fly by in a flash!

I hope you and Charlotte are frightfully well and happy. Arent you funny, preaching against marriage, and marrying. Against other things, and doing 'em! I shall be puzzled about everyone to the end. Can learn from no one. Men are as inconsistent as women, and so it goes. I'm going for a walk with the dogs. I believe it's going to snow. You wont forget the 17th and Brassbound rehearsals please, will you?

Yours affectionately,

NELLEN T.

CCLXXXIV: G. B. S. *to* E. T.

[The following message is written on a postcard.—Courtenay: Alfred Courtenay, Ellen Terry's business-manager.]

1 December 1906.
10 Adelphi Terrace, W. C. 2.

I HAVE neglected Brassbound disgracefully, but I have been so frightfully busy, that I desperately left it all to Courtenay. I will be ready on the 17th and see you again, again, again.   G. B. S.

CCLXXXV: E. T. *to* G. B. S.

[Written on tour in America. It was at "lovely" Pittsburg that Ellen Terry's third marriage had taken place on 22 March (see note to Letter CCLXXVIII). She kept it a secret from everyone until her return to England.]

7 April 1907

PITTSBURG, of all places in the world, is lovely! Surely, never was there more beautiful sunshine than to-day's! The smoke of the place was unendurable and so I just crossed the river and went up to the Allegheny hills and there found all the wonderfulness. It's a sort of day when one finds oneself blessing everything, to oneself of course! The children in the streets (of course) the policemen, the cabmen, and the poor little dingy bell-boys in the hotels. I feel I am ungrateful not to have written before this to say "thank you dear Mr Shaw for letting me have your Brassbound for the English Provinces" (and "on easy terms"). I cant tell you how much everyone here seems to like it, and some come again and again. I wish more came! If only once! Still, except during Lent, we have had great audiences, and they were greatly pleased.

I have taken three different days to write this and to-day it is the 7th
April and the snow is deep upon the ground and is still blinding the view
out of windows, and we are in Montreal now. My windows are wide
open and the hotel 'ot as 'ell! You would be pleased to see the 3 scenes
painted for Brassbound and my old Edy just makes the end of Act I as
you write it. I wish you would offer her some work on our return. She
is so able, and such a Duck. I've lots to tell you, but this must go off to
you to-day, just to say thank you. Much love to Bernard and Charlotte

from ELLEN

James Carew goes on trying and striving and acts better and better every
week. He is a splendid fellow and adores you, *and me!*

CCLXXXVI: G. B. S. *to* E. T.

[*Bobby Loraine: Colonel Robert Loraine, D.S.O. His first great success was
made in Man and Superman as Tanner. He played the part in the first performance in America (Hudson Theatre, New York, 1905). He won distinction as a soldier in the South African War and as an Ace in the World War
of 1914–18.*]

5 August 1907.
Hafod y Bryn, Llanbedr.
N. Wales

DEAREST EL— what am I saying?
Dear Mrs Carew,

IF JAMES loathes Brassbound, let him play the captain, and get Bobby
Loraine (he and I got carried out to sea and all but drowned here the
other day bathing) to play Brassbound. But I recommend James to stick
to his part: *he* will be the attraction as your latest victim; and unless
you have played him off the stage with your tricks or driven him down
the stage with his back to the footlights all the time, he ought to hold
his own.

In haste for post—G. B. S.

CCLXXXVII: E. T. *to* G. B. S.

[*Shaw, holidaying in Wales, had lost his way in the mountains and been
compelled to sleep at a strange hotel.—Ellen Terry, on her return from America, went on a tour of the English provinces with James Carew.*]

... **N**O, JAMES hasnt jilted me yet. He bosses me nicely instead! I must tell you he likes Capn. B. much better here in England than in America. Naturally, for the donkeys there didnt take any notice of him! We return to London to-morrow. . . . The night we heard news you were lost on the mountain was a bad time for me. Lord, I didnt know how fond I was of you, and said so to Jim, who said the same to Nell! All the play through I was thinking of Charlotte's anxiety and believing that somehow she would get a wire from you tho' all the party were ignorant of where you were. Oh, what a trial to have a precious boy like you to be anxious about. Oddly enough when they thought you were nearly drowned I just didnt believe it. I'm so sleepy I dont know what I am talking about. I'm very glad you are alive. Bless you, my dear.

This is just to congratulate Bobbie Loraine upon being nearly drowned with you!

I want, I long to play a mighty serious part in a play of yours in which you can show yourself as you really *are* very clearly to even the biggest idiots who go and sit in stuffy theatres.

I feel in despair sometimes when I realize that nearly all the audiences are quite as stupid as myself, and some few stupider!

Dont lose yourself any more.

ELLEN TERRY CAREW

CCLXXXVIII: E. T. *to* G. B. S.

DONT you think, Jim (and I too?) could have played in your Devil's Disciple. I should have loved it, for both of us. We *must* work, so I suppose we shall be wandering around the delectable Provinces making money as a last recourse against idleness. I did want Jim to act in London so much. It does not concern me if I dont act at all, altho' I should much like to do Mrs What's-her-name. Well, have you any work for us (or for him, Jim, at least) up your sleeve? The plays sent to us to read are beyond, beyond!

I do hope you are neither drowned nor hanged but that you flourish like a Bernard Shaw.

With love to you and to Charlotte

Yours

ELLEN CAREW

CCLXXXIX: G. B. S. *to* E. T.

[*Rudge Harding had played Sir Howard Hallam in Brassbound all through Ellen Terry's American tour. He has retired from the stage.—Drinkwater was played by George Elton.*]

14 October 1907

DEAREST ELLEN,

YOUR letter arrived this morning. The fact that I went to Fulham to see you in Brassbound before I received it shews that you have nothing to do but think about me at any time to attract me to you as a magnet. In fact that happens usually whether you think about me or not.

I was quite appalled on Saturday by the consequences of my writing Brassbound for you. At the Court, you were always merely trying to remember a part. But now you have realized that you are Lady Cicely. Her history has become your history; and instead of trying to remember somebody else's words, you simply say what is right to say in the situation (which, by the way, is mostly much better than my dialogue) and there you have the whole thing alive and perfect. It is really a very wonderful performance now; and the others are not half good enough for you.

But this involves frightful consequences for yourself and others. It puts an end to your career as an actress, because never again will you be able to play another part. The public will never stand anything now except the real Ellen and the real Cicely. It will be a worse case than Jefferson and Rip Van Winkle. It will be a part of everybody's education to go at least once a year and see Lady Cicely. This will be hard enough for you; but it will simply mean ruin for Jim, who cannot go on playing Brassbound all his life without utterly destroying himself as an actor.

Look at poor Rudge Harding: he is absolutely stupefied by repetition. Jim's brain is visibly half gone: he holds on to the part as if nothing but the grimmest determination could save him from going mad on the spot. Drinkwater is the only one who keeps fresh; and he only sterilizes himself by boiling furiously from time to time. You will have to engage a new company every year, and let Jim play Hamlet two evenings a week and Captain Kearney the rest of the time.

It is really a very difficult situation; and I dont quite see my way out.

Suppose one wanted Jim for anything at the Savoy or elsewhere, would you let him loose to do it, or is he tied to your apron strings for the rest of his life? This habit of getting married is the ruin of theatrical art: Vedrenne and Barker are almost shipwrecked by it already. Why could you not have been content with my adoration?

Ever, dear Ellen,
Yours devotedly.

CCXC: E. T. *to* G. B. S.

[F. K.: Frederick Kerr who had played Captain Brassbound at the Court.— The flat Edith Craig took and lived in for two years was in Adelphi Terrace House, as the old Caledonian Hotel was called when it was rebuilt. In 1909 Sir James Barrie bought her lease. When the late Joseph Pennell, the American artist, left the flat above, which had superior attractions, one of them a fine roof-garden, Barrie moved into it, and is still living there.]

15 October 1907.
215 King's Road,
Chelsea

I HAVE not read your letter to me to Jim. Thought it better not to. The part has got on his nerves (as it did on F. K.'s) and it is only by soothing him he'll be able to stick on till the end.

. . . He is not tied to my apron strings (nor is "his mother" tied to his) and if one of us is at work I shall be satisfied and so will he. I'd like you (for he loves you) to make him an offer. Oh, do be quick and ask him to play a fine part with a fair salary, or a mere good part with an unfair salary! Will you? Quick quick, oh, Shaw, and save us from the "Halls" or the Hells. (Not that I am going "on the 'alls" anyhow, but save me from rushing about the land when we both want to settle down in our country home to do nice work.) Edy is I believe about to take a flat which overlooks *your* bedroom at No. 10.

I'm late for the theatre. Farewell everywhere.

Yours, as you treat her, ELLEN

CCXCI: G. B. S. *to* E. T.

[Both "dearest Ellen" and "ever devotedly" have a line through them in the original letter.]

19 December 1907.
10 Adelphi Terrace, W. C.

DEAREST ELLEN,

My dear Mrs Carew,

THE writer of the note opposite is Alvin Langdon Coburn, the best photographer now living, a young American. I made him come over to Paris to photograph Rodin. He has photographed all your great contemporaries. He is as quiet as a mouse, the only young genius I ever met who was soothing. You will like him, and he will make wonderful photographs of you. May he come to see you?

Ever devotedly,
Yours faithfully,

G. B. S.

CCXCII: G. B. S. *to* E. T.

[*The reference to "James' wampum and feathers" perhaps needs the elucidation that James Carew's striking features bear a certain resemblance to those of the North American Indian.*]

30 January 1908.
10 Adelphi Terrace, W. C.

DEAREST MADAM,

I AM in high spirits today because you smiled at me from your taxi-cab. I also caught a glimpse of James' wampum and feathers through the back window. I still think he treated me rather badly in marrying you: after all, you were my leading lady and not his: still, I suppose it is no use keeping up a grudge against him.

Ever your devoted,

G. BERNARD SHAW

CCXCIII: E. T. *to* G. B. S.

[*"The new play"*: Getting Married, *produced at the Haymarket Theatre on 12 May 1908. Fanny Brough, an actress with a great reputation whose remarkable powers were in Shaw's opinion being wasted at the moment in supplying "vulgar comic relief" in melodrama at Drury Lane (she had in 1907 made a great success as Lady Goldbury in* The Sins of Society), *was persuaded by Shaw to play the clairvoyant Mrs Collins, mayoress and coalmerchant, an extraordinary part, which, says Shaw, "demands an actress who can combine inspiration with the broadest comic characterization. The chance came to Fanny Brough a little too late; but in many passages written expressly for her peculiar manner she was inimitable." When Getting*]

320

Married was put into the evening bill (after experimental matinées) Edith
Craig, at Shaw's suggestion, was engaged to play Mrs Bridgenorth, the
Bishop's wife. When he told her he was going to make the suggestion, he
said he had no doubt the management would think he was mad, but that on
hearing her call to her housemate one night, from the pavement outside
Adelphi Terrace House, immediately beneath his window, to "throw down
the latchkey," he had been convinced that she was the right person, with
the right voice, for the part.]

25 April 1908.
Grand Hotel,
Newcastle on Tyne

DEAR FRIEND,

I AM very sorry you have another bad attack of influenza. As you
could not lend me a copy of the new play to read perhaps you will
let me come to see the first performance.

I have booked an autumn tour. *More* Lady Cicely! But I am hoping
James will not be with me on that tour. I know I shall hate it without
him, but it is dreadful for a man at his age to be playing one part year
after year, and unless you write Lady Cicely in America, and give Jim
a tipping rousing part in it (an American) I shall carry out the engagements made for the autumn, alone. We are both quite extraordinarily
happy together (unberufen!) and it seems a pity to go different ways for
a while, but I think he would become a lunatic if he played Captain B.
much longer. He has settled down to it now, altho' he hates it so (only
because he thinks he does it badly) but he must do other work.

I hope you are staying in town during your rehearsals since the
weather is so blustifurious, for waiting about at stations is a fine recipe
for the grave. I *am* a low comedian, tell Fanny, but she is splendid I
own, whilst I envy her her rehearsals.

E. C.

CCXCIV: G. B. S. *to* E. T.

[The following message is written on a postcard.—E. G. C.: Gordon Craig.
—The Repertory Theatre experiment at the Duke of York's, in which Charles
Frohman was interested, failed. One of its productions was Shaw's Misalli-
ance.—Earlier in the year (1909) there are letters giving glimpses of Ellen
Terry's peaceful life at Small Hythe, of Shaw touring in Algeria, of Edith
Craig being strenuous in the famous militant agitation for votes for women.
They have been omitted for no other reason than that they are "scrappy" and
not of much general interest.]

[Some time in 1909.]
Care of Col. Cholmondeley, C. B.
Edstaston, Wem, Shrops

C ANT E. G. C. be coerced into coming along and doing a man's work with Barker and Barrie and myself at the Duke of York's? Barker writes that it is not good enough for him. And it is good enough for ME. And it was good enough for YOU. I feel like Falstaff when Pistol stood on his honor about carrying the letter to Mrs Ford. Laziness! Infinite dishonorable laziness! Tell him I said so. G. B. S.

CCXCV: E. T. *to* G. B. S.

[*Shaw was certainly "on the wrong tack." Ellen Terry often said: "Whatever my children are not, they* are *industrious," and she was right. At this time Gordon Craig was working hard and producing a great number of fine woodcuts and drawings.*]

[Not dated. Traced to 1909 by contents.]
215 King's Road,
Chelsea

T ED IS not in the least lazy. He knows not lazy. I do wish he would act (always have wished it). There is a little show of Beauty at his rooms which can convince anyone at least he is not lazy. Will you come with me some evening about 6 or 9 o'clock and see it? I think Ted imagines you dont like him, and so wont ask you about anything, and so I didnt show him either your card or your letter concerning him. You see you are on the wrong tack in thinking he is lazy. That would make him laugh charmingly. It makes *me* laugh, and you'd laugh too *if you knew!*

Enough "laugh"—

Why doesnt Granville Barker offer *me* a part? I keep on refusing big sums of money, tho' I want money. But I want a *part* more. Yours ever, my dear, the usual   OLD ELLEN

CCXCVI: E. T. *to* G. B. S.

6 August 1910.
215 King's Road,
Chelsea

DEAR G. B. S.,

F OR beginning to write to you again (in *these* terrible days of pen and ink gone mad!) I crave your pardon *d'avance!!* That means *in advance!* It is French, and I never had any.)

322

A friend of mine—a courageous creature of 40, might have the very thorny path made less unendurable if she could get some work on a London Newspaper. Do you think she writes well enough for that? Tell me, please, dear man. I loathe to trouble you with this note, but *do* glance through these newspaper cuttings and tell me what she ought to do. You once brought peace and some good fortune by your advice to a young singer-friend of mine. Therefore I write you now! Think of the privilege of helping. (Lordy, Lordy! As if you didnt think of everything.) I can no more. I think I have a skewer in my right eye. Or is it a mere neuralgic pain? I send you my love. I send Charlotte my love. Dont fight over the delectable thing. I have plenty more.

ELLEN

CCXCVII: E. T. *to* G. B. S.

28 August 1910.
215 Kings Road, Chelsea.
Sunday

DEAREST G. B. S.,

I SHOULD like to pay my debt to you, but I cannot. Gratitude seems worthless. *My* sort of gratitude has no results, no benefit to you. I can only just say thank you very much for troubling to answer my note about my friend. I did not show her your letter but told her bits of it as advice from a frightfully wise one who seemed to me to be always terribly right! I fear she is beyond help. I have just bought a little play of hers (an all wrong, delicately wrong, one) for a little money, but one *has* to do something! Great Scott, what a number of good people want things done for them! What should be done with the very feeble ones? No, I'm not asking for your advice this time. I'm only wondering! Also I wonder shall I ever act in a Play of yours again! I know you didnt like me in Brassbound, and indeed I didnt like myself, but sometimes nowadays I feel as if I *could* act! But that's only in Moon-y time, when the Marshes look all silver, and I feel very calm and happy. (It's more, I find, than most people can say, that they are quite happy for about 3 days in every month! On other days I cant say that, for I'd rather like to murder now and again! Some of your imitators to begin with!)

Thanks and thanks from

ELLEN

CCXCVIII: E. T. *to* G. B. S.

[*The "2 plays" must mean The Dark Lady of the Sonnets, a plea for a National Theatre, and The Shewing Up of Blanco Posnet, which was banned*

323

7 February 1911

WELL! There *will* be a rush for the 2 plays and your review of "B.'s" work. Perhaps *that* is what the whole fuss means? I'm far away and would be mightily grateful to you if you would secure me a copy of each and forgive me for taxing you. No Booksellers can be depended upon, and Edy, the scamp, forgets me 'cos she's busy helping all the other females!

I'm starting for England on the 25th of this month. God knows how America will get on without me, and if you will secure me these things to read when I come home it will ensure work for James for *he* will save my eyesight. I'm sure (if you cant find time) that Charlotte would undertake the job for you and perhaps for me!

All blessings on your dear head

ELLEN

CCXCIX: G. B. S. *to* E. T.

28 February 1911.
10 Adelphi Terrace, W. C.

I SEND you a private and particular copy of The Dark Lady to keep; but the English Review reprint is in much larger type; so read it in that if James is off duty.

When I went to coax you to play Queen Elizabeth I found that you were on the high seas on your way to America

Just like you to run away when I wanted you!

G. B. S.

CCC: E. T. *to* G. B. S.

were acting together at the Haymarket Theatre in 1891. Subsequently they went into management, and for a period of thirty years have appeared frequently in London and the provinces with their own company. Phyllis Terry made her first appearance as Juliet in a production of Romeo and Juliet at the New Theatre in September 1911. Ellen Terry was not the Nurse on this occasion, but she played the part a few years later in Doris Kean's production at the Lyric Theatre. It was the last but not the least of her triumphs in Shakespear. Innocently she, in the jargon of the theatre, "stole the play" from Romeo and Juliet.—Phyllis Neilson-Terry appeared as Candida at the Malvern Festival in 1930, to the great satisfaction of the author.]

18 March 1911.
215 King's Road,
Chelsea

"**W**HAT can you do"? (Thank you for asking.) Why let me play a fine part written by you so I may abide in England!

The Lieblers offer me a fine engagement for the autumn and winter coming, but I'd rather not go *next* season to America. Then I can play "the Nurse" to Phil Terry in Romeo and Juliet.

That is all I have for my *business* look out, but I dont care much for it. Can you enlarge my prospect? Do if you can. I must work and I'd like to work.

My little house wants a righting. Then I'll sit down and read a while. Not a book, not a newspaper have I looked at for a week! The days fly! I like being here. The people are so nice and dull, not so shine-y and brittle as the American folk. The voices here go up and down, not that *one dum-dum* on *one* spot inside your head until you fly to scream in another room, or burst! But they are kind over there and quick and eager.

Pardon, Pardon!

Yes, a part in a play by you, in early autumn. That's what you can do. Dont reply *please*. You waste your time in reading me.

E. C.

CCCI: G. B. S. *to* E. T.

[The play referred to is Pygmalion. Its first performance took place, not in England, but in Germany at the Lessing Theatre, Berlin, in 1913. In April

1914 it was produced at His Majesty's Theatre, with Mrs Patrick Campbell as Eliza Doolittle, and Sir Herbert Tree as Professor Higgins.—Gertrude Kingston revived Captain Brassbound's Conversion at the Little Theatre on 12 October 1915.—"Reeking from Bella Donna": not the drug but the play of that name in which Mrs Campbell was then appearing.]

13 August 1912.
Hotel Excelsior, Nancy,
Meurthe-et-Moselle, France

DEAREST ELLEN,

WHAT is a Philomathic Society? It sounds like stamp collecting. When you said you had no personal influence with me you told a wicked lie; but it served the man right for bothering you.

I am languishing here alone, with a broken automobile. I left Charlotte at Kissingen doing a cure (mud baths and such like) with her sister, and made a dash for the Alps. Unluckily the dash broke something vital in the auto; and I had to drag it here by rail through custom houses and over frontiers and all sorts of bothers to get it to the factory of its makers.

I now have a grotesque confession to make to you. I wrote a play for Alexander which was really a play for Mrs Patrick Campbell. It is almost as wonderful a fit as Brassbound; for I am a good ladies' tailor, whatever my shortcomings may be. And the part is SO different, not a bit in the world like Lady Cicely. ("I should think not" you will say.) Then came the question, would *she* stand it? For, I repeat, this heroine wasnt a Lady Cicely Waynflete: she was Liza Doolittle, a flower girl, using awful language and wearing an apron and three ostrich feathers, and having her hat put in the oven to slay the creepy-crawlies, and being taken off the stage and washed, like Drinkwater. I simply didnt dare offer it to her. Well, I read it to a good friend of mine [Dame Edith Lyttelton], and contrived that she should be there. And she *was* there, reeking from Bella Donna. She saw through it like a shot. "You beast, you wrote this for me, every line of it: I can hear you mimicking my voice in it, etc. etc." And she rose to the occasion, quite fine and dignified for a necessary moment, and said unaffectedly she was flattered. And then—and then—oh Ellen; and then? Why, then I went calmly to her house to discuss business with her, as hard as nails, and, as I am a living man, fell head over ears in love with her in thirty seconds. And it lasted more than thirty hours. I made no struggle: I went in head over ears, and dreamed and dreamed and walked on air for all that afternoon and the next day as if my next birthday were my twentieth. And I said, among other things (to myself) "Now I shall amuse and interest Ellen again for at least one letter or two." Which I am accordingly trying to do.

One thing she said pleased me better than she knew. She said that Duse has leaden feet, and that the perfect people walked on air, "like Ellen Terry." I was tempted to reply that Ellen's feet were heavy enough when she was trampling on a man's heart; but I didnt.

Storms soon arose. She was clever enough to see that her business was not to accept the offers of Frohman and the others, but to get the profits of the play herself by going into management. Then came a terrible conflict over the question of the leading man. She wanted—whom do you think? Your Jim! I wouldnt have him at any price, because the part is essentially an English part of a certain type; and he would have been at a disadvantage in it. She proposed all sorts of impossible people. I proposed Loraine. She would not hear of him. I pressed my choice. She said awful things about him. I repeated them to him. He said unpardonable things about her. I repeated them to her. This sort of Shavian horseplay startled her: she said I was a mischief-maker. I made some more; and finally they had to assure one another of their undying esteem and admiration, which was what I wanted. But Loraine had to go to America to Supermanage himself into a solvent condition before coming back to play with her. And she said that she would never never never play Liza. And so she went off to Aix-les-Bains, where she is at present. And I am plying her with the most wonderful love letters. To write love letters to you was like giving tracts to a missionary (not that I could help doing it for all that) for you could hold me at letter writing and play with me at love making; but there cannot be two women alive at the same time who could do that: she is a wonderful person in her way; but there is only one Ellen.

And now Gertrude Kingston is going to do Brassbound, having got an hour's start of Marie Tempest, who was that much too late. I suppose it must be let go now that you have exhausted it; but what will it be to me without you?

I shall be here for a few days still. Be my good angel to the extent of throwing me a scrap of your beloved writing.

G. B. S.

CCCII: E. T. *to* G. B. S.

["The V. Inheritance": Granville-Barker's play The Voysey Inheritance]

16 September 1912.
215 King's Road,
Chelsea

DEAR G. B. S.,

THIS photograph is such a dear thing. I'd love **to see** *it,* and your writing together. So will you put your name on it for me. *You* are to write it, please. The Edy-devil says you never do. Your "Secretary always." I tell her she lies.

It was a joy to get your letter. *I'm* in love with Mrs Campbell too, or rather I'd like to be, but something tugs me back. She is amusing and was nice to me in America. The flower-girl idea is thrilling.

I suppose an old woman would not attract as a centre piece in a play, and that you never could write such a thing for—*me?* (for this old woman?) But I wish it were possible that your dear noddle could contrive it. As it is 3 o'clock in the morning, and most old folk are asleep, and I'm nearly asleep myself, this shall end.

Your blessing, Sir.

ELLEN

Just seen The V. Inheritance, first time. I like it. Bits of it are fine.

CCCIII: E. T. *to* G. B. S.

[Ellen Terry had been pressing Shaw to find her some work in London and this had evidently made him anxious about his friend's financial situation. We may surmise, too, that in his answer, which is missing, he had discussed her difficult situation with his usual care. He has alluded to its problems in his preface. His own situation had again changed. The firm of Vedrenne and Barker had overreached itself in an expansion of its activities and was wound up, solvent only by Shaw and Granville-Barker paying its debts. Granville-Barker had gone to America and met the lady whose husband he afterwards became, an event which ended his association with Shaw and with the pioneer movement in the theatre. Shaw was for the moment free from the need for supplying it with potboilers: he reacted, not by writing a play for Ellen Terry, but by turning his back on all the apparent possibilities of the nineteenth century theatre in the composition of his Heartbreak House and Back to Methuselah, the latter requiring three nights and two afternoons for its performance.]

328

M Y DEAR friend neighbour, you must not trouble your dear heart for a moment about me in that way, for I am really quite rich! My worldly possessions positively hamper me! I could get on quite nicely without them (but having them there's no being without them). I am grateful for the loan of your light which shows me that I see a little all the while. I see how unintelligent I am. That fact is so near me, that I must be careful I dont break my heart against it. But your flashlight shows me one or two other usefuls, and after a little more plodding in hope, all may be well. Thank you, very dear friend, for the loan of your light. My eyes pain me. Good Lord, my poor eyes! Teddy is afloat now, and my son all along has been my sun. Without the warmth of him many a time I would have died and died, I know! When I cannot see I'll get dear little Barrie to adopt me! Thank you for writing me so kindest and helpfullest a letter.

ELLEN

CCCIV: E. T. *to* G. B. S.

[*During the first years of the war Ellen Terry went on a lecture tour, first in Australia and then in the United States. Young readers who were children in 1914 can hardly be expected to realize what fearless independence Ellen Terry showed in saying then that Shaw was "splendid about the war." The old and the middle-aged who remember how far from "splendid" about it he was generally considered after the publication of Commonsense About The War in November 1914, how many of his friends and admirers joined in the public chorus of vulgar abuse, may agree with me that there is no letter in this correspondence which affords a more striking proof that Ellen Terry did, as she claims, "know Shaw," and had the courage of her knowledge. Adapting Milton's lines about the Seraph Abdiel, let us say that in 1914 "her loyalty she kept, her love, her zeal . . . among the faithless, faithful only she—."—Ellen Terry stayed "here" (New York) until the end of April 1915. Charles Frohman, who was sailing in the* Lusitania *on 1 May, offered her a passage on that swift and luxurious boat as a present, but she declined to accept it and cancel the passage she had booked on an American liner. She had promised her daughter not to take the risk of coming home on an English steamer. She confessed when she was safe home that she had been very much tempted to break her promise. Frohman had assured her that the rumours current about the Germans and the* Lusitania *were absurd. It was not, indeed, until the morning of 1 May that the official German warning to travellers intending to embark on her was issued. By that time Ellen Terry had sailed.*]

DEAREST G. B. S. (who is splendid about the war)
Very strange people are all over the world. I thought they
knew you! But, they are strange. I dont know *them*. I know *you!* (The
impudence of saying that, but I *do*.) I send you and Charlotte all Christ-
massy love from New York. I trust to you to keep bombs from Edy's
head. You know everything, so there's no excuse if you dont take care
of her for me and send her out of the way of violence, if any nears
her. I'm so surely, so simply aware that you have blessed, infernal, wisdom that, please, I'll ask you to tell her what to do—*if* she wants to
know!

ELLEN ELLEN

Australia is a Garden. Heaps of lovely people, and heaps of uninteresting
ones too! I want to stay here until March or April.

CCCV: G. B. S. *to* E. T.

[*"On the roof"*: *the roof referred to is the roof of the Coliseum. After a
performance there in aid of a war charity, the stars who had appeared in
it assembled on the roof to be photographed. I am informed that certain of
these stars shot madly from their spheres with indignation at the presence
of G. B. S. and requested that no photograph showing them in the company
of the author of* Commonsense About The War *should be published in the
press.*]

15 June 1916.
Wyndham Croft,
Turners Hill, Essex

MY BLESSED darling Ellen, for such were the feelings that rushed over
me when you appeared, willow slender, on the roof the other
day. I have been away from London ever since the book came out, and
so have been unable to send a single copy to anyone. When I return you
shall have your own copy; so you may give away the sordid commercial
sample you have acquired.

Why do I make you nervous? I know why *you* make *me* nervous.
It is because people are looking on, and the way I want to and ought to
behave would be ridiculous and indecorous. But meet me by moonlight
alone;—and—my word!—you shall see.

G. B. S.

CCCVI: G. B. S. *to* E. T.

[*"Ayot": Ayot St Lawrence, Shaw's home in Hertfordshire where he still lives. The "album," full of picture postcards of Ayot with ridiculous rhymes, was carefully preserved by Ellen Terry with Shaw's letters. A macabre specimen sticks in the memory. It was appended to a view of the graveyard, and runs:*

Tread softly, Nell. Here Ayot's deaders
Into eternity take headers.]

23 August 1916.
10 Adelphi Terrace, W. C.

DEAREST ELLEN,

I T WAS in the last degree wicked of you to come to Ayot and leave a message with the postmistress instead of coming in to tea. How can you be so barbarous?

As you ordered postcards, I send you a real Ayot album to put them in, and have filled up half the leaves with my own productions. If you want a picture of any particular place about there, tell me, and I'll take one for you. Probably I shall have one already: I have stacks of them.

I am off now for a month in the provinces by way of holiday.

Ever your

G. B. S.

CCCVII: G. B. S. *to* E. T.

[*The Inca of Perusalem, "an almost historical comedietta" in one act, was first produced at the Birmingham Repertory Theatre on 9 October 1916. The first performance in London was given by the Pioneer Players at the Criterion Theatre on Sunday, 16 December 1917. This was produced by Edith Craig, and Ellen Terry, who was the Pioneer Players' President, was present in a box. Randle Ayrton played the Inca, Gertrude Kingston Ermyntrude, and Nigel Playfair the Waiter.*]

7 January 1918

DEAREST ELLEN,

S O YOU still remember this old party. You looked very nice, and very young at The Inca. I scan the rising generations of women for another Ellen; but Nature seems really to have broken the mould this time: nobody replaces you in my heart.

I learnt to dance for the first time last August. Or stop! Was it really the first time? I recollect that when I was a very minute kid indeed, a lady named Magrane, who lived a few doors off, taught me the 5 positions; and I can still remember three of them. That is what they did in those days: they taught you positions but did not teach you to dance. Thus I learnt the positions at, say, seven, and how to dance (rather like a tank) at 61.

Such is my year's record.

None of the wildest expressions I have ever addressed to you are to be considered in any way withdrawn. I am incurable.

Ever

G. B. S.

CCCVIII: E. T. *to* G. B. S.

[*"A Church by Daylight": the reference is to Beatrice's line in Much Ado About Nothing: "I have a good eye, uncle. I can see a church by daylight."—* *"Your Play"*: Pygmalion, *which was revived at the Aldwych Theatre on 10 February 1920. Mrs Patrick Campbell again played Eliza Doolittle. Marion Terry was the new Mrs Higgins.*]

[Not dated. Assigned to February 1920]

IF ANYTHING can be done surely you would do it to stay horrible cruelty to the poor animals who can speak to us only with their eyes. Is it true—the horrible things written in a book I took up by chance yesterday by "Jack London." It was on a table in the dentist's waiting-room. "Who would, who could do this or that," often comes into my head when I am moved strongly to call "help help" to right some wrong or another, and Shaw the fearless could do anything. Will he do this?

It was mighty pleasant seeing you and your Play the other evening. I should like to see it again next week if I may. If you please. Only, most of all things to happen, is the staying of this cruelty business. How very old I am to be so ignorant about such obvious ills under my very nose for nearly 72 years! It makes me crazy. "A Church by Daylight" indeed!

I have actually delighted in "Animal Turns." And I travelled with a wonderful little Seal not long ago and even then—what a blind fool am I!

Dont trouble to write to me for you are sure to be slaving at work. Only remember me, and the other animals.

ELLEN

CCCIX: G. B. S. *to* E. T.

1 March 1920.
10 Adelphi Terrace, W. C. 2

DEAREST ELLEN,

THE agitation against performing animals is an old story for me. Mrs Hayden Coffin worked hard at it. Alas! it is only a drop in the ocean of cruelty which makes me wonder that the animals do not either conspire to exterminate the human race as we exterminate tigers or else commit suicide in despair.

Performing dog trainers should be shot at sight: their faces betray them far more than their whips and their way of handling the wretched animals. The only animals which seem to enjoy performing are seals and sea lions: apparently they wont do it unless they get promptly rewarded with fish to gobble. Perhaps the twenty lions in whose midst our modern lion taming ladies swagger may enjoy being fed until the offer of even a plump and tender baby would make them sick; but their boredom is pitiable; and when the lady slashes them across the eyes to make them growl "Oh *do* for God's sake leave me alone," I always hope they will tear her limb from limb, and am always disappointed: they hate her too much to touch her. Captive birds and tigers are worse than prisoners of the Bastille in old romances; but there is one maneless lion (the majestic Trafalgar Square sort; *you* wouldnt call him maneless) in the Zoo (born there) who likes to have an audience and be admired, and will let you pet him. Except for the softness of his chest fur it is rather like trying to shove Primrose Hill over on its side with one hand; but he makes Androcles credible. The maned lion, Dick, is a furious brute. I pitied his poor cruelly bullied wife (judging by appearances) until she yawned, walked under his chin, and hit it up—perhaps trying to make him bite his tongue—with a toss of her head that would have lifted the dome off St Paul's. After that I understood what had spoiled his temper and pitied *him*.

Marion did not arrive at the Aldwych until the production stage was over; so she had to produce herself, which she did very well, as she knew as much about it as I. Clever family, the Terries! When she found that I was not as detestable as my reputation (an impossibility) she was angelic to me. I needed kindness, as Beatrice Stella excelled herself in perfect hellishness. You need not brag of being 72. *I'm* 63¾.

G. B. S.

CCCX: E. T. *to* G. B. S.

[Ellen Terry received the honorary degree of LL.D. of St Andrews University on 5 May 1922. Other recipients were Earl Haig and John Galsworthy. Sir James Barrie was then Lord Rector. This is the last letter from her Bernard Shaw kept and probably the last he received. During the last six years of her life (she died on 21 July 1928) she wrote but few letters to anyone. In April 1922 she visited Stratford-on-Avon for the Shakespear Birthday Festival, and alludes in this letter to having met the Shaws there. The last words, a simple and spontaneous expression of abiding love, are the last words of the correspondence, for there are no more letters from Shaw after March 1920.]

L AID up—a cold—*Have* to communicate with you somehow, my dear. If only you had seen J. M. B. yesterday! He was *almost* as beautiful and adorable as my 5 months old kitten. If only you had been there to watch him! He seems to me to be so ill, the poor mite. How he kept up all the while! Haig is a pet, and the two together were—well I'm glad I was there to see two such boys! Their fun! I loved 'em, not so much of course as *you*—but there! Will you tell Charlotte I am feeling the "miss" of Stratford-on-Avon and of her and *you*. My old Edy had charge of me at St Andrews, and has now put me to bed, and says I must *rest* now.

Ever and ever yours,

E. T.

[A few days after Ellen Terry's death, her daughter found a piece of paper labelled My Friends. In this roll of honour which there was evidence was of very recent date, the name of Charles Reade was written first. Directly underneath it was the name of Bernard Shaw.]